My First Summer in the Sierra and Selected Essays

D0121663

John Muir

My First Summer in the Sierra

and Selected Essays

WITH AN INTRODUCTION BY

Bill McKibben

LIBRARY OF AMERICA PAPERBACK CLASSICS

WILLIAM CRONON
WROTE THE NOTES FOR THIS VOLUME

Contents

INTRODUCTION

by Bill McKibben

When we consider John Muir, we consider one of the small handful of Americans who truly changed the world. He belongs with the Founding Fathers whose words gave shape to an inchoate but bracing sense of political liberty, and with the great political reformers of the women's and civil rights movements. Like all of them he added a new dimension to the quintessential American idea of freedom, a dimension we're still exploring a century and a half after that epochal first summer in the Sierras. And he did it, above all, with words—with a new grammar and rhetoric and vocabulary of wildness, a burst of ecstasy in whose echo we yet live.

To make sense of that summer, it pays to understand a little of Muir's life beforehand, the first thirty years that wound the spring that was about to uncoil with such power. Muir was born in Scotland, in the coastal town of Dunbar. He learned some of the climbing skills that he'd later put to good use in Yosemite on the ruins of the town's old castle, and he spent long hours wandering its seashore (where you can wander now, along the John Muir Way). His family moved to Wisconsin when he was ten—his father, who was a religious zealot, had apparently found the Church of Scotland not harsh enough in its orthodoxy, and so emigrated, joining the Disciples of Christ. Frontier life was hard, both because they were carving out a homestead (Muir's recollection of digging a well is . . . well worth reading) and because he and his nine siblings were doing it under the shadow of a spooky father. Muir learned his Bible—learned it "by heart and by sore flesh." Which was a gift for his later readers who savored his high strong language, but also I think a perverse gift for the development of his thinking. For it was in reaction, conscious and unconscious, to the narrowness of his father's theology that he developed his broadest themes.

His first escape was to Madison, already the home of the University of Wisconsin. He took an irregular scattering of courses, developing deep interests in chemistry, botany, and geology, the latter two of which were to be invaluable in his later career. In 1864, at the age of twenty-five, he struck out for Canada, apparently to avoid the draft; he tramped the shores of Lake Huron gathering plants. When he returned to the States, it was to Indianapolis, where he worked as a sawyer at a wheelwright's; an accident there in the spring of 1867 injured his eye, and left him confined to a dark room for weeks on end, unsure whether he'd see again. When he finally emerged, it was into the true light of his life. "This affliction has driven me to the sweet fields," he said. "God has to nearly kill us sometimes, to teach us lessons."

Muir began his new life with a walk, a long one. He set off from Indiana with plans to wander to the Gulf of Mexico, and the vague intention of continuing from there to South America. His trek took him through hardscrabble and discouraging country, in those days after the Civil War—Kentucky, the hills of North Carolina, Georgia. It's worth quoting at some length from the account he much later compiled from his journals of those youthful travels, for they reveal a good deal about his character and his thinking. Early on, for instance, he eats cornbread and bacon at the home of one hardworking local:

> "Well, young man," he queried, "you mean to say that you are not employed by the Government on some private business?" "No," I said, "I am not employed by any one except just myself. I love all kinds of plants, and I came down here to these Southern States to get acquainted with as many of them as possible." "You look like a strong-minded man," he replied, "and surely you are able to do something better than wander over the country and look at weeds and blossoms. These are hard times, and real work is required of every man that is able. Picking up blossoms doesn't seem to be a man's work at all in any kind of times."
>
> To this I replied, "You are a believer in the Bible, are you not?" "Oh, yes." "Well, you know Solomon was a strong-minded man, and he is generally believed to have been the very wisest man the world ever saw, and yet he considered it was worth while to study plants; not only to

go and pick them up as I am doing, but to study them; and you know we are told that he wrote a book about plants, not only of the great cedars of Lebanon, but of little bits of things growing in the cracks of the walls.

"Therefore, you see that Solomon differed very much more from you than from me in this matter. I'll warrant you he had many a long ramble in the mountains of Judea, and had he been a Yankee he would likely have visited every weed in the land. And again, do you not remember that Christ told his disciples to 'consider the lilies how they grow,' and compared their beauty with Solomon in all his glory? Now, whose advice am I to take, yours or Christ's? Christ says, 'Consider the lilies.' You say, 'Don't consider them. It isn't worth while for any strong-minded man.'"

This evidently satisfied him, and he acknowledged that he had never thought of blossoms in that way before. He repeated again and again that I must be a very strong-minded man, and admitted that no doubt I was fully justified in picking up blossoms. He then told me that although the war was over, walking across the Cumberland Mountains still was far from safe on account of small bands of guerrillas who were in hiding along the roads, and earnestly entreated me to turn back and not to think of walking so far as the Gulf of Mexico until the country became quiet and orderly once more.

I replied that I had no fear, that I had but very little to lose, and that nobody was likely to think it worth while to rob me; that, anyhow, I always had good luck.

As he wandered out of the straight safe paths, so too his mind wandered out of the safe orthodoxies that defined his time. The prevailing orthodoxy about the natural world, the one he would eventually explode, was, in his words, that the world

was made especially for man—a presumption not supported by all the facts. A numerous class of men are painfully astonished whenever they find anything, living or dead, in all God's universe, which they cannot eat or render in some way what they call useful to themselves. They have precise dogmatic insight into the intentions of the Creator, and it is hardly possible to be guilty of irreverence in speaking of their God any more than of heathen idols. He is regarded as a civilized, law-abiding gentlemen in favor either of a republican form of government or of a limited monarchy; believes in the literature and language of England; is a warm supporter of the English constitution and Sunday schools and missionary societies; and is as purely a manufactured article as any puppet at a half-penny theater.

With such views of the Creator it is, of course, not surprising that erroneous views should be entertained of the creation. To such properly trimmed people, the sheep, for example, is an easy problem—food and clothing "for us," eating grass and daisies white by divine appointment for this predestined purpose, on perceiving the demand for wool that would be occasioned by the eating of the apple in the Garden of Eden. In the same pleasant plan, whales are storehouses of oil for us, to help out the stars in lighting our dark ways until the discovery of the Pennsylvania oil wells.

But it's very hard to keep this particular view of the world as you're wandering through some of the harshest and most inhospitable country on the continent. By the time he gets to Florida, it's humid, there are bugs everywhere, not to mention snakes, not to mention thorny vines, not to mention . . . alligators. Clearly this place wasn't made for man (Muir lacks the imagination to picture a state full of vacation homes and retiree compounds). Indeed, after spending a night worrying about the possibilities of alligator attack, Muir pens what may be the first western hymn to a biocentric world view, and one of the most radical ever.

Many good people believe that alligators were created by the Devil, thus accounting for their all-consuming appetite and ugliness. But doubtless these creatures are happy and fill the place assigned them by the great Creator of us all. Fierce and cruel they appear to us, but beautiful in the eyes of God. They, also, are his children, for He hears their cries, cares for them tenderly, and provides their daily bread.

The antipathies existing in the Lord's great animal family must be wisely planned, like balanced repulsion and attraction in the mineral kingdom. How narrow we selfish, conceited creatures are in our sympathies! how blind to the rights of all the rest of creation! With what dismal irreverence we speak of our fellow mortals! Though alligators, snakes, etc., naturally repel us, they are not mysterious evils. They dwell happily in these flowery wilds, are part of God's family, unfallen, undepraved, and cared for with the same species of tenderness and love as is bestowed on angels in heaven or saints on earth.

I think that most of the antipathies which haunt and terrify us are morbid productions of ignorance and weakness. I have better thoughts of those alligators now that I have seen them at home. Honorable representatives of the great saurians of an older creation, may you long enjoy your lilies and rushes, and be blessed now and then with a mouthful of terror-stricken man by way of dainty!

Read that last line carefully. Muir is endorsing the idea of occasional death-by-alligator. He's reached some deep, even remarkable, understanding of what it means to be a human—not the center of creation, but a small part of it. He's traded the conventional Genesis understanding—dominion for man—with a deep ecology that would make Ed Abbey proud. And he's done it, as far as I can tell, pretty much on his own.

But there's one thing he hasn't done at this point, which is give us a new paradise. Muir clearly enjoys his walk through the backwoods of the south, but if you're going to argue for a new theology, it better not be all alligators. This is where the Sierras come in.

Muir ended his walk at the Gulf Coast port of Cedar Key (whose cedar groves eventually produced most of nation's pencils!). Muir recovered from a bout of malaria there, and instead of heading for South America he did what so many other Americans would eventually do: light out for California. Arriving in San Francisco, he immediately headed for Yosemite, and in some sense he never left.

It's hard, if you've never been in the high Sierras, to quite understand their magic. These are not the highest mountains of the continent, but they must be the most charming. The weather is almost always blue-sky perfect, with an occasional late-afternoon thundershower to keep things cool. Bugs are few, lakes are many. The smooth granite jumbles in every direction. Thanks to Ansel Adams you've seen the pictures, but if you've never felt the air . . . Well, no matter. John Muir has felt it for you.

July 9—Exhilarated with the mountain air, I feel like shouting this morning with excess of wild animal joy.
July 14—How deathlike is sleep in this mountain air, and quick the awakening into newness of life! A calm dawn, yellow and purple, then floods of sun-gold, making everything tingle and glow.
July 19.—Watching the daybreak and sunrise. The pale rose and purple sky changing softly to daffodil yellow and white, sunbeams pouring through the passes between the peaks and over the Yosemite domes, making their edges burn; the silver firs in the middle ground catching the glow on their spiry tops, and our camp grove fills and thrills with the glorious light. . . . The whole landscape glows like a human face in a glory of enthusiasm, and the blue sky, pale around the horizon, bends peacefully down over all like one vast flower.

A few weeks into his sojourn, he writes that it "seems the greatest of all the months of my life, the most truly, divinely free, boundless like eternity, immortal. Everything in it seems equally divine—one smooth, pure, wild glow of Heaven's love, never to be blotted or blurred by anything past or to come." And it gets better after that. The essays in this book are a serial love letter to this wildness. Muir on a glacier, Muir on top of a tree in a windstorm, Muir at the canyon's edge in an earthquake—always the same transcendental delight. If in Florida he realized that man was a small part of creation, in California, caught up in a sea of sequoia and wildflower, rock and ice, he recognized just how glorious that creation was.

That summer was the most important moment of Muir's life, and perhaps, along with Thoreau's year in his cabin, the most crucial stretch of time in the history of what we now call the environmental movement. Muir invented a new grammar, a contagious vocabulary for communicating the splendor of the natural world.

And then, as if that wasn't enough, he created the modern campaigning nonprofit, the model for so much else that came afterwards. In 1892 the Sierra Club was formed as an "alpine club" for those that loved the mountains. Muir was elected president, a post he held for the twenty-two years until his death. From the beginning it sponsored hikes and camp-outs—but it also plunged into politics, opposing efforts to slash the size of the park in half, and helping persuade the state to transfer the land to the control of the federal government. Muir lost his most famous battle when San Francisco dammed the Tuolumne River and flooded Hetch Hetchy Canyon, but in a way he won the war: his preservationist call echoed down through the century. "As well dam for water-tanks the people's cathedrals and churches, for no holier temple has ever been consecrated by the hearts of man." That's what Muir said in 1897, and it's more or less what his great successor as head of the Sierra Club, David Brower, said in the 1960s when he led the successful fight to save the Grand Canyon of the Colorado from a similar fate: "Should we also flood the Sistine Chapel so tourists can get nearer the ceiling?"

Muir was not completely prescient, of course. He could see the damage sheep were doing to Yosemite as they grazed, for instance, but no one had yet imagined just how bad our environmental woes would get:

> They cannot hurt the trees, though some of the seedlings suffer, and should the woolly locusts be greatly multi-plied, as on account of dollar value they are likely to be, then the forests, too, may in time be destroyed. Only the sky will then be safe, though hid from view by dust and smoke, incense of a bad sacrifice.

Needless to say, in an age of global warming, the sky is no longer safe; indeed the Sierra Club now spends the bulk of its time fighting to save the climate. The glaciers of the high Sierra are dwindling fast; I camped not long ago in a place behind Tuolumne where I can remember the snow fields, but they are no more. Indeed, when last I camped there the blue sky was darkened by the smoke of a massive drought-caused forest fire in the adjoining valley. For related reasons, Muir's marvelous rhetoric of glorious wildness is no longer the main vocabulary of environmentalism; more and more we speak the language of utility, of survival, of fear.

And yet the explosive charge of that first summer still detonates in a thousand souls each day—people who arrive for the first time on the north rim of the Grand Canyon or the shore at Acadia or the high peaks of the Adirondacks or the overlook at Half Dome and find themselves overcome by the feeling of rightness that Muir first articulated, at least for those westerners who had to return to the consciousness that had been the birthright of most humans over most of prehistory. These essays are crucial documents of the human experience, a declaration of something even deeper than independence.

MY FIRST SUMMER
IN THE SIERRA

TO
THE SIERRA CLUB OF CALIFORNIA
FAITHFUL DEFENDER OF THE
PEOPLE'S PLAYGROUNDS

Contents

Illustrations

Chapter I

IN the great Central Valley of California there are only two seasons—spring and summer. The spring begins with the first rain-storm, which usually falls in November. In a few months the wonderful flowery vegetation is in full bloom, and by the end of May it is dead and dry and crisp, as if every plant had been roasted in an oven.

Then the lolling, panting flocks and herds are driven to the high, cool, green pastures of the Sierra. I was longing for the mountains about this time, but money was scarce and I couldn't see how a bread supply was to be kept up. While I was anxiously brooding on the bread problem, so troublesome to wanderers, and trying to believe that I might learn to live like the wild animals, gleaning nourishment here and there from seeds, berries, etc., sauntering and climbing in joyful independence of money or baggage, Mr. Delaney, a sheep-owner, for whom I had worked a few weeks, called on me, and offered to engage me to go with his shepherd and flock to the headwaters of the Merced and Tuolumne Rivers—the very region I had most in mind. I was in the mood to accept work of any kind that would take me into the mountains whose treasures I had tasted last summer in the Yosemite region. The flock, he explained, would be moved gradually higher through the successive forest belts as the snow melted, stopping for a few weeks at the best places we came to. These I thought would be good centers of observation from which I might be able to make many telling excursions within a radius of eight or ten miles of the camps to learn something of the plants, animals, and rocks; for he assured me that I should be left perfectly free to follow my studies. I judged, however, that I was in no way the right man for the place, and freely explained my shortcomings, confessing that I was wholly unacquainted with the topography of the upper mountains, the streams that would have to be crossed, and the wild sheep-eating animals, etc.; in short that, what with bears, coyotes, rivers, cañons, and thorny, bewildering chaparral, I feared that half or more of his flock would be lost. Fortunately

7

these shortcomings seemed insignificant to Mr. Delaney. The main thing, he said, was to have a man about the camp whom he could trust to see that the shepherd did his duty, and he assured me that the difficulties that seemed so formidable at a distance would vanish as we went on; encouraging me further by saying that the shepherd would do all the herding, that I could study plants and rocks and scenery as much as I liked, and that he would himself accompany us to the first main camp and make occasional visits to our higher ones to replenish our store of provisions and see how we prospered. Therefore I concluded to go, though still fearing, when I saw the silly sheep bouncing one by one through the narrow gate of the home corral to be counted, that of the two thousand and fifty many would never return.

I was fortunate in getting a fine St. Bernard dog for a companion. His master, a hunter with whom I was slightly acquainted, came to me as soon as he heard that I was going to spend the summer in the Sierra and begged me to take his favorite dog, Carlo, with me, for he feared that if he were compelled to stay all summer on the plains the fierce heat might be the death of him. "I think I can trust you to be kind to him," he said, "and I am sure he will be good to you. He knows all about the mountain animals, will guard the camp, assist in managing the sheep, and in every way be found able and faithful." Carlo knew we were talking about him, watched our faces, and listened so attentively that I fancied he understood us. Calling him by name, I asked him if he was willing to go with me. He looked me in the face with eyes expressing wonderful intelligence, then turned to his master, and after permission was given by a wave of the hand toward me and a farewell patting caress, he quietly followed me as if he perfectly understood all that had been said and had known me always.

June 3, 1869. This morning provisions, camp-kettles, blankets, plant-press, etc., were packed on two horses, the flock headed for the tawny foothills, and away we sauntered in a cloud of dust: Mr. Delaney, bony and tall, with sharply hacked profile like Don Quixote, leading the pack-horses, Billy, the proud shepherd, a Chinaman and a Digger Indian to assist in driving for the first few days in the brushy foothills, and myself with notebook tied to my belt.

The home ranch from which we set out is on the south side of the Tuolumne River near French Bar, where the foothills of metamorphic gold-bearing slates dip below the stratified deposits of the Central Valley. We had not gone more than a mile before some of the old leaders of the flock showed by the eager, inquiring way they ran and looked ahead that they were thinking of the high pastures they had enjoyed last summer. Soon the whole flock seemed to be hopefully excited, the mothers calling their lambs, the lambs replying in tones wonderfully human, their fondly quavering calls interrupted now and then by hastily snatched mouthfuls of withered grass. Amid all this seeming babel of baas as they streamed over the hills every mother and child recognized each other's voice. In case a tired lamb, half asleep in the smothering dust, should fail to answer, its mother would come running back through the flock toward the spot whence its last response was heard, and refused to be comforted until she found it, the one of a thousand, though to our eyes and ears all seemed alike.

The flock traveled at the rate of about a mile an hour, outspread in the form of an irregular triangle, about a hundred yards wide at the base, and a hundred and fifty yards long, with a crooked, ever-changing point made up of the strongest foragers, called the "leaders," which, with the most active of those scattered along the ragged sides of the "main body," hastily explored nooks in the rocks and bushes for grass and leaves; the lambs and feeble old mothers dawdling in the rear were called the "tail end."

About noon the heat was hard to bear; the poor sheep panted pitifully and tried to stop in the shade of every tree they came to, while we gazed with eager longing through the dim burning glare toward the snowy mountains and streams, though not one was in sight. The landscape is only wavering foothills roughened here and there with bushes and trees and outcropping masses of slate. The trees, mostly the blue oak (*Quercus Douglasii*), are about thirty to forty feet high, with pale blue-green leaves and white bark, sparsely planted on the thinnest soil or in crevices of rocks beyond the reach of grass fires. The slates in many places rise abruptly through the tawny grass in sharp lichen-covered slabs like tombstones in deserted burying-grounds. With the exception of the oak and four or five species of manzanita and ceanothus, the vegetation of the foothills is mostly the same as that of the plains. I saw this region in the early spring, when it was a charming landscape garden full of birds and bees and flowers. Now the scorching weather makes everything dreary. The ground is full of cracks, lizards glide about on the rocks, and ants in amazing numbers, whose tiny sparks of life only burn the brighter with the heat, fairly quiver with unquenchable energy as they run in long lines to fight and gather food. How it comes that they do not dry to a crisp in a few seconds' exposure to such sun-fire is mar-velous. A few rattlesnakes lie coiled in out-of-the-way places, but are seldom seen. Magpies and crows, usually so noisy, are silent now, standing in mixed flocks on the ground beneath the best shade trees, with bills wide open and wings drooped, too breathless to speak; the quails also are trying to keep in the shade about the few tepid alkaline water-holes; cottontail rabbits are running from shade to shade among the ceanothus brush, and occasionally the long-eared hare is seen cantering gracefully across the wider openings.

After a short noon rest in a grove, the poor dust-choked flock was again driven ahead over the brushy hills, but the dim roadway we had been following faded away just where it was most needed, compelling us to stop to look about us and get our bearings. The Chinaman seemed to think we were lost, and chattered in pidgin English concerning the abundance of "litty stick" (chaparral), while the Indian silently scanned the billowy ridges and gulches for openings. Pushing through the thorny jungle, we at length discovered a road trending toward Coulterville, which we followed until an hour before sunset, when we reached a dry ranch and camped for the night.

Camping in the foothills with a flock of sheep is simple and easy, but far from pleasant. The sheep were allowed to pick what they could find in the neighborhood until after sunset, watched by the shepherd, while the others gathered wood, made a fire, cooked, unpacked and fed the horses, etc. About dusk the weary sheep were gathered on the highest open spot near camp, where they willingly bunched close together, and after each mother had found her lamb and suckled it, all lay down and required no attention until morning.

Supper was announced by the call, "Grub!" Each with a tin plate helped himself direct from the pots and pans while chatting about such camp studies as sheep-feed, mines, coyotes, bears, or adventures during the memorable gold days of pay dirt. The Indian kept in the background, saying never a word, as if he belonged to another species. The meal finished, the dogs were fed, the smokers smoked by the fire, and under the influences of fullness and tobacco the calm that settled on their faces seemed almost divine, something like the mellow meditative glow portrayed on the countenances of saints. Then suddenly, as if awakening from a dream, each with a sigh or a grunt knocked the ashes out of his pipe, yawned, gazed at the fire a few moments, said, "Well, I believe I'll turn in," and straightway vanished beneath his blankets. The fire smouldered and flickered an hour or two longer; the stars shone brighter; coons, coyotes, and owls stirred the silence here and there, while crickets and hylas made a cheerful, continuous music, so fitting and full that it seemed a part of the very body of the night. The only discordance came from a snoring sleeper, and the coughing sheep with dust in their throats. In the starlight the flock looked like a big gray blanket.

June 4. The camp was astir at daybreak; coffee, bacon, and beans formed the breakfast, followed by quick dish-washing and packing. A general bleating began about sunrise. As soon as a mother ewe arose, her lamb came bounding and bunting for its breakfast, and after the thousand youngsters had been suckled the flock began to nibble and spread. The restless wethers with ravenous appetites were the first to move, but dared not go far from the main body. Billy and the Indian and the Chinaman kept them headed along the weary road, and allowed them to pick up what little they could find on a breadth of about a quarter of a mile. But as several flocks had already gone ahead of us, scarce a leaf, green or dry, was left; therefore the starving flock had to be hurried on over the bare, hot hills to the nearest of the green pastures, about twenty or thirty miles from here.

The pack-animals were led by Don Quixote, a heavy rifle over his shoulder intended for bears and wolves. This day has been as hot and dusty as the first, leading over gently sloping brown hills, with mostly the same vegetation, excepting the strange-looking Sabine pine (*Pinus Sabiniana*), which here forms small groves or is scattered among the blue oaks. The trunk divides at a height of fifteen or twenty feet into two or more stems, outleaning or nearly upright, with many straggling branches and long gray needles, casting but little shade. In general appearance this tree looks more like a palm than a pine. The cones are about six or seven inches long, about five in diameter, very heavy, and last long after they fall, so that the ground beneath the trees is covered with them. They make fine resiny, light-giving camp-fires, next to ears of Indian corn the most beautiful fuel I've ever seen. The nuts, the Don tells me, are gathered in large quantities by the Digger Indians for food. They are about as large and hard-shelled as hazelnuts—food and fire fit for the gods from the same fruit.

June 5. This morning a few hours after setting out with the crawling sheep-cloud, we gained the summit of the first well-defined bench on the mountain-flank at Pino Blanco. The Sabine pines interest me greatly. They are so airy and strangely palm-like I was eager to sketch them, and was in a fever of excitement without accomplishing much. I managed to halt long enough, however, to make a tolerably fair sketch of Pino Blanco peak from the southwest side, where there is a small field and vineyard irrigated by a stream that makes a pretty fall on its way down a gorge by the roadside.

After gaining the open summit of this first bench, feeling the natural exhilaration due to the slight elevation of a thousand feet or so, and the hopes excited concerning the outlook to be obtained, a magnificent section of the Merced Valley at what is called Horseshoe Bend came full in sight—a glorious wilderness that seemed to be calling with a thousand songful voices. Bold, down-sweeping slopes, feathered with pines and clumps of manzanita with sunny, open spaces between them, make up most of the foreground; the middle and background present fold beyond fold of finely modeled hills and ridges rising into mountain-like masses in the distance, all covered with a shaggy growth of chaparral, mostly adenostoma, planted so marvelously close and even that it looks like soft, rich plush without a

Horseshoe Bend, Merced River

On second bench. Edge of the main forest belt, above Coulterville,
near Greeley's Mill

single tree or bare spot. As far as the eye can reach it extends, a heaving, swelling sea of green as regular and continuous as that produced by the heaths of Scotland. The sculpture of the landscape is as striking in its main lines as in its lavish richness of detail; a grand congregation of massive heights with the river shining between, each carved into smooth, graceful folds without leaving a single rocky angle exposed, as if the delicate fluting and ridging fashioned out of metamorphic slates had been carefully sandpapered. The whole landscape showed design, like man's noblest sculptures. How wonderful the power of its beauty! Gazing awe-stricken, I might have left everything for it. Glad, endless work would then be mine tracing the forces that have brought forth its features, its rocks and plants and animals and glorious weather. Beauty beyond thought everywhere, beneath, above, made and being made forever. I gazed and gazed and longed and admired until the dusty sheep and packs were far out of sight, made hurried notes and a sketch, though there was no need of either, for the colors and lines and expression of this divine landscape-countenance are so burned into mind and heart they surely can never grow dim.

The evening of this charmed day is cool, calm, cloudless, and full of a kind of lightning I have never seen before—white glowing cloud-shaped masses down among the trees and bushes, like quick-throbbing fireflies in the Wisconsin meadows rather than the so-called "wild fire." The spreading hairs of the horses' tails and sparks from our blankets show how highly charged the air is.

June 6. We are now on what may be called the second bench or plateau of the Range, after making many small ups and downs over belts of hill-waves, with, of course, corresponding changes in the vegetation. In open spots many of the lowland compositæ are still to be found, and some of the Mariposa tulips and other conspicuous members of the lily family; but the characteristic blue oak of the foothills is left below, and its place is taken by a fine large species (*Quercus Californica*) with deeply lobed deciduous leaves, picturesquely divided trunk, and broad, massy, finely lobed and modeled head. Here also at a height of about twenty-five hundred feet we come to the edge of the great coniferous forest, made up mostly of yellow pine with just a few sugar pines. We are now in the mountains and they are in us, kindling enthusiasm, making every nerve quiver, filling every pore and cell of us. Our flesh-and-bone tabernacle seems transparent as glass to the beauty about us, as if truly an inseparable part of it, thrilling with the air and trees, streams and rocks, in the waves of the sun,—a part of all nature, neither old nor young, sick nor well, but immortal. Just now I can hardly conceive of any bodily condition dependent on food or breath any more than the ground or the sky. How glorious a conversion, so complete and wholesome it is, scarce memory enough of old bondage days left as a standpoint to view it from! In this newness of life we seem to have been so always.

Through a meadow opening in the pine woods I see snowy peaks about the head-waters of the Merced above Yosemite. How near they seem and how clear their outlines on the blue air, or rather *in* the blue air; for they seem to be saturated with it. How consuming strong the invitation they extend! Shall I be allowed to go to them? Night and day I'll pray that I may, but it seems too good to be true. Some one worthy will go, able for the Godful work, yet as far as I can I must drift about these love-monument mountains, glad to be a servant of servants in so holy a wilderness.

Found a lovely lily (*Calochortus albus*) in a shady adenostoma thicket near Coulterville, in company with *Adiantum Chilense*. It is white with a faint purplish tinge inside at the base of the petals, a most impressive plant, pure as a snow crystal, one of the plant saints that all must love and be made so much the purer by it every time it is seen. It puts the roughest mountaineer on his good behavior. With this plant the whole world would seem rich though none other existed. It is not easy to keep on with the camp cloud while such plant people are standing preaching by the wayside.

During the afternoon we passed a fine meadow bounded by stately pines, mostly the arrowy yellow pine, with here and there a noble sugar pine, its feathery arms outspread above the spires of its companion species in marked contrast; a glorious tree, its cones fifteen to twenty inches long, swinging like tassels at the ends of the branches with superb ornamental effect. Saw some logs of this species at the Greeley Mill. They are round and regular as if turned in a lathe, excepting the butt cuts, which have a few buttressing projections. The fragrance of the sugary sap is delicious and scents the mill and lumber yard. How beautiful the ground beneath this pine thickly strewn with slender needles and grand cones, and the piles of cone-scales, seed-wings and shells around the instep of each tree where the squirrels have been feasting! They get the seeds by cutting off the scales at the base in regular order, following their spiral arrangement, and the two seeds at the base of each scale, a hundred or two in a cone, must make a good meal. The yellow pine cones and those of most other species and genera are held upside down on the ground by the Douglas squirrel, and turned around gradually until stripped, while he sits usually with his back to a tree, probably for safety. Strange to say, he never seems to get himself smeared with gum, not even his paws or whiskers—and how cleanly and beautiful in color the cone-litter kitchen-middens he makes.

We are now approaching the region of clouds and cool streams. Magnificent white cumuli appeared about noon above the Yosemite region,—floating fountains refreshing the glorious wilderness,—sky mountains in whose pearly hills and dales the streams take their rise,—blessing with cooling shadows and rain. No rock landscape is more varied in sculpture, none more delicately modeled than these landscapes of the sky; domes and peaks rising, swelling, white as finest marble and firmly outlined, a most impressive manifestation of world building. Every rain-cloud, however fleeting, leaves its mark, not only on trees and flowers whose pulses are quickened, and on the replenished streams and lakes, but also on the rocks are its marks engraved whether we can see them or not.

I have been examining the curious and influential shrub *Adenostoma fasciculata*, first noticed about Horseshoe Bend. It is very abundant on the lower slopes of the second plateau near Coulterville, forming a dense, almost impenetrable growth that looks dark in the distance. It belongs to the rose family, is about six or eight feet high, has small white flowers in racemes eight to twelve inches long, round needle-like leaves, and reddish bark that becomes shreddy when old. It grows on sun-beaten slopes, and like grass is often swept away by running fires, but is quickly renewed from the roots. Any trees that may have established themselves in its midst are at length killed by these fires, and this no doubt is the secret of the unbroken character of its broad belts. A few manzanitas, which also rise again from the root after consuming fires, make out to dwell with it, also a few bush compositæ—baccharis and linosyris, and some liliaceous plants, mostly calochortus and brodiæa, with deepset bulbs safe from fire. A multitude of birds and "wee, sleekit, cow'rin', tim'rous beasties" find good homes in its deepest thickets, and the open bays and lanes that fringe the margins of its main belts offer shelter and food to the deer when winter storms drive them down from their high mountain pastures. A most admirable plant! It is now in bloom, and I like to wear its pretty fragrant racemes in my buttonhole.

Azalea occidentalis, another charming shrub, grows beside cool streams hereabouts and much higher in the Yosemite region. We found it this evening in bloom a few miles above Greeley's Mill, where we are camped for the night. It is closely related to the rhododendrons, is very showy and fragrant, and everybody must like it not only for itself but for the shady alders and willows, ferny meadows, and living water associated with it.

Another conifer was met to-day—incense cedar (*Libocedrus decurrens*), a large tree with warm yellow-green foliage in flat plumes like those of arborvitæ, bark cinnamon-colored, and as the boles of the old trees are without limbs they make striking pillars in the woods where the sun chances to shine on them— a worthy companion of the kingly sugar and yellow pines. I feel strangely attracted to this tree. The brown close-grained wood, as well as the small scale-like leaves, is fragrant, and the flat over-lapping plumes make fine beds, and must shed the rain well. It would be delightful to be storm-bound beneath one of these noble, hospitable, inviting old trees, its broad sheltering arms bent down like a tent, incense rising from the fire made from its dry fallen branches, and a hearty wind chanting overhead. But the weather is calm to-night, and our camp is only a sheep camp. We are near the North Fork of the Merced. The night wind is telling the wonders of the upper mountains, their snow fountains and gardens, forests and groves; even their topography is in its tones. And the stars, the everlasting sky lilies, how bright they are now that we have climbed above the lowland dust! The horizon is bounded and adorned by a spiry wall of pines, every tree harmoniously related to every other; definite symbols, divine hieroglyphics written with sunbeams. Would I could understand them! The stream flowing past the camp through ferns and lilies and alders makes sweet music to the ear, but the pines marshaled around the edge of the sky make a yet sweeter music to the eye. Divine beauty all. Here I could stay tethered forever with just bread and water, nor would I be lonely; loved friends and neighbors, as love for everything increased, would seem all the nearer however many the miles and mountains between us.

June 7. The sheep were sick last night, and many of them are still far from well, hardly able to leave camp, coughing, groaning, looking wretched and pitiful, all from eating the leaves of the blessed azalea. So at least say the shepherd and the Don. Having had but little grass since they left the plains, they are starving, and so eat anything green they can get. "Sheep-men" call azalea "sheep-poison," and wonder what the Creator was thinking about when he made it—so desperately does sheep business blind and degrade, though supposed to have a refining influence in the good old days we read of. The California sheep owner is in haste to get rich, and often does, now that pasturage costs nothing, while the climate is so favorable that no winter food supply, shelter-pens, or barns are required. Therefore large flocks may be kept at slight expense, and large profits realized, the money invested doubling, it is claimed, every other year. This quickly acquired wealth usually creates desire for more. Then indeed the wool is drawn close down over the poor fellow's eyes, dimming or shutting out almost everything worth seeing.

As for the shepherd, his case is still worse, especially in winter when he lives alone in a cabin. For, though stimulated at times by hopes of one day owning a flock and getting rich like his boss, he at the same time is likely to be degraded by the life he leads, and seldom reaches the dignity or advantage—or disadvantage—of ownership. The degradation in his case has for cause one not far to seek. He is solitary most of the year, and solitude to most people seems hard to bear. He seldom has much good mental work or recreation in the way of books. Coming into his dingy hovel-cabin at night, stupidly weary, he finds nothing to balance and level his life with the universe. No, after his dull drag all day after the sheep, he must get his supper; he is likely to slight this task and try to satisfy his hunger with whatever comes handy. Perhaps no bread is baked; then he just makes a few grimy flapjacks in his unwashed frying-pan, boils a handful of tea, and perhaps fries a few strips of rusty bacon. Usually there are dried peaches or apples in the cabin, but he hates to be bothered with the cooking of them, just swallows the bacon and flapjacks, and depends on the genial stupefaction of tobacco for the rest. Then to bed, often without removing the clothing worn during the day. Of course his health suffers, reacting on his mind; and seeing nobody for weeks or months, he finally becomes semi-insane or wholly so.

The shepherd in Scotland seldom thinks of being anything but a shepherd. He has probably descended from a race of shepherds and inherited a love and aptitude for the business almost as marked as that of his collie. He has but a small flock to look after, sees his family and neighbors, has time for reading in fine weather, and often carries books to the fields with which he may converse with kings. The oriental shepherd, we read, called his sheep by name; they knew his voice and followed him. The flocks must have been small and easily managed, allowing piping on the hills and ample leisure for reading and thinking. But whatever the blessings of sheep-culture in other times and countries, the California shepherd, as far as I've seen or heard, is never quite sane for any considerable time. Of all Nature's voices baa is about all he hears. Even the howls and ki-yis of coyotes might be blessings if well heard, but he hears them only through a blur of mutton and wool, and they do him no good.

The sick sheep are getting well, and the shepherd is discoursing on the various poisons lurking in these high pastures—azalea, kalmia, alkali. After crossing the North Fork of the Merced we turned to the left toward Pilot Peak, and made a considerable ascent on a rocky, brush-covered ridge to Brown's Flat, where for the first time since leaving the plains the flock is enjoying plenty of green grass. Mr. Delaney intends to seek a permanent camp somewhere in the neighborhood, to last several weeks.

Before noon we passed Bower Cave, a delightful marble palace, not dark and dripping, but filled with sunshine, which pours into it through its wide-open mouth facing the south. It has a fine, deep, clear little lake with mossy banks embowered with broad-leaved maples, all under ground, wholly unlike anything I have seen in the cave line even in Kentucky, where a large part of the State is honeycombed with caves. This curious specimen of subterranean scenery is located on a belt of marble that is said to extend from the north end of the Range to the extreme south. Many other caves occur on the belt, but none like this, as far as I have learned, combining as it does sunny outdoor brightness and vegetation with the crystalline beauty of the underworld. It is claimed by a Frenchman, who has fenced and locked it, placed a boat on the lakelet and seats on the mossy bank under the maple trees, and charges a dollar admission fee. Being on one of the ways to the Yosemite Valley, a good many tourists visit it during the travel months of summer, regarding it as an interesting addition to their Yosemite wonders.

Poison oak or poison ivy (*Rhus diversiloba*), both as a bush and a scrambler up trees and rocks, is common throughout the foothill region up to a height of at least three thousand feet above the sea. It is somewhat troublesome to most travelers, inflaming the skin and eyes, but blends harmoniously with its companion plants, and many a charming flower leans confidingly upon it for protection and shade. I have oftentimes found the curious twining lily (*Stropholirion Californicum*) climbing its branches, showing no fear but rather congenial companionship. Sheep eat it without apparent ill effects; so do horses to some extent, though not fond of it, and to many persons it is harmless. Like most other things not apparently useful to man, it has few friends, and the blind question, "Why was it made?" goes on and on with never a guess that first of all it might have been made for itself.

Brown's Flat is a shallow fertile valley on the top of the divide between the North Fork of the Merced and Bull Creek, commanding magnificent views in every direction. Here the adventurous pioneer David Brown made his headquarters for many years, dividing his time between gold-hunting and bear-hunting. Where could lonely hunter find a better solitude? Game in the woods, gold in the rocks, health and exhilaration in the air, while the colors and cloud furniture of the sky are ever inspiring through all sorts of weather. Though sternly practical, like most pioneers, old David seems to have been uncommonly fond of scenery. Mr. Delaney, who knew him well, tells me that he dearly loved to climb to the summit of a commanding ridge to gaze abroad over the forest to the snow-clad peaks and sources of the rivers, and over the foreground valleys and gulches to note where miners were at work or claims were abandoned, judging by smoke from cabins and camp-fires, the sounds of axes, etc.; and when a rifle-shot was heard, to guess who was the hunter, whether Indian or some poacher on his wide domain. His dog Sandy accompanied him everywhere, and well the little hairy mountaineer knew and loved his master and his master's aims. In deer-hunting he had but little to do, trotting behind his master as he slowly made his way through the wood, careful not to step heavily on dry twigs, scanning open spots in the chaparral, where the game loves to feed in the early morning and towards sunset; peering cautiously over ridges as new outlooks were reached, and along the meadowy borders of streams. But when bears were hunted, little Sandy became more important, and it was as a bear-hunter that Brown became famous. His hunting method, as described by Mr. Delaney, who had passed many a night with him in his lonely cabin and learned his stories, was simply to go slowly and silently through the best bear pastures, with his dog and rifle and a few pounds of flour, until he found a fresh track and then follow it to the death, paying no heed to the time required. Wherever the bear went he followed, led by little Sandy, who had a keen nose and never lost the track, however rocky the ground. When high open points were reached, the likeliest places were carefully scanned. The time of year enabled the hunter to determine approximately where the bear would be found,—in the spring and early summer on open spots about the banks of streams and springy places eating grass and clover and lupines, or in dry meadows feasting on strawberries; toward the end of summer, on dry ridges, feasting on manzanita berries, sitting on his haunches, pulling down the laden branches with his paws, and pressing them together so as to get good compact mouthfuls however much mixed with twigs and leaves; in the Indian summer, beneath the pines, chewing the cones cut off by the squirrels, or occasionally climbing a tree to gnaw and break off the fruitful branches. In late autumn, when acorns are ripe, Bruin's favorite feeding-grounds are groves of the California oak in park-like cañon flats. Always the cunning hunter knew where to look, and seldom came upon Bruin unawares. When the hot scent showed the dangerous game was nigh, a long halt was made, and the intricacies of the topography and vegetation leisurely scanned to catch a glimpse of the shaggy wanderer, or to at least determine where he was most likely to be.

"Whenever," said the hunter, "I saw a bear before it saw me I had no trouble in killing it. I just studied the lay of the land and got to leeward of it no matter how far around I had to go, and then worked up to within a few hundred yards or so, at the foot of a tree that I could easily climb, but too small for the bear to climb. Then I looked well to the condition of my rifle, took off my boots so as to climb well if necessary, and waited until the bear turned its side in clear view when I could make a sure or at least a good shot. In case it showed fight I climbed out of reach. But bears are slow and awkward with their eyes, and being to leeward of them they could not scent me, and I often got in a second shot before they noticed the smoke. Usually, however, they run when wounded and hide in the brush. I let them run a good safe time before I ventured to follow them, and Sandy was pretty sure to find them dead. If not, he barked and drew their attention, and occasionally rushed in for a distracting bite, so that I was able to get to a safe distance for a final shot. Oh, yes, bear-hunting is safe enough when followed in a safe way, though like every other business it has its accidents, and little doggie and I have had some close calls. Bears like to keep out of the way of men as a general thing, but if an old, lean, hungry mother with cubs met a man on her own ground she would, in my opinion, try to catch and eat him. This would be only fair play anyhow, for we eat them, but nobody hereabout has been used for bear grub that I know of."

Brown had left his mountain home ere we arrived, but a considerable number of Digger Indians still linger in their cedar-bark huts on the edge of the flat. They were attracted in the first place by the white hunter whom they had learned to respect, and to whom they looked for guidance and protection against their enemies the Pah Utes, who sometimes made raids across from the east side of the Range to plunder the stores of the comparatively feeble Diggers and steal their wives.

Chapter II

JUNE 8. The sheep, now grassy and good-natured, slowly nibbled their way down into the valley of the North Fork of the Merced at the foot of Pilot Peak Ridge to the place selected by the Don for our first central camp, a picturesque hopper-shaped hollow formed by converging hill slopes at a bend of the river. Here racks for dishes and provisions were made in the shade of the river-bank trees, and beds of fern fronds, cedar plumes, and various flowers, each to the taste of its owner, and a corral back on the open flat for the wool.

June 9. How deep our sleep last night in the mountain's heart, beneath the trees and stars, hushed by solemn-sounding waterfalls and many small soothing voices in sweet accord whispering peace! And our first pure mountain day, warm, calm, cloudless,—how immeasurable it seems, how serenely wild! I can scarcely remember its beginning. Along the river, over the hills, in the ground, in the sky, spring work is going on with joyful enthusiasm, new life, new beauty, unfolding, unrolling in glorious exuberant extravagance,—new birds in their nests, new winged creatures in the air, and new leaves, new flowers, spreading, shining, rejoicing everywhere.

The trees about the camp stand close, giving ample shade for ferns and lilies, while back from the bank most of the sunshine reaches the ground, calling up the grasses and flowers in glorious array, tall bromus waving like bamboos, starry compositæ, monardella, Mariposa tulips, lupines, gilias, violets, glad children of light. Soon every fern frond will be unrolled, great beds of common pteris and woodwardia along the river, wreaths and rosettes of pellæa and cheilanthes on sunny rocks. Some of the woodwardia fronds are already six feet high.

A handsome little shrub, *Chamæbatia foliolosa*, belonging to the rose family, spreads a yellow-green mantle beneath the sugar pines for miles without a break, not mixed or roughened with other plants. Only here and there a Washington lily may be seen nodding above its even surface, or a bunch or two of tall bromus as if for ornament. This fine carpet shrub begins to appear at, say, twenty-five hundred or three thousand feet above sea level, is about knee high or less, has brown branches, and the largest stems are only about half an inch in diameter. The leaves, light yellow green, thrice pinnate and finely cut, give them a rich ferny appearance, and they are dotted with minute glands that secrete wax with a peculiar pleasant odor that blends finely with the spicy fragrance of the pines. The flowers are white, five eighths of an inch in diameter, and look like those of the strawberry. Am delighted with this little bush. It is the only true carpet shrub of this part of the Sierra. The manzanita, rhamnus, and most of the species of ceanothus make shaggy rugs and border fringes rather than carpets or mantles.

The sheep do not take kindly to their new pastures, perhaps from being too closely hemmed in by the hills. They are never fully at rest. Last night they were frightened, probably by bears or coyotes prowling and planning for a share of the grand mass of mutton.

June 10. Very warm. We get water for the camp from a rock basin at the foot of a picturesque cascading reach of the river where it is well stirred and made lively without being beaten into dusty foam. The rock here is black metamorphic slate, worn into smooth knobs in the stream channels, contrasting with the fine gray and white cascading water as it glides and glances and falls in lace-like sheets and braided overfolding currents. Tufts of sedge growing on the rock knobs that rise above the surface produce a charming effect, the long elastic leaves arching over in every direction, the tips of the longest drooping into the current, which dividing against the projecting rocks makes still finer lines, uniting with the sedges to see how beautiful the happy stream can be made. Nor is this all, for the giant saxifrage also is growing on some of the knob rock islets, firmly anchored and displaying their broad, round, umbrella-like leaves in showy groups by themselves, or above the sedge tufts. The flowers of this species (*Saxifraga peltata*) are purple, and form tall glandular racemes that are in bloom before the appearance of the leaves. The fleshy root-stocks grip the rock in cracks and hollows, and thus enable the plant to hold on against occasional floods,—a marked species employed by Nature to make yet more beautiful the most interesting portions of these cool clear streams. Near camp the trees arch over from bank to bank, making a leafy tunnel full of soft subdued light, through which the young river sings and shines like a happy living creature.

Heard a few peals of thunder from the upper Sierra, and saw firm white bossy cumuli rising back of the pines. This was about noon.

June 11. On one of the eastern branches of the river discovered some charming cascades with a pool at the foot of each of them. White dashing water, a few bushes and tufts of carex on ledges leaning over with fine effect, and large orange lilies assembled in superb groups on fertile soil-beds beside the pools.

There are no large meadows or grassy plains near camp to supply lasting pasture for our thousands of busy nibblers. The main dependence is ceanothus brush on the hills and tufted grass patches here and there, with lupines and pea-vines among the flowers on sunny open spaces. Large areas have already been stripped bare, or nearly so, compelling the poor hungry wool bundles to scatter far and wide, keeping the shepherds and dogs at the top of their speed to hold them within bounds. Mr. Delaney has gone back to the plains, taking the Indian and Chinaman with him, leaving instruction to keep the flock here or hereabouts until his return, which he promised would not be long delayed.

How fine the weather is! Nothing more celestial can I conceive. How gently the winds blow! Scarce can these tranquil air-currents be called winds. They seem the very breath of Nature, whispering peace to every living thing. Down in the camp dell there is no swaying of tree-tops; most of the time not a leaf moves. I don't remember having seen a single lily swinging on its stalk, though they are so tall the least breeze would rock them. What grand bells these lilies have! Some of them big enough for children's bonnets. I have been sketching them, and would fain draw every leaf of their wide shining whorls and every curved and spotted petal. More beautiful, better kept gardens cannot be imagined. The species *Lilium pardalinum*, five to six feet high leaf-whorls a foot wide flowers about six inches wide, bright orange, purple spotted in the throat, segments revolute—a majestic plant.

June 12. A slight sprinkle of rain—large drops far apart, falling with hearty pat and plash on leaves and stones and into the mouths of the flowers. Cumuli rising to the eastward. How beautiful their pearly bosses! How well they harmonize with the upswelling rocks beneath them. Mountains of the sky, solid-looking, finely sculptured, their richly varied topography wonderfully defined. Never before have I seen clouds so substantial looking in form and texture. Nearly every day toward noon they rise with visible swelling motion as if new worlds were being created. And how fondly they brood and hover over the gardens and forests with their cooling shadows and showers, keeping every petal and leaf in glad health and heart. One may fancy the clouds themselves are plants, springing up in the skyfields at the call of the sun, growing in beauty until they reach their prime, scattering rain and hail like berries and seeds, then wilting and dying.

The mountain live oak, common here and a thousand feet or so higher, is like the live oak of Florida, not only in general appearance, foliage, bark, and wide-branching habit, but in its tough, knotty, unwedgeable wood. Standing alone with plenty of elbow room, the largest trees are about seven to eight feet in diameter near the ground, sixty feet high, and as wide or wider across the head. The leaves are small and undivided, mostly without teeth or wavy edging, though on young shoots some are sharply serrated, both kinds being found on the same tree. The cups of the medium-sized acorns are shallow, thick walled, and covered with a golden dust of minute hairs. Some of the trees have hardly any main trunk, dividing near the ground into large wide-spreading limbs, and these, dividing again and again, terminate in long, drooping, cordlike branchlets, many of which reach nearly to the ground, while a dense canopy of short, shining, leafy branchlets forms a round head which looks something like a cumulus cloud when the sunshine is pouring over it.

A marked plant is the bush poppy (*Dendromecon rigidum*), found on the hot hillsides near camp, the only woody member of the order I have yet met in all my walks. Its flowers are bright orange yellow, an inch to two inches wide, fruit-pods three or four inches long, slender and curving,—height of bushes about four feet, made up of many slim, straight branches, radiating from the root,—a companion of the manzanita and other sun-loving chaparral shrubs.

Camp, North Fork of the Merced

Mountain Live Oak (Quercus chrysolepis), eight feet in diameter

June 13. Another glorious Sierra day in which one seems to be dissolved and absorbed and sent pulsing onward we know not where. Life seems neither long nor short, and we take no more heed to save time or make haste than do the trees and stars. This is true freedom, a good practical sort of immortality. Yonder rises another white skyland. How sharply the yellow pine spires and the palm-like crowns of the sugar pines are outlined on its smooth white domes. And hark! the grand thunder billows booming, rolling from ridge to ridge, followed by the faithful shower.

A good many herbaceous plants come thus far up the mountains from the plains, and are now in flower, two months later than their lowland relatives. Saw a few columbines to-day. Most of the ferns are in their prime,—rock ferns on the sunny hillsides, cheilanthes, pellæa, gymnogramme; woodwardia, aspidium, woodsia along the stream banks, and the common *Pteris aquilina* on sandy flats. This last, however common, is here making shows of strong, exuberant, abounding beauty to set the botanist wild with admiration. I measured some scarce full grown that are more than seven feet high. Though the commonest and most widely distributed of all the ferns, I might almost say that I never saw it before. The broad-shouldered fronds held high on smooth stout stalks growing close together, overleaning and overlapping, make a complete ceiling, beneath which one may walk erect over several acres without being seen, as if beneath a roof. And how soft and lovely the light streaming through this living ceiling, revealing the arching branching ribs and veins of the fronds as the framework of countless panes of pale green and yellow plant-glass nicely fitted together—a fairyland created out of the commonest fern-stuff.

The smaller animals wander about as if in a tropical forest. I saw the entire flock of sheep vanish at one side of a patch and reappear a hundred yards farther on at the other, their progress betrayed only by the jerking and trembling of the fronds; and strange to say very few of the stout woody stalks were broken. I sat a long time beneath the tallest fronds, and never enjoyed anything in the way of a bower of wild leaves more strangely impressive. Only spread a fern frond over a man's head and worldly cares are cast out, and freedom and beauty and peace come in. The waving of a pine tree on the top of a mountain,—a magic wand in Nature's hand,—every devout mountaineer knows its power; but the marvelous beauty value of what the Scotch call a breckan in a still dell, what poet has sung this? It would seem impossible that any one, however incrusted with care, could escape the Godful influence of these sacred fern forests. Yet this very day I saw a shepherd pass through one of the finest of them without betraying more feeling than his sheep. "What do you think of these grand ferns?" I asked. "Oh, they're only d——d big brakes," he replied.

Lizards of every temper, style, and color dwell here, seemingly as happy and companionable as the birds and squirrels. Lowly, gentle fellow mortals, enjoying God's sunshine, and doing the best they can in getting a living, I like to watch them at their work and play. They bear acquaintance well, and one likes them the better the longer one looks into their beautiful, innocent eyes. They are easily tamed, and one soon learns to love them, as they dart about on the hot rocks, swift as dragon-flies. The eye can hardly follow them; but they never make long-sustained runs, usually only about ten or twelve feet, then a sudden stop, and as sudden a start again; going all their journeys by quick, jerking impulses. These many stops I find are necessary as rests, for they are short-winded, and when pursued steadily are soon out of breath, pant pitifully, and are easily caught. Their bodies are more than half tail, but these tails are well managed, never heavily dragged nor curved up as if hard to carry; on the contrary, they seem to follow the body lightly of their own will. Some are colored like the sky, bright as bluebirds, others gray like the lichened rocks on which they hunt and bask. Even the horned toad of the plains is a mild, harmless creature, and so are the snake-like species which glide in curves with true snake motion, while their small, undeveloped limbs drag as useless appendages. One specimen fourteen inches long which I observed closely made no use whatever of its tender, sprouting limbs, but glided with all the soft, sly ease and grace of a snake. Here comes a little, gray, dusty fellow who seems to know and trust me, running about my feet, and looking up cunningly into my face. Carlo is watching, makes a quick pounce on him, for the fun of the thing I suppose; but Liz has shot away from his paws like an arrow, and is safe in the recesses of a clump of chaparral. Gentle saurians, dragons, descendants of an ancient and mighty race, Heaven bless you all and make your virtues known! for few of us know as yet that scales may cover fellow creatures as gentle and lovable as feathers, or hair, or cloth.

Mastodons and elephants used to live here no great geological time ago, as shown by their bones, often discovered by miners in washing gold-gravel. And bears of at least two species are here now, besides the California lion or panther, and wild cats, wolves, foxes, snakes, scorpions, wasps, tarantulas; but one is almost tempted at times to regard a small savage black ant as the master existence of this vast mountain world. These fearless, restless, wandering imps, though only about a quarter of an inch long, are fonder of fighting and biting than any beast I know. They attack every living thing around their homes, often without cause as far as I can see. Their bodies are mostly jaws curved like ice-hooks, and to get work for these weapons seems to be their chief aim and pleasure. Most of their colonies are established in living oaks somewhat decayed or hollowed, in which they can conveniently build their cells. These are chosen probably because of their strength as opposed to the attacks of animals and storms. They work both day and night, creep into dark caves, climb the highest trees, wander and hunt through cool ravines as well as on hot, unshaded ridges, and extend their highways and byways over everything but water and sky. From the foothills to a mile above the level of the sea nothing can stir without their knowledge; and alarms are spread in an incredibly short time, without any howl or cry that we can hear. I can't understand the need of their ferocious courage; there seems to be no common sense in it. Sometimes, no doubt, they fight in defense of their homes, but they fight anywhere and always wherever they can find anything to bite. As soon as a vulnerable spot is discovered on man or beast, they stand on their heads and sink their jaws, and though torn limb from limb, they will yet hold on and die biting deeper. When I contemplate this fierce creature so widely distributed and strongly intrenched, I see that much remains to be done ere the world is brought under the rule of universal peace and love.

On my way to camp a few minutes ago, I passed a dead pine nearly ten feet in diameter. It has been enveloped in fire from top to bottom so that now it looks like a grand black pillar set up as a monument. In this noble shaft a colony of large jet-black ants have established themselves, laboriously cutting tunnels and cells through the wood, whether sound or decayed. The entire trunk seems to have been honey-combed, judging by the size of the talus of gnawed chips like sawdust piled up around its base. They are more intelligent looking than their small, belligerent, strong-scented brethren, and have better manners, though quick to fight when required. Their towns are carved in fallen trunks as well as in those left standing, but never in sound, living trees or in the ground. When you happen to sit down to rest or take notes near a colony, some wandering hunter is sure to find you and come cautiously forward to discover the nature of the intruder and what ought to be done. If you are not too near the town and keep perfectly still he may run across your feet a few times, over your legs and hands and face, up your trousers, as if taking your measure and getting comprehensive views, then go in peace without raising an alarm. If, however, a tempting spot is offered or some suspicious movement excites him, a bite follows, and such a bite! I fancy that a bear or wolf bite is not to be compared with it. A quick electric flame of pain flashes along the outraged nerves, and you discover for the first time how great is the capacity for sensation you are possessed of. A shriek, a grab for the animal, and a bewildered stare follow this bite of bites as one comes back to consciousness from sudden eclipse. Fortunately, if careful, one need not be bitten oftener than once or twice in a lifetime. This wonderful electric species is about three fourths of an inch long. Bears are fond of them, and tear and gnaw their home-logs to pieces, and roughly devour the eggs, larvæ, parent ants, and the rotten or sound wood of the cells, all in one spicy acid hash. The Digger Indians also are fond of the larvæ and even of the perfect ants, so I have been told by old mountaineers. They bite off and reject the head, and eat the tickly acid body with keen relish. Thus are the poor biters bitten, like every other biter, big or little, in the world's great family.

There is also a fine, active, intelligent-looking red species, intermediate in size between the above. They dwell in the ground, and build large piles of seed husks, leaves, straw, etc., over their nests. Their food seems to be mostly insects and plant leaves, seeds and sap. How many mouths Nature has to fill, how many neighbors we have, how little we know about them, and how seldom we get in each other's way! Then to think of the infinite numbers of smaller fellow mortals, invisibly small, compared with which the smallest ants are as mastodons.

June 14. The pool-basins below the falls and cascades here-abouts, formed by the heavy down-plunging currents, are kept nicely clean and clear of detritus. The heavier parts of the material swept over the falls are heaped up a short distance in front of the basins in the form of a dam, thus tending, together with erosion, to increase their size. Sudden changes, however, are effected during the spring floods, when the snow is melting and the upper tributaries are roaring loud from "bank to brae." Then boulders that have fallen into the channels, and which the ordinary summer and winter currents were unable to move, are suddenly swept forward as by a mighty besom, hurled over the falls into these pools, and piled up in a new dam together with part of the old one, while some of the smaller boulders are carried farther down stream and variously lodged according to size and shape, all seeking rest where the force of the current is less than the resistance they are able to offer. But the great-est changes made in these relations of fall, pool, and dam are caused, not by the ordinary spring floods, but by extraordinary ones that occur at irregular intervals. The testimony of trees growing on flood boulder deposits shows that a century or more has passed since the last master flood came to awaken everything movable to go swirling and dancing on wonderful journeys. These floods may occur during the summer, when heavy thunder-showers, called "cloud-bursts," fall on wide, steeply inclined stream basins furrowed by converging chan-nels, which suddenly gather the waters together into the main trunk in booming torrents of enormous transporting power, though short lived.

One of these ancient flood boulders stands firm in the middle of the stream channel, just below the lower edge of the pool dam at the foot of the fall nearest our camp. It is a nearly cubical mass of granite about eight feet high, plushed with mosses over the top and down the sides to ordinary high-water mark. When I climbed on top of it to-day and lay down to rest, it seemed the most romantic spot I had yet found—the one big stone with its mossy level top and smooth sides standing square and firm and solitary, like an altar, the fall in front of it bathing it lightly with the finest of the spray, just enough to keep its moss cover fresh; the clear green pool beneath, with its foam-bells and its half circle of lilies leaning forward like a band of admirers, and flowering dogwood and alder trees leaning over all in sun-sifted arches. How soothingly, restfully cool it is beneath that leafy, translucent ceiling, and how delightful the water music—the deep bass tones of the fall, the clashing, ringing spray, and infinite variety of small low tones of the current gliding past the side of the boulder-island, and glinting against a thousand smaller stones down the ferny channel! All this shut in; every one of these influences acting at short range as if in a quiet room. The place seemed holy, where one might hope to see God.

After dark, when the camp was at rest, I groped my way back to the altar boulder and passed the night on it,—above the water, beneath the leaves and stars,—everything still more impressive than by day, the fall seen dimly white, singing Nature's old love song with solemn enthusiasm, while the stars peering through the leaf-roof seemed to join in the white water's song. Precious night, precious day to abide in me forever. Thanks be to God for this immortal gift.

June 15. Another reviving morning. Down the long mountain-slopes the sunbeams pour, gilding the awakening pines, cheering every needle, filling every living thing with joy. Robins are singing in the alder and maple groves, the same old song that has cheered and sweetened countless seasons over almost all of our blessed continent. In this mountain hollow they seem as much at home as in farmers' orchards. Bullock's oriole and the Louisiana tanager are here also, with many warblers and other little mountain troubadours, most of them now busy about their nests.

Discovered another magnificent specimen of the goldcup oak six feet in diameter, a Douglas spruce seven feet, and a twining lily (*Stropholirion*), with stem eight feet long, and sixty rose-colored flowers.

Sugar pine cones are cylindrical, slightly tapered at the end and rounded at the base. Found one to-day nearly twenty-four inches long and six in diameter, the scales being open. Another specimen nineteen inches long; the average length of full-grown cones on trees favorably situated is nearly eighteen inches. On the lower edge of the belt at a height of about twenty-five hundred feet above the sea they are smaller, say a foot to fifteen inches long, and at a height of seven thousand feet or more near the upper limits of its growth in the Yosemite region they are about the same size. This noble tree is an inexhaustible study and source of pleasure. I never weary of gazing at its grand tassel cones, its perfectly round bole one hundred feet or more without a limb, the fine purplish color of its bark, and its

Sugar Pine

magnificent outsweeping, down-curving feathery arms forming
a crown always bold and striking and exhilarating. In habit and
general port it looks somewhat like a palm, but no palm that I
have yet seen displays such majesty of form and behavior either
when poised silent and thoughtful in sunshine, or wide-awake
waving in storm winds with every needle quivering. When
young it is very straight and regular in form like most other
conifers; but at the age of fifty to one hundred years it begins
to acquire individuality, so that no two are alike in their prime
or old age. Every tree calls for special admiration. I have been
making many sketches, and regret that I cannot draw every
needle. It is said to reach a height of three hundred feet, though
the tallest I have measured falls short of this stature sixty feet or
more. The diameter of the largest near the ground is about ten
feet, though I've heard of some twelve feet thick or even fifteen.
The diameter is held to a great height, the taper being almost
imperceptibly gradual. Its companion, the yellow pine, is almost
as large. The long silvery foliage of the younger specimens forms
magnificent cylindrical brushes on the top shoots and the ends
of the upturned branches, and when the wind sways the needles
all one way at a certain angle every tree becomes a tower of
white quivering sun-fire. Well may this shining species be called
the silver pine. The needles are sometimes more than a foot
long, almost as long as those of the long-leaf pine of Florida.
But though in size the yellow pine almost equals the sugar pine,
and in rugged enduring strength seems to surpass it, it is far less
marked in general habit and expression, with its regular conventional spire and its comparatively small cones clustered stiffly
among the needles. Were there no sugar pine, then would this
be the king of the world's eighty or ninety species, the brightest
of the bright, waving, worshiping multitude. Were they mere
mechanical sculptures, what noble objects they would still be!
How much more throbbing, thrilling, overflowing, full of life
in every fiber and cell, grand glowing silver-rods—the very gods
of the plant kingdom, living their sublime century lives in sight
of Heaven, watched and loved and admired from generation
to generation! And how many other radiant resiny sun trees
are here and higher up,—libocedrus, Douglas spruce, silver fir,
sequoia. How rich our inheritance in these blessed mountains,
the tree pastures into which our eyes are turned!

Now comes sundown. The west is all a glory of color trans-figuring everything. Far up the Pilot Peak Ridge the radiant host of trees stand hushed and thoughtful, receiving the Sun's good-night, as solemn and impressive a leave-taking as if sun and trees were to meet no more. The daylight fades, the color spell is broken, and the forest breathes free in the night breeze beneath the stars.

June 16. One of the Indians from Brown's Flat got right into the middle of the camp this morning, unobserved. I was seated on a stone, looking over my notes and sketches, and happening to look up, was startled to see him standing grim and silent within a few steps of me, as motionless and weather-stained as an old tree-stump that had stood there for centuries. All Indians seem to have learned this wonderful way of walking unseen,—making themselves invisible like certain spiders I have been observing here, which, in case of alarm, caused, for example, by a bird alighting on the bush their webs are spread upon, imme-diately bounce themselves up and down on their elastic threads so rapidly that only a blur is visible. The wild Indian power of escaping observation, even where there is little or no cover to hide in, was probably slowly acquired in hard hunting and fighting lessons while trying to approach game, take enemies by surprise, or get safely away when compelled to retreat. And this experience transmitted through many generations seems at length to have become what is vaguely called instinct.

How smooth and changeless seems the surface of the moun-tains about us! Scarce a track is to be found beyond the range of the sheep except on small open spots on the sides of the streams, or where the forest carpets are thin or wanting. On the smoothest of these open strips and patches deer tracks may be seen, and the great suggestive footprints of bears, which, with those of the many small animals, are scarce enough to answer as a kind of light ornamental stitching or embroidery. Along the main ridges and larger branches of the river Indian trails may be traced, but they are not nearly as distinct as one would expect to find them. How many centuries Indians have roamed these woods nobody knows, probably a great many, extending far beyond the time that Columbus touched our shores, and it seems strange that heavier marks have not been made. Indians walk softly and hurt the landscape hardly more than the birds and squirrels, and their brush and bark huts last hardly longer than those of wood rats, while their more enduring monuments, excepting those wrought on the forests by the fires they made to improve their hunting grounds, vanish in a few centuries.

How different are most of those of the white man, especially on the lower gold region—roads blasted in the solid rock, wild streams dammed and tamed and turned out of their channels and led along the sides of cañons and valleys to work in mines like slaves. Crossing from ridge to ridge, high in the air, on long straddling trestles as if flowing on stilts, or down and up across valleys and hills, imprisoned in iron pipes to strike and wash away hills and miles of the skin of the mountain's face, riddling, stripping every gold gully and flat. These are the white man's marks made in a few feverish years, to say nothing of mills, fields, villages, scattered hundreds of miles along the flank of the Range. Long will it be ere these marks are effaced, though Nature is doing what she can, replanting, gardening, sweeping away old dams and flumes, leveling gravel and boulder piles, patiently trying to heal every raw scar. The main gold storm is over. Calm enough are the gray old miners scratching a bare living in waste diggings here and there. Thundering underground blasting is still going on to feed the pounding quartz mills, but their influence on the landscape is light as compared with that of the pick-and-shovel storms waged a few years ago. Fortunately for Sierra scenery the gold-bearing slates are mostly restricted to the foothills. The region about our camp is still wild, and higher lies the snow about as trackless as the sky.

Only a few hills and domes of cloudland were built yesterday and none at all to-day. The light is peculiarly white and thin, though pleasantly warm. The serenity of this mountain weather in the spring, just when Nature's pulses are beating highest, is one of its greatest charms. There is only a moderate breeze from the summits of the Range at night, and a slight breathing from the sea and the lowland hills and plains during the day, or stillness so complete no leaf stirs. The trees hereabouts have but little wind history to tell.

Sheep, like people, are ungovernable when hungry. Excepting my guarded lily gardens, almost every leaf that these hoofed locusts can reach within a radius of a mile or two from camp has been devoured. Even the bushes are stripped bare, and in spite of dogs and shepherds the sheep scatter to all points of the compass and vanish in dust. I fear some are lost, for one of the sixteen black ones is missing.

June 17. Counted the wool bundles this morning as they bounced through the narrow corral gate. About three hundred are missing, and as the shepherd could not go to seek them, I had to go. I tied a crust of bread to my belt, and with Carlo set out for the upper slopes of the Pilot Peak Ridge, and had a good day, notwithstanding the care of seeking the silly runaways. I went out for wool, and did not come back shorn. A peculiar light circled around the horizon, white and thin like that often seen over the auroral corona, blending into the blue of the upper sky. The only clouds were a few faint flossy pencilings like combed silk. I pushed direct to the boundary of the usual range of the flock, and around it until I found the outgoing trail of the wanderers. It led far up the ridge into an open place surrounded by a hedge-like growth of ceanothus chaparral. Carlo knew what I was about, and eagerly followed the scent until we came up to them, huddled in a timid, silent bunch. They had evidently been here all night and all the forenoon, afraid to go out to feed. Having escaped restraint, they were, like some people we know of, afraid of their freedom, did not know what to do with it, and seemed glad to get back into the old familiar bondage.

June 18. Another inspiring morning, nothing better in any world can be conceived. No description of Heaven that I have ever heard or read of seems half so fine. At noon the clouds occupied about .05 of the sky, white filmy touches drawn delicately on the azure.

The high ridges and hilltops beyond the woolly locusts are now gay with monardella, clarkia, coreopsis, and tall tufted grasses, some of them tall enough to wave like pines. The lupines, of which there are many ill-defined species, are now mostly out of flower, and many of the compositæ are beginning to fade, their radiant corollas vanishing in fluffy pappus like stars in mist.

We had another visitor from Brown's Flat to-day, an old Indian woman with a basket on her back. Like our first caller from the village, she got fairly into camp and was standing in plain view when discovered. How long she had been quietly looking on, I cannot say. Even the dogs failed to notice her stealthy approach. She was on her way, I suppose, to some wild garden, probably for lupine and starchy saxifrage leaves and rootstocks. Her dress was calico rags, far from clean. In every way she seemed sadly unlike Nature's neat well-dressed animals, though living like them on the bounty of the wilderness. Strange that mankind alone is dirty. Had she been clad in fur, or cloth woven of grass or shreddy bark, like the juniper and libocedrus mats, she might then have seemed a rightful part of the wilderness; like a good wolf at least, or bear. But from no point of view that I have found are such debased fellow beings a whit more natural than the glaring tailored tourists we saw that frightened the birds and squirrels.

June 19. Pure sunshine all day. How beautiful a rock is made by leaf shadows! Those of the live oak are particularly clear and distinct, and beyond all art in grace and delicacy, now still as if painted on stone, now gliding softly as if afraid of noise, now dancing, waltzing in swift, merry swirls, or jumping on and off sunny rocks in quick dashes like wave embroidery on seashore cliffs. How true and substantial is this shadow beauty, and with what sublime extravagance is beauty thus multiplied! The big orange lilies are now arrayed in all their glory of leaf and flower. Noble plants, in perfect health, Nature's darlings.

June 20. Some of the silly sheep got caught fast in a tangle of chaparral this morning, like flies in a spider's web, and had to be helped out. Carlo found them and tried to drive them from the trap by the easiest way. How far above sheep are intelligent dogs! No friend and helper can be more affectionate and constant than Carlo. The noble St. Bernard is an honor to his race.

The air is distinctly fragrant with balsam and resin and mint,—every breath of it a gift we may well thank God for. Who could ever guess that so rough a wilderness should yet be so fine, so full of good things. One seems to be in a majestic domed pavilion in which a grand play is being acted with scenery and music and incense,—all the furniture and action so interesting we are in no danger of being called on to endure one dull moment. God himself seems to be always doing his best here, working like a man in a glow of enthusiasm.

June 21. Sauntered along the river-bank to my lily gardens. The perfection of beauty in these lilies of the wilderness is a never-ending source of admiration and wonder. Their rhizomes are set in black mould accumulated in hollows of the metamorphic slates beside the pools, where they are well watered without being subjected to flood action. Every leaf in the level whorls around the tall polished stalks is as finely finished as the petals, and the light and heat required are measured for them and tempered in passing through the branches of over-leaning trees. However strong the winds from the noon rainstorms, they are securely sheltered. Beautiful hypnum carpets bordered with ferns are spread beneath them, violets too, and a few daisies. Everything around them sweet and fresh like themselves.

Cloudland to-day is only a solitary white mountain; but it is so enriched with sunshine and shade, the tones of color on its big domed head and bossy outbulging ridges, and in the hollows and ravines between them, are ineffably fine.

June 22. Unusually cloudy. Besides the periodical shower-bearing cumuli there is a thin, diffused, fog-like cloud overhead. About .75 in all.

June 23. Oh, these vast, calm, measureless mountain days, inciting at once to work and rest! Days in whose light everything seems equally divine, opening a thousand windows to show us God. Nevermore, however weary, should one faint by the way who gains the blessings of one mountain day; whatever his fate, long life, short life, stormy or calm, he is rich forever.

June 24. Our regular allowance of clouds and thunder. Shepherd Billy is in a peck of trouble about the sheep; he declares that they are possessed with more of the evil one than any other flock from the beginning of the invention of mutton and wool to the last batch of it. No matter how many are missing, he will not, he says, go a step to seek them, because, as he reasons, while getting back one wanderer he would probably lose ten. Therefore runaway hunting must be Carlo's and mine. Billy's little dog Jack is also giving trouble by leaving camp every night to visit his neighbors up the mountain at Brown's Flat. He is a common-looking cur of no particular breed, but tremendously enterprising in love and war. He has cut all the ropes and leather straps he has been tied with, until his master in desperation, after climbing the brushy mountain again and again to drag him back, fastened him with a pole attached to his collar under his chin at one end, and to a stout sapling at the other. But the pole gave good leverage, and by constant twisting during the night, the fastening at the sapling end was chafed off, and he set out on his usual journey, dragging the pole through the brush, and reached the Indian settlement in safety. His master followed, and making no allowance, gave him a beating, and swore in bad terms that next evening he would "fix that infatuated pup" by anchoring him unmercifully to the heavy cast-iron lid of our Dutch oven, weighing about as much as the dog. It was linked directly to his collar close up under the chin, so that the poor fellow seemed unable to stir. He stood quite discouraged until after dark, unable to look about him, or even to lie down unless he stretched himself out with his front feet across the lid, and his head close down between his paws. Before morning, however, Jack was heard far up the height howling Excelsior, cast-iron anchor to the contrary notwithstanding. He must have walked, or rather climbed, erect on his hind legs, clasping the heavy lid like a shield against his breast, a formidable ironclad condition in which to meet his rivals. Next night, dog, pot-lid, and all, were tied up in an old bean-sack, and thus at last angry Billy gained the victory. Just before leaving home, Jack was bitten in the lower jaw by a rattlesnake, and for a week or so his head and neck were swollen to more than double the normal size; nevertheless he ran about as brisk and lively as ever, and is now completely recovered. The only treatment he got was fresh milk—a gallon or two at a time forcibly poured down his sore, poisoned throat.

June 25. Though only a sheep-camp, this grand mountain hollow is home, sweet home, every day growing sweeter, and I shall be sorry to leave it. The lily gardens are safe as yet from the trampling flock. Poor, dusty, raggedy, famishing creatures, I heartily pity them. Many a mile they must go every day to gather their fifteen or twenty tons of chaparral and grass.

June 26. Nuttall's flowering dogwood makes a fine show when in bloom. The whole tree is then snowy white. The involucres are six to eight inches wide. Along the streams it is a good-sized tree thirty to fifty feet high, with a broad head when not crowded by companions. Its showy involucres attract a crowd of moths, butterflies, and other winged people about it for their own, and, I suppose, the tree's advantage. It likes plenty of cool water, and is a great drinker like the alder, willow, and cottonwood, and flourishes best on stream banks, though it often wanders far from streams in damp shady glens beneath the pines, where it is much smaller. When the leaves ripen in the fall, they become more beautiful than the flowers, displaying charming tones of red, purple, and lavender. Another species grows in abundance as a chaparral shrub on the shady sides of the hills, probably *Cornus sessilis*. The leaves are eaten by the sheep.—Heard a few lightning strokes in the distance, with rumbling, mumbling reverberations.

June 27. The beaked hazel (*Corylus rostrata*, var. *Californica*) is common on cool slopes up toward the summit of the Pilot Peak Ridge. There is something peculiarly attractive in the hazel, like the oaks and heaths of the cool countries of our forefathers, and through them our love for these plants has, I suppose, been transmitted. This species is four or five feet high, leaves soft and hairy, grateful to the touch, and the delicious nuts are eagerly gathered by Indians and squirrels. The sky as usual adorned with white noon clouds.

June 28. Warm, mellow summer. The glowing sunbeams make every nerve tingle. The new needles of the pines and firs are nearly full grown and shine gloriously. Lizards are glinting about on the hot rocks; some that live near the camp are more than half tame. They seem attentive to every movement on our part, as if curious to simply look on without suspicion of harm, turning their heads to look back, and making a variety of pretty gestures. Gentle, guileless creatures with beautiful eyes, I shall be sorry to leave them when we leave camp.

June 29. I have been making the acquaintance of a very interesting little bird that flits about the falls and rapids of the main branches of the river. It is not a water-bird in structure, though it gets its living in the water, and never leaves the streams. It is not web-footed, yet it dives fearlessly into deep swirling rapids, evidently to feed at the bottom, using its wings to swim with under water just as ducks and loons do. Sometimes it wades about in shallow places, thrusting its head under from time to time in a jerking, nodding, frisky way that is sure to attract attention. It is about the size of a robin, has short crisp wings serviceable for flying either in water or air, and a tail of moderate size slanted upward, giving it, with its nodding, bobbing manners, a wrennish look. Its color is plain bluish ash, with a tinge of brown on the head and shoulders. It flies from fall to fall, rapid to rapid, with a solid whir of wing-beats like those of a quail, follows the windings of the stream, and usually alights on some rock jutting up out of the current, or on some stranded snag, or rarely on the dry limb of an overhanging tree, perching like regular tree birds when it suits its convenience. It has the oddest, daintiest mincing manners imaginable; and the little fellow can sing too, a sweet, thrushy, fluty song, rather low, not the least boisterous, and much less keen and accentuated than from its vigorous briskness one would be led to look for. What a romantic life this little bird leads on the most beautiful portions of the streams, in a genial climate with shade and cool water and spray to temper the summer heat. No wonder it is a fine singer, considering the stream songs it hears day and night. Every breath the little poet draws is part of a song, for all the air about the rapids and falls is beaten into music, and its first lessons must begin before it is born by the thrilling and quivering of the eggs in unison with the tones of the falls. I have not yet found its nest, but it must be near the streams, for it never leaves them.

June 30. Half cloudy, half sunny, clouds lustrous white. The tall pines crowded along the top of the Pilot Peak Ridge look like six-inch miniatures exquisitely outlined on the satiny sky. Average cloudiness for the day about .25. No rain. And so this memorable month ends, a stream of beauty unmeasured, no more to be sectioned off by almanac arithmetic than sun-radiance or the currents of seas and rivers—a peaceful, joyful stream of beauty. Every morning, arising from the death of sleep, the happy plants and all our fellow animal creatures great and small, and even the rocks, seemed to be shouting, "Awake, awake, rejoice, rejoice, come love us and join in our song. Come! Come!" Looking back through the stillness and romantic enchanting beauty and peace of the camp grove, this June seems the greatest of all the months of my life, the most truly, divinely free, boundless like eternity, immortal. Everything in it seems equally divine—one smooth, pure, wild glow of Heaven's love, never to be blotted or blurred by anything past or to come.

July 1. Summer is ripe. Flocks of seeds are already out of their cups and pods seeking their predestined places. Some will strike root and grow up beside their parents, others flying on the wings of the wind far from them, among strangers. Most of the young birds are full feathered and out of their nests, though still looked after by both father and mother, protected and fed and to some extent educated. How beautiful the home life of birds! No wonder we all love them.

I like to watch the squirrels. There are two species here, the large California gray and the Douglas. The latter is the brightest of all the squirrels I have ever seen, a hot spark of life, making every tree tingle with his prickly toes, a condensed nugget of fresh mountain vigor and valor, as free from disease as a sunbeam. One cannot think of such an animal ever being weary or sick. He seems to think the mountains belong to him, and at first tried to drive away the whole flock of sheep as well as the shepherd and dogs. How he scolds, and what faces he makes, all eyes, teeth, and whiskers! If not so comically small,

Douglas Squirrel observing Brother Man

he would indeed be a dreadful fellow. I should like to know more about his bringing up, his life in the home knot-hole, as well as in the treetops, throughout all seasons. Strange that I have not yet found a nest full of young ones. The Douglas is nearly allied to the red squirrel of the Atlantic slope, and may have been distributed to this side of the continent by way of the great unbroken forests of the north.

The California gray is one of the most beautiful, and, next to the Douglas, the most interesting of our hairy neighbors. Compared with the Douglas he is twice as large, but far less lively and influential as a worker in the woods and he manages to make his way through leaves and branches with less stir than his small brother. I have never heard him bark at anything except our dogs. When in search of food he glides silently from branch to branch, examining last year's cones, to see whether some few seeds may not be left between the scales, or gleans fallen ones among the leaves on the ground, since none of the present season's crop is yet available. His tail floats now behind him, now above him, level or gracefully curled like a wisp of cirrus cloud, every hair in its place, clean and shining and radiant as thistle-down in spite of rough, gummy work. His whole body seems about as unsubstantial as his tail. The little Douglas is fiery, peppery, full of brag and fight and show, with movements so quick and keen they almost sting the onlooker, and the harlequin gyrating show he makes of himself turns one giddy to see. The gray is shy, and oftentimes stealthy in his movements, as if half expecting an enemy in every tree and bush, and back of every log, wishing only to be let alone apparently, and manifesting no desire to be seen or admired or feared. The Indians hunt this species for food, a good cause for caution, not to mention other enemies—hawks, snakes, wild cats. In woods where food is abundant they wear paths through sheltering thickets and over prostrate trees to some favorite pool where in hot and dry weather they drink at nearly the same hour every day. These pools are said to be narrowly watched, especially by the boys, who lie in ambush with bow and arrow, and kill without noise. But, in spite of enemies, squirrels are happy fellows, forest favorites, types of tireless life. Of all Nature's wild beasts, they seem to me the wildest. May we come to know each other better.

The chaparral-covered hill-slope to the south of the camp, besides furnishing nesting-places for countless merry birds, is the home and hiding-place of the curious wood rat (*Neotoma*), a handsome, interesting animal, always attracting attention wherever seen. It is more like a squirrel than a rat, is much larger, has delicate, thick, soft fur of a bluish slate color, white on the belly; ears large, thin, and translucent; eyes soft, full, and liquid; claws slender, sharp as needles; and as his limbs are strong, he can climb about as well as a squirrel. No rat or squirrel has so innocent a look, is so easily approached, or expresses such confidence in one's good intentions. He seems too fine for the thorny thickets he inhabits, and his hut also is as unlike himself as may be, though softly furnished inside. No other animal inhabitant of these mountains builds houses so large and striking in appearance. The traveler coming suddenly upon a group of them for the first time will not be likely to forget them. They are built of all kinds of sticks, old rotten pieces picked up anywhere, and green prickly twigs bitten from the nearest bushes, the whole mixed with miscellaneous odds and ends of everything movable, such as bits of cloddy earth, stones, bones, deerhorn, etc., piled up in a conical mass as if it were got ready for burning. Some of these curious cabins are six feet high and as wide at the base, and a dozen or more of them are occasionally grouped together, less perhaps for the sake of society than for advantages of food and shelter. Coming through the dense shaggy thickets of some lonely hillside, the solitary explorer happening into one of these strange villages is startled at the sight, and may fancy himself in an Indian settlement, and begin to wonder what kind of reception he is likely to get. But no savage face will he see, perhaps not a single inhabitant, or at most two or three seated on top of their wigwams, looking at the stranger with the mildest of wild eyes, and allowing a near approach. In the center of the rough spiky hut a soft nest is made of the inner fibers of bark chewed to tow, and lined with feathers and the down of various seeds, such as willow and milkweed. The delicate creature in its prickly, thick-walled home suggests a tender flower in a thorny involucre. Some of the nests are built in trees thirty or forty feet from the ground, and even in garrets, as if seeking the company and protection of man, like swallows and linnets, though accustomed to the wildest solitude. Among house-keepers Neotoma has the reputation of a thief, because he carries away everything transportable to his queer hut,—knives, forks, combs, nails, tin cups, spectacles, etc.,—merely, however, to strengthen his fortifications, I guess. His food at home, as far as I have learned, is nearly the same as that of the squirrels—nuts, berries, seeds, and sometimes the bark and tender shoots of the various species of ceanothus.

July 2. Warm, sunny day, thrilling plants and animals and rocks alike, making sap and blood flow fast, and making every particle of the crystal mountains throb and swirl and dance in glad accord like star-dust. No dullness anywhere visible or thinkable. No stagnation, no death. Everything kept in joyful rhythmic motion in the pulses of Nature's big heart.

Pearl cumuli over the higher mountains—clouds, not with a silver lining, but all silver. The brightest, crispest, rockiest-looking clouds, most varied in features and keenest in outline I ever saw at any time of year in any country. The daily building and unbuilding of these snowy cloud-ranges—the highest Sierra—is a prime marvel to me, and I gaze at the stupendous white domes, miles high, with ever fresh admiration. But in the midst of these sky and mountain affairs a change of diet is pulling us down. We have been out of bread a few days, and begin to miss it more than seems reasonable, for we have plenty of meat and sugar and tea. Strange we should feel food-poor in so rich a wilderness. The Indians put us to shame, so do the squirrels,—starchy roots and seeds and bark in abundance, yet the failure of the meal sack disturbs our bodily balance, and threatens our best enjoyments.

July 3. Warm. Breeze just enough to sift through the woods and waft fragrance from their thousand fountains. The pine and fir cones are growing well, resin and balsam dripping from every tree, and seeds are ripening fast, promising a fine harvest. The squirrels will have bread. They eat all kinds of nuts long before they are ripe, and yet never seem to suffer in stomach.

Chapter III

A BREAD FAMINE

JULY 4. The air beyond the flock range, full of the essences of the woods, is growing sweeter and more fragrant from day to day, like ripening fruit.

Mr. Delaney is expected to arrive soon from the lowlands with a new stock of provisions, and as the flock is to be moved to fresh pastures we shall all be well fed. In the mean time our stock of beans as well as flour has failed—everything but mutton, sugar, and tea. The shepherd is somewhat demoralized, and seems to care but little what becomes of his flock. He says that since the boss has failed to feed him he is not rightly bound to feed the sheep, and swears that no decent white man can climb these steep mountains on mutton alone. "It's not fittin' grub for a white man really white. For dogs and coyotes and Indians it's different. Good grub, good sheep. That's what I say." Such was Billy's Fourth of July oration.

July 5. The clouds of noon on the high Sierra seem yet more marvelously, indescribably beautiful from day to day as one becomes more wakeful to see them. The smoke of the gunpowder burned yesterday on the lowlands, and the eloquence of the orators has probably settled or been blown away by this time. Here every day is a holiday, a jubilee ever sounding with serene enthusiasm, without wear or waste or cloying weariness. Everything rejoicing. Not a single cell or crystal unvisited or forgotten.

July 6. Mr. Delaney has not arrived, and the bread famine is sore. We must eat mutton a while longer, though it seems hard to get accustomed to it. I have heard of Texas pioneers living without bread or anything made from the cereals for months without suffering, using the breast-meat of wild turkeys for bread. Of this kind they had plenty in the good old days when life, though considered less safe, was fussed over the less. The trappers and fur traders of early days in the Rocky Mountain regions lived on bison and beaver meat for months. Salmon-eaters, too, there are among both Indians and whites who seem to suffer little or not at all from the want of bread. Just at this moment mutton seems the least desirable of food, though of good quality. We pick out the leanest bits, and down they go against heavy disgust, causing nausea and an effort to reject the offensive stuff. Tea makes matters worse, if possible. The stomach begins to assert itself as an independent creature with a will of its own. We should boil lupine leaves, clover, starchy petioles, and saxifrage rootstocks like the Indians. We try to ignore our gastric troubles, rise and gaze about us, turn our eyes to the mountains, and climb doggedly up through brush and rocks into the heart of the scenery. A stifled calm comes on, and the day's duties and even enjoyments are languidly got through with. We chew a few leaves of ceanothus by way of luncheon, and smell or chew the spicy monardella for the dull headache and stomach-ache that now lightens, now comes muffling down upon us and into us like fog. At night more mutton, flesh to flesh, down with it, not too much, and there are the stars shining through the cedar plumes and branches above our beds.

July 7. Rather weak and sickish this morning, and all about a piece of bread. Can scarce command attention to my best studies, as if one couldn't take a few days' saunter in the Godful woods without maintaining a base on a wheat-field and grist-mill. Like caged parrots we want a cracker, any of the hundred kinds—the remainder biscuit of a voyage around the world would answer well enough, nor would the wholesomeness of saleratus biscuit be questioned. Bread without flesh is a good diet, as on many botanical excursions I have proved. Tea also may easily be ignored. Just bread and water and delightful toil is all I need,—not unreasonably much, yet one ought to be trained and tempered to enjoy life in these brave wilds in full independence of any particular kind of nourishment. That this may be accomplished is manifest, as far as bodily welfare is concerned, in the lives of people of other climes. The Eskimo, for example, gets a living far north of the wheat line, from oily seals and whales. Meat, berries, bitter weeds, and blubber, or only the last, for months at a time; and yet these people all around the frozen shores of our continent are said to be hearty, jolly, stout, and brave. We hear, too, of fish-eaters, carnivorous as spiders, yet well enough as far as stomachs are concerned, while we are so ridiculously helpless, making wry faces over our fare, looking sheepish in digestive distress amid rumbling, grumbling sounds that might well pass for smothered baas. We have a large supply of sugar, and this evening it occurred to me that these belligerent stomachs might possibly, like complaining children, be coaxed with candy. Accordingly the frying-pan was cleansed, and a lot of sugar cooked in it to a sort of wax, but this stuff only made matters worse.

Man seems to be the only animal whose food soils him, making necessary much washing and shield-like bibs and napkins. Moles living in the earth and eating slimy worms are yet as clean as seals or fishes, whose lives are one perpetual wash. And, as we have seen, the squirrels in these resiny woods keep themselves clean in some mysterious way; not a hair is sticky, though they handle the gummy cones, and glide about apparently without care. The birds, too, are clean, though they seem to make a good deal of fuss washing and cleaning their feathers. Certain flies and ants I see are in a fix, entangled and sealed up in the sugar-wax we threw away, like some of their ancestors in amber. Our stomachs, like tired muscles, are sore with long squirming. Once I was very hungry in the Bonaventure graveyard near Savannah, Georgia, having fasted for several days; then the empty stomach seemed to chafe in much the same way as now, and a somewhat similar tenderness and aching was produced, hard to bear, though the pain was not acute. We dream of bread, a sure sign we need it. Like the Indians, we ought to know how to get the starch out of fern and saxifrage stalks, lily bulbs, pine bark, etc. Our education has been sadly neglected for many generations. Wild rice would be good. I noticed a leersia in wet meadow edges, but the seeds are small. Acorns are not ripe, nor pine nuts, nor filberts. The inner bark of pine or spruce might be tried. Drank tea until half intoxicated. Man seems to crave a stimulant when anything extraordinary is going on, and this is the only one I use. Billy chews great quantities of tobacco, which I suppose helps to stupefy and moderate his misery. We look and listen for the Don every hour. How beautiful upon the mountains his big feet would be!

In the warm, hospitable Sierra, shepherds and mountain men in general, as far as I have seen, are easily satisfied as to food supplies and bedding. Most of them are heartily content

to "rough it," ignoring Nature's fineness as bothersome or
unmanly. The shepherd's bed is often only the bare ground
and a pair of blankets, with a stone, a piece of wood, or a pack-
saddle for a pillow. In choosing the spot, he shows less care
than the dogs, for they usually deliberate before making up
their minds in so important an affair, going from place to place,
scraping away loose sticks and pebbles, and trying for comfort
by making many changes, while the shepherd casts himself
down anywhere, seemingly the least skilled of all rest seekers.
His food, too, even when he has all he wants, is usually far from
delicate, either in kind or cooking. Beans, bread of any sort,
bacon, mutton, dried peaches, and sometimes potatoes and
onions, make up his bill-of-fare, the two latter articles being
regarded as luxuries on account of their weight as compared
with the nourishment they contain; a half-sack or so of each
may be put into the pack in setting out from the home ranch
and in a few days they are done. Beans are the main standby,
portable, wholesome, and capable of going far, besides being
easily cooked, although curiously enough a great deal of mystery is supposed to lie about the bean-pot. No two cooks quite
agree on the methods of making beans do their best, and, after
petting and coaxing and nursing the savory mess,—well oiled
and mellowed with bacon boiled into the heart of it,—the
proud cook will ask, after dishing out a quart or two for trial,
"Well, how do you like *my* beans?" as if by no possibility could
they be like any other beans cooked in the same way, but must
needs possess some special virtue of which he alone is master.
Molasses, sugar, or pepper may be used to give desired flavors;
or the first water may be poured off and a spoonful or two
of ashes or soda added to dissolve or soften the skins more
fully, according to various tastes and notions. But, like casks of
wine, no two potfuls are exactly alike to every palate. Some are
supposed to be spoiled by the moon, by some unlucky day, by
the beans having been grown on soil not suitable; or the whole
year may be to blame as not favorable for beans.

Coffee, too, has its marvels in the camp kitchen, but not
so many, and not so inscrutable as those that beset the bean-
pot. A low, complacent grunt follows a mouthful drawn in
with a gurgle, and the remark cast forth aimlessly, "That's
good coffee." Then another gurgling sip and repetition of the

judgment, "*Yes, sir*, that *is* good coffee." As to tea, there are
but two kinds, weak and strong, the stronger the better. The
only remark heard is, "That tea's weak," otherwise it is good
enough and not worth mentioning. If it has been boiled an
hour or two or smoked on a pitchy fire, no matter,—who cares
for a little tannin or creosote? they make the black beverage
all the stronger and more attractive to tobacco-tanned palates.

Sheep-camp bread, like most California camp bread, is
baked in Dutch ovens, some of it in the form of yeast powder
biscuit, an unwholesome sticky compound leading straight to
dyspepsia. The greater part, however, is fermented with sour
dough, a handful from each batch being saved and put away in
the mouth of the flour sack to inoculate the next. The oven is
simply a cast-iron pot, about five inches deep and from twelve
to eighteen inches wide. After the batch has been mixed and
kneaded in a tin pan the oven is slightly heated and rubbed
with a piece of tallow or pork rind. The dough is then placed in
it, pressed out against the sides, and left to rise. When ready for
baking a shovelful of coals is spread out by the side of the fire
and the oven set upon them, while another shovelful is placed
on top of the lid, which is raised from time to time to see that
the requisite amount of heat is being kept up. With care good
bread may be made in this way, though it is liable to be burned
or to be sour, or raised too much, and the weight of the oven
is a serious objection.

At last Don Delaney comes doon the lang glen—hunger
vanishes, we turn our eyes to the mountains, and to-morrow
we go climbing toward cloudland.

Never while anything is left of me shall this first camp be
forgotten. It has fairly grown into me, not merely as memory
pictures, but as part and parcel of mind and body alike. The
deep hopper-like hollow, with its majestic trees through which
all the wonderful nights the stars poured their beauty. The
flowery wildness of the high steep slope toward Brown's Flat,
and its bloom-fragrance descending at the close of the still days.
The embowered river-reaches with their multitude of voices
making melody, the stately flow and rush and glad exulting
onsweeping currents caressing the dipping sedge-leaves and
bushes and mossy stones, swirling in pools, dividing against
little flowery islands, breaking gray and white here and there,

ever rejoicing, yet with deep solemn undertones recalling the ocean—the brave little bird ever beside them, singing with sweet human tones among the waltzing foam-bells, and like a blessed evangel explaining God's love. And the Pilot Peak Ridge, its long withdrawing slopes gracefully modeled and braided, reaching from climate to climate, feathered with trees that are the kings of their race, their ranks nobly marshaled to view, spire above spire, crown above crown, waving their long, leafy arms, tossing their cones like ringing bells—blessed sun-fed mountaineers rejoicing in their strength, every tree tuneful, a harp for the winds and the sun. The hazel and buckthorn pastures of the deer, the sun-beaten brows purple and yellow with mint and golden-rods, carpeted with chamœbatia, humming with bees. And the dawns and sunrises and sundowns of these mountains days,—the rose light creeping higher among the stars, changing to daffodil yellow, the level beams bursting forth, streaming across the ridges, touching pine after pine, awakening and warming all the mighty host to do gladly their shining day's work. The great sun-gold noons, the alabaster cloud-mountains, the landscape beaming with consciousness like the face of a god. The sunsets, when the trees stood hushed awaiting their good-night blessings. Divine, enduring, unwastable wealth.

Chapter IV

TO THE HIGH MOUNTAINS

JULY 8. Now away we go toward the topmost mountains. Many still, small voices, as well as the noon thunder, are calling, "Come higher." Farewell, blessed dell, woods, gardens, streams, birds, squirrels, lizards, and a thousand others. Farewell. Farewell.

Up through the woods the hoofed locusts streamed beneath a cloud of brown dust. Scarcely were they driven a hundred yards from the old corral ere they seemed to know that at last they were going to new pastures, and rushed wildly ahead, crowding through gaps in the brush, jumping, tumbling like exulting hurrahing flood-waters escaping through a broken dam. A man on each flank kept shouting advice to the leaders, who in their famishing condition were behaving like Gadarene swine; two other drivers were busy with stragglers, helping them out of brush tangles; the Indian, calm, alert, silently watched for wanderers likely to be overlooked; the two dogs ran here and there, at a loss to know what was best to be done, while the Don, soon far in the rear, was trying to keep in sight of his troublesome wealth.

As soon as the boundary of the old eaten-out range was passed the hungry horde suddenly became calm, like a mountain stream in a meadow. Thenceforward they were allowed to eat their way as slowly as they wished, care being taken only to keep them headed toward the summit of the Merced and Tuolumne divide. Soon the two thousand flattened paunches were bulged out with sweet-pea vines and grass, and the gaunt, desperate creatures, more like wolves than sheep, became bland and governable, while the howling drivers changed to gentle shepherds, and sauntered in peace.

Toward sundown we reached Hazel Green, a charming spot on the summit of the dividing ridge between the basins of the Merced and Tuolumne, where there is a small brook flowing through hazel and dogwood thickets beneath magnificent silver firs and pines. Here, we are camped for the night, our big fire, heaped high with rosiny logs and branches, is blazing

like a sunrise, gladly giving back the light slowly sifted from
the sunbeams of centuries of summers; and in the glow of
that old sunlight how impressively surrounding objects are
brought forward in relief against the outer darkness! Grasses,
larkspurs, columbines, lilies, hazel bushes, and the great trees
form a circle around the fire like thoughtful spectators, gazing
and listening with human-like enthusiasm. The night breeze
is cool, for all day we have been climbing into the upper sky,
the home of the cloud mountains we so long have admired.
How sweet and keen the air! Every breath a blessing. Here the
sugar pine reaches its fullest development in size and beauty
and number of individuals, filling every swell and hollow and
down-plunging ravine almost to the exclusion of other species.
A few yellow pines are still to be found as companions, and in
the coolest places silver firs; but noble as these are, the sugar
pine is king, and spreads long protecting arms above them
while they rock and wave in sign of recognition.

We have now reached a height of six thousand feet. In the
forenoon we passed along a flat part of the dividing ridge that
is planted with manzanita (*Arctostaphylos*), some specimens
the largest I have seen. I measured one, the bole of which is
four feet in diameter and only eighteen inches high from the
ground, where it dissolves into many wide-spreading branches
forming a broad round head about ten or twelve feet high,

Divide between the Tuolumne and the Merced, below Hazel Green

covered with clusters of small narrow-throated pink bells. The leaves are pale green, glandular, and set on edge by a twist of the petiole. The branches seem naked; for the chocolate-colored bark is very smooth and thin, and is shed off in flakes that curl when dry. The wood is red, close-grained, hard, and heavy. I wonder how old these curious tree-bushes are, probably as old as the great pines. Indians and bears and birds and fat grubs feast on the berries, which look like small apples, often rosy on one side, green on the other. The Indians are said to make a kind of beer or cider out of them. There are many species. This one, *Arctostaphylos pungens*, is common hereabouts. No need have they to fear the wind, so low they are and steadfastly rooted. Even the fires that sweep the woods seldom destroy them utterly, for they rise again from the root, and some of the dry ridges they grow on are seldom touched by fire. I must try to know them better.

I miss my river songs to-night. Here Hazel Creek at its topmost springs has a voice like a bird. The wind-tones in the great trees overhead are strangely impressive, all the more because not a leaf stirs below them. But it grows late, and I must to bed. The camp is silent; everybody asleep. It seems extravagant to spend hours so precious in sleep. "He giveth his beloved sleep." Pity the poor beloved needs it, weak, weary, forspent; oh, the pity of it, to sleep in the midst of eternal, beautiful motion instead of gazing forever, like the stars.

July 9. Exhilarated with the mountain air, I feel like shouting this morning with excess of wild animal joy. The Indian lay down away from the fire last night, without blankets, having nothing on, by way of clothing, but a pair of blue overalls and a calico shirt wet with sweat. The night air is chilly at this eleva-tion, and we gave him some horse-blankets, but he didn't seem to care for them. A fine thing to be independent of clothing where it is so hard to carry. When food is scarce, he can live on whatever comes in his way—a few berries, roots, bird eggs, grasshoppers, black ants, fat wasp or bumblebee larvæ, without feeling that he is doing anything worth mention, so I have been told.

Our course to-day was along the broad top of the main ridge to a hollow beyond Crane Flat. It is scarce at all rocky, and is covered with the noblest pines and spruces I have yet seen. Sugar pines from six to eight feet in diameter are not uncommon, with a height of two hundred feet or even more. The silver firs (*Abies concolor* and *A. magnifica*) are exceedingly beautiful, especially the *magnifica*, which becomes more abundant the higher we go. It is of great size, one of the most notable in every way of the giant conifers of the Sierra. I saw specimens that measured seven feet in diameter and over two hundred feet in height, while the average size for what might be called full-grown mature trees can hardly be less than one hundred and eighty or two hundred feet high and five or six feet in diameter; and with these noble dimensions there is a symmetry and perfection of finish not to be seen in any other tree, hereabout at least. The branches are whorled in fives mostly, and stand out from the tall, straight, exquisitely tapered bole in level collars, each branch regularly pinnated like the fronds of ferns, and densely clad with leaves all around the branchlets, thus giving them a singularly rich and sumptuous appearance. The extreme top of the tree is a thick blunt shoot pointing straight to the zenith like an admonishing finger. The cones stand erect like casks on the upper branches. They are about six inches long, three in diameter, blunt, velvety, and cylindrical in form, and very rich and precious looking. The seeds are about three quarters of an inch long, dark reddish brown with brilliant iridescent purple wings, and when ripe, the cone falls to pieces, and the seeds thus set free at a height of one hundred and fifty or two hundred feet have a good send off and may fly considerable distances in a good breeze; and it is when a good breeze is blowing that most of them are shaken free to fly.

The other species, *Abies concolor*, attains nearly as great a height and thickness as the *magnifica*, but the branches do not form such regular whorls, nor are they so exactly pinnated or richly leaf-clad. Instead of growing all around the branchlets, the leaves are mostly arranged in two flat horizontal rows. The cones and seeds are like those of the *magnifica* in form but less than half as large. The bark of the *magnifica* is reddish purple and closely furrowed, that of the *concolor* gray and widely furrowed. A noble pair.

At Crane Flat we climbed a thousand feet or more in a distance of about two miles, the forest growing more dense and the silvery *magnifica* fir forming a still greater portion of the whole. Crane Flat is a meadow with a wide sandy border lying on the top of the divide. It is often visited by blue cranes to rest and feed on their long journeys, hence the name. It is about half a mile long, draining into the Merced, sedgy in the middle, with a margin bright with lilies, columbines, larkspurs, lupines, castilleia, then an outer zone of dry, gently sloping ground starred with a multitude of small flowers—eunanus, mimulus, gilia, with rosettes of spraguea, and tufts of several species of eriogonum and the brilliant zauschneria. The noble forest wall about it is made up of the two silver firs and the yellow and sugar pines, which here seem to reach their highest pitch of beauty and grandeur; for the elevation, six thousand feet or a little more, is not too great for the sugar and yellow pines or too low for the *magnifica* fir, while the *concolor* seems to find this elevation the best possible. About a mile from the north end of the flat there is a grove of *Sequoia gigantea*, the king of all the conifers. Furthermore, the Douglas spruce (*Pseudotsuga Douglasii*) and *Libocedrus decurrens*, and a few two-leaved pines, occur here and there, forming a small part of the forest. Three pines, two silver firs, one Douglas spruce, one sequoia,—all of them, except the two-leaved pine, colossal trees,—are found here together, an assemblage of conifers unrivaled on the globe.

We passed a number of charming garden-like meadows lying on top of the divide or hanging like ribbons down its sides, imbedded in the glorious forest. Some are taken up chiefly with the tall white-flowered *Veratrum Californicum*, with boat-shaped leaves about a foot long, eight or ten inches wide, and veined like those of cypripedium,—a robust, hearty, liliaceous plant, fond of water and determined to be seen. Columbine and larkspur grow on the dryer edges of the meadows, with a tall handsome lupine standing waist-deep in long grasses and sedges. Castilleias, too, of several species make a bright show with beds of violets at their feet. But the glory of these forest meadows is a lily (*L. parvum*). The tallest are from seven to eight feet high with magnificent racemes of ten to twenty or more small orange-colored flowers; they stand out free in open ground, with just enough grass and other companion plants about them to fringe their feet, and show them off to best advantage. This is a grand addition to my lily acquaintances,—a true mountaineer, reaching prime vigor and beauty at a height of seven thousand feet or thereabouts. It varies, I find, very much in size even in the same meadow, not only with the soil, but with age. I saw a specimen that had only one flower, and another within a stone's throw had twenty-five. And to think that the sheep should be allowed in these lily meadows! after how many centuries of Nature's care planting and watering them, tucking the bulbs in snugly below winter frost, shading the tender shoots with clouds drawn above them like curtains, pouring refreshing rain, making them perfect in beauty, and keeping them safe by a thousand miracles; yet, strange to say, allowing the trampling of devastating sheep. One might reasonably look for a wall of fire to fence such gardens. So extravagant is Nature with her choicest treasures, spending plant beauty as she spends sunshine, pouring it forth into land and sea, garden and desert. And so the beauty of lilies falls on angels and men, bears and squirrels, wolves and sheep, birds and bees, but as far as I have seen, man alone, and the animals he tames, destroy these gardens. Awkward, lumbering bears, the Don tells me, love to wallow in them in hot weather, and deer with their sharp feet cross them again and again, sauntering and feeding, yet never a lily have I seen spoiled by them. Rather, like gardeners, they seem to cultivate them, pressing and dibbling as required. Anyhow not a leaf or petal seems misplaced.

The trees round about them seem as perfect in beauty and form as the lilies, their boughs whorled like lily leaves in exact order. This evening, as usual, the glow of our camp-fire is working enchantment on everything within reach of its rays. Lying beneath the firs, it is glorious to see them dipping their spires in the starry sky, the sky like one vast lily meadow in bloom! How can I close my eyes on so precious a night?

July 10. A Douglas squirrel, peppery, pungent autocrat of the woods, is barking overhead this morning, and the small forest birds, so seldom seen when one travels noisily, are out on sunny branches along the edge of the meadow getting warm, taking a sun bath and dew bath—a fine sight. How charming the sprightly confident looks and ways of these little feathered people of the trees! They seem sure of dainty, wholesome breakfasts, and where are so many breakfasts to come from? How helpless should we find ourselves should we try to set a table for them of such buds, seeds, insects, etc., as would keep them in the pure wild health they enjoy! Not a headache or any other ache amongst them, I guess. As for the irrepressible Douglas squirrels, one never thinks of their breakfasts or the possibility of hunger, sickness or death; rather they seem like stars above chance or change, even though we may see them at times busy gathering burrs, working hard for a living.

On through the forest ever higher we go, a cloud of dust dimming the way, thousands of feet trampling leaves and flowers, but in this mighty wilderness they seem but a feeble band, and a thousand gardens will escape their blighting touch. They cannot hurt the trees, though some of the seedlings suffer, and should the woolly locusts be greatly multiplied, as on account of dollar value they are likely to be, then the forests, too, may in time be destroyed. Only the sky will then be safe, though hid from view by dust and smoke, incense of a bad sacrifice. Poor, helpless, hungry sheep, in great part misbegotten, without good right to be, semi-manufactured, made less by God than man, born out of time and place, yet their voices are strangely human and call out one's pity.

Our way is still along the Merced and Tuolumne divide, the streams on our right going to swell the songful Yosemite River, those on our left to the songful Tuolumne, slipping through sunny carex and lily meadows, and breaking into song down a thousand ravines almost as soon as they are born. A more tuneful set of streams surely nowhere exists, or more sparkling crystal pure, now gliding with tinkling whisper, now with merry dimpling rush, in and out through sunshine and shade, shimmering in pools, uniting their currents, bouncing, dancing from form to form over cliffs and inclines, ever more beautiful the farther they go until they pour into the main glacial rivers.

All day I have been gazing in growing admiration at the noble groups of the magnificent silver fir which more and more is taking the ground to itself. The woods above Crane Flat still continue comparatively open, letting in the sunshine on the brown needle-strewn ground. Not only are the individual trees admirable in symmetry and superb in foliage and port, but half a dozen or more often form temple groves in which the trees are so nicely graded in size and position as to seem one. Here, indeed, is the tree-lover's paradise. The dullest eye in the world must surely be quickened by such trees as these.

Fortunately the sheep need little attention, as they are driven slowly and allowed to nip and nibble as they like. Since leaving Hazel Green we have been following the Yosemite trail; visitors to the famous valley coming by way of Coulterville and Chinese Camp pass this way—the two trails uniting at Crane Flat—and enter the valley on the north side. Another trail enters on the south side by way of Mariposa. The tourists we saw were in parties of from three or four to fifteen or twenty, mounted on mules or small mustang ponies. A strange show they made, winding single file through the solemn woods in gaudy attire, scaring the wild creatures, and one might fancy that even the great pines would be disturbed and groan aghast. But what may we say of ourselves and the flock?

We are now camped at Tamarack Flat, within four or five miles of the lower end of Yosemite. Here is another fine meadow embosomed in the woods, with a deep, clear stream gliding through it, its banks rounded and beveled with a thatch of dipping sedges. The flat is named after the two-leaved pine (*Pinus contorta*, var. *Murrayana*), common here, especially around the cool margin of the meadow. On rocky ground it is a rough, thickset tree, about forty to sixty feet high and one to three feet in diameter, bark thin and gummy, branches rather naked, tassels, leaves, and cones small. But in damp, rich soil it grows close and slender, and reaches a height at times of nearly a hundred feet. Specimens only six inches in diameter at the ground are often fifty or sixty feet in height, as slender and sharp in outline as arrows, like the true tamarack (larch) of the Eastern States; hence the name, though it is a pine.

July 11. The Don has gone ahead on one of the pack animals to spy out the land to the north of Yosemite in search of the best point for a central camp. Much higher than this we cannot now go, for the upper pastures, said to be better than any hereabouts, are still buried in heavy winter snow. Glad I am that camp is to be fixed in the Yosemite region, for many a glorious ramble I'll have along the top of the walls, and then what landscapes I shall find with their new mountains and cañons, forests and gardens, lakes and streams and falls.

We are now about seven thousand feet above the sea, and the nights are so cool we have to pile coats and extra clothing on top of our blankets. Tamarack Creek is icy cold, delicious, exhilarating champagne water. It is flowing bank-full in the meadow with silent speed, but only a few hundred yards below our camp the ground is bare gray granite strewn with boulders, large spaces being without a single tree or only a small one here and there anchored in narrow seams and cracks. The boulders, many of them very large, are not in piles or scattered like rubbish among loose crumbling débris as if weathered out of the solid as boulders of disintegration; they mostly occur singly, and are lying on a clean pavement on which the sunshine falls in a glare that contrasts with the shimmer of light and shade we have been accustomed to in the leafy woods. And, strange to say, these boulders lying so still and deserted, with no moving force near them, no boulder carrier anywhere in sight, were nevertheless brought from a distance, as difference in color and composition shows, quarried and carried and laid down here each in its place; nor have they stirred, most of them, through calm and storm since first they arrived. They look lonely here, strangers in a strange land,—huge blocks, angular mountain chips, the largest twenty or thirty feet in diameter, the chips that Nature has made in modeling her landscapes, fashioning the forms of her mountains and valleys. And with what tool were they quarried and carried? On the pavement we find its marks. The most resisting unweathered portion of the surface is scored and striated in a rigidly parallel way, indicating that the region has been overswept by a glacier from the northeastward, grinding down the general mass of the mountains, scoring and polishing, producing a strange, raw, wiped appearance, and dropping whatever boulders it chanced to be carrying at the time it was melted at the close of the Glacial Period. A fine discovery this. As for the forests we have been passing through, they are probably growing on deposits of soil most of which has been laid down by this same ice agent in the form of moraines of different sorts, now in great part disintegrated and outspread by post-glacial weathering.

Out of the grassy meadow and down over this ice-planed granite runs the glad young Tamarack Creek, rejoicing, exulting, chanting, dancing in white, glowing, irised falls and cascades on its way to the Merced Cañon, a few miles below Yosemite, falling more than three thousand feet in a distance of about two miles.

All the Merced streams are wonderful singers, and Yosemite is the centre where the main tributaries meet. From a point about half a mile from our camp we can see into the lower end of the famous valley, with its wonderful cliffs and groves, a grand page of mountain manuscript that I would gladly give my life to be able to read. How vast it seems, how short human life when we happen to think of it, and how little we may learn, however hard we try! Yet why bewail our poor inevitable ignorance? Some of the external beauty is always in sight, enough to keep every fibre of us tingling, and this we are able to gloriously enjoy though the methods of its creation may lie beyond our ken. Sing on, brave Tamarack Creek, fresh from your snowy fountains, plash and swirl and dance to your fate in the sea; bathing, cheering every living thing along your way.

Have greatly enjoyed all this huge day, sauntering and seeing, steeping in the mountain influences, sketching, noting, pressing flowers, drinking ozone and Tamarack water. Found the white fragrant Washington lily, the finest of all the Sierra lilies. Its bulbs are buried in shaggy chaparral tangles, I suppose for safety from pawing bears; and its magnificent panicles sway and rock over the top of the rough snow-pressed bushes, while big, bold, blunt-nosed bees drone and mumble in its polleny bells. A lovely flower, worth going hungry and footsore endless miles to see. The whole world seems richer now that I have found this plant in so noble a landscape.

A log house serves to mark a claim to the Tamarack meadow, which may become valuable as a station in case travel to Yosemite should greatly increase. Belated parties occasionally stop here. A white man with an Indian woman is holding possession of the place.

Sauntered up the meadow about sundown, out of sight of camp and sheep and all human mark, into the deep peace of the solemn old woods, everything glowing with Heaven's unquenchable enthusiasm.

July 12. The Don has returned, and again we go on pilgrimage. "Looking over the Yosemite Creek country," he said, "from the tops of the hills you see nothing but rocks and patches of trees; but when you go down into the rocky desert you find no end of small grassy banks and meadows, and so the country is not half so lean as it looks. There we'll go and stay until the snow is melted from the upper country."

I was glad to hear that the high snow made a stay in the Yosemite region necessary, for I am anxious to see as much of it as possible. What fine times I shall have sketching, studying plants and rocks, and scrambling about the brink of the great valley alone, out of sight and sound of camp!

We saw another party of Yosemite tourists to-day. Somehow most of these travelers seem to care but little for the glorious objects about them, though enough to spend time and money and endure long rides to see the famous valley. And when they are fairly within the mighty walls of the temple and hear the psalms of the falls, they will forget themselves and become devout. Blessed, indeed, should be every pilgrim in these holy mountains!

We moved slowly eastward along the Mono Trail, and early in the afternoon unpacked and camped on the bank of Cascade Creek. The Mono Trail crosses the range by the Bloody Cañon Pass to gold mines near the north end of Mono Lake. These mines were reported to be rich when first discovered, and a grand rush took place, making a trail necessary. A few small bridges were built over streams where fording was not practicable on account of the softness of the bottom, sections of fallen trees cut out, and lanes made through thickets wide enough to allow the passage of bulky packs; but over the greater part of the way scarce a stone or shovelful of earth has been moved.

The woods we passed through are composed almost wholly of *Abies magnifica*, the companion species, *concolor*, being mostly left behind on account of altitude, while the increasing elevation seems grateful to the charming *magnifica*. No words can do anything like justice to this noble tree. At one place many had fallen during some heavy wind-storm, owing to the loose sandy character of the soil, which offered no secure anchorage. The soil is mostly decomposed and disintegrated moraine material.

The sheep are lying down on a bare rocky spot such as they like, chewing the cud in grassy peace. Cooking is going on, appetites growing keener every day. No lowlander can appreciate the mountain appetite, and the facility with which heavy food called "grub" is disposed of. Eating, walking, resting, seem alike delightful, and one feels inclined to shout lustily on rising in the morning like a crowing cock. Sleep and digestion as clear as the air. Fine spicy plush boughs for bedding we shall have to-night, and a glorious lullaby from this cascading creek. Never was stream more fittingly named, for as far as I have traced it above and below our camp it is one continuous bouncing, dancing, white bloom of cascades. And at the very last unwearied it finishes its wild course in a grand leap of three hundred feet or more to the bottom of the main Yosemite cañon near the fall of Tamarack Creek, a few miles below the foot of the valley. These falls almost rival some of the far-famed Yosemite falls. Never shall I forget these glad cascade songs, the low booming, the roaring, the keen, silvery clashing of the cool water rushing exulting from form to form beneath irised spray; or in the deep still night seen white in the darkness, and its multitude of voices sounding still more impressively sublime. Here I find the little water ouzel as much at home as any linnet in a leafy grove, seeming to take the greater delight the more boisterous the stream. The dizzy precipices, the swift dashing energy displayed, and the thunder tones of the sheer falls are awe-inspiring, but there is nothing awful about this little bird. Its song is sweet and low, and all its gestures, as it flits about amid the loud uproar, bespeak strength and peace and joy. Contemplating these darlings of Nature coming forth from spray-sprinkled nests on the brink of savage streams, Samson's riddle comes to mind, "Out of the strong cometh forth sweetness." A yet finer bloom is this little bird than the foam-bells in eddying pools. Gentle bird, a precious message you bring me. We may miss the meaning of the torrent, but thy sweet voice, only love is in it.

July 13. Our course all day has been eastward over the rim of Yosemite Creek basin and down about halfway to the bottom, where we have encamped on a sheet of glacier-polished granite, a firm foundation for beds. Saw the tracks of a very large bear on the trail, and the Don talked of bears in general. I said I should like to see the maker of these immense tracks as he marched along, and follow him for days, without disturbing him, to learn something of the life of this master beast of the wilderness. Lambs, the Don told me, born in the lowland, that never saw or heard a bear, snort and run in terror when they catch the scent, showing how fully they have inherited a knowledge of their enemy. Hogs, mules, horses, and cattle are afraid of bears, and are seized with ungovernable terror when they approach, particularly hogs and mules. Hogs are frequently driven to pastures in the foothills of the Coast Range and Sierra where acorns are abundant, and are herded in droves of hundreds like sheep. When a bear comes to the range they promptly leave it, emigrating in a body, usually in the night time, the keepers being powerless to prevent; they thus show more sense than sheep, that simply scatter in the rocks and brush and await their fate. Mules flee like the wind with or without riders when they see a bear, and, if picketed, sometimes break their necks in trying to break their ropes, though I have not heard of bears killing mules or horses. Of hogs they are said to be particularly fond, bolting small ones, bones and all, without choice of parts. In particular, Mr. Delaney assured me that all kinds of bears in the Sierra are very shy, and that hunters found far greater difficulty in getting within gunshot of them than of deer or indeed any other animal in the Sierra, and if I was anxious to see much of them I should have to wait and watch with endless Indian patience and pay no attention to anything else.

Night is coming on, the gray rock waves are growing dim in the twilight. How raw and young this region appears! Had the ice sheet that swept over it vanished but yesterday, its traces on the more resisting portions about our camp could hardly be more distinct than they now are. The horses and sheep and all of us, indeed, slipped on the smoothest places.

July 14. How deathlike is sleep in this mountain air, and quick the awakening into newness of life! A calm dawn, yellow and purple, then floods of sun-gold, making everything tingle and glow.

In an hour or two we came to Yosemite Creek, the stream that makes the greatest of all the Yosemite falls. It is about forty feet wide at the Mono Trail crossing, and now about four feet in average depth, flowing about three miles an hour. The distance to the verge of the Yosemite wall, where it makes its tremendous plunge, is only about two miles from here. Calm, beautiful, and nearly silent, it glides with stately gestures, a dense growth of the slender two-leaved pine along its banks, and a fringe of willow, purple spirea, sedges, daisies, lilies, and columbines. Some of the sedges and willow boughs dip into the current, and just outside of the close ranks of trees there is a sunny flat of washed gravelly sand which seems to have been deposited by some ancient flood. It is covered with millions of erethrea, eriogonum, and oxytheca, with more flowers than leaves, forming an even growth, slightly dimpled and ruffled here and there by rosettes of *Spraguea umbellata*. Back of this flowery strip there is a wavy upsloping plain of solid granite, so smoothly ice-polished in many places that it glistens in the sun like glass. In shallow hollows there are patches of trees, mostly the rough form of the two-leaved pine, rather scrawny looking where there is little or no soil. Also a few junipers (*Juniperus occidentalis*), short and stout, with bright cinnamon-colored bark and gray foliage, standing alone mostly, on the sun-beaten pavement, safe from fire, clinging by slight joints,—a sturdy storm-enduring mountaineer of a tree, living on sunshine and snow, maintaining tough health on this diet for perhaps more than a thousand years.

Up towards the head of the basin I see groups of domes rising above the wavelike ridges, and some picturesque castellated masses, and dark strips and patches of silver fir, indicating deposits of fertile soil. Would that I could command the time to study them! What rich excursions one could make in this well-defined basin! Its glacial inscriptions and sculptures, how marvelous they seem, how noble the studies they offer! I tremble with excitement in the dawn of these glorious mountain sublimities, but I can only gaze and wonder, and, like a child, gather here and there a lily, half hoping I may be able to study and learn in years to come.

The drivers and dogs had a lively, laborious time getting the sheep across the creek, the second large stream thus far that they have been compelled to cross without a bridge; the first being the North Fork of the Merced near Bower Cave. Men and dogs, shouting and barking, drove the timid, water-fearing creatures in a close crowd against the bank, but not one of the flock would launch away. While thus jammed, the Don and the shepherd rushed through the frightened crowd to stampede those in front, but this would only cause a break backward, and away they would scamper through the stream-bank trees and scatter over the rocky pavement. Then with the aid of the dogs the runaways would again be gathered and made to face the stream, and again the compacted mass would break away, amid wild shouting and barking that might well have disturbed the stream itself and marred the music of its falls, to which visitors no doubt from all quarters of the globe were listening. "Hold them there! Now hold them there!" shouted the Don; "the front ranks will soon tire of the pressure, and be glad to take to the water, then all will jump in and cross in a hurry." But they did nothing of the kind; they only avoided the pressure by breaking back in scores and hundreds, leaving the beauty of the banks sadly trampled.

If only one could be got to cross over, all would make haste to follow; but that one could not be found. A lamb was caught, carried across, and tied to a bush on the opposite bank, where it cried piteously for its mother. But though greatly concerned, the mother only called it back. That play on maternal affection failed, and we began to fear that we should be forced to make a long roundabout drive and cross the wide-spread tributaries of the creek in succession. This would require several days, but it had its advantages, for I was eager to see the sources of so famous a stream. Don Quixote, however, determined that they must ford just here, and immediately began a sort of siege by cutting down slender pines on the bank and building a corral barely large enough to hold the flock when well pressed together. And as the stream would form one side of the corral he believed that they could easily be forced into the water.

In a few hours the inclosure was completed, and the silly animals were driven in and rammed hard against the brink of the ford. Then the Don, forcing a way through the compacted mass, pitched a few of the terrified unfortunates into the stream by main strength; but instead of crossing over, they swam about close to the bank, making desperate attempts to get back into the flock. Then a dozen or more were shoved off, and the Don, tall like a crane and a good natural wader, jumped in after them, seized a struggling wether, and dragged it to the opposite shore. But no sooner did he let it go than it jumped into the stream and swam back to its frightened companions in the corral, thus manifesting sheep-nature as unchangeable as gravitation. Pan with his pipes would have had no better luck, I fear. We were now pretty well baffled. The silly creatures would suffer any sort of death rather than cross that stream. Calling a council, the dripping Don declared that starvation was now the only likely scheme to try, and that we might as well camp here in comfort and let the besieged flock grow hungry and cool, and come to their senses, if they had any. In a few minutes after being thus let alone, an adventurer in the foremost rank plunged in and swam bravely to the farther shore. Then suddenly all rushed in pell-mell together, trampling one another under water, while we vainly tried to hold them back. The Don jumped into the thickest of the gasping, gurgling, drowning mass, and shoved them right and left as if each sheep was a piece of floating timber. The current also served to drift them apart; a long bent column was soon formed, and in a few minutes all were over and began baaing and feeding as if nothing out of the common had happened. That none were drowned seems wonderful. I fully expected that hundreds would gain the romantic fate of being swept into Yosemite over the highest waterfall in the world.

As the day was far spent, we camped a little way back from the ford, and let the dripping flock scatter and feed until sundown. The wool is dry now, and calm, cud-chewing peace has fallen on all the comfortable band, leaving no trace of the watery battle. I have seen fish driven out of the water with less ado than was made in driving these animals into it. Sheep brain must surely be poor stuff. Compare to-day's exhibition with the performances of deer swimming quietly across broad and rapid rivers, and from island to island in seas and lakes; or with dogs, or even with the squirrels that, as the story goes, cross the Mississippi River on selected chips, with tails for sails comfortably trimmed to the breeze. A sheep can hardly be called an animal; an entire flock is required to make one foolish individual.

Chapter V

THE YOSEMITE

JULY 15. Followed the Mono Trail up the eastern rim of the basin nearly to its summit, then turned off southward to a small shallow valley that extends to the edge of the Yosemite, which we reached about noon, and encamped. After luncheon I made haste to high ground, and from the top of the ridge on the west side of Indian Cañon gained the noblest view of the summit peaks I have ever yet enjoyed. Nearly all the upper basin of the Merced was displayed, with its sublime domes and cañons, dark upsweeping forests, and glorious array of white peaks deep in the sky, every feature glowing, radiating beauty that pours into our flesh and bones like heat rays from fire. Sunshine over all; no breath of wind to stir the brooding calm. Never before had I seen so glorious a landscape, so boundless an affluence of sublime mountain beauty. The most extravagant description I might give of this view to any one who has not seen similar landscapes with his own eyes would not so much as hint its grandeur and the spiritual glow that covered it. I shouted and gesticulated in a wild burst of ecstasy, much to the astonishment of St. Bernard Carlo, who came running up to me, manifesting in his intelligent eyes a puzzled concern that was very ludicrous, which had the effect of bringing me to my senses. A brown bear, too, it would seem, had been a spectator of the show I had made of myself, for I had gone but a few yards when I started one from a thicket of brush. He evidently considered me dangerous, for he ran away very fast, tumbling over the tops of the tangled manzanita bushes in his haste. Carlo drew back, with his ears depressed as if afraid, and kept looking me in the face, as if expecting me to pursue and shoot, for he had seen many a bear battle in his day.

Following the ridge, which made a gradual descent to the south, I came at length to the brow of that massive cliff that stands between Indian Cañon and Yosemite Falls, and here the far-famed valley came suddenly into view throughout almost its whole extent. The noble walls—sculptured into endless variety of domes and gables, spires and battlements and plain mural precipices—all a-tremble with the thunder tones of the falling water. The level bottom seemed to be dressed like a garden—sunny meadows here and there, and groves of pine and oak; the river of Mercy sweeping in majesty through the midst of them and flashing back the sunbeams. The great Tissiack, or Half-Dome, rising at the upper end of the valley to a height of nearly a mile, is nobly proportioned and life-like, the most impressive of all the rocks, holding the eye in devout admiration, calling it back again and again from falls or meadows, or even the mountains beyond,—marvelous cliffs, marvelous in sheer dizzy depth and sculpture, types of endurance. Thousands of years have they stood in the sky exposed to rain, snow, frost, earthquake and avalanche, yet they still wear the bloom of youth.

I rambled along the valley rim to the westward; most of it is rounded off on the very brink, so that it is not easy to find places where one may look clear down the face of the wall to the bottom. When such places were found, and I had cautiously set my feet and drawn my body erect, I could not help fearing a little that the rock might split off and let me down, and what a down!—more than three thousand feet. Still my limbs did not tremble, nor did I feel the least uncertainty as to the reliance to be placed on them. My only fear was that a flake of the granite, which in some places showed joints more or less open and running parallel with the face of the cliff, might give way. After withdrawing from such places, excited with the view I had got, I would say to myself, "Now don't go out on the verge again." But in the face of Yosemite scenery cautious remonstrance is vain; under its spell one's body seems to go where it likes with a will over which we seem to have scarce any control.

After a mile or so of this memorable cliff work I approached Yosemite Creek, admiring its easy, graceful, confident gestures as it comes bravely forward in its narrow channel, singing the last of its mountain songs on its way to its fate—a few rods more over the shining granite, then down half a mile in showy foam to another world, to be lost in the Merced, where climate, vegetation, inhabitants, all are different. Emerging from its last gorge, it glides in wide lace-like rapids down a smooth incline into a pool where it seems to rest and compose its gray, agitated waters before taking the grand plunge, then slowly slipping over the lip of the pool basin, it descends another glossy slope with rapidly accelerated speed to the brink of the tremendous cliff, and with sublime, fateful confidence springs out free in the air.

I took off my shoes and stockings and worked my way cautiously down alongside the rushing flood, keeping my feet and hands pressed firmly on the polished rock. The booming, roaring water, rushing past close to my head, was very exciting. I had expected that the sloping apron would terminate with the perpendicular wall of the valley, and that from the foot of it, where it is less steeply inclined, I should be able to lean far enough out to see the forms and behavior of the fall all the way down to the bottom. But I found that there was yet another small brow over which I could not see, and which appeared to be too steep for mortal feet. Scanning it keenly, I discovered a narrow shelf about three inches wide on the very brink, just wide enough for a rest for one's heels. But there seemed to be no way of reaching it over so steep a brow. At length, after careful scrutiny of the surface, I found an irregular edge of a flake of the rock some distance back from the margin of the torrent. If I was to get down to the brink at all that rough edge, which might offer slight finger-holds, was the only way. But the slope beside it looked dangerously smooth and steep, and the swift roaring flood beneath, overhead, and beside me was very nerve-trying. I therefore concluded not to venture farther, but did nevertheless. Tufts of artemisia were growing in clefts of the rock near by, and I filled my mouth with the bitter leaves, hoping they might help to prevent giddiness. Then, with a caution not known in ordinary circumstances, I crept down safely to the little ledge, got my heels well planted on it, then shuffled in a horizontal direction twenty or thirty feet until close to the outplunging current, which, by the time it had descended thus far, was already white. Here I obtained a perfectly free view down into the heart of the snowy, chanting throng of comet-like streamers, into which the body of the fall soon separates.

While perched on that narrow niche I was not distinctly conscious of danger. The tremendous grandeur of the fall in form and sound and motion, acting at close range, smothered the sense of fear, and in such places one's body takes keen care for safety on its own account. How long I remained down there, or how I returned, I can hardly tell. Anyhow I had a glorious time, and got back to camp about dark, enjoying triumphant exhilaration soon followed by dull weariness. Hereafter I'll try to keep from such extravagant, nerve-straining places. Yet such a day is well worth venturing for. My first view of the High Sierra, first view looking down into Yosemite, the death song of Yosemite Creek, and its flight over the vast cliff, each one of these is of itself enough for a great life-long landscape fortune—a most memorable day of days—enjoyment enough to kill if that were possible.

July 16. My enjoyments yesterday afternoon, especially at the head of the fall, were too great for good sleep. Kept starting up last night in a nervous tremor, half awake, fancying that the foundation of the mountain we were camped on had given way and was falling into Yosemite Valley. In vain I roused myself to make a new beginning for sound sleep. The nerve strain had been too great, and again and again I dreamed I was rushing through the air above a glorious avalanche of water and rocks. One time, springing to my feet, I said, "This time it is real—all must die, and where could mountaineer find a more glorious death!"

Left camp soon after sunrise for an all-day ramble eastward. Crossed the head of Indian Basin, forested with *Abies magnifica*, underbrush mostly *Ceanothus cordulatus* and manzanita, a mixture not easily trampled over or penetrated, for the ceanothus is thorny and grows in dense snow-pressed masses, and the manzanita has exceedingly crooked, stubborn branches. From the head of the cañon continued on past North Dome into the basin of Dome or Porcupine Creek. Here are many fine meadows imbedded in the woods, gay with *Lilium parvum* and its companions; the elevation, about eight thousand feet, seems to be best suited for it—saw specimens that were a foot or two higher than my head. Had more magnificent views of the upper mountains, and of the great South Dome, said to be the grandest rock in the world. Well it may be, since it is of such noble dimensions and sculpture. A wonderfully impressive monument, its lines exquisite in fineness, and though sublime in size, is finished like the finest work of art, and seems to be alive.

July 17. A new camp was made to-day in a magnificent silver fir grove at the head of a small stream that flows into Yosemite by way of Indian Cañon. Here we intend to stay several weeks,—a fine location from which to make excursions about the great valley and its fountains. Glorious days I'll have sketching, pressing plants, studying the wonderful topography and the wild animals, our happy fellow mortals and neighbors. But the vast mountains in the distance, shall I ever know them, shall I be allowed to enter into their midst and dwell with them?

We were pelted about noon by a short, heavy rainstorm, sublime thunder reverberating among the mountains and cañons,—some strokes near, crashing, ringing in the tense crisp air with startling keenness, while the distant peaks loomed gloriously through the cloud fringes and sheets of rain. Now the storm is past, and the fresh washed air is full of the essences of the flower gardens and groves. Winter storms in Yosemite must be glorious. May I see them!

Have got my bed made in our new camp,—plushy, sumptuous, and deliciously fragrant, most of it *magnifica* fir plumes, of course, with a variety of sweet flowers in the pillow. Hope to sleep to-night without tottering nerve-dreams. Watched a deer eating ceanothus leaves and twigs.

July 18. Slept pretty well; the valley walls did not seem to fall, though I still fancied myself at the brink, alongside the white, plunging flood, especially when half asleep. Strange the danger of that adventure should be more troublesome now that I am in the bosom of the peaceful woods, a mile or more from the fall, than it was while I was on the brink of it.

Bears seem to be common here, judging by their tracks. About noon we had another rainstorm with keen startling thunder, the metallic, ringing, clashing, clanging notes gradually fading into low bass rolling and muttering in the distance. For a few minutes the rain came in a grand torrent like a waterfall, then hail; some of the hailstones an inch in diameter, hard, icy, and irregular in form, like those oftentimes seen in Wisconsin. Carlo watched them with intelligent astonishment as they came pelting and thrashing through the quivering branches of the trees. The cloud scenery sublime. Afternoon calm, sunful, and clear, with delicious freshness and fragrance from the firs and flowers and steaming ground.

July 19. Watching the daybreak and sunrise. The pale rose and purple sky changing softly to daffodil yellow and white, sunbeams pouring through the passes between the peaks and over the Yosemite domes, making their edges burn; the silver firs in the middle ground catching the glow on their spiry tops, and our camp grove fills and thrills with the glorious light. Everything awakening alert and joyful; the birds begin to stir and innumerable insect people. Deer quietly withdraw into leafy hiding-places in the chaparral; the dew vanishes, flowers spread their petals, every pulse beats high, every life cell rejoices, the very rocks seem to thrill with life. The whole landscape glows like a human face in a glory of enthusiasm, and the blue sky, pale around the horizon, bends peacefully down over all like one vast flower.

About noon, as usual, big bossy cumuli began to grow above the forest, and the rainstorm pouring from them is the most imposing I have yet seen. The silvery zigzag lightning lances are longer than usual, and the thunder gloriously impressive, keen, crashing, intensely concentrated, speaking with such tremendous energy it would seem that an entire mountain is being shattered at every stroke, but probably only a few trees are being shattered, many of which I have seen on my walks hereabouts strewing the ground. At last the clear ringing strokes are succeeded by deep low tones that grow gradually fainter as they roll afar into the recesses of the echoing mountains, where they seem to be welcomed home. Then another and another peal, or rather crashing, splintering stroke, follows in quick succession, perchance splitting some giant pine or fir from top to bottom into long rails and slivers, and scattering them to all points of the compass. Now comes the rain, with corresponding extravagant grandeur, covering the ground high and low with a sheet of flowing water, a transparent film fitted like a skin upon the rugged anatomy of the landscape, making the rocks glitter and glow, gathering in the ravines, flooding the streams, and making them shout and boom in reply to the thunder.

How interesting to trace the history of a single raindrop! It is not long, geologically speaking, as we have seen, since the first raindrops fell on the newborn leafless Sierra landscapes. How different the lot of these falling now! Happy the showers that fall on so fair a wilderness,—scarce a single drop can fail to find a beautiful spot,—on the tops of the peaks, on the shining glacier pavements, on the great smooth domes, on forests and gardens and brushy moraines, plashing, glinting, pattering, laving. Some go to the high snowy fountains to swell their well-saved stores; some into the lakes, washing the mountain windows, patting their smooth glassy levels, making dimples and bubbles and spray; some into the waterfalls and cascades, as if eager to join in their dance and song and beat their foam yet finer; good luck and good work for the happy mountain raindrops, each one of them a high waterfall in itself, descending from the cliffs and hollows of the clouds to the cliffs and hollows of the rocks, out of the sky-thunder into the thunder of the falling rivers. Some, falling on meadows and bogs, creep silently out of sight to the grass roots, hiding softly as in a nest, slipping, oozing hither, thither, seeking and finding their appointed work. Some, descending through the spires of the woods, sift spray through the shining needles, whispering peace and good cheer to each one of them. Some drops with happy aim glint on the sides of crystals,—quartz, hornblende, garnet, zircon, tourmaline, feldspar,—patter on grains of gold and heavy way-worn nuggets; some, with blunt plap-plap and low bass drumming, fall on the broad leaves of veratrum, saxifrage, cypripedium. Some happy drops fall straight into the cups of flowers, kissing the lips of lilies. How far they have to go, how many cups to fill, great and small, cells too small to be seen, cups holding half a drop as well as lake basins between the hills, each replenished with equal care, every drop in all the blessed throng a silvery newborn star with lake and river, garden and grove, valley and mountain, all that the landscape holds reflected in its crystal depths, God's messenger, angel of love sent on its way with majesty and pomp and display of power that make man's greatest shows ridiculous.

Now the storm is over, the sky is clear, the last rolling thunder-wave is spent on the peaks, and where are the raindrops now—what has become of all the shining throng? In winged vapor rising some are already hastening back to the sky, some have gone into the plants, creeping through invisible doors into the round rooms of cells, some are locked in crystals of ice, some in rock crystals, some in porous moraines to keep their small springs flowing, some have gone journeying on in the rivers to join the larger raindrop of the ocean. From form to form, beauty to beauty, ever changing, never resting, all are speeding on with love's enthusiasm, singing with the stars the eternal song of creation.

July 20. Fine calm morning; air tense and clear; not the slightest breeze astir; everything shining, the rocks with wet crystals, the plants with dew, each receiving its portion of irised dewdrops and sunshine like living creatures getting their breakfast, their dew manna coming down from the starry sky like swarms of smaller stars. How wondrous fine are the particles in showers of dew, thousands required for a single drop, growing in the dark as silently as the grass! What pains are taken to keep this wilderness in health,—showers of snow, showers of rain, showers of dew, floods of light, floods of invisible vapor, clouds, winds, all sorts of weather, interaction of plant on plant, animal on animal, etc., beyond thought! How fine Nature's methods! How deeply with beauty is beauty overlaid! the ground covered with crystals, the crystals with mosses and lichens and low-spreading grasses and flowers, these with larger plants leaf over leaf with ever-changing color and form, the broad palms of the firs outspread over these, the azure dome over all like a bell-flower, and star above star.

Yonder stands the South Dome, its crown high above our camp, though its base is four thousand feet below us; a most noble rock, it seems full of thought, clothed with living light, no sense of dead stone about it, all spiritualized, neither heavy looking nor light, steadfast in serene strength like a god.

Our shepherd is a queer character and hard to place in this wilderness. His bed is a hollow made in red dry-rot punky dust beside a log which forms a portion of the south wall of the corral. Here he lies with his wonderful everlasting clothing on, wrapped in a red blanket, breathing not only the dust of the decayed wood but also that of the corral, as if determined to take ammoniacal snuff all night after chewing tobacco all day. Following the sheep he carries a heavy six-shooter swung from his belt on one side and his luncheon on the other. The ancient cloth in which the meat, fresh from the frying-pan, is tied serves as a filter through which the clear fat and gravy juices drip down on his right hip and leg in clustering stalactites. This oleaginous formation is soon broken up, however, and diffused and rubbed evenly into his scanty apparel, by sitting down, rolling over, crossing his legs while resting on logs, etc., making shirt and trousers water-tight and shiny. His trousers, in particular, have become so adhesive with the mixed fat and resin that pine needles, thin flakes and fibres of bark, hair, mica scales and minute grains of quartz, hornblende, etc., feathers, seed wings, moth and butterfly wings, legs and antennæ of innumerable insects, or even whole insects such as the small beetles, moths and mosquitoes, with flower petals, pollen dust and indeed bits of all plants, animals, and minerals of the region adhere to them and are safely imbedded, so that though far from being a naturalist he collects fragmentary specimens of everything and becomes richer than he knows. His specimens are kept passably fresh, too, by the purity of the air and the resiny bituminous beds into which they are pressed. Man is a microcosm, at least our shepherd is, or rather his trousers. These precious overalls are never taken off, and nobody knows how old they are, though one may guess by their thickness and concentric structure. Instead of wearing thin they wear thick, and in their stratification have no small geological significance.

Besides herding the sheep, Billy is the butcher, while I have agreed to wash the few iron and tin utensils and make the bread. Then, these small duties done, by the time the sun is fairly above the mountain-tops I am beyond the flock, free to rove and revel in the wilderness all the big immortal days.

Sketching on the North Dome. It commands views of nearly all the valley besides a few of the high mountains. I would fain draw everything in sight—rock, tree, and leaf. But little can I do beyond mere outlines,—marks with meanings like words, readable only to myself,—yet I sharpen my pencils and work on as if others might possibly be benefited. Whether these picture-sheets are to vanish like fallen leaves or go to friends like letters, matters not much; for little can they tell to those who have not themselves seen similar wildness, and like a language have learned it. No pain here, no dull empty hours, no fear of the past, no fear of the future. These blessed mountains are so compactly filled with God's beauty, no petty personal hope or experience has room to be. Drinking this champagne water is pure pleasure, so is breathing the living air, and every movement of limbs is pleasure, while the whole body seems to feel beauty when exposed to it as it feels the camp-fire or sunshine, entering not by the eyes alone, but equally through all one's flesh like radiant heat, making a passionate ecstatic pleasure-glow not explainable. One's body then seems homogeneous throughout, sound as a crystal.

Perched like a fly on this Yosemite dome, I gaze and sketch and bask, oftentimes settling down into dumb admiration without definite hope of ever learning much, yet with the longing, unresting effort that lies at the door of hope, humbly prostrate before the vast display of God's power, and eager to offer self-denial and renunciation with eternal toil to learn any lesson in the divine manuscript.

It is easier to feel than to realize, or in any way explain, Yosemite grandeur. The magnitudes of the rocks and trees and streams are so delicately harmonized they are mostly hidden. Sheer precipices three thousand feet high are fringed with tall trees growing close like grass on the brow of a lowland hill, and extending along the feet of these precipices a ribbon of meadow a mile wide and seven or eight long, that seems like a strip a farmer might mow in less than a day. Waterfalls, five hundred to one or two thousand feet high, are so subordinated to the mighty cliffs over which they pour that they seem like wisps of smoke, gentle as floating clouds, though their voices fill the valley and make the rocks tremble. The mountains, too, along the eastern sky, and the domes in front of them, and the succession of smooth rounded waves between, swelling higher, higher, with dark woods in their hollows, serene in massive exuberant bulk and beauty, tend yet more to hide the grandeur of the Yosemite temple and make it appear as a subdued subordinate feature of the vast harmonious landscape. Thus every attempt to appreciate any one feature is beaten down by the overwhelming influence of all the others. And, as if this were not enough, lo! in the sky arises another mountain range with topography as rugged and substantial-looking as the one beneath it—snowy peaks and domes and shadowy Yosemite valleys—another version of the snowy Sierra, a new creation heralded by a thunder-storm. How fiercely, devoutly wild is

Nature in the midst of her beauty-loving tenderness!—painting lilies, watering them, caressing them with gentle hand,
going from flower to flower like a gardener while building
rock mountains and cloud mountains full of lightning and
rain. Gladly we run for shelter beneath an overhanging cliff and
examine the reassuring ferns and mosses, gentle love tokens
growing in cracks and chinks. Daisies, too, and ivesias, confiding wild children of light, too small to fear. To these one's
heart goes home, and the voices of the storm become gentle.
Now the sun breaks forth and fragrant steam arises. The birds
are out singing on the edges of the groves. The west is flaming
in gold and purple, ready for the ceremony of the sunset, and
back I go to camp with my notes and pictures, the best of
them printed in my mind as dreams. A fruitful day, without
measured beginning or ending. A terrestrial eternity. A gift of
good God.

Wrote to my mother and a few friends, mountain hints to
each. They seem as near as if within voice-reach or touch. The
deeper the solitude the less the sense of loneliness, and the
nearer our friends. Now bread and tea, fir bed and good-night
to Carlo, a look at the sky lilies, and death sleep until the dawn
of another Sierra to-morrow.

July 21. Sketching on the Dome—no rain; clouds at noon
about quarter filled the sky, casting shadows with fine effect
on the white mountains at the heads of the streams, and a
soothing cover over the gardens during the warm hours.

Saw a common house-fly and a grasshopper and a brown
bear. The fly and grasshopper paid me a merry visit on the top
of the Dome, and I paid a visit to the bear in the middle of a
small garden meadow between the Dome and the camp where
he was standing alert among the flowers as if willing to be seen
to advantage. I had not gone more than half a mile from camp
this morning, when Carlo, who was trotting on a few yards
ahead of me, came to a sudden, cautious standstill. Down went
tail and ears, and forward went his knowing nose, while he
seemed to be saying, "Ha, what's this? A bear, I guess." Then
a cautious advance of a few steps, setting his feet down softly
like a hunting cat, and questioning the air as to the scent he
had caught until all doubt vanished. Then he came back to
me, looked me in the face, and with his speaking eyes reported

a bear near by; then led on softly, careful, like an experienced hunter, not to make the slightest noise, and frequently looking back as if whispering, "Yes, it's a bear; come and I'll show you." Presently we came to where the sunbeams were streaming through between the purple shafts of the firs, which showed that we were nearing an open spot, and here Carlo came behind me, evidently sure that the bear was very near. So I crept to a low ridge of moraine boulders on the edge of a narrow garden meadow, and in this meadow I felt pretty sure the bear must be. I was anxious to get a good look at the sturdy mountaineer without alarming him; so drawing myself up noiselessly back of one of the largest of the trees I peered past its bulging buttresses, exposing only a part of my head, and there stood neighbor Bruin within a stone's throw, his hips covered by tall grass and flowers, and his front feet on the trunk of a fir that had fallen out into the meadow, which raised his head so high that he seemed to be standing erect. He had not yet seen me, but was looking and listening attentively, showing that in some way he was aware of our approach. I watched his gestures and tried to make the most of my opportunity to learn what I could about him, fearing he would catch sight of me and run away. For I had been told that this sort of bear, the cinnamon, always ran from his bad brother man, never showing fight unless wounded or in defense of young. He made a telling picture standing alert in the sunny forest garden. How well he played his part, harmonizing in bulk and color and shaggy hair with the trunks of the trees and lush vegetation, as natural a feature as any other in the landscape. After examining at leisure, noting the sharp muzzle thrust inquiringly forward, the long shaggy hair on his broad chest, the stiff, erect ears nearly buried in hair, and the slow, heavy way he moved his head, I thought I should like to see his gait in running, so I made a sudden rush at him, shouting and swinging my hat to frighten him, expecting to see him make haste to get away. But to my dismay he did not run or show any sign of running. On the contrary, he stood his ground ready to fight and defend himself, lowered his head, thrust it forward, and looked sharply and fiercely at me. Then I suddenly began to fear that upon me would fall the work of running; but I was afraid to run, and therefore, like the bear, held my ground. We stood staring at each other in solemn silence within a dozen yards or thereabouts, while I fervently hoped that the power of the human eye over wild beasts would prove as great as it is said to be. How long our awfully strenuous interview lasted, I don't know; but at length in the slow fullness of time he pulled his huge paws down off the log, and with magnificent deliberation turned and walked leisurely up the meadow, stopping frequently to look back over his shoulder to see whether I was pursuing him, then moving on again, evidently neither fearing me very much nor trusting me. He was probably about five hundred pounds in weight, a broad, rusty bundle of ungovernable wildness, a happy fellow whose lines have fallen in pleasant places. The flowery glade in which I saw him so well, framed like a picture, is one of the best of all I have yet discovered, a conservatory of Nature's precious plant people. Tall lilies were swinging their bells over that bear's back, with geraniums, larkspurs, columbines, and daisies brushing against his sides. A place for angels, one would say, instead of bears.

In the great cañons Bruin reigns supreme. Happy fellow, whom no famine can reach while one of his thousand kinds of food is spared him. His bread is sure at all seasons, ranged on the mountain shelves like stores in a pantry. From one to the other, up or down he climbs, tasting and enjoying each in turn in different climates, as if he had journeyed thousands of miles to other countries north or south to enjoy their varied productions. I should like to know my hairy brothers better—though after this particular Yosemite bear, my very neighbor, had sauntered out of sight this morning, I reluctantly went back to camp for the Don's rifle to shoot him, if necessary, in defense of the flock. Fortunately I couldn't find him, and after tracking him a mile or two towards Mount Hoffman I bade him Godspeed and gladly returned to my work on the Yosemite Dome.

The house-fly also seemed at home and buzzed about me as I sat sketching, and enjoying my bear interview now it was over. I wonder what draws house-flies so far up the mountains, heavy gross feeders as they are, sensitive to cold, and fond of domestic ease. How have they been distributed from continent to continent, across seas and deserts and mountain chains, usually so influential in determining boundaries of species both of plants and animals. Beetles and butterflies are sometimes restricted to small areas. Each mountain in a range, and even the different zones of a mountain, may have its own peculiar species. But the house-fly seems to be everywhere. I wonder if any island in mid-ocean is flyless. The bluebottle is abundant in these Yosemite woods, ever ready with his marvelous store of eggs to make all dead flesh fly. Bumblebees are here, and are well fed on boundless stores of nectar and pollen. The honeybee, though abundant in the foothills, has not yet got so high. It is only a few years since the first swarm was brought to California.

A queer fellow and a jolly fellow is the grasshopper. Up the mountains he comes on excursions, how high I don't know, but at least as far and high as Yosemite tourists. I was much interested with the hearty enjoyment of the one that danced and sang for me on the Dome this afternoon. He seemed brimful of glad, hilarious energy, manifested by springing into

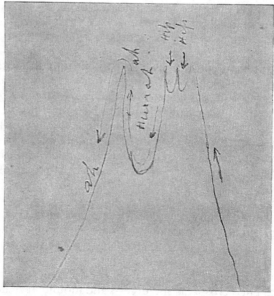

Track of singing dancing grasshopper in the air over North Dome

the air to a height of twenty or thirty feet, then diving and springing up again and making a sharp musical rattle just as the lowest point in the descent was reached. Up and down a dozen times or so he danced and sang, then alighted to rest, then up and at it again. The curves he described in the air in diving and rattling resembled those made by cords hanging loosely and attached at the same height at the ends, the loops nearly covering each other. Braver, heartier, keener, care-free enjoyment of life I have never seen or heard in any creature, great or small. The life of this comic red-legs, the mountain's merriest child, seems to be made up of pure, condensed gayety. The Douglas squirrel is the only living creature that I can compare him with in exuberant, rollicking, irrepressible jollity. Wonderful that these sublime mountains are so loudly cheered and brightened by a creature so queer. Nature in him seems to be snapping her fingers in the face of all earthly dejection and melancholy with a boyish hip-hip-hurrah. How the sound is made I do not understand. When he was on the ground he made not the slightest noise, nor when he was simply flying from place to place, but only when diving in curves, the motion seeming to be required for the sound; for the more vigorous the diving the more energetic the corresponding outbursts of jolly rattling. I tried to observe him closely while he was resting in the intervals of his performances; but he would not allow a near approach, always getting his jumping legs ready to spring for immediate flight, and keeping his eyes on me. A fine sermon the little fellow danced for me on the Dome, a likely place to look for sermons in stones, but not for grasshopper sermons. A large and imposing pulpit for so small a preacher. No danger of weakness in the knees of the world while Nature can spring such a rattle as this. Even the bear did not express for me the mountain's wild health and strength and happiness so tellingly as did this comical little hopper. No cloud of care in his day, no winter of discontent in sight. To him every day is a holiday; and when at length his sun sets, I fancy he will cuddle down on the forest floor and die like the leaves and flowers, and like them leave no unsightly remains calling for burial.

Sundown, and I must to camp. Good-night, friends three,— brown bear, rugged boulder of energy in groves and gardens fair as Eden; restless, fussy fly with gauzy wings stirring the air around all the world; and grasshopper, crisp, electric spark of joy enlivening the massy sublimity of the mountains like the laugh of a child. Thank you, thank you all three for your quickening company. Heaven guide every wing and leg. Good-night friends three, good-night.

July 22. A fine specimen of the black-tailed deer went bounding past camp this morning. A buck with wide spread of antlers, showing admirable vigor and grace. Wonderful the beauty, strength, and graceful movements of animals in wildernesses, cared for by Nature only, when our experience with domestic animals would lead us to fear that all the so-called neglected wild beasts would degenerate. Yet the upshot of Nature's method of breeding and teaching seems to lead to excellence of every sort. Deer, like all wild animals, are as clean as plants. The beauties of their gestures and attitudes, alert or in repose, surprise yet more than their bounding exuberant strength. Every movement and posture is graceful, the very poetry of manners and motion. Mother Nature is too often spoken of as in reality no mother at all. Yet how wisely, sternly, tenderly she loves and looks after her children in all sorts of weather and wildernesses. The more I see of deer the more I admire them as mountaineers. They make their way into the heart of the roughest solitudes with smooth reserve of strength, through dense belts of brush and forest encumbered with fallen trees and boulder piles, across cañons, roaring streams, and snow-fields, ever showing forth beauty and cour-age. Over nearly all the continent the deer find homes. In the Florida savannas and hummocks, in the Canada woods, in the far north, roaming over mossy tundras, swimming lakes and rivers and arms of the sea from island to island washed with waves, or climbing rocky mountains, everywhere healthy and able, adding beauty to every landscape,—a truly admirable creature and great credit to Nature.

Have been sketching a silver fir that stands on a granite ridge a few hundred yards to the eastward of camp—a fine tree with a particular snow-storm story to tell. It is about one hundred feet high, growing on bare rock, thrusting its roots into a weathered joint less than an inch wide, and bulging out to form a base to bear its weight. The storm came from the north while it was young and broke it down nearly to the ground, as is shown by the old, dead, weather-beaten top leaning out from the living trunk built up from a new shoot below the break. The annual rings of the trunk that have overgrown the dead sapling tell the year of the storm. Wonderful that a side branch forming a portion of one of the level collars that encircle the trunk of this species (*Abies magnifica*) should bend upward, grow erect, and take the place of the lost axis to form a new tree.

Mt. Clark   Mt. Starr King

Top of S. Dome

Abies magnifica

Many others, pines as well as firs, bear testimony to the crushing severity of this particular storm. Trees, some of them fifty to seventy-five feet high, were bent to the ground and buried like grass, whole groves vanishing as if the forest had been cleared away, leaving not a branch or needle visible until the spring thaw. Then the more elastic undamaged saplings rose

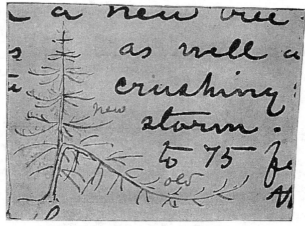

Illustrating growth of new pine from branch below the break of axis of snow-crushed tree

again, aided by the wind, some reaching a nearly erect attitude, others remaining more or less bent, while those with broken backs endeavored to specialize a side branch below the break and make a leader of it to form a new axis of development. It is as if a man, whose back was broken or nearly so and who was compelled to go bent, should find a branch backbone sprouting straight up from below the break and should gradually develop new arms and shoulders and head, while the old damaged portion of his body died.

Grand white cloud mountains and domes created about noon as usual, ridges and ranges of endless variety, as if Nature dearly loved this sort of work, doing it again and again nearly every day with infinite industry, and producing beauty that never palls. A few zigzags of lightning, five minutes' shower, then a gradual wilting and clearing.

July 23. Another midday cloudland, displaying power and beauty that one never wearies in beholding, but hopelessly unsketchable and untellable. What can poor mortals say about clouds? While a description of their huge glowing domes and ridges, shadowy gulfs and cañons, and feather-edged ravines is being tried, they vanish, leaving no visible ruins. Nevertheless, these fleeting sky mountains are as substantial and significant as the more lasting upheavals of granite beneath them. Both alike are built up and die, and in God's calendar difference of duration is nothing. We can only dream about them in wondering, worshiping admiration, happier than we dare tell even to friends who see farthest in sympathy, glad to know that not a crystal or vapor particle of them, hard or soft, is lost; that they sink and vanish only to rise again and again in higher and higher beauty. As to our own work, duty, influence, etc., concerning which so much fussy pother is made, it will not fail of its due effect, though, like a lichen on a stone, we keep silent.

July 24. Clouds at noon occupying about half the sky gave half an hour of heavy rain to wash one of the cleanest landscapes in the world. How well it is washed! The sea is hardly less dusty than the ice-burnished pavements and ridges, domes and cañons, and summit peaks plashed with snow like waves with foam. How fresh the woods are and calm after the last films of clouds have been wiped from the sky! A few minutes ago every tree was excited, bowing to the roaring storm, waving, swirling, tossing their branches in glorious enthusiasm like worship. But though to the outer ear these trees are now silent, their songs never cease. Every hidden cell is throbbing with music and life, every fibre thrilling like harp strings, while incense is ever flowing from the balsam bells and leaves. No wonder the hills and groves were God's first temples, and the more they are cut down and hewn into cathedrals and churches, the farther off and dimmer seems the Lord himself. The same may be said of stone temples. Yonder, to the eastward of our camp grove, stands one of Nature's cathedrals, hewn from the living rock, almost conventional in form, about two thousand feet high, nobly adorned with spires and pinnacles, thrilling under floods of sunshine as if alive like a grove-temple, and well named "Cathedral Peak." Even Shepherd Billy turns at times to this wonderful mountain building, though apparently deaf to all stone sermons. Snow that refused to melt in fire would hardly be more wonderful than unchanging dullness in the rays of God's beauty. I have been trying to get him to walk to the brink of Yosemite for a view, offering to watch the sheep for a day, while he should enjoy what tourists come from all over the world to see. But though within a mile of the famous valley, he will not go to it even out of mere curiosity. "What," says he, "is Yosemite but a cañon—a lot of rocks—a hole in the ground—a place dangerous about falling into—a d—d good place to keep away from." "But think of the waterfalls, Billy—just think of that big stream we crossed the other day, falling half a mile through the air—think of that, and the sound it makes. You can hear it now like the roar of the sea." Thus I pressed Yosemite upon him like a missionary offering the gospel, but he would have none of it. "I should be afraid to look over so high a wall," he said. "It would make my head swim. There is nothing worth seeing anywhere, only rocks, and I see plenty of them here. Tourists that spend their money to see rocks and falls are fools, that's all. You can't humbug me. I've been in this country too long for that." Such souls, I suppose, are asleep, or smothered and befogged beneath mean pleasures and cares.

July 25. Another cloudland. Some clouds have an over-ripe decaying look, watery and bedraggled and drawn out into wind-torn shreds and patches, giving the sky a littered appearance; not so these Sierra summer midday clouds. All are beautiful with smooth definite outlines and curves like those of glacier-polished domes. They begin to grow about eleven o'clock, and seem so wonderfully near and clear from this high camp one is tempted to try to climb them and trace the streams that pour like cataracts from their shadowy fountains. The rain to which they give birth is often very heavy, a sort of waterfall as imposing as if pouring from rock mountains. Never in all my travels have I found anything more truly novel and interesting than these midday mountains of the sky, their fine tones of color, majestic visible growth, and ever-changing scenery and general effects, though mostly as well let alone as far as description goes. I oftentimes think of Shelley's cloud poem, "I sift the snow on the mountains below."

Chapter VI

JULY 26. Ramble to the summit of Mount Hoffman, eleven thousand feet high, the highest point in life's journey my feet have yet touched. And what glorious landscapes are about me, new plants, new animals, new crystals, and multitudes of new mountains far higher than Hoffman, towering in glorious array along the axis of the range, serene, majestic, snow-laden, sun-drenched, vast domes and ridges shining below them, forests, lakes, and meadows in the hollows, the pure blue bell-flower sky brooding them all,—a glory day of admission into a new realm of wonders as if Nature had wooingly whispered, "Come higher." What questions I asked, and how little I know of all the vast show, and how eagerly, tremulously hopeful of some day knowing more, learning the meaning of these divine symbols crowded together on this wondrous page.

Mount Hoffman is the highest part of a ridge or spur about fourteen miles from the axis of the main range, perhaps a remnant brought into relief and isolated by unequal denudation. The southern slopes shed their waters into Yosemite Valley by Tenaya and Dome Creeks, the northern in part into the Tuolumne River, but mostly into the Merced by Yosemite Creek. The rock is mostly granite, with some small piles and crests rising here and there in picturesque pillared and castellated remnants of red metamorphic slates. Both the granite and slates are divided by joints, making them separable into blocks like the stones of artificial masonry, suggesting the Scripture "He hath builded the mountains." Great banks of snow and ice are piled in hollows on the cool precipitous north side forming the highest perennial sources of Yosemite Creek. The southern slopes are much more gradual and accessible. Narrow slot-like gorges extend across the summit at right angles, which look like lanes, formed evidently by the erosion of less resisting beds. They are usually called "devil's slides," though they lie far above the region usually haunted by the devil; for though we read that he once climbed an exceeding high mountain, he cannot be much of a mountaineer, for his tracks are seldom seen above the timber-line.

The broad gray summit is barren and desolate-looking in general views, wasted by ages of gnawing storms; but looking at the surface in detail, one finds it covered by thousands and millions of charming plants with leaves and flowers so small they form no mass of color visible at a distance of a few hundred yards. Beds of azure daisies smile confidingly in moist hollows, and along the banks of small rills, with several species of eriogonum, silky-leaved ivesia, pentstemon, orthocarpus, and patches of *Primula suffruticosa*, a beautiful shrubby species.

Approach of Dome Creek to Yosemite

Here also I found bryanthus, a charming heathwort covered with purple flowers and dark green foliage like heather, and three trees new to me—a hemlock and two pines. The hemlock (*Tsuga Mertensiana*) is the most beautiful conifer I have ever seen; the branches and also the main axis droop in a singularly graceful way, and the dense foliage covers the delicate, sensitive, swaying branchlets all around. It is now in full bloom, and the flowers, together with thousands of last season's cones still clinging to the drooping sprays, display wonderful wealth of color, brown and purple and blue. Gladly I climbed the first tree I found to revel in the midst of it. How the touch of the flowers makes one's flesh tingle! The pistillate are dark, rich purple, and almost translucent, the staminate blue,—a vivid, pure tone of blue like the mountain sky,—the most uncommonly beautiful of all the Sierra tree flowers I have seen. How wonderful that, with all its delicate feminine grace and beauty of form and dress and behavior, this lovely tree up here, exposed to the wildest blasts, has already endured the storms of centuries of winters!

The two pines also are brave storm-enduring trees, the mountain pine (*Pinus monticola*) and the dwarf pine (*Pinus albicaulis*). The mountain pine is closely related to the sugar pine, though the cones are only about four to six inches long. The largest trees are from five to six feet in diameter at four feet above the ground, the bark rich brown. Only a few storm-beaten adventurers approach the summit of the mountain. The dwarf or white-bark pine is the species that forms the timber-line, where it is so completely dwarfed that one may walk over the top of a bed of it as over snow-pressed chaparral.

How boundless the day seems as we revel in these storm-beaten sky gardens amid so vast a congregation of onlooking mountains! Strange and admirable it is that the more savage and chilly and storm-chafed the mountains, the finer the glow on their faces and the finer the plants they bear. The myriads of flowers tingeing the mountain-top do not seem to have grown out of the dry, rough gravel of disintegration, but rather they appear as visitors, a cloud of witnesses to Nature's love in what we in our timid ignorance and unbelief call howling desert. The surface of the ground, so dull and forbidding at first sight, besides being rich in plants, shines and sparkles with crystals:

mica, hornblende, feldspar, quartz, tourmaline. The radiance in some places is so great as to be fairly dazzling, keen lance rays of every color flashing, sparkling in glorious abundance, joining the plants in their fine, brave beauty-work—every crystal, every flower a window opening into heaven, a mirror reflecting the Creator.

From garden to garden, ridge to ridge, I drifted enchanted, now on my knees gazing into the face of a daisy, now climbing again and again among the purple and azure flowers of the hemlocks, now down into the treasuries of the snow, or gazing afar over domes and peaks, lakes and woods, and the billowy glaciated fields of the upper Tuolumne, and trying to sketch them. In the midst of such beauty, pierced with its rays, one's body is all one tingling palate. Who wouldn't be a mountaineer! Up here all the world's prizes seem nothing.

The largest of the many glacier lakes in sight, and the one with the finest shore scenery, is Tenaya, about a mile long, with an imposing mountain dipping its feet into it on the south side, Cathedral Peak a few miles above its head, many smooth swelling rock-waves and domes on the north, and in the distance southward a multitude of snowy peaks, the fountain-heads of rivers. Lake Hoffman lies shimmering beneath my feet, mountain pines around its shining rim. To the northward the picturesque basin of Yosemite Creek glitters with lakelets and pools; but the eye is soon drawn away from these bright mirror wells, however attractive, to revel in the glorious congregation of peaks on the axis of the range in their robes of snow and light.

Carlo caught an unfortunate woodchuck when it was running from a grassy spot to its boulder-pile home—one of the hardiest of the mountain animals. I tried hard to save him, but in vain. After telling Carlo that he must be careful not to kill anything, I caught sight, for the first time, of the curious pika, or little chief hare, that cuts large quantities of lupines and other plants and lays them out to dry in the sun for hay, which it stores in underground barns to last through the long, snowy winter. Coming upon these plants freshly cut and lying in handfuls here and there on the rocks has a startling effect of busy life on the lonely mountain-top. These little haymakers, endowed with brain stuff something like our own,—God up here looking after them,—what lessons they teach, how they widen our sympathy!

An eagle soaring above a sheer cliff, where I suppose its nest is, makes another striking show of life, and helps to bring to mind the other people of the so-called solitude—deer in the forest caring for their young; the strong, well-clad, well-fed bears; the lively throng of squirrels; the blessed birds, great and small, stirring and sweetening the groves; and the clouds of happy insects filling the sky with joyous hum as part and parcel of the down-pouring sunshine. All these come to mind, as well as the plant people, and the glad streams singing their way to the sea. But most impressive of all is the vast glowing countenance of the wilderness in awful, infinite repose.

Toward sunset, enjoyed a fine run to camp, down the long south slopes, across ridges and ravines, gardens and avalanche gaps, through the firs and chaparral, enjoying wild excitement and excess of strength, and so ends a day that will never end.

July 27. Up and away to Lake Tenaya,—another big day, enough for a lifetime. The rocks, the air, everything speaking with audible voice or silent; joyful, wonderful, enchanting, banishing weariness and sense of time. No longing for anything now or hereafter as we go home into the mountain's heart. The level sunbeams are touching the fir-tops, every leaf shining with dew. Am holding an easterly course, the deep cañon of Tenaya Creek on the right hand, Mount Hoffman on the left, and the lake straight ahead about ten miles distant, the summit of Mount Hoffman about three thousand feet above me, Tenaya Creek four thousand feet below and separated from the shallow, irregular valley, along which most of the way lies, by smooth domes and wave-ridges. Many mossy emerald bogs, meadows, and gardens in rocky hollows to wade and saunter through—and what fine plants they give me, what joyful streams I have to cross, and how many views are displayed of the Hoffman and Cathedral Peak masonry, and what a wondrous breadth of shining granite pavement to walk over for the first time about the shores of the lake! On I sauntered in freedom complete; body without weight as far as I was aware; now wading through starry parnassia bogs, now through gardens shoulder deep in larkspur and lilies, grasses and rushes, shaking off showers of dew; crossing piles of crystalline moraine boulders, bright mirror pavements, and cool, cheery streams going to Yosemite; crossing bryanthus carpets and the scoured pathways of avalanches, and thickets of snow-pressed ceanothus; then down a broad, majestic stairway into the ice-sculptured lake-basin.

The snow on the high mountains is melting fast, and the streams are singing bank-full, swaying softly through the level meadows and bogs, quivering with sun-spangles, swirling in pot-holes, resting in deep pools, leaping, shouting in wild, exulting energy over rough boulder dams, joyful, beautiful in all their forms. No Sierra landscape that I have seen holds anything truly dead or dull, or any trace of what in manufactories is called rubbish or waste; everything is perfectly clean and pure and full of divine lessons. This quick, inevitable interest attaching to everything seems marvelous until the hand of God becomes visible; then it seems reasonable that what interests Him may well interest us. When we try to pick out anything by itself, we find it hitched to everything else in the universe. One fancies a heart like our own must be beating in every crystal and cell, and we feel like stopping to speak to the plants and animals as friendly fellow mountaineers. Nature as a poet, an enthusiastic workingman, becomes more and more visible the farther and higher we go; for the mountains are fountains—beginning places, however related to sources beyond mortal ken.

I found three kinds of meadows: (1) Those contained in basins not yet filled with earth enough to make a dry surface. They are planted with several species of carex, and have their margins diversified with robust flowering plants such as veratrum, larkspur, lupine, etc. (2) Those contained in the same sort of basins, once lakes like the first, but so situated in relation to the streams that flow through them and beds of transportable sand, gravel, etc., that they are now high and dry and well drained. This dry condition and corresponding difference in their vegetation may be caused by no superiority of position, or power of transporting filling material in the streams that belong to them, but simply by the basin being shallow and therefore sooner filled. They are planted with grasses, mostly fine, silky, and rather short-leaved, *Calamagrostis* and *Agrostis* being the principal genera. They form delightfully smooth, level sods in which one finds two or three species of gentian and as many of purple and yellow orthocarpus, violet, vaccinium, kalmia, bryanthus, and lonicera. (3) Meadows hanging on ridge and mountain slopes, not in basins at all, but made and held in place by masses of boulders and fallen trees, which, forming dams one above another in close succession on small, outspread, channelless streams, have collected soil enough for the growth of grasses, carices, and many flowering plants, and being kept well watered, without being subject to currents sufficiently strong to carry them away, a hanging or sloping meadow is the result. Their surfaces are seldom so smooth as the others, being roughened more or less by the projecting tops of the dam rocks or logs; but at a little distance this roughness is not noticed, and the effect is very striking— bright green, fluent, down-sweeping flowery ribbons on gray slopes. The broad shallow streams these meadows belong to are mostly derived from banks of snow and because the soil is well drained in some places, while in others the dam rocks are packed close and caulked with bits of wood and leaves, making boggy patches; the vegetation, of course, is correspondingly varied. I saw patches of willow, bryanthus, and a fine show of lilies on some of them, not forming a margin, but scattered about among the carex and grass. Most of these meadows are now in their prime. How wonderful must be the temper of the elastic leaves of grasses and sedges to make curves so perfect and fine. Tempered a little harder, they would stand erect, stiff and bristly, like strips of metal; a little softer, and every leaf would lie flat. And what fine painting and tinting there is on the glumes and pales, stamens and feathery pistils. Butterflies colored like the flowers waver above them in wonderful profusion, and many other beautiful winged people, numbered and known and loved only by the Lord, are waltzing together high over head, seemingly in pure play and hilarious enjoyment of their little sparks of life. How wonderful they are! How do they get a living, and endure the weather? How are their little bodies, with muscles, nerves, organs, kept warm and jolly in such admirable exuberant health? Regarded only as mechanical inventions, how wonderful they are! Compared with these, Godlike man's greatest machines are as nothing

Most of the sandy gardens on moraines are in prime beauty like the meadows, though some on the north sides of rocks and beneath groves of sapling pines have not yet bloomed. On sunny sheets of crystal soil along the slopes of the Hoffman Mountains, I saw extensive patches of ivesia and purple gilia with scarce a green leaf, making fine clouds of color. Ribes bushes, vaccinium, and kalmia, now in flower, make beautiful rugs and borders along the banks of the streams. Shaggy beds of dwarf oak (*Quercus chrysolepis*, var. *vaccinifolia*) over which one may walk are common on rocky moraines, yet this is the same species as the large live oak seen near Brown's Flat. The most beautiful of the shrubs is the purple-flowered bryanthus, here making glorious carpets at an elevation of nine thousand feet.

The principal tree for the first mile or two from camp is the magnificent silver fir, which reaches perfection here both in size and form of individual trees, and in the mode of grouping in groves with open spaces between. So trim and tasteful are these silvery, spiry groves one would fancy they must have been placed in position by some master landscape gardener, their regularity seeming almost conventional. But Nature is the only gardener able to do work so fine. A few noble specimens two hundred feet high occupy central positions in the groups with younger trees around them; and outside of these another circle of yet smaller ones, the whole arranged like tastefully symmetrical bouquets, every tree fitting nicely the place assigned to it as if made especially for it; small roses and eriogonums are usually found blooming on the open spaces about the groves, forming charming pleasure grounds. Higher, the firs gradually become smaller and less perfect, many showing double summits, indicating storm stress. Still, where good moraine soil is found, even on the rim of the lake-basin, specimens one hundred and fifty feet in height and five feet in diameter occur nearly nine thousand feet above the sea. The saplings, I find, are mostly bent with the crushing weight of the winter snow, which at this elevation must be at least eight or ten feet deep, judging by marks on the trees; and this depth of compacted snow is heavy enough to bend and bury young trees twenty or thirty feet in height and hold them down for four or five months. Some are broken; the others spring up when the snow melts and at length attain a size that enables them to withstand the snow pressure. Yet even in trees five feet thick the traces of this early discipline are still plainly to be seen in their curved insteps, and frequently in old dried saplings protruding from the trunk, partially overgrown by the new axis developed from a branch below the break. Yet through all this stress the forest is maintained in marvelous beauty.

Beyond the silver firs I find the two-leaved pine (*Pinus contorta*, var. *Murrayana*) forms the bulk of the forest up to an elevation of ten thousand feet or more—the highest timber-belt of the Sierra. I saw a specimen nearly five feet in diameter growing on deep, well-watered soil at an elevation of about nine thousand feet. The form of this species varies very much with position, exposure, soil, etc. On stream-banks, where it is closely planted, it is very slender; some specimens seventy-five feet high do not exceed five inches in diameter at the ground, but the ordinary form, as far as I have seen, is well proportioned. The average diameter when full grown at this elevation is about twelve or fourteen inches, height forty or fifty feet, the straggling branches bent up at the end, the bark thin and bedraggled with amber-colored resin. The pistillate flowers form little crimson rosettes a fourth of an inch in diameter on the ends of the branchlets, mostly hidden in the leaf-tassels; the staminate are about three eighths of an inch in diameter, sulphur-yellow, in showy clusters, giving a remarkably rich effect—a brave, hardy mountaineer pine, growing cheerily on rough beds of avalanche boulders and joints of rock pavements, as well as in fertile hollows, standing up to the waist in snow every winter for centuries, facing a thousand storms and blooming every year in colors as bright as those worn by the sun-drenched trees of the tropics.

A still hardier mountaineer is the Sierra juniper (*Juniperus occidentalis*), growing mostly on domes and ridges and glacier pavements. A thickset, sturdy, picturesque highlander, seemingly content to live for more than a score of centuries on sunshine and snow; a truly wonderful fellow, dogged endurance expressed in every feature, lasting about as long as the granite he stands on. Some are nearly as broad as high. I saw one on the shore of the lake nearly ten feet in diameter, and many six to eight feet. The bark, cinnamon-colored, flakes off in long

Junipers in Tenaya Cañon

ribbon-like strips with a satiny luster. Surely the most enduring of all tree mountaineers, it never seems to die a natural
death, or even to fall after it has been killed. If protected from
accidents, it would perhaps be immortal. I saw some that had
withstood an avalanche from snowy Mount Hoffman cheerily
putting out new branches, as if repeating, like Grip, "Never
say die." Some were simply standing on the pavement where
no fissure more than half an inch wide offered a hold for its
roots. The common height for these rock-dwellers is from ten
to twenty feet; most of the old ones have broken tops, and are
mere stumps, with a few tufted branches, forming picturesque
brown pillars on bare pavements, with plenty of elbow-room
and a clear view in every direction. On good moraine soil it
reaches a height of from forty to sixty feet, with dense gray
foliage. The rings of the trunk are very thin, eighty to an
inch of diameter in some specimens I examined. Those ten
feet in diameter must be very old—thousands of years. Wish
I could live, like these junipers, on sunshine and snow, and
stand beside them on the shore of Lake Tenaya for a thousand

years. How much I should see, and how delightful it would be! Everything in the mountains would find me and come to me, and everything from the heavens like light.

The lake was named for one of the chiefs of the Yosemite tribe. Old Tenaya is said to have been a good Indian to his tribe. When a company of soldiers followed his band into Yosemite to punish them for cattle-stealing and other crimes, they fled to this lake by a trail that leads out of the upper end of the valley, early in the spring, while the snow was still deep; but being pursued, they lost heart and surrendered. A fine monument the old man has in this bright lake, and likely to last a long time, though lakes die as well as Indians, being gradually filled with detritus carried in by the feeding streams, and to some extent also by snow avalanches and rain and wind. A considerable portion of the Tenaya basin is already changed into a forested flat and meadow at the upper end, where the main tributary enters from Cathedral Peak. Two other tributaries come from the Hoffman Range. The outlet flows westward through Tenaya Cañon to join the Merced River in Yosemite. Scarce a handful of loose soil is to be seen on the north shore. All is bare, shining granite, suggesting the Indian name of the lake, Pywiack, meaning shining rock. The basin seems to have been slowly excavated by the ancient glaciers, a marvelous work requiring countless thousands of years. On the south side an imposing mountain rises from the water's edge to a height of three thousand feet or more, feathered with hemlock and pine; and huge shining domes on the east, over the tops of which the grinding, wasting, molding glacier must have swept as the wind does to-day.

July 28. No cloud mountains, only curly cirrus wisps scarce perceptible, and the want of thunder to strike the noon hour seems strange, as if the Sierra clock had stopped. Have been studying the *magnifica* fir—measured one near two hundred and forty feet high, the tallest I have yet seen. This species is the most symmetrical of all conifers, but though gigantic in size it seldom lives more than four or five hundred years. Most of the trees die from the attacks of a fungus at the age of two or three centuries. This dry-rot fungus perhaps enters the trunk by way of the stumps of limbs broken off by the snow that loads the broad palmate branches. The younger specimens are marvels of symmetry, straight and erect as a plumbline, their branches in regular level whorls of five mostly, each branch as exact in its divisions as a fern frond, and thickly covered by the leaves, making a rich plush over all the tree, excepting only the trunk and a small portion of the main limbs. The leaves turn upward, especially on the branchlets, and are stiff and sharp, pointed on all the upper portion of the tree. They remain on the tree about eight or ten years, and as the growth is rapid it is not rare to find the leaves still in place on the upper part of the axis where it is three to four inches in diameter, wide apart of course, and their spiral arrangement beautifully displayed. The leaf-scars are conspicuous for twenty years or more, but there is a good deal of variation in different trees as to the thickness and sharpness of the leaves.

After the excursion to Mount Hoffman I had seen a complete cross-section of the Sierra forest, and I find that *Abies magnifica* is the most symmetrical tree of all the noble coniferous company. The cones are grand affairs, superb in form, size, and color, cylindrical, stand erect on the upper branches like casks, and are from five to eight inches in length by three or four in diameter, greenish gray, and covered with fine down which has a silvery luster in the sunshine, and their brilliance is augmented by beads of transparent balsam which seems to have been poured over each cone, bringing to mind the old ceremonies of anointing with oil. If possible, the inside of the cone is more beautiful than the outside; the scales, bracts, and seed wings are tinted with the loveliest rosy purple with a bright lustrous iridescence; the seeds, three fourths of an inch long, are dark brown. When the cones are ripe the scales and bracts fall off, setting the seeds free to fly to their predestined places, while the dead spike-like axes are left on the branches for many years to mark the positions of the vanished cones, excepting those cut off when green by the Douglas squirrel. How he gets his teeth under the broad bases of the sessile cones, I don't know. Climbing these trees on a sunny day to visit the growing cones and to gaze over the tops of the forest is one of my best enjoyments.

July 29. Bright, cool, exhilarating. Clouds about .05. Another glorious day of rambling, sketching, and universal enjoyment.

July 30. Clouds .20, but the regular shower did not reach us, though thunder was heard a few miles off striking the noon hour. Ants, flies, and mosquitoes seem to enjoy this fine climate. A few house-flies have discovered our camp. The Sierra mosquitoes are courageous and of good size, some of them measuring nearly an inch from tip of sting to tip of folded wings. Though less abundant than in most wildernesses, they occasionally make quite a hum and stir, and pay but little attention to time or place. They sting anywhere, any time of day, wherever they can find anything worth while, until they are themselves stung by frost. The large, jet-black ants are only ticklish and troublesome when one is lying down under the trees. Noticed a borer drilling a silver fir. Ovipositor about an inch and a half in length, polished and straight like a needle. When not in use, it is folded back in a sheath, which extends straight behind like the legs of a crane in flying. This drilling, I suppose, is to save nest building, and the after care of feeding the young. Who would guess that in the brain of a fly so much knowledge could find lodgment? How do they know that their eggs will hatch in such holes, or, after they hatch, that the soft, helpless grubs will find the right sort of nourishment in silver fir sap? This domestic arrangement calls to mind the curious family of gallflies. Each species seems to know what kind of plant will respond to the irritation or stimulus of the puncture it makes and the eggs it lays, in forming a growth that not only answers for a nest and home but also provides food for the young. Probably these gallflies make mistakes at times, like anybody else; but when they do, there is simply a failure of that particular brood, while enough to perpetuate the species do find the proper plants and nourishment. Many mistakes of this kind might be made without being discovered by us. Once a pair of wrens made the mistake of building a nest in the sleeve of a workman's coat, which was called for at sundown, much to the consternation and discomfiture of the birds. Still the marvel remains that any of the children of such small people as gnats and mosquitoes should escape their own and their parents' mistakes, as well as the vicissitudes of the weather and hosts of enemies, and come forth in full vigor and perfection to enjoy the sunny world. When we think of the small creatures that are visible, we are led to think of many that are smaller still and lead us on and on into infinite mystery.

July 31. Another glorious day, the air as delicious to the lungs as nectar to the tongue; indeed the body seems one palate, and tingles equally throughout. Cloudiness about .05, but our ordinary shower has not yet reached us, though I hear thunder in the distance.

The cheery little chipmunk, so common about Brown's Flat, is common here also, and perhaps other species. In their light, airy habits they recall the familiar species of the Eastern States, which we admired in the oak openings of Wisconsin as they skimmed along the zigzag rail fences. These Sierra chipmunks are more arboreal and squirrel-like. I first noticed them on the lower edge of the coniferous belt, where the Sabine and yellow pines meet,—exceedingly interesting little fellows, full of odd, funny ways, and without being true squirrels, have most of their acomplishments without their aggressive quarrel-someness. I never weary watching them as they frisk about in the bushes gathering seeds and berries, like song sparrows poising daintily on slender twigs, and making even less stir than most birds of the same size. Few of the Sierra animals interest me more; they are so able, gentle, confiding, and beautiful, they take one's heart, and get themselves adopted as darlings. Though weighing hardly more than field mice, they are laborious collectors of seeds, nuts, and cones, and are therefore well fed, but never in the least swollen with fat or lazily full. On the contrary, of their frisky, birdlike liveliness there is no end. They have a great variety of notes corresponding with their movements, some sweet and liquid, like water dripping with tinkling sounds into pools. They seem dearly to love teasing a dog, coming frequently almost within reach, then frisking away with lively chipping, like sparrows, beating time to their music with their tails, which at each chip describe half circles from side to side. Not even the Douglas squirrel is surer-footed or more fearless. I have seen them running about on sheer precipices of the Yosemite walls seemingly holding on with as little effort as flies, and as unconscious of danger, where, if the slightest slip were made, they would have fallen two or three thousand feet. How fine it would be could we mountaineers climb these tremendous cliffs with the same sure grip! The venture I made the other day for a view of the Yosemite Fall, and which tried my nerves so sorely, this little Tamias would have made for an ear of grass.

The woodchuck (*Arctomys monax*) of the bleak mountain-tops is a very different sort of mountaineer—the most bovine of rodents, a heavy eater, fat, aldermanic in bulk and fairly bloated, in his high pastures, like a cow in a clover field. One woodchuck would outweigh a hundred chipmunks, and yet he is by no means a dull animal. In the midst of what we regard as storm-beaten desolation he pipes and whistles right cheerily, and enjoys long life in his skyland homes. His burrow is made in disintegrated rocks or beneath large boulders. Coming out of his den in the cold hoarfrost mornings, he takes a sun-bath on some favorite flat-topped rock, then goes to breakfast in garden hollows, eats grass and flowers until comfortably swollen, then goes a-visiting to fight and play. How long a woodchuck lives in this bracing air I don't know, but some of them are rusty and gray like lichen-covered boulders.

August 1. A grand cloudland and five-minute shower, refreshing the blessed wilderness, already so fragrant and fresh, steeping the black meadow mold and dead leaves like tea.

The waycup, or flicker, so familiar to every boy in the old Middle West States, is one of the most common of the woodpeckers hereabouts, and makes one feel at home. I can see no difference in plumage or habits from the Eastern species, though the climate here is so different,—a fine, brave, confiding, beautiful bird. The robin, too, is here, with all his familiar notes and gestures, tripping daintily on open garden spots and high meadows. Over all America he seems to be at home, moving from the plains to the mountains and from north to south, back and forth, up and down, with the march of the seasons and food supply. How admirable the constitution and temper of this brave singer, keeping in cheery health over so vast and varied a range! Oftentimes, as I wander through these solemn woods, awe-stricken and silent, I hear the reassuring voice of this fellow wanderer ringing out, sweet and clear, "Fear not! fear not!"

The mountain quail (*Oreortyx ricta*) I often meet in my walks—a small brown partridge with a very long, slender, ornamental crest worn jauntily like a feather in a boy's cap, giving it a very marked appearance. This species is considerably larger than the valley quail, so common on the hot foothills. They seldom alight in trees, but love to wander in flocks of from five or six to twenty through the ceanothus and manzanita thickets and over open, dry meadows and rocks of the ridges where the forest is less dense or wanting, uttering a low clucking sound to enable them to keep together. When disturbed they rise with a strong birr of wing-beats, and scatter as if exploded to a distance of a quarter of a mile or so. After the danger is past they call one another together with a loud piping note—Nature's beautiful mountain chickens. I have not yet found their nests. The young of this season are already hatched and away—new broods of happy wanderers half as large as their parents. I wonder how they live through the long winters, when the ground is snow-covered ten feet deep. They must go down towards the lower edge of the forest, like the deer, though I have not heard of them there.

The blue, or dusky, grouse is also common here. They like the deepest and closest fir woods, and when disturbed, burst from the branches of the trees with a strong, loud whir of wing-beats, and vanish in a wavering, silent slide, without moving a feather—a stout, beautiful bird about the size of the prairie chicken of the old west, spending most of the time in the trees, excepting the breeding season, when it keeps to the ground. The young are now able to fly. When scattered by man or dog, they keep still until the danger is supposed to be passed, then the mother calls them together. The chicks can hear the call a distance of several hundred yards, though it is not loud. Should the young be unable to fly, the mother feigns desperate lameness or death to draw one away, throwing herself at one's feet within two or three yards, rolling over on her back, kicking and gasping, so as to deceive man or beast. They are said to stay all the year in the woods hereabouts, taking shelter in dense tufted branches of fir and yellow pine during snowstorms, and feeding on the young buds of these trees. Their legs are feathered down to their toes, and I have never heard of their suffering in any sort of weather. Able to live on pine and fir buds, they are forever independent in the matter of food, which troubles so many of us and controls our movements. Gladly, if I could, I would live forever on pine buds, however full of turpentine and pitch, for the sake of this grand independence. Just to think of our sufferings last month merely for grist-mill flour. Man seems to have more difficulty in gaining food than any other of the Lord's creatures. For many in towns it is a consuming, lifelong struggle; for others, the danger of coming to want is so great, the deadly habit of endless hoarding for the future is formed, which smothers all real life, and is continued long after every reasonable need has been over-supplied.

On Mount Hoffman I saw a curious dove-colored bird that seemed half woodpecker, half magpie, or crow. It screams something like a crow, but flies like a woodpecker, and has a long, straight bill, with which I saw it opening the cones of the mountain and white-barked pines. It seems to keep to the heights, though no doubt it comes down for shelter during winter, if not for food. So far as food is concerned, these bird-mountaineers, I guess, can glean nuts enough, even in winter, from the different kinds of conifers; for always there are a few that have been unable to fly out of the cones and remain for hungry winter gleaners.

Chapter VII

A STRANGE EXPERIENCE

AUGUST 2. Clouds and showers, about the same as yesterday. Sketching all day on the North Dome until four or five o'clock in the afternoon, when, as I was busily employed thinking only of the glorious Yosemite landscape, trying to draw every tree and every line and feature of the rocks, I was suddenly, and without warning, possessed with the notion that my friend, Professor J. D. Butler, of the State University of Wisconsin, was below me in the valley, and I jumped up full of the idea of meeting him, with almost as much startling excitement as if he had suddenly touched me to make me look up. Leaving my work without the slightest deliberation, I ran down the western slope of the Dome and along the brink of the valley wall, looking for a way to the bottom, until I came to a side cañon, which, judging by its apparently continuous growth of trees and bushes, I thought might afford a practical way into the valley, and immediately began to make the descent, late as it was, as if drawn irresistibly. But after a little, common sense stopped me and explained that it would be long after dark ere I could possibly reach the hotel, that the visitors would be asleep, that nobody would know me, that I had no money in my pockets, and moreover was without a coat. I therefore compelled myself to stop, and finally succeeded in reasoning myself out of the notion of seeking my friend in the dark, whose presence I only felt in a strange, telepathic way. I succeeded in dragging myself back through the woods to camp, never for a moment wavering, however, in my determination to go down to him next morning. This I think is the most unexplainable notion that ever struck me. Had some one whispered in my ear while I sat on the Dome, where I had spent so many days, that Professor Butler was in the valley, I could not have been more surprised and startled. When I was leaving the university, he said, "Now, John, I want to hold you in sight and watch your career. Promise to write me at least once a year." I received a letter from him in July, at our first camp in the Hollow, written in May, in which he said that he might possibly visit California some time this summer, and therefore hoped to meet me. But inasmuch as he named no meeting-place, and gave no directions as to the course he would probably follow, and as I should be in the wilderness all summer, I had not the slightest hope of seeing him, and all thought of the matter had vanished from my mind until this afternoon, when he seemed to be wafted bodily almost against my face. Well, to-morrow I shall see; for, reasonable or unreasonable, I feel I must go.

August 3. Had a wonderful day. Found Professor Butler as the compass-needle finds the pole. So last evening's telepathy, transcendental revelation, or whatever else it may be called, was true; for, strange to say, he had just entered the valley by way of the Coulterville Trail and was coming up the valley past El Capitan when his presence struck me. Had he then looked toward the North Dome with a good glass when it first came in sight, he might have seen me jump up from my work and run toward him. This seems the one well-defined marvel of my life of the kind called supernatural; for, absorbed in glad Nature, spirit-rappings, second sight, ghost stories, etc., have never interested me since boyhood, seeming comparatively useless and infinitely less wonderful than Nature's open, harmonious, songful, sunny, everyday beauty.

This morning, when I thought of having to appear among tourists at a hotel, I was troubled because I had no suitable clothes, and at best am desperately bashful and shy. I was determined to go, however, to see my old friend after two years among strangers; got on a clean pair of overalls, a cashmere shirt, and a sort of jacket,—the best my camp wardrobe afforded,—tied my notebook on my belt, and strode away on my strange journey, followed by Carlo. I made my way through the gap discovered last evening, which proved to be Indian Cañon. There was no trail in it, and the rocks and brush were so rough that Carlo frequently called me back to help him down precipitous places. Emerging from the cañon shadows, I found a man making hay on one of the meadows, and asked him whether Professor Butler was in the valley. "I don't know," he replied; "but you can easily find out at the hotel. There are but few visitors in the valley just now. A small party came in yesterday afternoon, and I heard some one called Professor Butler, or Butterfield, or some name like that."

In front of the gloomy hotel I found a tourist party adjusting their fishing tackle. They all stared at me in silent wonderment, as if I had been seen dropping down through the trees from the clouds, mostly, I suppose, on account of my strange garb. Inquiring for the office, I was told it was locked, and that the landlord was away, but I might find the landlady, Mrs. Hutchings, in the parlor. I entered in a sad state of embarrassment, and after I had waited in the big, empty room and knocked at several doors the landlady at length appeared, and in reply to my question said she rather thought Professor Butler *was* in the valley, but to make sure, she would bring the register from the office. Among the names of the last arrivals I soon discovered the Professor's familiar handwriting, at the sight of which bashfulness vanished; and having learned that his party had gone up the valley,—probably to the Vernal and Nevada Falls,—I pushed on in glad pursuit, my heart now sure of its prey. In less than an hour I reached the head of the Nevada Cañon at the Vernal Fall, and just outside of the spray discovered a distinguished-looking gentleman, who, like everybody else I have seen to-day, regarded me curiously as I approached. When I made bold to inquire if he knew where Professor Butler was, he seemed yet more curious to know what could possibly have happened that required a messenger for the Professor, and instead of answering my question he asked with military sharpness, "Who wants him?" "I want him," I replied with equal sharpness. "Why? Do *you* know him?" "Yes," I said. "Do *you* know him?" Astonished that any one in the mountains could possibly know Professor Butler and find him as soon as he had reached the valley, he came down to meet the strange mountaineer on equal terms, and courteously replied, "Yes, I know Professor Butler very well. I am General Alvord, and we were fellow students in Rutland, Vermont, long ago, when we were both young." "But where is he now?" I persisted, cutting short his story. "He has gone beyond the falls with a companion, to try to climb that big rock, the top of which you see from here." His guide now volunteered the information that it was the Liberty Cap Professor Butler and his companion had gone to climb, and that if I waited at the head of the fall I should be sure to find them on their way down. I therefore climbed the ladders alongside the Vernal Fall, and was pushing

forward, determined to go to the top of Liberty Cap rock in
my hurry, rather than wait, if I should not meet my friend
sooner. So heart-hungry at times may one be to see a friend in
the flesh, however happily full and care-free one's life may be. I
had gone but a short distance, however, above the brow of the
Vernal Fall when I caught sight of him in the brush and rocks,
half erect, groping his way, his sleeves rolled up, vest open,
hat in his hand, evidently very hot and tired. When he saw
me coming he sat down on a boulder to wipe the perspiration
from his brow and neck, and taking me for one of the valley
guides, he inquired the way to the fall ladders. I pointed out
the path marked with little piles of stones, on seeing which
he called his companion, saying that the way was found; but
he did not yet recognize me. Then I stood directly in front
of him, looked him in the face, and held out my hand. He
thought I was offering to assist him in rising. "Never mind,"
he said. Then I said, "Professor Butler, don't you know me?"
"I think not," he replied; but catching my eye, sudden recognition followed, and astonishment that I should have found him
just when he was lost in the brush and did not know that I
was within hundreds of miles of him. "John Muir, John Muir,
where have you come from?" Then I told him the story of my
feeling his presence when he entered the valley last evening,
when he was four or five miles distant, as I sat sketching on
the North Dome. This, of course, only made him wonder the
more. Below the foot of the Vernal Fall the guide was waiting
with his saddle-horse, and I walked along the trail, chatting
all the way back to the hotel, talking of school days, friends
in Madison, of the students, how each had prospered, etc.,
ever and anon gazing at the stupendous rocks about us, now
growing indistinct in the gloaming, and again quoting from
the poets—a rare ramble.

It was late ere we reached the hotel, and General Alvord
was waiting the Professor's arrival for dinner. When I was
introduced he seemed yet more astonished than the Professor at my descent from cloudland and going straight to my
friend without knowing in any ordinary way that he was even
in California. They had come on direct from the East, had
not yet visited any of their friends in the state, and considered
themselves undiscoverable. As we sat at dinner, the General

leaned back in his chair, and looking down the table, thus introduced me to the dozen guests or so, including the staring fisherman mentioned above: "This man, you know, came down out of these huge, trackless mountains, you know, to find his friend Professor Butler here, the very day he arrived; and how did he know he was here? He just felt him, he says. This is the queerest case of Scotch farsightedness I ever heard of," etc., etc. While my friend quoted Shakespeare: "More things in heaven and earth, Horatio, than are dreamt of in your philosophy," "As the sun, ere he has risen, sometimes paints his image in the firmament, e'en so the shadows of events precede the events, and in to-day already walks to-morrow."

Had a long conversation, after dinner, over Madison days. The Professor wants me to promise to go with him, sometime, on a camping trip in the Hawaiian Islands, while I tried to get him to go back with me to camp in the high Sierra. But he says, "Not now." He must not leave the General; and I was surprised to learn they are to leave the valley to-morrow or next day. I'm glad I'm not great enough to be missed in the busy world.

August 4. It seemed strange to sleep in a paltry hotel chamber after the spacious magnificence and luxury of the starry sky and silver fir grove. Bade farewell to my friend and the General. The old soldier was very kind, and an interesting talker. He told me long stories of the Florida Seminole war, in which he took part, and invited me to visit him in Omaha. Calling Carlo, I scrambled home through the Indian Cañon gate, rejoicing, pitying the poor Professor and General, bound by clocks, almanacs, orders, duties, etc., and compelled to dwell with lowland care and dust and din, where Nature is covered and her voice smothered, while the poor, insignificant wanderer enjoys the freedom and glory of God's wilderness.

Apart from the human interest of my visit to-day, I greatly enjoyed Yosemite, which I had visited only once before, having spent eight days last spring in rambling amid its rocks and waters. Wherever we go in the mountains, or indeed in any of God's wild fields, we find more than we seek. Descending four thousand feet in a few hours, we enter a new world—climate, plants, sounds, inhabitants, and scenery all new or changed. Near camp the goldcup oak forms sheets of chaparral, on top of which we may make our beds. Going down the Indian Cañon we observe this little bush changing by regular gradations to a large bush, to a small tree, and then larger, until on the rocky taluses near the bottom of the valley we find it developed into a broad, wide-spreading, gnarled, picturesque tree from four to eight feet in diameter, and forty or fifty feet high. Innumerable are the forms of water displayed. Every gliding reach, cascade, and fall has characters of its own. Had a good view of the Vernal and Nevada, two of the main falls of the valley, less than a mile apart, and offering striking differences in voice, form, color, etc. The Vernal, four hundred feet high and about seventy-five or eighty feet wide, drops smoothly over a round-lipped precipice and forms a superb apron of embroidery, green and white, slightly folded and fluted, maintaining this form nearly to the bottom, where it is suddenly veiled in quick-flying billows of spray and mist, in which the afternoon sunbeams play with ravishing beauty of rainbow colors. The Nevada is white from its first appearance as it leaps out into the freedom of the air. At the head it presents a twisted appearance, by an overfolding of the current from striking on the side of its channel just before the first free outbounding leap is made. About two thirds of the way down, the hurrying throng of comet-shaped masses glance on an inclined part of the face of the precipice and are beaten into yet whiter foam, greatly expanded, and sent bounding outward, making an indescribably glorious show, especially when the afternoon sunshine is pouring into it. In this fall—one of the most wonderful in the world—the water does not seem to be under the dominion of ordinary laws, but rather as if it were a living creature, full of the strength of the mountains and their huge, wild joy.

From beneath heavy throbbing blasts of spray the broken river is seen emerging in ragged boulder-chafed strips. These are speedily gathered into a roaring torrent, showing that the young river is still gloriously alive. On it goes, shouting, roaring, exulting in its strength, passes through a gorge with sublime display of energy, then suddenly expands on a gently inclined pavement, down which it rushes in thin sheets and folds of lace-work into a quiet pool,—"Emerald Pool," as it is called,—a stopping-place, a period separating two grand sentences. Resting here long enough to part with its foam-bells and gray mixtures of air, it glides quietly to the verge of the

Vernal precipice in a broad sheet and makes its new display in the Vernal Fall; then more rapids and rock tossings down the cañon, shaded by live oak, Douglas spruce, fir, maple, and dogwood. It receives the Illilouette tributary, and makes a long sweep out into the level, sun-filled valley to join the other streams which, like itself, have danced and sung their way down from snowy heights to form the main Merced—the river of Mercy. But of this there is no end, and life, when one thinks of it, is so short. Never mind, one day in the midst of these divine glories is well worth living and toiling and starving for.

Before parting with Professor Butler he gave me a book, and I gave him one of my pencil sketches for his little son Henry, who is a favorite of mine. He used to make many visits to my room when I was a student. Never shall I forget his patriotic speeches for the Union, mounted on a tall stool, when he was only six years old.

It seems strange that visitors to Yosemite should be so little influenced by its novel grandeur, as if their eyes were bandaged and their ears stopped. Most of those I saw yesterday were looking down as if wholly unconscious of anything going on about them, while the sublime rocks were trembling with the tones of the mighty chanting congregation of waters gathered from all the mountains round about, making music that might draw angels out of heaven. Yet respectable-looking, even wise-looking people were fixing bits of worms on bent pieces of wire to catch trout. Sport they called it. Should church-goers try to pass the time fishing in baptismal fonts while dull sermons were being preached, the so-called sport might not be so bad; but to play in the Yosemite temple, seeking pleasure in the pain of fishes struggling for their lives, while God himself is preaching his sublimest water and stone sermons!

Now I'm back at the camp-fire, and cannot help thinking about my recognition of my friend's presence in the valley while he was four or five miles away, and while I had no means of knowing that he was not thousands of miles away. It seems supernatural, but only because it is not understood. Anyhow, it seems silly to make so much of it, while the natural and common is more truly marvelous and mysterious than the so-called supernatural. Indeed most of the miracles we hear of are infinitely less wonderful than the commonest of natural phenomena, when fairly seen. Perhaps the invisible rays that struck me while I sat at work on the Dome are something like those which attract and repel people at first sight, concerning which so much nonsense has been written. The worst apparent effect of these mysterious odd things is blindness to all that is divinely common. Hawthorne, I fancy, could weave one of his weird romances out of this little telepathic episode, the one strange marvel of my life, probably replacing my good old Professor by an attractive woman.

August 5. We were awakened this morning before daybreak by the furious barking of Carlo and Jack and the sound of stampeding sheep. Billy fled from his punk bed to the fire, and refused to stir into the darkness to try to gather the scattered flock, or ascertain the nature of the disturbance. It was a bear attack, as we afterward learned, and I suppose little was gained by attempting to do anything before daylight. Nevertheless, being anxious to know what was up, Carlo and I groped our way through the woods, guided by the rustling sound made by fragments of the flock, not fearing the bear, for I knew that the runaways would go from their enemy as far as possible and Carlo's nose was also to be depended upon. About half a mile east of the corral we overtook twenty or thirty of the flock and succeeded in driving them back; then turning to the westward, we traced another band of fugitives and got them back to the flock. After daybreak I discovered the remains of a sheep carcass, still warm, showing that Bruin must have been enjoying his early mutton breakfast while I was seeking the runaways. He had eaten about half of it. Six dead sheep lay in the corral, evidently smothered by the crowding and piling up of the flock against the side of the corral wall when the bear entered. Making a wide circuit of the camp, Carlo and I discovered a third band of fugitives and drove them back to camp. We also discovered another dead sheep half eaten, showing there had been two of the shaggy freebooters at this early breakfast. They were easily traced. They had each caught a sheep, jumped over the corral fence with them, carrying them as a cat carries a mouse, laid them at the foot of fir trees a hundred yards or so back from the corral, and eaten their fill. After breakfast I set out to seek more of the lost, and found seventy-five at a considerable distance from camp. In the afternoon I succeeded, with

Carlo's help, in getting them back to the flock. I don't know whether all are together again or not. I shall make a big fire this evening and keep watch.

When I asked Billy why he made his bed against the corral in rotten wood, when so many better places offered, he replied that he "wished to be as near the sheep as possible in case bears should attack them." Now that the bears have come, he has moved his bed to the far side of the camp, and seems afraid that he may be mistaken for a sheep.

This has been mostly a sheep day, and of course studies have been interrupted. Nevertheless, the walk through the gloom of the woods before the dawn was worth while, and I have learned something about these noble bears. Their tracks are very telling, and so are their breakfasts. Scarce a trace of clouds to-day, and of course our ordinary midday thunder is wanting.

August 6. Enjoyed the grand illumination of the camp grove, last night, from the fire we made to frighten the bears—compensation for loss of sleep and sheep. The noble pillars of verdure, vividly aglow, seemed to shoot into the sky like the flames that lighted them. Nevertheless, one of the bears paid us another visit, as if more attracted than repelled by the fire, climbed into the corral, killed a sheep and made off with it without being seen, while still another was lost by trampling and suffocation against the side of the corral. Now that our mutton has been tasted, I suppose it will be difficult to put a stop to the ravages of these freebooters.

The Don arrived to-day from the lowlands with provisions and a letter. On learning the losses he had sustained, he determined to move the flock at once to the Upper Tuolumne region, saying that the bears would be sure to visit the camp every night as long as we stayed, and that no fire or noise we might make would avail to frighten them. No clouds save a few thin, lustrous touches on the eastern horizon. Thunder heard in the distance.

Chapter VIII

THE MONO TRAIL

August 7. Early this morning bade good-bye to the bears and blessed silver fir camp, and moved slowly eastward along the Mono Trail. At sundown camped for the night on one of the many small flowery meadows so greatly enjoyed on my excursion to Lake Tenaya. The dusty, noisy flock seems outrageously foreign and out of place in these nature gardens, more so than bears among sheep. The harm they do goes to the heart, but glorious hope lifts above all the dust and din and bids me look forward to a good time coming, when money enough will be earned to enable me to go walking where I like in pure wildness, with what I can carry on my back, and when the bread-sack is empty, run down to the nearest point on the bread-line for more. Nor will these run-downs be blanks, for, whether up or down, every step and jump on these blessed mountains is full of fine lessons.

August 8. Camp at the west end of Lake Tenaya. Arriving early, I took a walk on the glacier-polished pavements along the north shore, and climbed the magnificent mountain rock at the east end of the lake, now shining in the late afternoon light. Almost every yard of its surface shows the scoring and polishing action of a great glacier that enveloped it and swept heavily over its summit, though it is about two thousand feet high above the lake and ten thousand above sea-level. This majestic, ancient ice-flood came from the eastward, as the scoring and crushing of the surface shows. Even below the waters of the lake the rock in some places is still grooved and polished; the lapping of the waves and their disintegrating action have not as yet obliterated even the superficial marks of glaciation. In climbing the steepest polished places I had to take off shoes and stockings. A fine region this for study of glacial action in mountain-making. I found many charming plants: arctic daisies, phlox, white spiræa, bryanthus, and rock-ferns,—pellæa, cheilanthes, allosorus,—fringing weathered seams all the way up to the summit; and sturdy junipers, grand old gray and brown monuments, stood bravely erect on fissured spots here

View of Tenaya Lake showing Cathedral Peak

*One of the tributary fountains of the Tuolumne Cañon waters,
on the north side of the Hoffman Range*

and there, telling storm and avalanche stories of hundreds of winters. The view of the lake from the top is, I think, the best of all. There is another rock, more striking in form than this, standing isolated at the head of the lake, but it is not more than half as high. It is a knob or knot of burnished granite, perhaps about a thousand feet high, apparently as flawless and strong in structure as a wave-worn pebble, and probably owes its existence to the superior resistance it offered to the action of the overflowing ice-flood.

Made sketch of the lake, and sauntered back to camp, my iron-shod shoes clanking on the pavements disturbing the chipmunks and birds. After dark went out to the shore,—not a breath of air astir, the lake a perfect mirror reflecting the sky and mountains with their stars and trees and wonderful sculpture, all their grandeur refined and doubled,—a marvelously impressive picture, that seemed to belong more to heaven than earth.

August 9. I went ahead of the flock, and crossed over the divide between the Merced and Tuolumne Basins. The gap between the east end of the Hoffman spur and the mass of mountain rocks about Cathedral Peak, though roughened by ridges and waving folds, seems to be one of the channels of a broad ancient glacier that came from the mountains on the summit of the range. In crossing this divide the ice-river made an ascent of about five hundred feet from the Tuolumne meadows. This entire region must have been overswept by ice.

From the top of the divide, and also from the big Tuolumne Meadows, the wonderful mountain called Cathedral Peak is in sight. From every point of view it shows marked individuality. It is a majestic temple of one stone, hewn from the living rock, and adorned with spires and pinnacles in regular cathedral style. The dwarf pines on the roof look like mosses. I hope some time to climb to it to say my prayers and hear the stone sermons.

The big Tuolumne Meadows are flowery lawns, lying along the south fork of the Tuolumne River at a height of about eighty-five hundred to nine thousand feet above the sea, partially separated by forests and bars of glaciated granite. Here the mountains seem to have been cleared away or set back, so that wide-open views may be had in every direction. The upper end of the series lies at the base of Mount Lyell, the lower below the east end of the Hoffman Range, so the length must be about ten or twelve miles. They vary in width from a quarter of a mile to perhaps three quarters, and a good many branch meadows put out along the banks of the tributary streams. This is the most spacious and delightful high pleasure-ground I have yet seen. The air is keen and bracing, yet warm during the day; and though lying high in the sky, the surrounding mountains are so much higher, one feels protected as if in a grand hall. Mounts Dana and Gibbs, massive red mountains, perhaps thirteen thousand feet high or more, bound the view on the east, the Cathedral and Unicorn Peaks, with many nameless peaks, on the south, the Hoffman Range on the west, and a number of peaks unnamed, as far as I know, on the north. One of these last is much like the Cathedral. The grass of the meadows is mostly fine and silky, with exceedingly slender leaves, making a close sod, above which the panicles of minute purple flowers seem to float in airy, misty lightness, while the sod is enriched with at least three species of gentian and as many or more of orthocarpus, potentilla, ivesia, solidago, pentstemon, with their gay colors,—purple, blue, yellow, and red,—all of which I may know better ere long. A central camp will probably be made in this region, from which I hope to make long excursions into the surrounding mountains.

On the return trip I met the flock about three miles east of Lake Tenaya. Here we camped for the night near a small lake lying on top of the divide in a clump of the two-leaved pine. We are now about nine thousand feet above the sea. Small lakes abound in all sorts of situations,—on ridges, along mountain sides, and in piles of moraine boulders, most of them mere pools. Only in those cañons of the larger streams at the foot of declivities, where the down thrust of the glaciers was heaviest, do we find lakes of considerable size and depth. How grateful a task it would be to trace them all and study them! How pure their waters are, clear as crystal in polished stone basins! None of them, so far as I have seen, have fishes, I suppose on account of falls making them inaccessible. Yet one would think their eggs might get into these lakes by some chance or other; on ducks' feet, for example, or in their mouths, or in their crops, as some plant seeds are distributed. Nature has so many ways of doing such things. How did the frogs, found in all the bogs and pools and lakes, however high, manage to get up these mountains? Surely not by jumping. Such excursions through miles of dry brush and boulders would be very hard on frogs. Perhaps their stringy gelatinous spawn is occasionally entangled or glued on the feet of water birds. Anyhow, they are here and in hearty health and voice. I like their cheery tronk and crink. They take the place of song-birds at a pinch.

August 10. Another of those charming exhilarating days that make the blood dance and excite nerve currents that render one unweariable and well-nigh immortal. Had another view of the broad ice-ploughed divide, and gazed again and again at the Sierra temple and the great red mountains east of the meadows.

We are camped near the Soda Springs on the north side of the river. A hard time we had getting the sheep across. They were driven into a horseshoe bend and fairly crowded off the bank. They seemed willing to suffer death rather than risk getting wet, though they swim well enough when they have to. Why sheep should be so unreasonably afraid of water, I don't know, but they do fear it as soon as they are born and perhaps before. I once saw a lamb only a few hours old approach a shallow stream about two feet wide and an inch deep, after it had walked only about a hundred yards on its life journey. All the flock to which it belonged had crossed this inch-deep stream, and as the mother and her lamb were the last to cross, I had a good opportunity to observe them. As soon as the flock was out of the way, the anxious mother crossed over and called the youngster. It walked cautiously to the brink, gazed at the water, bleated piteously, and refused to venture. The patient mother went back to it again and again to encourage it, but long without avail. Like the pilgrim on Jordan's stormy bank it feared to launch away. At length, gathering its trembling inexperienced legs for the mighty effort, throwing up its head as if it knew all about drowning, and was anxious to keep its nose above water, it made the tremendous leap, and landed in the middle of the inch-deep stream. It seemed astonished to find that, instead of sinking over head and ears, only its toes were wet, gazed at the shining water a few seconds, and then sprang to the shore safe and dry through the dreadful adventure. All kinds of wild sheep are mountain animals, and their descendants' dread of water is not easily accounted for.

August 11. Fine shining weather, with a ten minutes' noon thunderstorm and rain. Rambling all day getting acquainted with the region north of the river. Found a small lake and many charming glacier meadows embosomed in an extensive forest of the two-leaved pine. The forest is growing on broad, almost continuous deposits of moraine material, is remarkably even in its growth, and the trees are much closer together than in any of the fir or pine woods farther down the range. The evenness of the growth would seem to indicate that the trees are all of the same age or nearly so. This regularity has probably been in great part the result of fire. I saw several large patches and strips of dead bleached spars, the ground beneath them covered with a young even growth. Fire can run in these woods, not only because the thin bark of the trees is dripping with resin, but because the growth is close, and the comparatively rich soil produces good crops of tall broad-leaved grasses on which fire can travel, even when the weather is calm. Besides these fire-killed patches there are a good many fallen uprooted trees here and there, some with the bark and needles still on, as if they had lately been blown down in some thunderstorm blast. Saw a large black-tailed deer, a buck with antlers like the upturned roots of a fallen pine.

After a long ramble through the dense encumbered woods I emerged upon a smooth meadow full of sunshine like a lake of light, about a mile and a half long, a quarter to half a mile wide, and bounded by tall arrowy pines. The sod, like that of all the glacier meadows hereabouts, is made of silky agrostis and calamagrostis chiefly; their panicles of purple flowers and purple stems, exceedingly light and airy, seem to float above the green plush of leaves like a thin misty cloud, while the sod is brightened by several species of gentian, potentilla, ivesia, orthocarpus, and their corresponding bees and butterflies. All the glacier meadows are beautiful, but few are so perfect as this one. Compared with it the most carefully leveled, licked, snipped artificial lawns of pleasure-grounds are coarse things. I should like to live here always. It is so calm and withdrawn while open to the universe in full communion with everything good. To the north of this glorious meadow I discovered the camp of some Indian hunters. Their fire was still burning, but they had not yet returned from the chase.

Glacier meadow, on the headwaters of the Tuolumne,
9500 feet above the sea

From meadow to meadow, every one beautiful beyond telling, and from lake to lake through groves and belts of arrowy trees, I held my way northward toward Mount Conness, finding telling beauty everywhere, while the encompassing mountains were calling "Come." Hope I may climb them all.

August 12. The sky-scenery has changed but little so far with the change in elevation. Clouds about .05. Glorious pearly cumuli tinted with purple of ineffable fineness of tone. Moved camp to the side of the glacier meadow mentioned above. To let sheep trample so divinely fine a place seems barbarous. Fortunately they prefer the succulent broad-leaved triticum and other woodland grasses to the silky species of the meadows, and therefore seldom bite them or set foot on them.

The shepherd and the Don cannot agree about methods of herding. Billy sets his dog Jack on the sheep far too often, so the Don thinks; and after some dispute to-day, in which the shepherd loudly claimed the right to dog the sheep as often as he pleased, he started for the plains. Now I suppose the care of the sheep will fall on me, though Mr. Delaney promises to do the herding himself for a while, then return to the lowlands and bring another shepherd, so as to leave me free to rove as I like.

Had another rich ramble. Pushed northward beyond the forests to the head of the general basin, where traces of glacial action are strikingly clear and interesting. The recesses among the peaks look like quarries, so raw and fresh are the moraine chips and boulders that strew the ground in Nature's glacial workshops.

Soon after my return to camp we received a visit from an Indian, probably one of the hunters whose camp I had discovered. He came from Mono, he said, with others of his tribe, to hunt deer. One that he had killed a short distance from here he was carrying on his back, its legs tied together in an ornamental bunch on his forehead. Throwing down his burden, he gazed stolidly for a few minutes in silent Indian fashion, then cut off eight or ten pounds of venison for us, and begged a "lill" (little) of everything he saw or could think of—flour, bread, sugar, tobacco, whiskey, needles, etc. We gave a fair price for the meat in flour and sugar and added a few needles. A strangely dirty and irregular life these dark-eyed, dark-haired, half-happy savages lead in this clean wilderness,—starvation and abundance, deathlike calm, indolence, and admirable, indefatigable action succeeding each other in stormy rhythm like winter and summer. Two things they have that civilized toilers might well envy them—pure air and pure water. These go far to cover and cure the grossness of their lives. Their food is mostly good berries, pine nuts, clover, lily bulbs, wild sheep, antelope, deer, grouse, sage hens, and the larvæ of ants, wasps, bees, and other insects.

August 13. Day all sunshine, dawn and evening purple, noon gold, no clouds, air motionless. Mr. Delaney arrived with two shepherds, one of them an Indian. On his way up from the plains he left some provisions at the Portuguese camp on Porcupine Creek near our old Yosemite camp, and I set out this morning with one of the pack animals to fetch them. Arrived at the Porcupine camp at noon, and might have returned to the Tuolumne late in the evening, but concluded to stay over night with the Portuguese shepherds at their pressing invitation. They had sad stories to tell of losses from the Yosemite bears, and were so discouraged they seemed on the point of leaving the mountains; for the bears came every night and helped themselves to one or several of the flock in spite of all their efforts to keep them off.

I spent the afternoon in a grand ramble along the Yosemite walls. From the highest of the rocks called the Three Brothers, I enjoyed a magnificent view comprehending all the upper half of the floor of the valley and nearly all the rocks of the walls on both sides and at the head, with snowy peaks in the background. Saw also the Vernal and Nevada Falls, a truly glorious picture,—rocky strength and permanence combined with beauty of plants frail and fine and evanescent; water descending in thunder, and the same water gliding through meadows and groves in gentlest beauty. This standpoint is about eight thousand feet above the sea, or four thousand feet above the floor of the valley, and every tree, though looking small and feathery, stands in admirable clearness, and the shadows they cast are as distinct in outline as if seen at a distance of a few yards. They appeared even more so. No words will ever describe the exquisite beauty and charm of this mountain park—Nature's landscape garden at once tenderly beautiful and sublime. No wonder it draws nature-lovers from all over the world.

Glacial action even on this lofty summit is plainly displayed. Not only has all the lovely valley now smiling in sunshine been filled to the brim with ice, but it has been deeply overflowed.

I visited our old Yosemite camp-ground on the head of Indian Creek, and found it fairly patted and smoothed down with bear-tracks. The bears had eaten all the sheep that were smothered in the corral, and some of the grand animals must have died, for Mr. Delaney, before leaving camp, put a large quantity of poison in the carcasses. All sheep-men carry strychnine to kill coyotes, bears, and panthers, though neither coyotes nor panthers are at all numerous in the upper mountains. The little dog-like wolves are far more numerous in the foothill region and on the plains, where they find a better supply of food,—saw only one panther-track above eight thousand feet.

On my return after sunset to the Portuguese camp I found the shepherds greatly excited over the behavior of the bears that have learned to like mutton. "They are getting worse and worse," they lamented. Not willing to wait decently until after dark for their suppers, they come and kill and eat their fill in broad daylight. The evening before my arrival, when the two shepherds were leisurely driving the flock toward camp half an hour before sunset, a hungry bear came out of the chaparral within a few yards of them and shuffled deliberately toward the flock. "Portuguese Joe," who always carried a gun loaded with buckshot, fired excitedly, threw down his gun, fled to the nearest suitable tree, and climbed to a safe height without waiting to see the effect of his shot. His companion also ran, but said that he saw the bear rise on its hind legs and throw out its arms as if feeling for somebody, and then go into the brush as if wounded.

At another of their camps in this neighborhood, a bear with two cubs attacked the flock before sunset, just as they were approaching the corral. Joe promptly climbed a tree out of danger, while Antone, rebuking his companion for cowardice in abandoning his charge, said that he was not going to let bears "eat up his sheeps" in daylight, and rushed towards the bears, shouting and setting his dog on them. The frightened cubs climbed a tree, but the mother ran to meet the shepherd and seemed anxious to fight. Antone stood astonished for a moment, eyeing the oncoming bear, then turned and fled, closely pursued. Unable to reach a suitable tree for climbing, he ran to the camp and scrambled up to the roof of the little cabin; the bear followed, but did not climb to the roof,—only stood glaring up at him for a few minutes, threatening him and holding him in mortal terror, then went to her cubs, called them down, went to the flock, caught a sheep for supper, and vanished in the brush. As soon as the bear left the cabin, the trembling Antone begged Joe to show him a good safe tree, up which he climbed like a sailor climbing a mast, and remained as long as he could hold on, the tree being almost branchless. After these disastrous experiences the two shepherds chopped and gathered large piles of dry wood and made a ring of fire around the corral every night, while one with a gun kept watch from a comfortable stage built on a neighboring pine that commanded a view of the corral. This evening the show made by the circle of fire was very fine, bringing out the surrounding trees in most impressive relief, and making the thousands of sheep eyes glow like a glorious bed of diamonds.

August 14. Up to the time I went to bed last night all was quiet, though we expected the shaggy freebooters every minute. They did not come till near midnight, when a pair walked boldly to the corral between two of the great fires, climbed in, killed two sheep and smothered ten, while the frightened watcher in the tree did not fire a single shot, saying that he was afraid he might kill some of the sheep, for the bears got into the corral before he got a good clear view of them. I told the shepherds they should at once move the flock to another camp. "Oh, no use, no use," they lamented; "where we go, the bears go too. See my poor dead sheeps—soon all dead. No use try another camp. We go down to the plains." And as I afterwards learned, they were driven out of the mountains a month before the usual time. Were bears much more numerous and destructive, the sheep would be kept away altogether.

It seems strange that bears, so fond of all sorts of flesh, running the risks of guns and fires and poison, should never attack men except in defense of their young. How easily and safely a bear could pick us up as we lie asleep! Only wolves and tigers seem to have learned to hunt man for food, and perhaps sharks and crocodiles. Mosquitoes and other insects would, I suppose, devour a helpless man in some parts of the world, and so might lions, leopards, wolves, hyenas, and panthers at times if pressed by hunger,—but under ordinary circumstances, perhaps, only the tiger among land animals may be said to be a man-eater,—unless we add man himself.

Clouds as usual about .05. Another glorious Sierra day, warm, crisp, fragrant, and clear. Many of the flowering plants have gone to seed, but many others are unfolding their petals every day, and the firs and pines are more fragrant than ever. Their seeds are nearly ripe, and will soon be flying in the merriest flocks that ever spread a wing.

On the way back to our Tuolumne camp, I enjoyed the scenery if possible more than when it first came to view. Every feature already seems familiar as if I had lived here always. I never weary gazing at the wonderful Cathedral. It has more individual character than any other rock or mountain I ever saw, excepting perhaps the Yosemite South Dome. The forests, too, seem kindly familiar, and the lakes and meadows and glad singing streams. I should like to dwell with them forever. Here with bread and water I should be content. Even if not allowed to roam and climb, tethered to a stake or tree in some meadow or grove, even then I should be content forever. Bathed in such beauty, watching the expressions ever varying on the faces of the mountains, watching the stars, which here have a glory that the lowlander never dreams of, watching the circling seasons, listening to the songs of the waters and winds and birds, would be endless pleasure. And what glorious cloudlands I should see, storms and calms,—a new heaven and a new earth every day, aye and new inhabitants. And how many visitors I should have. I feel sure I should not have one dull moment. And why should this appear extravagant? It is only common sense, a sign of health, genuine, natural, all-awake health. One would be at an endless Godful play, and what speeches and music and acting and scenery and lights!—sun, moon, stars, auroras. Creation just beginning, the morning stars "still singing together and all the sons of God shouting for joy."

Chapter IX

AUGUST 21. Have just returned from a fine wild excursion across the range to Mono Lake, by way of the Mono or Bloody Cañon Pass. Mr. Delaney has been good to me all summer, lending a helping, sympathizing hand at every opportunity, as if my wild notions and rambles and studies were his own. He is one of those remarkable California men who have been overflowed and denuded and remodeled by the excitements of the gold fields, like the Sierra landscapes by grinding ice, bringing the harder bosses and ridges of character into relief,—a tall, lean, big-boned, big-hearted Irishman, educated for a priest in Maynooth College,—lots of good in him, shining out now and then in this mountain light. Recognizing my love of wild places, he told me one evening that I ought to go through Bloody Cañon, for he was sure I should find it wild enough. He had not been there himself, he said, but had heard many of his mining friends speak of it as the wildest of all the Sierra passes. Of course I was glad to go. It lies just to the east of our camp and swoops down from the summit of the range to the edge of the Mono Desert, making a descent of about four thousand feet in a distance of about four miles. It was known and traveled as a pass by wild animals and the Indians long before its discovery by white men in the gold year of 1858, as is shown by old trails which come together at the head of it. The name may have been suggested by the red color of the metamorphic slates in which the cañon abounds, or by the blood stains on the rocks from the unfortunate animals that were compelled to slide and shuffle over the sharp-angled boulders.

Early in the morning I tied my notebook and some bread to my belt, and strode away full of eager hope, feeling that I was going to have a glorious revel. The glacier meadows that lay along my way served to soothe my morning speed, for the sod was full of blue gentians and daisies, kalmia and dwarf vaccinium, calling for recognition as old friends, and I had to stop many times to examine the shining rocks over which the ancient glacier had passed with tremendous pressure, polishing them so well that they reflected the sunlight like glass in some places, while fine striæ, seen clearly through a lens, indicated the direction in which the ice had flowed. On some of the sloping polished pavements abrupt steps occur, showing that occasionally large masses of the rock had given way before the glacial pressure, as well as small particles; moraines too, some scattered, others regular like long curving embankments and dams, occur here and there, giving the general surface of the region a young, new-made appearance. I watched the gradual dwarfing of the pines as I ascended, and the corresponding dwarfing of nearly all the rest of the vegetation. On the slopes of Mammoth Mountain, to the south of the pass, I saw many gaps in the woods reaching from the upper edge of the timber-line down to the level meadows, where avalanches of snow had descended, sweeping away every tree in their paths as well as the soil they were growing in, leaving the bed-rock bare. The trees are nearly all uprooted, but a few that had been extremely well anchored in clefts of the rock were broken off near the ground. It seems strange at first sight that trees that had been allowed to grow for a century or more undisturbed should in their old age be thus swished away at a stroke. Such avalanches can only occur under rare conditions of weather and snowfall. No doubt on some positions of the mountain slopes the inclination and smoothness of the surface is such that avalanches must occur every winter, or even after every heavy snowstorm, and of course no trees or even bushes can grow in their channels. I noticed a few clean-swept slopes of this kind. The uprooted trees that had grown in the pathway of what might be called "century avalanches" were piled in windrows, and tucked snugly against the wall-trees of the gaps, heads downward, excepting a few that were carried out into the open ground of the meadows, where the heads of the avalanches had stopped. Young pines, mostly the two-leaved and the white-barked, are already springing up in these cleared gaps. It would be interesting to ascertain the age of these saplings, for thus we should gain a fair approximation to the year that the great avalanches occurred. Perhaps most or all of them occurred the same winter. How glad I should be if free to pursue such studies!

Near the summit at the head of the pass I found a species of dwarf willow lying perfectly flat on the ground, making a nice, soft, silky gray carpet, not a single stem or branch more than three inches high; but the catkins, which are now nearly ripe, stand erect and make a close, nearly regular gray growth, being larger than all the rest of the plants. Some of these interesting dwarfs have only one catkin—willow bushes reduced to their lowest terms. I found patches of dwarf vaccinium also forming smooth carpets, closely pressed to the ground or against the sides of stones, and covered with round pink flowers in lavish abundance as if they had fallen from the sky like hail. A little higher, almost at the very head of the pass, I found the blue arctic daisy and purple-flowered bryanthus, the mountain's own darlings, gentle mountaineers face to face with the sky, kept safe and warm by a thousand miracles, seeming always the finer and purer the wilder and stormier their homes. The trees, tough and resiny, seem unable to go a step farther; but up and up, far above the tree-line, these tender plants climb, cheerily spreading their gray and pink carpets right up to the very edges of the snow-banks in deep hollows and shadows. Here, too, is the familiar robin, tripping on the flowery lawns, bravely singing the same cheery song I first heard when a boy in Wisconsin newly arrived from old Scotland. In this fine company sauntering enchanted, taking no heed of time, I at length entered the gate of the pass, and the huge rocks began to close around me in all their mysterious impressiveness. Just then I was startled by a lot of queer, hairy, muffled creatures coming shuffling, shambling, wallowing toward me as if they had no bones in their bodies. Had I discovered them while they were yet a good way off, I should have tried to avoid them. What a picture they made contrasted with the others I had just been admiring. When I came up to them, I found that they were only a band of Indians from Mono on their way to Yosemite for a load of acorns. They were wrapped in blankets made of the skins of sage-rabbits. The dirt on some of the faces seemed almost old enough and thick enough to have a geo-logical significance; some were strangely blurred and divided into sections by seams and wrinkles that looked like cleavage joints, and had a worn abraded look as if they had lain exposed to the weather for ages. I tried to pass them without stopping, but they wouldn't let me; forming a dismal circle about me, I was closely besieged while they begged whiskey or tobacco, and it was hard to convince them that I hadn't any. How glad I was to get away from the gray, grim crowd and see them vanish down the trail! Yet it seems sad to feel such desperate repulsion from one's fellow beings, however degraded. To prefer the society of squirrels and woodchucks to that of our own species must surely be unnatural. So with a fresh breeze and a hill or mountain between us I must wish them Godspeed and try to pray and sing with Burns, "It's coming yet, for a' that, that man to man, the warld o'er, shall brothers be for a' that."

How the day passed I hardly know. By the map I have come only about ten or twelve miles, though the sun is already low in the west, showing how long I must have lingered, observing, sketching, taking notes among the glaciated rocks and moraines and Alpine flower-beds.

At sundown the somber crags and peaks were inspired with the ineffable beauty of the alpenglow, and a solemn, awful stillness hushed everything in the landscape. Then I crept into a hollow by the side of a small lake near the head of the cañon, smoothed a sheltered spot, and gathered a few pine tassels for a bed. After the short twilight began to fade I kindled a sunny fire, made a tin cupful of tea, and lay down to watch the stars. Soon the night-wind began to flow from the snowy peaks overhead, at first only a gentle breathing, then gaining strength, in less than an hour rumbled in massive volume something like a boisterous stream in a boulder-choked channel, roaring and moaning down the cañon as if the work it had to do was tremendously important and fateful; and mingled with these storm tones were those of the waterfalls on the north side of the cañon, now sounding distinctly, now smothered by the heavier cataracts of air, making a glorious psalm of savage wildness. My fire squirmed and struggled as if ill at ease, for though in a sheltered nook, detached masses of icy wind often fell like icebergs on top of it, scattering sparks and coals, so that I had to keep well back to avoid being burned. But the big resiny roots and knots of the dwarf pine could neither be beaten out nor blown away, and the flames, now rushing up in long lances, now flattened and twisted on the rocky ground, roared as if trying to tell the storm stories of the trees they belonged to, as the light given out was telling the story of the sunshine they had gathered in centuries of summers.

The stars shone clear in the strip of sky between the huge dark cliffs; and as I lay recalling the lessons of the day, suddenly the full moon looked down over the cañon wall, her face apparently filled with eager concern, which had a startling effect, as if she had left her place in the sky and had come down to gaze on me alone, like a person entering one's bedroom. It was hard to realize that she was in her place in the sky, and was looking abroad on half the globe, land and sea, mountains, plains, lakes, rivers, oceans, ships, cities with their myriads of inhabitants sleeping and waking, sick and well. No, she seemed to be just on the rim of Bloody Cañon and looking only at me. This was indeed getting near to Nature. I remember watching the harvest moon rising above the oak trees in Wisconsin apparently as big as a cart-wheel and not farther than half a mile distant. With these exceptions I might say I never before had seen the moon, and this night she seemed so full of life and so near, the effect was marvelously impressive and made me forget the Indians, the great black rocks above me, and the wild uproar of the winds and waters making their way down the huge jagged gorge. Of course I slept but little and gladly welcomed the dawn over the Mono Desert. By the time I had made a cupful of tea the sunbeams were pouring through the cañon, and I set forth, gazing eagerly at the tremendous walls of red slates savagely hacked and scarred and apparently ready to fall in avalanches great enough to choke the pass and fill up the chain of lakelets. But soon its beauties came to view, and I bounded lightly from rock to rock, admiring the polished bosses shining in the slant sunshine with glorious effect in the general roughness of moraines and avalanche taluses, even toward the head of the cañon near the highest fountains of the ice. Here, too, are most of the lowly plant people seen yesterday on the other side of the divide now opening their beautiful eyes. None could fail to glory in Nature's tender care for them in so wild a place. The little ouzel is flitting from rock to rock along the rapid swirling Cañon Creek, diving for breakfast in icy pools, and merrily singing as if the huge rugged avalanche-swept gorge was the most delightful of all its mountain homes. Besides a high fall on the north wall of the cañon, apparently coming direct from the sky, there are many narrow cascades, bright silvery ribbons zigzagging down the red cliffs, tracing the diagonal cleavage joints of the metamorphic slates, now contracted and out of sight, now leaping from ledge to ledge in filmy sheets through which the sunbeams sift. And on the main Cañon Creek, to which all these are tributary, is a series of small falls, cascades, and rapids extending all the way down to the foot of the cañon, interrupted only by the lakes in which the tossed and beaten waters rest. One of the finest of the cascades is outspread on the face of a precipice, its waters separated into ribbon-like strips, and woven into a diamondlike pattern by tracing the cleavage joints of the rock, while tufts of bryanthus, grass, sedge, saxifrage form beautiful fringes. Who could imagine beauty so fine in so savage a place? Gardens are blooming in all sorts of nooks and hollows,—at the head alpine eriogonums, erigerons, saxifrages, gentians, cowania, bush primula; in the middle region larkspur, columbine, orthocarpus, castilleia, harebell, epilobium, violets, mints, yarrow; near the foot sunflowers, lilies, brier rose, iris, lonicera, clematis.

One of the smallest of the cascades, which I name the Bower Cascade, is in the lower region of the pass, where the vegetation is snowy and luxuriant. Wild rose and dogwood form dense masses overarching the stream, and out of this bower the creek, grown strong with many indashing tributaries, leaps forth into the light, and descends in a fluted curve thick-sown with crisp flashing spray. At the foot of the cañon there is a lake formed in part at least by the damming of the stream by a terminal moraine. The three other lakes in the cañon are in basins eroded from the solid rock, where the pressure of the glacier was greatest, and the most resisting portions of the basin rims are beautifully, tellingly polished. Below Moraine Lake at the foot of the cañon there are several old lake-basins lying between the large lateral moraines which extend out into the desert. These basins are now completely filled up by the material carried in by the streams, and changed to dry sandy flats covered mostly by grass and artemisia and sun-loving flowers. All these lower lake-basins were evidently formed by terminal moraine dams deposited where the receding glacier had lingered during short periods of less waste, or greater snowfall, or both.

Looking up the cañon from the warm sunny edge of the Mono plain my morning ramble seems a dream, so great is the change in the vegetation and climate. The lilies on the bank of Moraine Lake are higher than my head, and the sunshine is hot enough for palms. Yet the snow round the arctic gardens at the summit of the pass is plainly visible, only about four miles away, and between lie specimen zones of all the principal climates of the globe. In little more than an hour one may swoop down from winter to summer, from an Arctic to a torrid region, through as great changes of climate as one would encounter in traveling from Labrador to Florida.

The Indians I had met near the head of the cañon had camped at the foot of it the night before they made the ascent, and I found their fire still smoking on the side of a small tributary stream near Moraine Lake; and on the edge of what is called the Mono Desert, four or five miles from the lake, I came to a patch of elymus, or wild rye, growing in magnificent waving clumps six or eight feet high, bearing heads six to eight inches long. The crop was ripe, and Indian women were gathering the grain in baskets by bending down large handfuls, beating out the seed, and fanning it in the wind. The grains are about five eighths of an inch long, dark-colored and sweet. I fancy the bread made from it must be as good as wheat bread. A fine squirrelish employment this wild grain gathering seems, and the women were evidently enjoying it, laughing and chattering and looking almost natural, though most Indians I have seen are not a whit more natural in their lives than we civilized whites. Perhaps if I knew them better I should like them better. The worst thing about them is their uncleanliness. Nothing truly wild is unclean. Down on the shore of Mono Lake I saw a number of their flimsy huts on the banks of streams that dash swiftly into that dead sea,—mere brush tents where they lie and eat at their ease. Some of the men were feasting on buffalo berries, lying beneath the tall bushes now red with fruit. The berries are rather insipid, but they must needs be wholesome, since for days and weeks the Indians, it is said, eat nothing else. In the season they in like manner depend chiefly on the fat larvæ of a fly that breeds in the salt water of the lake, or on the big fat corrugated caterpillars of a species of silkworm that feeds on the leaves of the yellow pine. Occasionally a grand rabbit-drive is organized and hundreds are slain with clubs on the lake shore, chased and frightened into a dense crowd by dogs, boys, girls, men and women, and rings of sage brush fire, when of course they are quickly killed. The skins are made into blankets. In the autumn the more enterprising of the hunters bring in a good many deer, and rarely a wild sheep from the high peaks. Antelopes used to be abundant on the desert at the base of the interior mountain-ranges. Sage hens, grouse, and squirrels help to vary their wild diet of worms; pine nuts also from the small interesting *Pinus monophylla*, and good bread and good mush are made from acorns and wild rye. Strange to say, they seem to like the lake larvæ best of all. Long windrows are washed up on the shore, which they gather and dry like grain for winter use. It is said that wars, on account of encroachments on each other's worm-grounds, are of common occurrence among the various tribes and families. Each claims a certain marked portion of the shore. The pine nuts are delicious—large quantities are gathered every autumn. The tribes of the west flank of the range trade acorns for worms and pine nuts. The squaws carry immense loads on their backs across the rough passes and down the range, making journeys of about forty or fifty miles each way.

The desert around the lake is surprisingly flowery. In many places among the sage bushes I saw mentzelia, abronia, aster, bigelovia, and gilia, all of which seemed to enjoy the hot sunshine. The abronia, in particular, is a delicate, fragrant, and most charming plant.

Opposite the mouth of the cañon a range of volcanic cones extends southward from the lake, rising abruptly out of the desert like a chain of mountains. The largest of the cones are about twenty-five hundred feet high above the lake level, have well-formed craters, and all of them are evidently comparatively recent additions to the landscape. At a distance of a few miles they look like heaps of loose ashes that have never been blest by either rain or snow, but, for a' that and a' that, yellow pines are climbing their gray slopes, trying to clothe them and give beauty for ashes. A country of wonderful contrasts.

Mono Lake and volcanic cones, looking south

Highest Mono volcanic cones (near view)

Hot deserts bounded by snow-laden mountains,—cinders and ashes scattered on glacier-polished pavements,—frost and fire working together in the making of beauty. In the lake are several volcanic islands, which show that the waters were once mingled with fire.

Glad to get back to the green side of the mountains, though I have greatly enjoyed the gray east side and hope to see more of it. Reading these grand mountain manuscripts displayed through every vicissitude of heat and cold, calm and storm, upheaving volcanoes and down-grinding glaciers, we see that everything in Nature called destruction must be creation—a change from beauty to beauty.

Our glacier meadow camp north of the Soda Springs seems more beautiful every day. The grass covers all the ground though the leaves are thread-like in fineness, and in walking on the sod it seems like a plush carpet of marvelous richness and softness, and the purple panicles brushing against one's feet are not felt. This is a typical glacier meadow, occupying the basin of a vanished lake, very definitely bounded by walls of the arrowy two-leaved pines drawn up in a handsome orderly array like soldiers on parade. There are many other meadows of the same kind hereabouts imbedded in the woods. The main big meadows along the river are the same in general and extend with but little interruption for ten or twelve miles, but none I have seen are so finely finished and perfect as this one. It is richer in flowering plants than the prairies of Wisconsin and Illinois were when in all their wild glory. The showy flowers are mostly three species of gentian, a purple and yellow orthocarpus, a golden-rod or two, a small blue pentstemon almost like a gentian, potentilla, ivesia, pedicularis, white violet, kalmia, and bryanthus. There are no coarse weedy plants. Through this flowery lawn flows a stream silently gliding, swirling, slipping as if careful not to make the slightest noise. It is only about three feet wide in most places, widening here and there into pools six or eight feet in diameter with no apparent current, the banks bossily rounded by the down-curving mossy sod, grass panicles over-leaning like miniature pine trees, and rugs of bryanthus spreading here and there over sunken boulders. At the foot of the meadow the stream, rich with the juices of the plants it has refreshed, sings merrily down over shelving rock ledges on its way to the Tuolumne River. The sublime, massive Mount Dana and its companions, green, red, and white, loom impressively above the pines along the eastern horizon; a range or spur of gray rugged granite crags and mountains on the north; the curiously crested and battlemented Mount Hoffman on the west; and the Cathedral Range on the south with its grand Cathedral Peak, Cathedral Spires, Unicorn Peak, and several others, gray and pointed or massively rounded.

Chapter X

THE TUOLUMNE CAMP

AUGUST 22. Clouds none, cool west wind, slight hoarfrost on the meadows. Carlo is missing; have been seeking him all day. In the thick woods between camp and the river, among tall grass and fallen pines, I discovered a baby fawn. At first it seemed inclined to come to me; but when I tried to catch it, and got within a rod or two, it turned and walked softly away, choosing its steps like a cautious, stealthy, hunting cat. Then, as if suddenly called or alarmed, it began to buck and run like a grown deer, jumping high above the fallen trunks, and was soon out of sight. Possibly its mother may have called it, but I did not hear her. I don't think fawns ever leave the home thicket or follow their mothers until they are called or frightened. I am distressed about Carlo. There are several other camps and dogs not many miles from here, and I still hope to find him. He never left me before. Panthers are very rare here, and I don't think any of these cats would dare touch him. He knows bears too well to be caught by them, and as for Indians, they don't want him.

August 23. Cool, bright day, hinting Indian summer. Mr. Delaney has gone to the Smith Ranch, on the Tuolumne below Hetch-Hetchy Valley, thirty-five or forty miles from here, so I'll be alone for a week or more,—not really alone, for Carlo has come back. He was at a camp a few miles to the north-westward. He looked sheepish and ashamed when I asked him where he had been and why he had gone away without leave. He is now trying to get me to caress him and show signs of forgiveness. A wondrous wise dog. A great load is off my mind. I could not have left the mountains without him. He seems very glad to get back to me.

Rose and crimson sunset, and soon after the stars appeared the moon rose in most impressive majesty over the top of Mount Dana. I sauntered up the meadow in the white light. The jet-black tree-shadows were so wonderfully distinct and substantial looking, I often stepped high in crossing them, taking them for black charred logs.

August 24. Another charming day, warm and calm soon after sunrise, clouds only about .01,—faint, silky cirrus wisps, scarcely visible. Slight frost, Indian summerish, the mountains growing softer in outline and dreamy looking, their rough angles melted off, apparently. Sky at evening with fine, dark, subdued purple, almost like the evening purple of the San Joaquin plains in settled weather. The moon is now gazing over the summit of Dana. Glorious exhilarating air. I wonder if in all the world there is another mountain range of equal height blessed with weather so fine, and so openly kind and hospitable and approachable.

August 25. Cool as usual in the morning, quickly changing to the ordinary serene generous warmth and brightness. Toward evening the west wind was cool and sent us to the camp-fire. Of all Nature's flowery carpeted mountain halls none can be finer than this glacier meadow. Bees and butterflies seem as abundant as ever. The birds are still here, showing no sign of leaving for winter quarters though the frost must bring them to mind. For my part I should like to stay here all winter or all my life or even all eternity.

August 26. Frost this morning; all the meadow grass and some of the pine needles sparkling with irised crystals,—flowers of light. Large picturesque clouds, craggy like rocks, are piled on Mount Dana, reddish in color like the mountain itself; the sky for a few degrees around the horizon is pale purple, into which the pines dip their spires with fine effect. Spent the day as usual looking about me, watching the changing lights, the ripening autumn colors of the grass, seeds, late-blooming gentians, asters, goldenrods; parting the meadow grass here and there and looking down into the underworld of mosses and liverworts; watching the busy ants and beetles and other small people at work and play like squirrels and bears in a forest; studying the formation of lakes and meadows, moraines, mountain sculpture; making small beginnings in these directions, charmed by the serene beauty of everything.

The day has been extra cloudy, though bright on the whole, for the clouds were brighter than common. Clouds about .15, which in Switzerland would be considered extra clear. Probably more free sunshine falls on this majestic range than on any other in the world I've ever seen or heard of. It has the brightest weather, brightest glacier-polished rocks, the greatest abundance of irised spray from its glorious waterfalls, the brightest forests of silver firs and silver pines, more star-shine, moonshine, and perhaps more crystal-shine than any other mountain chain, and its countless mirror lakes, having more light poured into them, glow and spangle most. And how glorious the shining after the short summer showers and after frosty nights when the morning sunbeams are pouring through the crystals on the grass and pine needles, and how ineffably spiritually fine is the morning-glow on the mountain-tops and the alpenglow of evening. Well may the Sierra be named, not the Snowy Range, but the Range of Light.

August 27. Clouds only .05,—mostly white and pink cumuli over the Hoffman spur towards evening,—frosty morning. Crystals grow in marvelous beauty and perfection of form these still nights, every one built as carefully as the grandest holiest temple, as if planned to endure forever.

Contemplating the lace-like fabric of streams outspread over the mountains, we are reminded that everything is flowing—going somewhere, animals and so-called lifeless rocks as well as water. Thus the snow flows fast or slow in grand beauty-making glaciers and avalanches; the air in majestic floods carrying minerals, plant leaves, seeds, spores, with streams of music and fragrance; water streams carrying rocks both in solution and in the form of mud particles, sand, pebbles, and boulders. Rocks flow from volcanoes like water from springs, and animals flock together and flow in currents modified by stepping, leaping, gliding, flying, swimming, etc. While the stars go streaming through space pulsed on and on forever like blood globules in Nature's warm heart.

August 28. The dawn a glorious song of color. Sky absolutely cloudless. A fine crop of hoarfrost. Warm after ten o'clock. The gentians don't mind the first frost though their petals seem so delicate; they close every night as if going to sleep, and awake fresh as ever in the morning sun-glory. The grass is a shade browner since last week, but there are no nipped wilted plants of any sort as far as I have seen. Butterflies and the grand host of smaller flies are benumbed every night, but they hover and dance in the sunbeams over the meadows before noon with no apparent lack of playful, joyful life. Soon they must all fall like petals in an orchard, dry and wrinkled, not a wing of all the mighty host left to tingle the air. Nevertheless new myriads will arise in the spring, rejoicing, exulting, as if laughing cold death to scorn.

August 29. Clouds about .05, slight frost. Bland serene Indian summer weather. Have been gazing all day at the mountains, watching the changing lights. More and more plainly are they clothed with light as a garment, white tinged with pale purple, palest during the midday hours, richest in the morning and evening. Everything seems consciously peaceful, thoughtful, faithfully waiting God's will.

August 30. This day just like yesterday. A few clouds motionless and apparently with no work to do beyond looking beautiful. Frost enough for crystal building,—glorious fields of ice-diamonds destined to last but a night. How lavish is Nature building, pulling down, creating, destroying, chasing every material particle from form to form, ever changing, ever beautiful.

Mr. Delaney arrived this morning. Felt not a trace of loneliness while he was gone. On the contrary, I never enjoyed grander company. The whole wilderness seems to be alive and familiar, full of humanity. The very stones seem talkative, sympathetic, brotherly. No wonder when we consider that we all have the same Father and Mother.

August 31. Clouds .05. Silky cirrus wisps and fringes so fine they almost escape notice. Frost enough for another crop of crystals on the meadows but none on the forests. The gentians, goldenrods, asters, etc., don't seem to feel it; neither petals nor leaves are touched though they seem so tender. Every day opens and closes like a flower, noiseless, effortless. Divine peace glows on all the majestic landscape like the silent enthusiastic joy that sometimes transfigures a noble human face.

September 1. Clouds .05—motionless, of no particular color —ornaments with no hint of rain or snow in them. Day all calm—another grand throb of Nature's heart, ripening late flowers and seeds for next summer, full of life and the thoughts and plans of life to come, and full of ripe and ready death beautiful as life, telling divine wisdom and goodness and immortality. Have been up Mount Dana, making haste to see as much as I can now that the time of departure is drawing nigh.

The views from the summit reach far and wide, eastward over the Mono Lake and Desert; mountains beyond mountains looking strangely barren and gray and bare like heaps of ashes dumped from the sky. The lake, eight or ten miles in diameter, shines like a burnished disk of silver, no trees about its gray, ashy, cindery shores. Looking westward, the glorious forests are seen sweeping over countless ridges and hills, girdling domes and subordinate mountains, fringing in long curving lines the dividing ridges, and filling every hollow where the glaciers have spread soil-beds however rocky or smooth. Looking northward and southward along the axis of the range, you see the glorious array of high mountains, crags and peaks and snow, the fountain-heads of rivers that are flowing west to the sea through the famous Golden Gate, and east to hot salt lakes and deserts to evaporate and hurry back into the sky. Innumerable lakes are shining like eyes beneath heavy rock brows, bare or tree fringed, or imbedded in black forests. Meadow openings in the woods seem as numerous as the lakes or perhaps more so. Far up the moraine-covered slopes and among

One of the highest Mount Ritter fountains

crumbling rocks I found many delicate hardy plants, some of them still in flower. The best gains of this trip were the lessons of unity and interrelation of all the features of the landscape revealed in general views. The lakes and meadows are located just where the ancient glaciers bore heaviest at the foot of the steepest parts of their channels, and of course their longest diameters are approximately parallel with each other and with the belts of forests growing in long curving lines on the lateral and medial moraines, and in broad outspreading fields on the terminal beds deposited toward the end of the ice period when the glaciers were receding. The domes, ridges, and spurs also show the influence of glacial action in their forms, which approximately seem to be the forms of greatest strength with reference to the stress of oversweeping, past-sweeping, down-grinding ice-streams; survivals of the most resisting masses, or those most favorably situated. How interesting everything is! Every rock, mountain, stream, plant, lake, lawn, forest, garden, bird, beast, insect seems to call and invite us to come and learn something of its history and relationship. But shall the poor ignorant scholar be allowed to try the lessons they offer? It seems too great and good to be true. Soon I'll be going to the lowlands. The bread camp must soon be removed. If I had a few sacks of flour, an axe, and some matches, I would build a cabin of pine logs, pile up plenty of firewood about it and stay all winter to see the grand fertile snow-storms, watch the birds and animals that winter thus high, how they live, how the forests look snow-laden or buried, and how the avalanches look and sound on their way down the mountains. But now I'll have to go, for there is nothing to spare in the way of provisions. I'll surely be back, however, surely I'll be back. No other place has ever so overwhelmingly attracted me as this hospitable, Godful wilderness.

September 2. A grand, red, rosy, crimson day,—a perfect glory of a day. What it means I don't know. It is the first marked change from tranquil sunshine with purple mornings and evenings and still, white noons. There is nothing like a storm, however. The average cloudiness only about .08, and there is no sighing in the woods to betoken a big weather change. The sky was red in the morning and evening, the

color not diffused like the ordinary purple glow, but loaded
upon separate well-defined clouds that remained motionless,
as if anchored around the jagged mountain-fenced horizon.
A deep-red cap, bluffy around its sides, lingered a long time
on Mount Dana and Mount Gibbs, drooping so low as to
hide most of their bases, but leaving Dana's round summit
free, which seemed to float separate and alone over the big
crimson cloud. Mammoth Mountain, to the south of Gibbs
and Bloody Cañon, striped and spotted with snow-banks and
clumps of dwarf pine, was also favored with a glorious crimson
cap, in the making of which there was no trace of economy—a
huge bossy pile colored with a perfect passion of crimson that
seemed important enough to be sent off to burn among the
stars in majestic independence. One is constantly reminded
of the infinite lavishness and fertility of Nature—inexhaustible
abundance amid what seems enormous waste. And yet when
we look into any of her operations that lie within reach of our
minds, we learn that no particle of her material is wasted or
worn out. It is eternally flowing from use to use, beauty to yet
higher beauty; and we soon cease to lament waste and death,
and rather rejoice and exult in the imperishable, unspendable
wealth of the universe, and faithfully watch and wait the reap-
pearance of everything that melts and fades and dies about us,
feeling sure that its next appearance will be better and more
beautiful than the last.

I watched the growth of these red-lands of the sky as eagerly
as if new mountain ranges were being built. Soon the group of
snowy peaks in whose recesses lie the highest fountains of the
Tuolumne, Merced, and North Fork of the San Joaquin were
decorated with majestic colored clouds like those already described, but more complicated, to correspond with the grand
fountain-heads of the rivers they overshadowed. The Sierra
Cathedral, to the south of camp, was overshadowed like Sinai.
Never before noticed so fine a union of rock and cloud in form
and color and substance, drawing earth and sky together as
one; and so human is it, every feature and tint of color goes to
one's heart, and we shout, exulting in wild enthusiasm as if all
the divine show were our own. More and more, in a place like
this, we feel ourselves part of wild Nature, kin to everything.
Spent most of the day high up on the north rim of the valley,

commanding views of the clouds in all their red glory spreading their wonderful light over all the basin, while the rocks and trees and small Alpine plants at my feet seemed hushed and thoughtful, as if they also were conscious spectators of the glorious new cloud-world.

Here and there, as I plodded farther and higher, I came to small garden-patches and ferneries just where one would naturally decide that no plant-creature could possibly live. But, as in the region about the head of Mono Pass and the top of Dana, it was in the wildest, highest places that the most beautiful and tender and enthusiastic plant-people were found. Again and again, as I lingered over these charming plants, I said, How came you here? How do you live through the winter? Our roots, they explained, reach far down the joints of the summer-warmed rocks, and beneath our fine snow mantle killing frosts cannot reach us, while we sleep away the dark half of the year dreaming of spring.

Ever since I was allowed entrance into these mountains I have been looking for cassiope, said to be the most beautiful and best loved of the heathworts, but, strange to say, I have not yet found it. On my high mountain walks I keep muttering, "Cassiope, cassiope." This name, as Calvinists say, is driven in upon me, notwithstanding the glorious host of plants that come about me uncalled as soon as I show myself. Cassiope seems the highest name of all the small mountain-heath people, and as if conscious of her worth, keeps out of my way. I must find her soon, if at all this year.

September 4. All the vast sky dome is clear, filled only with mellow Indian summer light. The pine and hemlock and fir cones are nearly ripe and are falling fast from morning to night, cut off and gathered by the busy squirrels. Almost all the plants have matured their seeds, their summer work done; and the summer crop of birds and deer will soon be able to follow their parents to the foothills and plains at the approach of winter, when the snow begins to fly.

September 5. No clouds. Weather cool, calm, bright as if no great thing was yet ready to be done. Have been sketching the North Tuolumne Church. The sunset gloriously colored.

September 6. Still another perfectly cloudless day, purple evening and morning, all the middle hours one mass of pure serene sunshine. Soon after sunrise the air grew warm, and there was no wind. One naturally halted to see what Nature intended to do. There is a suggestion of real Indian summer in the hushed brooding, faintly hazy weather. The yellow atmosphere, though thin, is still plainly of the same general character as that of eastern Indian summer. The peculiar mellowness is perhaps in part caused by myriads of ripe spores adrift in the sky.

Mr. Delaney now keeps up a solemn talk about the need of getting away from these high mountains, telling sad stories of flocks that perished in storms that broke suddenly into the midst of fine innocent weather like this we are now enjoying. "In no case," said he, "will I venture to stay so high and far back in the mountains as we now are later than the middle of this month, no matter how warm and sunny it may be." He would move the flock slowly at first, a few miles a day until the Yosemite Creek basin was reached and crossed, then while lingering in the heavy pine woods should the weather threaten he could hurry down to the foothills, where the snow never falls deep enough to smother a sheep. Of course I am anxious to see as much of the wilderness as possible in the few days left me, and I say again,—May the good time come when I can stay as long as I like with plenty of bread, far and free from trampling flocks, though I may well be thankful for this generous foodful inspiring summer. Anyhow we never know where we must go nor what guides we are to get,—men, storms, guardian angels, or sheep. Perhaps almost everybody in the least natural is guarded more than he is ever aware of. All the wilderness seems to be full of tricks and plans to drive and draw us up into God's Light.

Have been busy planning, and baking bread for at least one more good wild excursion among the high peaks, and surely none, however hopefully aiming at fortune or fame, ever felt so gloriously happily excited by the outlook.

September 7. Left camp at daybreak and made direct for Cathedral Peak, intending to strike eastward and southward from that point among the peaks and ridges at the heads of the Tuolumne, Merced, and San Joaquin Rivers. Down through the pine woods I made my way, across the Tuolumne River and meadows, and up the heavily timbered slope forming the south boundary of the upper Tuolumne basin, along the east side of Cathedral Peak, and up to its topmost spire, which I reached at noon, having loitered by the way to study the fine trees—two-leaved pine, mountain pine, albicaulis pine, silver fir, and the most charming, most graceful of all the evergreens, the mountain hemlock. High, cool, late-flowering meadows also detained me, and lakelets and avalanche tracks and huge quarries of moraine rocks above the forests.

All the way up from the Big Meadows to the base of the Cathedral the ground is covered with moraine material, the left lateral moraine of the great glacier that must have completely filled this upper Tuolumne basin. Higher there are several small terminal moraines of residual glaciers shoved forward at right angles against the grand simple lateral of the main Tuolumne Glacier. A fine place to study mountain sculpture and soil making. The view from the Cathedral Spires is very fine and telling in every direction. Innumerable peaks, ridges, domes, meadows, lakes, and woods; the forests extending in long curving lines and broad fields wherever the glaciers have left soil for them to grow on, while the sides of the highest mountains show a straggling dwarf growth clinging to rifts in the rocks apparently independent of soil. The dark heath-like growth on the Cathedral roof I found to be dwarf snow-pressed albicaulis pine, about three or four feet high, but very old looking. Many of them are bearing cones, and the noisy Clarke crow is eating the seeds, using his long bill like a woodpecker in digging them out of the cones. A good many flowers are still in bloom about the base of the peak, and even on the roof among the little pines, especially a woody yellow-flowered eriogonum and a handsome aster. The body of the Cathedral is nearly square, and the roof slopes are wonderfully regular and symmetrical, the ridge trending northeast and southwest. This direction has apparently been determined by structure joints in the granite. The gable on the northeast end is magnificent in size and simplicity, and at its base there is a big snow-bank protected by the shadow of the building. The front is adorned with many pinnacles and a tall spire of curious workmanship. Here too the joints in the rock are seen to have played an important part

*Glacier meadow strewn with moraine boulders, 10,000 feet
above the sea (near Mount Dana)*

Front of Cathedral Peak

in determining their forms and size and general arrangement. The Cathedral is said to be about eleven thousand feet above the sea, but the height of the building itself above the level of the ridge it stands on is about fifteen hundred feet. A mile or so to the westward there is a handsome lake, and the glacier-polished granite about it is shining so brightly it is not easy in some places to trace the line between the rock and water, both shining alike. Of this lake with its silvery basin and bits of meadow and groves I have a fine view from the spires; also of Lake Tenaya, Cloud's Rest and the South Dome of Yosemite, Mount Starr King, Mount Hoffman, the Merced peaks, and the vast multitude of snowy fountain peaks extending far north and south along the axis of the range. No feature, however, of all the noble landscape as seen from here seems more wonderful than the Cathedral itself, a temple displaying Nature's best masonry and sermons in stones. How often I have gazed at it from the tops of hills and ridges, and through openings in the forests on my many short excursions, devoutly wondering, admiring, longing! This I may say is the first time I have been at church in California, led here at last, every door graciously opened for the poor lonely worshiper. In our best times everything turns into religion, all the world seems a church and the mountains altars. And lo, here at last in front of the Cathedral is blessed cassiope, ringing her thousands of sweet-toned bells, the sweetest church music I ever enjoyed. Listening, admiring, until late in the afternoon I compelled myself to hasten away eastward back of rough, sharp, spiry, splintery peaks, all of them granite like the Cathedral, sparkling with crystals—feldspar, quartz, hornblende, mica, tourmaline. Had a rather difficult walk and creep across an immense snow and ice cliff which gradually increased in steepness as I advanced until it was almost impassable. Slipped on a dangerous place, but managed to stop by digging my heels into the thawing surface just on the brink of a yawning ice gulf. Camped beside a little pool and a group of crinkled dwarf pines; and as I sit by the fire trying to write notes the shallow pool seems fathomless with the infinite starry heavens in it, while the onlooking rocks and trees, tiny shrubs and daisies and sedges, brought forward in the fire-glow, seem full of thought as if about to speak aloud and tell all their wild stories. A marvelously impressive meeting in which every one has something worth while to tell. And beyond the fire-beams out in the solemn darkness, how impressive is the music of a choir of rills singing their way down from the snow to the river! And when we call to mind that thousands of these rejoicing rills are assembled in each one of the main streams, we wonder the less that our Sierra rivers are songful all the way to the sea.

About sundown saw a flock of dun grayish sparrows going to roost in crevices of a crag above the big snow-field. Charming

Mt Ritter

View of Upper Tuolumne Valley

little mountaineers! Found a species of sedge in flower within eight or ten feet of a snow-bank. Judging by the looks of the ground, it can hardly have been out in the sunshine much longer than a week, and it is likely to be buried again in fresh snow in a month or so, thus making a winter about ten months long, while spring, summer, and autumn are crowded and hurried into two months. How delightful it is to be alone here! How wild everything is—wild as the sky and as pure! Never shall I forget this big, divine day—the Cathedral and its thousands of cassiope bells, and the landscapes around them, and this camp in the gray crags above the woods, with its stars and streams and snow.

September 8. Day of climbing, scrambling, sliding on the peaks around the highest source of the Tuolumne and Merced. Climbed three of the most commanding of the mountains, whose names I don't know; crossed streams and huge beds of ice and snow more than I could keep count of. Neither could I keep count of the lakes scattered on tablelands and in the cirques of the peaks, and in chains in the cañons, linked together by the streams—a tremendously wild gray wilderness of hacked, shattered crags, ridges, and peaks, a few clouds drifting over and through the midst of them as if looking for work. In general views all the immense round landscape seems raw and lifeless as a quarry, yet the most charming flowers were found rejoicing in countless nooks and garden-like patches everywhere. I must have done three or four days' climbing work in this one. Limbs perfectly tireless until near sundown, when I descended into the main upper Tuolumne valley at the foot of Mount Lyell, the camp still eight or ten miles distant. Going up through the pine woods past the Soda Springs Dome in the dark, where there is much fallen timber, and when all the excitement of seeing things was wanting, I was tired. Arrived at the main camp at nine o'clock, and soon was sleeping sound as death.

Chapter XI

SEPTEMBER 9. Weariness rested away and I feel eager and ready for another excursion a month or two long in the same wonderful wilderness. Now, however, I must turn toward the lowlands, praying and hoping Heaven will shove me back again.

The most telling thing learned in these mountain excursions is the influence of cleavage joints on the features sculptured from the general mass of the range. Evidently the denudation has been enormous, while the inevitable outcome is subtle balanced beauty. Comprehended in general views, the features of the wildest landscape seem to be as harmoniously related as the features of a human face. Indeed, they look human and radiate spiritual beauty, divine thought, however covered and concealed by rock and snow.

Mr. Delaney has hardly had time to ask me how I enjoyed my trip, though he has facilitated and encouraged my plans all summer, and declares I'll be famous some day, a kind guess that seems strange and incredible to a wandering wilderness-lover with never a thought or dream of fame while humbly trying to trace and learn and enjoy Nature's lessons.

The camp stuff is now packed on the horses, and the flock is headed for the home ranch. Away we go, down through the pines, leaving the lovely lawn where we have camped so long. I wonder if I'll ever see it again. The sod is so tough and close it is scarcely at all injured by the sheep. Fortunately they are not fond of silky glacier meadow grass. The day is perfectly clear, not a cloud or the faintest hint of a cloud is visible, and there is no wind. I wonder if in all the world, at a height of nine thousand feet, weather so steadily, faithfully calm and bright and hospitable may anywhere else be found. We are going away fearing destructive storms, though it is difficult to conceive weather changes so great.

Though the water is now low in the river, the usual difficulty occurred in getting the flock across it. Every sheep seemed to be invincibly determined to die any sort of dry death rather than wet its feet. Carlo has learned the sheep business as perfectly as the best shepherd, and it is interesting to watch his intelligent efforts to push or frighten the silly creatures into the water. They had to be fairly crowded and shoved over the bank; and when at last one crossed because it could not push its way back, the whole flock suddenly plunged in headlong together, as if the river was the only desirable part of the world. Aside from mere money profit one would rather herd wolves than sheep. As soon as they clambered up the opposite bank, they began baaing and feeding as if nothing unusual had happened. We crossed the meadows and drove slowly up the south rim of the valley through the same woods I had passed on my way to Cathedral Peak, and camped for the night by the side of a small pond on top of the big lateral moraine.

September 10. In the morning at daybreak not one of the two thousand sheep was in sight. Examining the tracks, we discovered that they had been scattered, perhaps by a bear. In a few hours all were found and gathered into one flock again. Had fine view of a deer. How graceful and perfect in every way it seemed as compared with the silly, dusty, tousled sheep! From the high ground hereabouts had another grand view to the northward—a heaving, swelling sea of domes and round-backed ridges fringed with pines, and bounded by innumerable sharp-pointed peaks, gray and barren-looking, though so full of beautiful life. Another day of the calm, cloudless kind, purple in the morning and evening. The evening glow has been very marked for the last two or three weeks. Perhaps the "zodiacal light."

September 11. Cloudless. Slight frost. Calm. Fairly started downhill, and now are camped at the west end meadows of Lake Tenaya—a charming place. Lake smooth as glass, mirroring its miles of glacier-polished pavements and bold mountain walls. Find aster still in flower. Here is about the upper limit of the dwarf form of the goldcup oak,—eight thousand feet above sea-level,—reaching about two thousand feet higher than the California black oak (*Quercus Californica*). Lovely evening, the lake reflections after dark marvelously impressive.

September 12. Cloudless day, all pure sun-gold. Among the magnificent silver firs once more, within two miles of the brink of Yosemite, at the famous Portuguese bear camp. Chaparral of goldcup oak, manzanita, and ceanothus abundant hereabouts, wanting about the Tuolumne meadows, although the elevation is but little higher there. The two-leaved pine, though far more abundant about the Tuolumne meadow region, reaches its greatest size on stream-sides hereabouts and around meadows that are rather boggy. All the best dry ground is taken by the magnificent silver fir, which here reaches its greatest size and forms a well-defined belt. A glorious tree. Have fine bed of its boughs to-night.

September 13. Camp this evening at Yosemite Creek, close to the stream, on a little sand flat near our old camp-ground. The vegetation is already brown and yellow and dry; the creek almost dry also. The slender form of the two-leaved pine on its banks is, I think, the handsomest I have anywhere seen. It might easily pass at first sight for a distinct species, though surely only a variety (*Murrayana*), due to crowded and rapid growth on good soil. The yellow pine is as variable, or perhaps more so. The form here and a thousand feet higher, on crumbling rocks, is broad branching, with closely furrowed, reddish bark, large cones, and long leaves. It is one of the hardiest of pines, and has wonderful vitality. The tassels of long, stout needles shining silvery in the sun, when the wind is blowing them all in the same direction, is one of the most splendid spectacles these glorious Sierra forests have to show. This variety of *Pinus ponderosa* is regarded as a distinct species, *Pinus Jeffreyi*, by some botanists. The basin of this famous Yosemite stream is extremely rocky,—seems fairly to be paved with domes like a street with big cobblestones. I wonder if I shall ever be allowed to explore it. It draws me so strongly, I would make any sacrifice to try to read its lessons. I thank God for this glimpse of it. The charms of these mountains are beyond all common reason, unexplainable and mysterious as life itself.

September 14. Nearly all day in magnificent fir forest, the top branches laden with superb erect gray cones shining with beads of pure balsam. The squirrels are cutting them off at a great rate. Bump, bump, I hear them falling, soon to be gathered and stored for winter bread. Those that chance to be left by the industrious harvesters drop the scales and bracts when fully ripe, and it is fine to see the purple-winged seeds flying in swirling, merry-looking flocks seeking their fortunes. The bole and dead limbs of nearly every tree in the main forest-belt are ornamented by conspicuous tufts and strips of a yellow lichen.

Camped for the night at Cascade Creek, near the Mono Trail crossing. Manzanita berries now ripe. Cloudiness to-day about .10. The sunset very rich, flaming purple and crimson showing gloriously through the aisles of the woods.

September 15. The weather pure gold, cloudiness about .05, white cirrus fleets and pencilings around the horizon. Move two or three miles and camp at Tamarack Flat. Wandering in the woods here back of the pines which bound the meadows, I found very noble specimens of the magnificent silver fir, the tallest about two hundred and forty feet high and five feet in diameter four feet from the ground.

September 16. Crawled slowly four or five miles to-day through the glorious forest to Crane Flat, where we are camped for the night. The forests we so admired in summer seem still more beautiful and sublime in this mellow autumn light. Lovely starry night, the tall, spiring tree-tops relieved in jet black against the sky. I linger by the fire, loath to go to bed.

September 17. Left camp early. Ran over the Tuolumne divide and down a few miles to a grove of sequoias that I had heard of, directed by the Don. They occupy an area of perhaps less than a hundred acres. Some of the trees are noble, colossal old giants, surrounded by magnificent sugar pines and Douglas spruces. The perfect specimens not burned or broken are singularly regular and symmetrical, though not at all conventional, showing infinite variety in general unity and harmony; the noble shafts with rich purplish brown fluted bark, free of limbs for one hundred and fifty feet or so, ornamented here and there with leafy rosettes; main branches of the oldest trees very large, crooked and rugged, zigzagging stiffly outward seemingly lawless, yet unexpectedly stooping just at the right distance from the trunk and dissolving in dense bossy masses of branchlets, thus making a regular though greatly varied outline,—a cylinder of leafy, outbulging spray masses, terminating in a noble dome, that may be recognized while yet far off upheaved against the sky above the dark bed of pines and firs and spruces, the king of all conifers, not only in size but in sublime majesty of behavior and port. I found a black, charred stump about thirty feet in diameter and eighty or ninety feet

high—a venerable, impressive old monument of a tree that in
its prime may have been the monarch of the grove; seedlings
and saplings growing up here and there, thrifty and hopeful,
giving no hint of the dying out of the species. Not any unfavor-
able change of climate, but only fire, threatens the existence of
these noblest of God's trees. Sorry I was not able to get a count
of the old monument's annual rings.

Camp this evening at Hazel Green, on the broad back of the
dividing ridge near our old camp-ground when we were on the
way up the mountains in the spring. This ridge has the finest
sugar-pine groves and finest manzanita and ceanothus thickets
I have yet found on all this wonderful summer journey.

September 18. Made a long descent on the south side of the
divide to Brown's Flat, the grand forests now left above us,
though the sugar pine still flourishes fairly well, and with the
yellow pine, libocedrus, and Douglas spruce, makes forests
that would be considered most wonderful in any other part of
the world.

The Indians here, with great concern, pointed to an old
garden patch on the flat and told us to keep away from it.
Perhaps some of their tribe are buried here.

September 19. Camped this evening at Smith's Mill, on the
first broad mountain bench or plateau reached in ascending
the range, where pines grow large enough for good lumber.
Here wheat, apples, peaches, and grapes grow, and we were
treated to wine and apples. The wine I didn't like, but Mr.
Delaney and the Indian driver and the shepherd seemed to
think the stuff divine. Compared to sparkling Sierra water fresh
from the heavens, it seemed a dull, muddy, stupid drink. But
the apples, best of fruits, how delicious they were—fit for gods
or men.

On the way down from Brown's Flat we stopped at Bower
Cave, and I spent an hour in it—one of the most novel and
interesting of all Nature's underground mansions. Plenty of
sunlight pours into it through the leaves of the four maple
trees growing in its mouth, illuminating its clear, calm pool
and marble chambers,—a charming place, ravishingly beautiful, but the accessible parts of the walls sadly disfigured with
names of vandals.

September 20. The weather still golden and calm, but hot. We are now in the foot-hills, and all the conifers are left behind except the gray Sabine pine. Camped at the Dutch Boy's Ranch, where there are extensive barley fields now showing nothing save dusty stubble.

September 21. A terribly hot, dusty, sun-burned day, and as nothing was to be gained by loitering where the flock could find nothing to eat save thorny twigs and chaparral, we made a long drive, and before sundown reached the home ranch on the yellow San Joaquin plain.

September 22. The sheep were let out of the corral one by one, this morning, and counted, and strange to say, after all their adventurous wanderings in bewildering rocks and brush and streams, scattered by bears, poisoned by azalea, kalmia, alkali, all are accounted for. Of the two thousand and fifty that left the corral in the spring lean and weak, two thousand and twenty-five have returned fat and strong. The losses are: ten killed by bears, one by a rattlesnake, one that had to be killed after it had broken its leg on a boulder slope, and one that ran away in blind terror on being accidentally separated from the flock,—thirteen all told. Of the other twelve doomed never to return, three were sold to ranchmen and nine were made camp mutton.

Here ends my forever memorable first High Sierra excursion. I have crossed the Range of Light, surely the brightest and best of all the Lord has built; and rejoicing in its glory, I gladly, gratefully, hopefully pray I may see it again.

SELECTED ESSAYS

Contents

Yosemite Glaciers

YOSEMITE VALLEY, Cal., Sept. 28.—Two years ago, when picking flowers in the mountains back of Yosemite Valley, I found a book. It was blotted and storm-beaten; all of its outer pages were mealy and crumbly, the paper seeming to dissolve like the snow beneath which it had been buried; but many of the inner pages were well preserved, and though all were more or less stained and torn, whole chapters were easily readable. In just this condition is the great open book of Yosemite glaciers to-day; its granite pages have been torn and blurred by the same storms that wasted the castaway book. The grand central chapters of the Hoffman, and Tenaya, and Nevada glaciers are stained and corroded by the frosts and rains, yet, nevertheless, they contain scarce one unreadable page; but the outer chapters of the Pohono, and the Illilouette, and the Yosemite Creek, and Ribbon, and Cascade glaciers, are all dimmed and eaten away on the bottom, though the tops of their pages have not been so long exposed, and still proclaim in splendid characters the glorious actions of their departed ice. The glacier which filled the basin of Yosemite Creek was the fourth ice-stream that flowed to Yosemite Valley. It was about fifteen miles in length by five in breadth at the middle of the main stream, and in many places was not less than 1,000 feet in depth. It united with the central glaciers in the valley by a mouth reaching from the east side of El Capitan to Yosemite Point, east of the falls. Its western rim was rayed with short tributaries, and on the north its divide from the Tuolumne glacier was deeply grooved; but few if any of its ridges were here high enough to separate the descending ice into distinct tributaries. The main central trunk flowed nearly south, and, at a distance of about 10 miles, separated into three nearly equal branches, which were turned abruptly to the east.

BRANCH BASINS.

Those branch basins are laid among the highest spurs of the Hoffman range, and abound in small, bright lakes, set in the solid granite without the usual terminal moraine dam. The structure of those dividing spurs is exactly similar, all three appearing as if ruins of one mountain, or rather as perfect units hewn from one mountain rock during long ages of glacial activity. As their north sides are precipitous, and as they extend east and west, they were enabled to shelter and keep alive their hiding glaciers long after the death of the main trunk. Their basins are still dazzling bright, and their lakes have as yet accumulated but narrow rings of border meadow, because their feeding streams have had but little time to carry the sand of which they are made. The east bank of the main stream, all the way from the three forks to the mouth, is a continuous, regular wall, which also forms the west bank of Indian Cañon glacier-basin. The tributaries of the west side of the main basin touched the east tributaries of the cascade, and the great Tuolumne glacier from Mount Dana, the mightiest ice-river of this whole region, flowed past on the north. The declivity of the tributaries was great, especially those which flowed from the spurs of the Hoffman on the Tuolumne divide, but the main stream was rather level, and in approaching Yosemite was compelled to make a considerable ascent back of Eagle Cliff. To the concentrated currents of the central glaciers, and to the levelness and width of mouth of this one, we in a great measure owe the present height of the Yosemite Falls. Yosemite Creek lives the most tranquil life of all the large streams that leap into the valley, the others occupying the cañons of narrower and, consequently, of deeper glaciers, while yet far from the valley, abound in loud falls and snowy cascades, but Yosemite Creek flows straight on through smooth meadows and hollows, with only two or three gentle cascades, and now and then a row of soothing, rumbling rapids, biding its time, and hoarding up the best music and poetry of its life for the one anthem at Yosemite, as planned by the ice.

YOSEMITE BASIN.

When a birdseye view of Yosemite Basin is obtained from any of its upper domes, it is seen to possess a great number of dense patches of black forest, planted in abrupt contact with bare gray rocks. Those forest plots mark the number and the size of all the entire and fragmentary moraines of the basin, as the later eroding agents have not yet had sufficient time to form a soil fit for the vigorous life of large trees.

Wherever a deep-wombed tributary was laid against a narrow ridge, and was also shielded from the sun by compassing rock-shadows, there we invariably find one or more small terminal moraines, because when such tributaries were melted off from the trunk they retired to those upper strongholds of shade, and lived and worked in full independence, and the moraines which they built are left entire because the water-collecting basins behind them are too small to make streams large enough to wash them away; but in the basins of exposed tributaries there are no terminal moraines, because their glaciers died *with* the trunk. Medial and lateral moraines are common upon all the outside slopes, some of them nearly perfect in form; but down in the main basin there is not left one unaltered moraine of any kind, immense floods having washed down and leveled them into border meadows for the present stream, and into sandy flower-beds and fields for forests.

GLACIER HISTORY.

Such was Yosemite glacier, and such is its basin, the magnificent work of its hands. There is sublimity in the life of a glacier. Water rivers work openly, and so do the rains and the gentle dews, and the great sea also grasping all the world; and even this universal ocean of breath, though invisible, yet speaks aloud in a thousand voices, and proclaims its modes of working and its power; but glaciers work apart from men, exerting their tremendous energies in silence and darkness, outspread, spirit-like, brooding above predestined rocks unknown to light, unborn, working on unwearied through unmeasured times, unhalting as the stars, until at length, their creations complete, their mountains brought forth, homes made for the meadows and the lakes, moraine banks for chosen flowers, and fields for waiting forests, earnest, calm as when they came in crystals from the sky, they depart.

The great valley itself, together with all of its various domes and walls, was brought forth and fashioned by a grand combination of glaciers, acting in certain directions against granite of peculiar physical structure. All of the rocks and mountains and lakes and meadows of the whole upper Merced basin received their specific forms and carvings almost entirely from this same agency of ice.

I have been drifting about among the rocks of this region for several years, anxious to spell out some of the mountain truths which are written here; and since the number, and magnitude, and significance of these ice rivers began to appear, I have become anxious for more exact knowledge regarding them; with this object, supplying myself with blankets and bread, I climbed out of Yosemite by Indian Cañon, and am now searching the upper rocks and moraines for readable glacier manuscript.

I meant to begin by exploring the main trunk glacier of Yosemite Creek, together with all of its rim tributaries one by one, gathering what data I could find regarding their depth, direction of flow, the kind and amount of work which each had done, etc., but when I was upon the El Capitan Mountain, seeking for the western shore of the main stream, I discovered that the Yosemite Creek glacier was not the lowest ice stream which flowed to the valley, but that the Ribbon Stream basin west of El Capitan had also been occupied by a glacier, which flowed nearly south, and united with the main central glaciers of the summits in the valley below El Capitan.

RIBBON STREAM BASIN.

I spent two days in this new basin. It must have been one of the smallest ice streams that entered the valley being only about four miles in length by three in width. It received some small tributaries from the slopes of El Capitan ridge, which flowed south 35° west; but most of its ice was derived from a spur of the Hoffman group, running nearly south-west. The slope of its bed is steep and pretty regular, and it must have flowed with considerable velocity. I have not thus far discovered any of the original striated surfaces, though possibly some patches may still exist somewhere in the basin upon hard plates of quartz, or where a bowlder of protecting form has settled upon a rounded surface. I found many such patches in the basin of Yosemite Glacier; one within half a mile of the top of the falls—about two feet square in extent of surface, very perfect in polish, and its striæ distinct, although the surrounding unprotected rock is disintegrated to a depth of at least four inches. As this small glacier sloped fully with unsheltered bosom to the sun, it was one of the first to die, and of course its tablets have been longer exposed to blurring rains and dews, and all eroding agents; but notwithstanding the countless blotting, crumbling storms which have fallen upon the historic lithographs of its surface, the great truth of its former existence printed in characters of moraine and meadow and valley groove, is still as clear as when every one of its pebbles and new-born rocks gleamed forth the full unshadowed poetry of its whole life. With the exception of a few castled piles and broken domes upon its east banks, its basin is rather smooth and lake-like, but it has charming meadows, most interesting in their present flora and glacier history, and noble forests of the two silver firs (Picea Amabilis and P. grandis) planted upon moraines spread out and leveled by overflowing waters.

These researches in the basin of the Ribbon Creek recalled some observations made by me some time ago in the lower portions of the basins of the Cascade and Tamarac streams, and I now thought it probable that careful search would discover abundant traces of glacial action in those basins also. Accordingly, on reaching the highest northern slope of the Ribbon, I obtained comprehensive views of both the Cascade and Tamarac basins, and amid their countless adornments could note many forms of lake and rock which appeared as genuine glacier characters unmarred and unaltered. Running down the bare slope of an icy-looking cañon, in less than half an hour I came upon a large patch of the old glacier bed, polished and striated, with the direction of the flow of the long dead stream clearly written—South 40° West. This proved to be the lowest, easternmost tributary of the Cascade glacier. I proceeded westward as far as the Cascade meadows on the Mono trail, then turning to the right, entered the mouth of the tributary at the head of the meadows. Here there is a well-defined terminal moraine, and the ends of both ridges which formed the banks of the ice are broken and precipitous, giving evidence of great pressure. I followed up this tributary to its source on the west bank of the Yosemite glacier about two miles north of the Mono trail, and throughout its entire length there is abundance of polished tablets with moraines, rock sculpture, etc., giving glacier testimony as clear and indisputable as can be found in the most recent glacier pathways of the Alps.

VANISHED GLACIERS.

I would gladly have explored the main trunk of this beautiful basin, from its highest snows upon the divide of the Tuolumne, to its mouth in the Merced Cañon below Yosemite, but alas! I had not sufficient bread, besides I felt sure that I should also have to explore the Tamarac basin, and, following westward among the fainter, most changed, and covered glacier pathways, I might probably be called as far as the end of the Pilot Peak Ridge. Therefore, I concluded to leave those lower chapters for future lessons, and go on with the easier Yosemite pages which I had already begun.

But before taking leave of those lower streams let me distinctly state, that in my opinion future investigation will discover proofs of the existence in the earlier ages of Sierra Nevada ice, of vast glaciers which flowed to the very foot of the range. Already it is clear that all of the upper basins were filled with ice so deep and universal, that but few of the highest crests and ridges were sufficiently great to separate it into individual glaciers, many of the highest mountains having been flowed over and rounded like the bowlders in a river. Glaciers poured into Yosemite by every one of its cañons; and at a comparatively recent period of its history its northern wall, with perhaps the single exception of the crest of Eagle Cliff, was covered by one unbroken flow of ice, the several glaciers having united before they reached the wall.

SEPTEMBER 30.—Last evening I was camped in a small round glacier meadow, at the head of the easternmost tributary of the cascade. The meadow was velvet with grass, and circled with the most beautiful of all the coniferæ, the Williamson spruce. I built a great fire, and the daisies of the sod rayed as if conscious of a sun. As I lay on my back, feeling the presence of the trees—gleaming upon the dark, and gushing with life—coming closer and closer about me, and saw the small round sky coming down with its stars to dome my trees, I said, "Never was mountain mansion more beautiful, more spiritual; never was mortal wanderer more blessedly homed." When the sun rose, my charmed walls were taken down, the trees returned to the common fund of the forest, and my little sky fused back into the measureless blue, I was left upon common ground to follow my glacial labor.

YOSEMITE RIVER BASINS.

I followed the main Yosemite River northward, passing round the head of the second Yosemite tributary, which flowed about north-east until bent southward by the main current. About noon I came to the basin of the third ice tributary of the west rim, a place of domes which had long engaged my attention, and as I was anxious to study their structure, and the various moraines, &c., of the little glacier which had issued from their midst, I camped here close to the foot of two of the most beautiful of the domes, in a sheltered hollow, the womb of the glacier. At the foot of these two domes are two lakes exactly alike in size and history, beautiful as any I ever beheld; first there is the crystal water center, then a yellowish fringe of Carex, which has long arching leaves that dip to the water; then a beveled bossy border of yellow Sphagnum moss, exactly marking the limits of the lake; further back is a narrow zone of dryer meadow, smooth and purple with grasses which grow in soft plushy sods, interrupted here and there by clumpy gatherings of blue berry bushes. The purple Kalmia grows here also, and the splendidly flowered Phyllodoce; but these are small, and weave into the sod, spreading low in the grasses and glowing with them. Beside these flowering shrubs, the meadow is lightly sprinkled with daisies, and dodecatheons and white violets, most lovely meadows divinely adjusted to most lovely lakes.

In the afternoon I followed down the bed of the tributary to its junction with the main glacier; then, turning to the right, crossed the mouths of the first two tributaries which I had passed in the morning; then, bearing east, examined a cross section of the main trunk, and reached camp by following up the north bank of the tributary. Between the three tributaries above-mentioned are well-defined medial moraines, having been preserved from leveling floods by their position on the higher slopes, with but small water-collecting basins behind them. Down at their junctions, where they were swept round by the main stream, is a large, level field of moraine matter, which, like all the drift-fields of this basin, is planted with heavy forests, composed mainly of a pine and fir (Pinus contarta, and Picea amabilis). This forest is now on fire. I wanted to pass through it, but feared the falling trees. As I stood watching the flapping flames and estimating chances, a tall blazing pine crashed across the gap which I wished to pass, and in a few minutes two more fell. This stirred a broken thought about special providences, and caused me to go around out of danger. Pinus contorta is very susceptible of fire, as it grows very close, in grovy thickets, and usually every tree is trickled and beaded with gum. The summit forests are almost entirely composed of this pine.

DEER IN THE VALLEY.

Emerging from this wooded moraine I found a great quantity of loose separate bowlders upon a polished hilltop, which had formed a part of the bottom of the main ice stream. They were of extraordinary size, some large as houses, and I started northward to seek the mountain from which they had been torn. I had gone but a little way when I discovered a deer quietly feeding upon a narrow strip of green meadow about sixty or seventy yards ahead of me. As the wind blew gently toward it, I thought the opportunity good for testing the truth of hunters' accounts of the deer's wonderful keenness of scent, and stood quite still, and as the deer continued to feed tranquilly, only casting round his head upon his shoulder occasionally to drive away the flies. I began to think that his nose was no better than my own, when suddenly, as if pierced by a bullet, he sprang up into the air and galloped confusedly off without turning to look; but in a few seconds, as if doubtful of the direction of the danger, he came bounding back, caught a glimpse of me, and ran off a second time in a settled direction.

The Yosemite basin is a favorite Summer home of the deer. The leguminous vines and juicy grasses of the great moraines supply savory food, while the many high hidings of the Hoffman Mountains, accessible by narrow passes, afford favorite shelter. Grizzly and brown bears also love Yosemite Creek. Berries of the dwarf manzanita, and acorns of the dwarf live-oak are abundant upon the dry hilltops; and these with some plants, and the larvæ of black ants, are the favorite food of bears, if varied occasionally by a stolen sheep or a shepherd. The gorges of the Tuolumne Cañon, on the north end of the basin, are their principal hiding places in this region. Higher in the range their food is not plentiful, and lower they are molested by man.

On returning to camp I passed three of the domes of the north bank, and was struck with the exact similarity of their structure, the same concentric layers, with a perpendicular cleavage also, but less perfectly developed and more irregular. This little dome tributary, about 2½ miles long by 1½ wide, must have been one of the most beautiful of the basin; all of its upper circling rim is adorned with domes, some half-born, sunk in the parent rock; some broken and torn upon the sides by the ice, and a few nearly perfect, from their greater strength of structure or more favorable position. The two lakes above described are the only ones of the tributary basin, both domes and lakes handiwork of the glacier.

A GLACIER'S DEATH.

In the waning days of this mountain ice, when the main river began to shallow and break like a Summer cloud, its crests and domes rising higher and higher, and island rocks coming to light far out in the main current, then many a tributary died, and this one, cut off from its trunk, moved slowly back amid the gurgling and gushing of its bleeding rills, until, crouching in the shadows of this half-mile hollow, it lived a feeble separate life. Here its days come and go, and the hiding glacier lives and works. It brings bowlders and sand and fine dust polishings from its sheltering domes and cañons, building up a terminal moraine, which forms a dam for the waters which issue from it; and beneath, working in the dark, it scoops a shallow lake basin. Again the glacier retires, crouching under cooler shadows, and a cluster of steady years enables the dying glacier to make yet another moraine dam like the first; and, where the granite begins to rise in curves to form the upper dam, it scoops another lake. Its last work is done, and it dies. The twin lakes are full of pure green water, and floating masses of snow and broken ice. The domes, perfect in sculpture, gleam in new-born purity, lakes and domes reflecting each other bright as the ice which made them. God's seasons circle on, glad brooks born of the snow and the rain sing in the rocks, and carry sand to the naked lakes, and, in the fullness of time comes many a chosen plant; first a lowly carex with dark brown spikes, then taller sedges and rushes, fixing a shallow soil, and now come many grasses, and daisies, and blooming shrubs, until lake and meadow growing throughout the season like a flower in Summer, develop to the perfect beauty of to-day.

How softly comes night to the mountains. Shadows grow upon all the landscape; only the Hoffman Peaks are open to the sun. Down in this hollow it is twilight, and my two domes, more impressive than in broad day, seem to approach me. They are not vast and over-spiritual, like Yosemite Tissiack, but comprehensible and companionable, and susceptible of human affinities. The darkness grows, and all of their finer sculpture dims. Now the great arches and deep curves sink also, and the whole structure is massed in black against the starry sky.

I have set fire to two pine logs, and the neighboring trees are coming to my charmed circle of light. The two-leaved pine, with sprays and tassels innumerable, the silver fir, with magnificent frouded whorls of shining boughs, and the graceful nodding spruce, dripping with cones, and seeming yet more spiritual in this camp-fire light. Grandly do my logs give back their light, slow gleaned from suns of a hundred Summers, garnered beautifully away in dotted cells and in beads of amber gum; and, together with this outgush of light, seems to flow all the other riches of their life, and their living companions are looking down as if to witness their perfect and beautiful death. But I am weary and must rest. Good-night to my two logs and two lakes, and to my two domes high and black on the sky, with a cluster of stars between.

New-York Tribune, December 5, 1871

Yosemite Valley in Flood

MANY a joyful stream is born in the Sierras, but not one can sing like the Merced. In childhood, high on the mountains, her silver thread is a moving melody; of sublime Yosemite she is the voice; the blooming *chaparral* or the flowery plains owe to her fullness their plant-wealth of purple and gold, and to the loose dipping willows and broad green oaks she is bounteous in blessing. I think she is the most absorbing and readable of rivers. I have lived with her for three years, sharing all her life and fortunes, dreaming that I appreciated her; but I never have so much as imagined the sublimity, the majesty of her music, until seeing and listening at every pore I stood in her temple to-day.

December brought to Yosemite, first of all, a cluster of ripe, golden days and silvery nights—a radiant company of the sweetest winter children of the sun. The blue sky had Sabbath and slept in its high dome, and down in its many mansions of *cañon* and cave, crystals grew in the calm nights, and fringed the rocks like mosses. The November torrents were soothed, and settled tranquillity beamed from every feature of rock and sky.

In the afternoon of December 16th, 1871, an immense crimson cloud grew up in solitary grandeur above Cathedral Rocks. It resembled a fungus, with a bulging base like a sequoia, a smooth, tapering stalk, and a round, bossy, down-curled head like a mushroom—stalk, head, and root, in equal, glowing, half-transparent crimson: one of the most gorgeous and symmetrical clouds I ever beheld. Next morning, I looked eagerly at the weather, but all seemed tranquil; and whatever was being done in the deep places of the sky, little stir was visible below. An ill-defined dimness consumed the best of the sunbeams, and toward noon well-developed grayish clouds appeared, having a close, curly grain, like bird's-eye maple. Late in the night some rain fell, which changed to snow, and, in the morning, about ten inches remained unmelted on the meadows, and was still falling—a fine, cordial snow-storm; but the end was not yet.

On the night of the 18th rain fell in torrents, but, as it had a temperature of 34° Fahrenheit, the snow-line was only a few feet above the meadows, and there was no promise of flood; yet sometime after eleven o'clock the temperature was suddenly raised by a south wind to 42°, carrying the snow-line to the top of the wall and far beyond—out on the upper basins, perhaps, to the very summit of the range—and morning saw Yosemite in the glory of flood. Torrents of warm rain were washing the valley walls, and melting the upper snows of the surrounding mountains; and the liberated waters held jubilee. On both sides the Sentinel foamed a splendid cascade, and across the valley by the Three Brothers, down through the pine grove, I could see fragments of an unaccountable out-gush of snowy cascades. I ran for the open meadow, that I might hear and see the whole glowing circumference at once, but the tinkling brook was an unfordable torrent, bearing down snow and bowlders like a giant. Farther up on the *débris* I discovered a place where the stream was broken up into three or four strips among the bowlders, where I crossed easily, and ran for the meadows. But, on emerging from the bordering bushes, I found them filled with green lakes, edged and islanded with floating snow. I had to keep along the *débris* as far as Hutchings', where I crossed the river, and reached a wadable meadow in the midst of the most glorious congregation of water-falls ever laid bare to mortal eyes. Between Black's and Hutchings' there were ten snowy, majestic, loud-voiced cascades and falls; in the neighborhood of Glacier Point, six; from Three Brothers to Yosemite Falls, nine; between Yosemite and Arch Falls, ten; between Washington Column and Mount Watkins, ten; on the slopes of South Dome, facing Mirror Lake, eight; on the shoulder of South Dome, facing the main valley, three. Fifty-six new-born falls occupying this upper end of the valley; besides a countless host of silvery-netted arteries gleaming everywhere! I did not go down to the Ribbon or Pohono; but in the whole valley there must have been upward of a hundred. As if inspired with some great water purpose, cascades and falls had come thronging, in Yosemite costume, from every grove and *cañon* of the mountains; and be it remembered, that these falls and cascades were not small, dainty, momentary gushes, but broad, noble-mannered water creations; sublime in all their attributes, and well worthy Yosemite rocks, shooting in arrowy foam from a height of near three thousand feet; the very smallest of which could be heard several miles away: a perfect storm of water-falls throbbing out their lives in one stupendous song. I have criticised Hill's painting for having two large falls between the Sentinel and Cathedral rocks; now I would not be unbelieving against fifty. From my first standpoint on the meadow toward Lamon's only one fall is usually seen; now there are forty. A most glorious convention this of vocal waters—not remote and dim, as only half present, but with forms and voices wholly seen and felt, each throbbing out rays of beauty warm and palpable as those of the sun.

All who have seen Yosemite in summer will remember the comet forms of upper Yosemite Falls, and the laces of Nevada. In these waters of the jubilee, the lace tissue predominates; but there is also a plentiful mingling of arrowy comets. A cascade back of Black's is composed of two white shafts set against the dark wall about thirty feet apart, and filled in with chained and beaded gauze of splendid pattern, among the living meshes of which the dark, purple granite is dimly seen. A little above Glacier Point there is a half-woven, half-divided web of cascades, with warp and woof so similar in song and in gestures, that they appear as one existence: living and rejoicing by the pulsings of one heart. The row of cascades between Washington Column and the Arch Falls are so closely side by side that they form an almost continuous sheet; and those about Indian Cañon and the Brothers are not a whit less noble. Tissiack is crowned with surpassing glory. Her sculptured walls and bosses and her great dome are nobly adorned with clouds and waters, and her thirteen cascades give her voice of song.

The upper Yosemite is queen of all these mountain waters; nevertheless, in the first half-day of jubilee, her voice was scarce heard. Ever since the coming of the first November storms, Yosemite has flowed with a constant stream, although far from being equal to the high water in May and June. About three o'clock this afternoon I heard a sudden crash and booming, mixed with heavy gaspings and rocky, angular explosions, and I ran out, sure that a rock-avalanche had started near the top of the wall, and hoping to see some of the huge blocks journeying down; but I quickly discovered that these craggy, sharp-angled notes belonged to the flood-wave of the upper fall. The great wave, gathered from many a glacier-*cañon* of the Hoffman spurs, had just arrived, sweeping logs and ice before it, and, plunging over the tremendous verge, was blended with the storm-notes of crowning grandeur.

During the whole two days of storm no idle, unconscious water appeared, and the clouds, and winds, and rocks were inspired with corresponding activity and life. Clouds rose hastily, upon some errand, to the very summit of the walls, with a single effort, and as suddenly returned; or, sweeping horizontally, near the ground, draggled long-bent streamers through the pine-tops; while others traveled up and down Indian Cañon, and overtopped the highest brows, then suddenly drooped and condensed, or, thinning to gauze, veiled half the valley, leaving here and there a summit looming alone. These clouds, and the crooked cascades, raised the valley-rocks to double their usual height, for the eye, mounting from cloud to cloud, and from angle to angle upon the cascades, obtained a truer measure of their sublime stature.

The warm wind still poured in from the south, melting the snows far out on the highest mountains. Thermometer, at noon, 45°. The smaller streams of the valley edge are waning, by the slackening of the rain; but the far-reaching streams, coming in by the Tenaya, Nevada, and Illilouette *cañons*, are still increasing. The Merced, in some places, overflows its banks, having risen at once from a shallow, prattling, ill-proportioned stream, to a deep, majestic river. The upper Yosemite is in full, gushing, throbbing glory of prime; still louder spring its shafts of song; still deeper grows the intense whiteness of its mingled meteors; fearlessly blow the winds among its dark, shadowy chambers, now softly bearing away the outside sprays, now swaying and bending the whole massive column. So sings Yosemite, with her hundred fellow-falls, to the trembling bushes, and solemn-waving pines, and winds, and clouds, and living, pulsing rocks—one stupendous unit of mountain power—one harmonious storm of mountain love.

On the third day the storm ceased. Frost killed the new falls; the clouds are withered and empty; a score of light is drawn across the sky, and our chapter of flood is finished. Visions like these do not remain with us as mere maps and pictures—flat shadows cast upon our minds, to brighten, at times, when touched by association or will, and fade again from our view, like landscapes in the gloaming. They saturate every fibre of the body and soul, dwelling in us and with us, like holy spirits, through all of our after-deaths and after-lives.

The Overland Monthly, April 1872

A Geologist's Winter Walk

AFTER reaching Turlock, I sped afoot over the stubble-fields, and through miles of brown *Hemizonia* and purple *Erigeron*, to Hopeton, conscious of little more than that the town was behind and beneath me, and the mountains above and before me; on through the oaks and *chaparral* of the foothills to Coulterville, and then ascended the first great mountain step upon which grows the sugar-pine. Here I slackened pace, for I drank the spicy, resiny wind, and was at home—never did pine-trees seem so dear. How sweet their breath and their song, and how grandly they winnowed the sky. I tingled my fingers among their tassels, and rustled my feet among their brown needles and burrs.

When I reached the valley, all the rocks seemed talkative, and more lovable than ever. They are dear friends, and have warm blood gushing through their granite flesh; and I love them with a love intensified by long and close companionship. After I had bathed in the bright river, sauntered over the meadows, conversed with the domes, and played with the pines, I still felt muddy, and weary, and tainted with the sticky sky of your streets; I determined, therefore, to run out to the higher temples. "The days are sunful," I said, "and though now winter, no great danger need be encountered, and a sudden storm will not block my return, if I am watchful."

The morning after this decision, I started up the Cañon of Tenaya, caring little about the quantity of bread I carried; for, I thought, a fast and a storm and a difficult cañon are just the medicine I require. When I passed Mirror Lake, I scarcely noticed it, for I was absorbed in the great Tissiack—her crown a mile away in the hushed azure; her purple drapery flowing in soft and graceful folds low as my feet, embroidered gloriously around with deep, shadowy forest. I have gazed on Tissiack a thousand times—in days of solemn storms, and when her form shone divine with jewels of winter, or was veiled in living clouds; I have heard her voice of winds, or snowy, tuneful waters; yet never did her soul reveal itself more impressively than now. I hung about her skirts, lingering timidly, till the glaciers compelled me to push up the cañon. This cañon is accessible only to determined mountaineers, and I was anxious to carry my barometer and chronometer through it, to obtain sections and altitudes. After I had passed the tall groves that stretch a mile above Mirror Lake, and scrambled around the Tenaya Fall, which is just at the head of the lake groves, and crept through the dense and spiny *chaparral* that plushes the roots of all the mountains here for miles, in warm, unbroken green, and was ascending a precipitous rock-front, where the foot-holds were good, when I suddenly stumbled, for the first time since I touched foot to Sierra rocks. After several involuntary somersaults, I became insensible, and when consciousness returned, I found myself wedged among short, stiff bushes, not injured in the slightest. Judging by the sun, I could not have been insensible very long; probably not a minute, possibly an hour; and I could not remember what made me fall, or where I had fallen from; but I saw that if I had rolled a little further, my mountain-climbing would have been finished. "There," said I, addressing my feet, to whose separate skill I had learned to trust night and day on any mountain, "that is what you get by intercourse with stupid town stairs, and dead pavements." I felt angry and worthless. I had not reached yet the difficult portion of the cañon, but I determined to guide my humbled body over the highest practicable precipices, in the most intricate and nerve-trying places I could find; for I was now fairly awake, and felt confident that the last town-fog had been shaken from both head and feet.

I camped at the mouth of a narrow gorge, which is cut into the bottom of the main cañon, determined to take earnest exercise next day. No plush boughs did my ill-behaved bones receive that night, nor did my bumped head get any spicy cedar-plumes for pillow. I slept on a naked bowlder, and when I awoke all my nervous trembling was gone.

The gorged portion of the cañon, in which I spent all the next day, is about a mile and a half in length; and I passed the time very profitably in tracing the action of the forces that determined this peculiar bottom gorge, which is an abrupt, ragged-walled, narrow-throated cañon, formed in the bottom of a wide-mouthed, smooth, and beveled cañon. I will not stop now to tell you more; some day you may see it, like a shadowy line, from Cloud's Rest. In high water, the stream occupies all the bottom of the gorge, surging and chafing in glorious power from wall to wall, but the sound of the grinding was low as I entered the gorge, scarcely hoping to be able to pass through its entire length. By cool efforts, along glassy, ice-worn slopes, I reached the upper end in a little over a day, but was compelled to pass the second night in the gorge, and in the moonlight I wrote you this short pencil-letter in my note-book:

"The moon is looking down into the cañon, and how marvelously the great rocks kindle to her light—every dome, and brow, and swelling boss touched by her white rays, glows, as if lighted with snow. I am now only a mile from last night's camp; and have been climbing and sketching all day in this difficult but instructive gorge. It is formed in the bottom of the main cañon, among the roots of Cloud's Rest. It begins at the dead lake where I camped last night, and ends a few hundred yards above, in another dead lake. The walls everywhere are craggy and vertical, and in some places they over-lean. It is only from twenty to sixty feet wide, and not, though black and broken enough, the thin, crooked mouth of some mysterious abyss; for in many places I saw the solid, seamless floor. I am sitting on a big stone, against which the stream divides, and goes brawling by in rapids on both sides; half my rock is white in the light, half in shadow. Looking from the opening jaws of this shadowy gorge, South Dome is immediately in front—high in the stars, her face turned from the moon, with the rest of her body gloriously muffled in waved folds of granite. On the left, cut from Cloud's Rest, by the lip of the gorge, are three magnificent rocks, sisters of the great South Dome. On the right is the massive, moonlit front of Mount Watkins, and between, low down in the furthest distance, is Sentinel Dome, girdled and darkened with forest. In the near foreground is the joyous creek, Tenaya, singing against bowlders that are white with the snow. Now, look back twenty yards, and you will see a waterfall, fair as a spirit; the moonlight just touches it, bringing it in relief against the deepest, dark background. A little to the left, and a dozen steps this side of the fall, a flickering light marks my camp—and a precious camp it is. A huge, glacier-polished slab, in falling from the glassy flank of Cloud's Rest, happened to settle on edge against the wall of the gorge. I did not know that this slab was glacier-polished, until I lighted my fire. Judge of my delight. I think it was sent here by an earthquake. I wish I could take it down to the valley. It is about twelve feet square. Beneath this slab is the only place in this torrent-swept gorge where I have seen sand sufficient for a bed. I expected to sleep on the bowlders, for I spent most of the afternoon on the slippery wall of the cañon, endeavoring to get around this difficult part of the gorge, and was compelled to hasten down here for water before dark. I will sleep soundly on this sand; half of it is mica. Here, wonderful to behold, are a few green stems of prickly *Rubus*, and a tiny grass. They are here to meet us. Ay, even here, in this darksome gorge, 'frightful and tormented' with raging torrents and choking avalanches of snow. Can it be? As if the *Rubus* and the grass-leaf were not enough of God's tender prattle-words of love, which we so much need in these mighty temples of power, yonder in the 'benmost bore' are two blessed *Adiantums*. Listen to them. How wholly infused with God is this one big word of love that we call the world! Good-night. Do you see the fire-glow on my ice-smoothed slab, and on my two ferns? And do you hear how sweet a sleep-song the fall and cascades are singing?"

The water-ground chips and knots that I found fastened between rocks, kept my fire alive all through the night, and I rose nerved and ready for another day of sketching and noting, and any form of climbing. I escaped from the gorge about noon, after accomplishing some of the most delicate feats of mountaineering I ever attempted; and here the cañon is all broadly open again—a dead lake, luxuriantly forested with pine, and spruce, and silver fir, and brown-trunked *Librocedrus*. The walls rise in Yosemite forms, and the stream comes down 700 feet, in a smooth brush of foam. This is a genuine Yosemite valley. It is about 2,000 feet above the level of Yosemite, and about 2,400 below Lake Tenaya. Lake Tenaya was frozen, and the ice was so clear and unruffled, that the mountains and the groves that looked upon it were reflected almost as perfectly as I ever beheld them in the calm evening mirrors of summer. At a little distance, it was difficult to believe the lake frozen at all; and when I walked out on it, cautiously stamping at short intervals to test the strength of the ice, I seemed to walk mysteriously, without any adequate faith, on the surface of the water. The ice was so transparent, that I could see the beautifully wave-rippled, sandy bottom, and the scales of mica glinting back the down-pouring light. When I knelt down with my face close to the ice, through which clear sunshine was pouring, I was delighted to discover myriads of Tyndall's six-sided ice-flowers, magnificently colored. A grand old mountain mansion is this Tenaya region. In the glacier period, it was a *mer de glace*, far grander than the *mer de glace* of Switzerland, which is only about half a mile broad. The Tenaya *mer de glace* was not less than two miles broad, late in the glacier epoch, when all the principal dividing crests were bare; and its depth was not less than fifteen hundred feet. Ice-streams from Mounts Lyell and Dana, and all the mountains between, and from the nearer Cathedral Peak, flowed hither, welded into one, and worked together. After accomplishing this Tenaya Lake basin, and all the splendidly-sculptured rocks and mountains that surround and adorn it, and the great Tenaya Cañon, with its wealth of all that makes mountains sublime, they were welded with the vast South Lyell and Illilouette glaciers on one side, and with those of Hoffman on the other—thus forming a portion of a yet grander *mer de glace*.

Now your finger is raised admonishingly, and you say, "This letter-writing will not do." Therefore, I will not try to register my homeward ramblings; but since this letter is already so long, you must allow me to tell you of Cloud's Rest and Tissiack; then will I cast away my letter pen, and begin "Articles," rigid as granite and slow as glaciers.

I reached the Tenaya Cañon, on my way home, by coming in from the northeast, rambling down over the shoulders of Mount Watkins, touching bottom a mile above Mirror Lake. From thence home was but a saunter in the moonlight. After resting one day, and the weather continuing calm, I ran up over the east shoulder of the South Dome, and down in front of its grand split face, to make some measurements; completed my work, climbed to the shoulder again, and struck off along the ridge for Cloud's Rest, and reached the topmost sprays of her sunny wave in ample time for sunset. Cloud's Rest is a thousand feet higher than Tissiack. It is a wave-like crest upon a ridge, which begins at Yosemite with Tissiack, and runs continuously eastward to the thicket of peaks and crests around Tenaya. This lofty granite wall is bent this way and that by the restless and weariless action of glaciers, just as if it had been made of dough—semi-plastic, as Prof. Whitney would say. But the grand circumference of mountains and forests are coming from far and near, densing into one close assemblage; for the sun, their god and father, with love ineffable, is glowing a sunset farewell. Not one of all the assembled rocks or trees seemed remote. How impressively their faces shone with responsive love!

I ran home in the moonlight, with long, firm strides; for the sun-love made me strong. Down through the junipers—down through the firs; now in jet-shadows, now in white light; over sandy moraines and bare, clanking rock; past the huge ghost of South Dome, rising weird through the firs—past glorious Nevada—past the groves of Illilouette—through the pines of the valley; frost-crystals flashing all the sky beneath, as star-crystals on all the sky above. All of this big mountain-bread for one day! One of the rich, ripe days that enlarge one's life—so much of sun upon one side of it, so much of moon on the other.

The Overland Monthly, April 1873

Flood-Storm in the Sierra

B EARS, wild sheep, and other denizens of the mountains are usually driven down out of the high Sierra about the beginning of winter, and are seldom allowed to return before late spring. But the extraordinary sunfulness of last winter, and my eagerness to obtain general views of the geology and topography of the Feather River basin, caused me to make a reconnoissance of its upper tributary valleys in the month of January. I had just completed this hasty survey and pushed my way down to comfortable winter quarters, when that fine storm broke upon the mountains which gave rise to the Marysville flood. I was then at Knoxville, a small village on the divide between the waters of the Yuba and Feather, some twenty miles back from the edge of the plains, and about 2,000 feet above the level of the sea. The cause of this notable flood was simply a sudden and copious fall of warm rain and warm wind upon the basins of the Yuba and Feather rivers at a time when these contained a considerable quantity of snow. The rain was of itself sufficient to produce a vigorous flood, while the snow which was so suddenly melted on the upper and middle regions of the basins may have been sufficiently abundant for the production of another flood equal in size to that of the rain. Now, these two distinct harvests of flood-waters were gathered simultaneously and poured down upon the plain in one magnificent avalanche. In the pursuit of clear conceptions concerning the formation of floods upon mountain rivers, we soon perceive that it is essential, not only that the water delivered by the tributaries be sufficient in quantity, but that it be delivered so rapidly that the trunk will not be able to discharge it without becoming choked and overflowed.

The basins of the Feather and Yuba are admirably adapted for the growth of floods. Their numerous tributary valleys radiate far and wide, comprehending large areas, and the tributaries are steeply inclined, while the trunks are comparatively level. While the storm under consideration was in progress, the thermometer at Knoxville ranged between 44 and 50°, and when warm wind and warm rain fall simultaneously upon snow contained in basins like those of the Yuba and Feather, both the rain and that portion of the snow which the rain and wind melt are sponged up and held back until the combined mass becomes sludge, which at length, suddenly dissolving, descends all together to the trunk, where, heaping and swelling, flood over flood, they debouch upon the plain with a violence and suddenness that at first seem wholly unaccountable. The destructiveness of the Marysville portion of the flood was augmented somewhat by mining-gravel occupying the river channels, and by levees which gave way after having first restrained and accumulated a portion of the waters. These exaggerating conditions did not, however, greatly influence the general result, the main effect having been caused by the rare combination of flood-factors indicated above.

It is a pity that so few people were fortunate enough to fairly meet with and enjoy this noble storm in its own home among the mountains; for, dying as it did so little known, it will doubtless be remembered far more for the drifted bridges and houses that chanced to lie in its way than for its own beauty, or for the thousand thousand blessings it brought to the fields and gardens of nature. The impressions which storms excite in the minds of different individuals vary with the degree of development to which they have attained, and with the ever-changing accidents of health, business position, and so on. Nevertheless, there seemed to be much in the voices and aspects of the Marysville storm which was in every way proper to arouse universal admiration. I will, therefore, offer a few of the more characteristic outlines.

On the morning of the flood (January 19th of this year) all the Knoxville landscapes were covered with running water, muddy torrents descended every gulch and ravine, and the sky was thick with rain. The pines had long slept in sunshine; they were now awake, and with one accord waved time to the beatings of the storm. The winds swept along the music curves of many a hill and dale, streaming through the pines, cascading over rocks, and blending all their tones and chords in one grand harmony. After fairly going out into and joining the storm, it was easy to see that only a small portion of the rain reached the ground in the form of drops; most of it seemed to have been dashed and beaten into a kind of coarse spray, like

that into which small water-falls are broken when they strike
glancingly on rough rock-shelves. Never have I beheld water
falling from the sky in denser or more passionate streams. The
heavy wind beat forward the spray in suffocating drifts, often
compelling me to shelter in the copse or behind big pines.
Go where I would, on ridges or in hollows, water still flashed
and gurgled around my ankles, vividly recalling a wild storm
morning in Yosemite, when a hundred water-falls from 1,000
to 3,000 feet in height came and sung together, filling all the
valley with their sea-like roar.

After drifting compliantly an hour or two, I set out for the
summit of a hill some 900 feet high, with a view to getting
as far up into the storm as possible. This hill, which is the
highest in the neighborhood, lies immediately to the south of
Knoxville, and in order to reach it, I had to cross Dry Creek,
a small tributary of the Yuba, that goes brawling along its base
on the north-west. The creek was now a booming river as large
as the Tuolumne, its current brown with mining-mud washed
down from many a "claim," and mottled with sluice-boxes,
fence-rails, and many a ponderous log that had long lain above
its reach. A little distance below the village a slim foot-bridge
stretches across from bank to bank, scarcely above the current.
Here I was glad to linger, gazing and listening, while the storm
was in its finest mood—the gray driving rain-stream above, the
brown savage flood-river beneath. The storm-language of the
river was hardly less enchanting than that of the forest wind;
the sublime overboom of the main current, the swash and
gurgle of eddies, the keen clash of firm wave-masses breaking
against rocks, and the smooth hush of shallow currentlets feeling their way through the willows of the margin: and amid all
this throng of sounds I could hear the smothered bumping and
rumbling of bowlders down on the bottom, as they were shoving or rolling forward against one another. The glad strong
creek rose high above its banks and wandered from its channel
out over many a briery sand-flat and sedgy meadow. Alders and
willows were standing waist-deep, bearing up against the current with nervous gestures, as if fearful of being carried away,
while supple branches bending over the flood dipped lightly
and rose again as if stroking the wild waters in play. Leaving
the bridge and pushing on through the storm-swept forest,

all the ground seemed in motion. Pine-tassels, flakes of bark, soil, leaves, and broken branches were being borne down; and many a rock-fragment weathered from exposed ledges was now receiving its first rounding and polishing at the hands of the strong enthusiastic storm-streams. On they rushed through every gulch and hollow, leaping, gliding, working with a will, and rejoicing like living creatures.

Nor were the phenomena confined to the ground. Every tree possessed a water system of its own; streams of every species were pouring down the grooves of each trunk, organized as regularly as Amazons and Mississippis; their tributaries widely branched and distributed over the valleys and table-lands of the bark; their currents in flood-time choked with moss-pedicels and muddy with spores and pollen, spreading over shallows, deepening in gorges, dividing, conflowing, and leaping from ledge to ledge. When patiently explored, these tree-rivers are found to possess much the same scenery as the rivers of the ground. Their valleys abound in fine miniature landscapes, moss-bogs enliven their banks like meadows, and thickets of fruited hypnæ rise here and there like forests. And though nearly vertical, these minute tree-rivers are not all fall. They flow in most places with smooth currents that mirror the banks and break into a bloom of foam only in a few special places.

Toward midday, cloud, wind, and rain seemed to have reached their highest pitch of grandeur. The storm was wholly developed; it was in full bloom, and formed, from my commanding outlook on the hill-top, one of the most glorious spectacles I ever beheld. As far as the eye could reach—above, beneath, around—the dusty wind-beaten rain filled the air like one vast water-fall. Detached cloud-masses swept imposingly up the valley as if endowed with independent motion—now rising high above the pine-tops, now descending into their midst, fondling their dark arrowy spires, and soothing every leaf and branch with infinite gentleness. Others, keeping near the ground, glided behind separate groves and brought them forward into relief with admirable distinctness; or passing in front, eclipsed whole groves in succession, pine after pine gradually melting in their gray fringes and emerging again seemingly clearer than before.

The topography of storms is in great measure controlled by the topography of the regions where they rise, or over which they pass. When, therefore, we attempt to study storms from the valleys or from the gaps and openings of the forest, we are confounded by a multitude of separate and apparently antagonistic impressions. The bottom of the main wind-stream is broken up into innumerable waves and currents that surge against the hill-sides like sea-waves against a shore, and these wind irregularities react in turn upon the nether surface of the main storm-cloud, eroding immense cavernous hollows and rugged cañons, and sweeping forward the resulting *detritus* in long curving trains like the moraines of glaciers. But in proportion as we ascend, these partial and confusing effects disappear, we escape above the region of dashing wind-waves and broken clouds, and the phenomena are beheld altogether united and harmonious.

The longer I gazed out into the storm, the more visible it became. The numerous trains and heaps of cloud-*detritus* gave it a kind of visible body, which explained many perplexing phenomena and published its motions in plain terms. This cloud-body was rounded out and rendered more visible and complete by the texture of the falling rain-mass. Rain-drops differ in shape and size; therefore, they fall at different velocities, and overtake and clash against one another, producing white mist and spray. They, of course, yield unequal compliance to the force of the wind, which gives rise to a still greater degree of interference and clashing; strong passionate gusts also sweep off clouds of spray from the groves like that torn from wave-tops in a gale. And all these factors of irregularity in the density, color, and general texture of the rain-mass, tend to make the visible body of the storm with all its motions more complete and telling. It is then seen definitely as a river, rushing over bank and brae, bending the pines like weeds, curving this way and that, whirling in immense eddies in hollows and dells, while the main body pours grandly over all like an ocean current above the landscapes that lie hidden at the bottom of the sea.

I watched the gestures of the pines while the storm was at its height, and it was easy to see that they were not at all distressed.

Several large sugar-pines stood near the thicket in which I was sheltered, bowing solemnly and tossing their giant arms as if interpreting the very words of the storm while accepting its wildest onsets with a passionate exhilaration. The lions were feeding. Those who have observed sunflowers eating light during any of the golden days of autumn know that none of their gestures express thankfulness. Their divine food is too heartily given, too heartily taken, to leave room for thanks. The sugar-pines were evidently accepting the benefactions of the storm in the same whole-souled manner; and when I looked down among the budding hazels, and still lower to the young violets and fern-tufts on the rocks, I noticed the same divine methods of giving and taking, and the same exquisite adaptations of what seems an outbreak of violent and uncontrollable force to the purposes of beautiful and delicate life.

Calms resembling deep sleep come upon whole landscapes just as they do upon individual pines, and storms awaken them in the same way. All through the dry midsummer of the lower portion of the range the withered hills and valleys seem to lie as empty and expressionless as dead shells on a shore. Even the loftiest alps may occasionally be found dull and uncommunicative, as if in some way they had lost countenance and shrunk to less than half their real stature. But when the lightnings crash and echo among these cañons, and the clouds come down and wreathe and crown their jagged summits, every feature beams with expression, and they rise again and hold themselves erect in all their imposing nobleness.

Storms are fine speakers and tell all they know, but their voices of lightning, torrent, and rushing wind are infinitely less numerous than their nameless still small voices too low for human ears; and because we are poor listeners we fail to catch much that is even fairly within reach. Our best rains are heard mostly on roofs, and winds in chimneys; and when, by choice or compulsion, we are fairly stormed upon, the confusion made by cumbersome equipments, and our nervous haste, and the noise of hail or rain on hard-brimmed hats, prevent our hearing any other than the loudest expressions. Yet we may draw intense enjoyment from a knowledge of storm-sounds that we can not hear, and of storm-movements that we can not see. The sublime rush of planets around their suns is not heard any more than the oozing of rain-drops among the roots of plants.

How interesting would be the history of a single rain-drop followed back from the ground to its farthest fountains. It is hard to obtain clear general views of storms so extensive and seemingly so shapeless as the one under consideration, notwithstanding the aid derived from a thousand observers furnished with the best instruments. The smallest and most comprehensible species of Sierra storm is found growing in the middle region of the range, some specimens being so local and small that we can go round their bases and see them from all sides like a mountain. Like the rains of the greater portion of equatorial regions, they seem to obey a kind of rhythm, appearing day after day a little before noon, sometimes for weeks in succession, and forming one of the most imposing and characteristic features of the midday scenery. Their periods are well known and taken into account by Indians and mountaineers. It is not long, geologically speaking, since the first rain-drop fell upon the present landscapes of the Sierra; for, however old the range may be, regarded as a whole, its features are young. They date back only to the glacial period. Yet in the few tens of thousands of years that have elapsed since these foot-hill landscapes were left bare by the melting ice-sheet, great superficial changes have taken place. The first post-glacial rains fell upon bare rocks and plantless moraines, but under nature's stormy cultivation these cold fields became fruitful. The ridged soils were spread out and mellowed, the seasons became warmer, and vegetation came gradually on—sedge and rush and waving grass, pine and fir, flower after flower—to make the lavish beauty that fills them to-day.

In the present storm, as in every other, there were tones and gestures inexpressibly gentle manifested in the midst of what is called violence and fury, and easily recognized by all who look and listen for them. The rain brought out all the colors of the woods with the most delightful freshness—the rich browns of bark, and burs, and fallen leaves, and dead ferns; the grays of rocks and lichens; the light purple of swelling buds, and the fine warm yellow greens of mosses and libocedrus. The air was steaming with fragrance, not rising and wafting past in separate masses, but equally diffused throughout all the wind. Pine woods are at all times fragrant, but most in spring when putting out their tassels, and in warm weather when their gums and balsams are softened by the sun. The wind was now chafing their needles, and the warm rain was steeping them. Monardella grows here in large beds, in sunny openings among the pines; and there is plenty of bog in the dells, and manzanita on the hill-sides; and the rosy fragrant-leaved *chamæbatia* carpets the ground almost everywhere. These with the gums and balsams of the evergreens formed the chief local fragrance-fountains within reach of the wind. Sailors tell that the flowery woods of Colombia scent the breeze a hundred miles to sea. Our Sierra wind seemed so perfectly filled, it could hardly lose its wealth go where it would; for the ascending clouds of aroma when first set free were wind-rolled and washed and parted from all their heaviness, and they became pure, like light, and were diffused and fairly lodged in the body of the air, and worked with it in close accord as an essential part of it.

Toward the middle of the afternoon the main flood-cloud lifted along its western border, revealing a beautiful section of the Sacramento Valley lying some twenty or thirty miles away, brilliantly sunlighted and glistening with rain-pools as if it were paved with burnished silver. Soon afterward a remarkably jagged bluff-like cloud with a sheer face appeared over the valley of the Yuba, dark colored and roughened with numerous furrows like some huge lava table. The blue Coast Range was seen stretching along the sky like a beveled wall, and the sombre and craggy Marysville Buttes rose imposingly out of the flooded plain like an island out of the sea. The rain began to abate, and the whole body of the storm was evidently withering and going to pieces.

I sauntered down through the dripping bushes, reveling in the universal vigor and freshness with which all the life about me was inspired. The woods were born again. How clean and unworn and immortal the world seemed to be!—the lofty cedars in full bloom, laden with golden pollen, and their washed plumes tipped with glowing rain-beads; the pines rocking gently and settling back into rest; light spangling on the broad mirror-leaves of the magnolia, and its tracery of yellow boughs relieved against dusky thickets of chestnut oak; liverworts, lycopodiums, ferns, all exulting in their glorious revival, and every moss that had ever lived seemed to have come crowding back from the dead to clothe each trunk and stone in living green. Young violets, smilax, frutillaria, saxifrage, were pushing up through the steaming ground as if conscious of all their coming glory; and innumerable green and yellow buds, scarce visible before the storm, were smiling everywhere, making the whole ground throb and tingle with glad life. As for the birds and squirrels, not a wing or tail was to be seen. Squirrels are dainty fellows, and dislike wetness more than cats. They were, therefore, snug at home, rocking in their dry nests. The birds were down in the sheltered dells, out of the wind, some of the strongest pecking at acorns or madroña berries, but most sitting in low copses with breast-feathers puffed out and keeping each other company.

Arriving at the Knox House, the good people bestirred themselves, pitying my bedraggled condition as if I were some benumbed castaway snatched from the sea; while I, in turn, pitied them, and for pity proclaimed but half the exalted beauty and riches of the storm. A fire, dry clothing, and special food were provided, all of which attentions were, I suppose, sufficiently commonplace to many, but truly novel to me.

How terribly downright must seem the utterances of storms and earthquakes to those accustomed to the soft hypocrisies of society. Man's control is being steadily extended over the forces of nature, but it is well, at least for the present, that storms can still make themselves heard through our thickest walls. On the night of the Marysville flood the easy-going apathy of many persons was broken up, and some were made to think, and the stars were seen, and the earnest roar of a flood-torrent was heard for the first time—a fine lesson. True, some goods were destroyed, and a few rats and people were drowned, and some took cold on the house-tops and died, but the total loss was less than the gain.

The Knoxville I have spoken of—sometimes called Browns-ville—is a desirable place of resort, not so much for the regular tourist, as for tired town-dwellers seeking health and rest. It lies some thirty miles to the east of Marysville, and is easily reached from this point by stage. The elevation above sea-level (2,000 feet) gives a delightful spring and autumn climate, diversified with storms of the most gentle and picturesque species. The woods are everywhere open to saunterers, for the trees are grouped in groves, and the hazel-bushes and dogwoods and most species of *chapparal* are kept together in tidy thickets, allowing room to pass between. In the larger of these openings flower-lovers will find plenty of mint, smilax, lilies, and mariposa tulips, and beds of gilias, violets, and hosackias, laid out in sunny parterres with their various colors and expressions in beautiful accord. The adjacent mountains, though not lofty, command an endless series of charming landscapes, and though the booming of strong Yosemitic falls is not heard, many a fine-voiced streamlet may be found in the leafy dells, singing like a bird as it leaps lightly from linn to linn beneath the cool shadows of alders and maples and broad plumy ferns.

Willow Glen lies a few miles to the west of the village, and contains a thousand objects of interest, picturesque rocks, cascades, ferny nooks, acres of polypodium and aspidium, wild gardens charmingly laid out, slopes of blooming shrubs, iris-beds, vine-tangles, birds, groves, and so on, among which the appreciative tourist might revel for weeks.

The Fox Den is another noteworthy point lying a little to the north-west of the village, and about 500 feet above it. It is a picturesque rock-pile resembling the ruins of some old feudal stronghold, where the red foxes of the neighborhood find shelter and sun themselves in the early morning, and where they watch and plan concerning the squirrels and quails that feed beneath the trees. In the spring-time the Den rocks are singularly rich in ferns, pellæa, polypodium, gymnogramma, and cheilanthes. In autumn they are brightened with lavish bunches of scarlet photinia berries, which show finely among their own warm yellow leaves and the gray-lichened rock-fronts, and, besides its own especial attractions, it commands noble views of the Sacramento Valley, and of the surrounding pictures of hill and dale.

The operations of all kinds of gold-mining may be witnessed in the neighborhood within short walks, or drives, and one of the guides attached to the hotel is wise in plants, more especially in ferns, and knows well the hollows where wood-wardias are tallest, and the rocks most rosetted with pellæa and cheilanthes.

The house itself is about as fresh as the woods after rain, and full of home-like sunshine. One of its rooms is a fine marvel, well deserving special mention. It is built entirely of plain sugar-pine, and filled with apples of every tint and taste, from the floor to the ceiling, all nicely assorted, rising regularly above one another in tiers, and shining as if the sunniest side of every apple were facing you.

Knoxville, though not containing above a dozen houses, is said to be noted for ministers. This apple-room is at any rate a kind of church, free to all, where one may enjoy capital sermons on color, fragrance, and sweetness, with very direct enforcements of their moral and religious correlations.

The world needs the woods, and is beginning to come to them; but it is not yet ready for the fine banks and braes of the lower Sierra, any more than for storms. Tourists make their way through the foot-hill landscapes as if blind to all their best beauty, and like children seek the emphasized mountains—the big alpine capitals whitened with glaciers and adorned with conspicuous spires. In like manner rivers are ascended hundreds of miles to see the water-falls at their heads, because they are as yet the only portions of river beauty plainly visible to all. Nevertheless the world moves onward, and "it is coming yet for a' that" that the beauty of storms will be as visible as that of calms, and that lowlands will be loved more than alps, and lakes and level rivers more than water-falls.

The Overland Monthly, June 1875

Living Glaciers of California

THE Sierra Nevada of California may be regarded as one grand wrinkled sheet of glacial records. For the scriptures of the ancient glaciers cover every rock, mountain, and valley of the range, and are in many places so well preserved, and are written in so plain a hand, they have long been recognized even by those who were not seeking for them, while the small living glaciers, lying hidden away among the dark recesses of the loftiest and most inaccessible summits, remain almost wholly unknown.

Looking from the summit of Mount Diablo across the San Joaquin Valley, after the atmosphere has been washed with winter rains, the Sierra is beheld stretching along the plain in simple grandeur, like some immense wall, two and a half miles high, and colored almost as bright as a rainbow, in four horizontal bands—the lowest rose purple, the next higher dark purple, the next blue, and the topmost pearly white—all beautifully interblended, and varying in tone with the time of day and the advance of the seasons.

The rose purple band, rising out of the yellow plain, is the foot-hill region, sparsely planted with oak and pine, the color in great measure depending upon argillaceous soils exposed in extensive openings among the trees; the dark purple is the region of the yellow and sugar pines; the blue is the cool middle region of the silver-firs; and the pearly band of summits is the Sierra Alps, composed of a vast wilderness of peaks, variously grouped, and segregated by stupendous cañons and swept with torrents and avalanches. Here are the homes of all the glaciers left alive in the Sierra Nevada. During the last five years I have discovered no less than sixty-five in that portion of the range embraced between latitudes 36° 30′ and 39°. They occur scattered throughout this vast region singly or in small groups, on the north sides of the loftiest peaks, sheltered beneath broad, frosty shadows. Over two-thirds of the entire number are contained between latitudes 37° and 38°, and form the highest fountains of the San Joaquin, Tuolumne, and Owens rivers.

The first Sierra glacier was discovered in October, 1871, in a wide, shadowy amphitheatre, comprehended by the bases of Red and Black mountains, two of the dominating summits of the Merced group. This group consists of the highest portion of a long crooked spur that straggles out from the main axis of the range in the direction of Yosemite Valley. At the time of my discovery I was engaged in exploring its *névé* amphitheatres, and in tracing the channels of the ancient glaciers which they poured down into the basin of Illilouette. Beginning on the northwestern extremity of the group with Mount Clark, I examined the chief tributaries in succession, their moraines, *roches moutonnées*, and shining glacial pavements, taking them as they came in regular course without any reference to the time consumed in their study.

The monuments of the tributary that poured its ice from between Red and Black mountains I found to be far the grandest of them all; and when I beheld its magnificent moraines ascending in majestic curves to the dark, mysterious solitudes at its head, I was exhilarated with the work that lay before me, as if on the verge of some great discovery. It was one of the golden days of Indian summer, when the sun melts all the roughness from the rockiest alpine landscapes. The path of the dead glacier shone as if washed with silver, the pines stood transfigured in the living light, poplar groves were masses of orange and yellow, and solidagoes were in full bloom, adding gold to gold.

Pushing on over my glacial highway, I passed lake after lake set in solid basins of granite, and many a thicket and meadow watered by the stream; now clanking over naked rock where not a leaf tries to grow, now wading through plushy bogs knee-deep in yellow and purple sphagnum, or brushing through luxuriant garden patches among larkspurs eight feet high and lilies with thirty flowers on a single stalk. The main lateral moraines bounded the view on either side like artificial embankments, covered with a superb growth of silver-fir and pine, many specimens attaining a height of two hundred feet or more. But all this garden and forest luxuriance was speedily left behind. The trees were dwarfed. The gardens became exclusively alpine. Patches of the heathy bryanthus and cassiope began to appear, and arctic willows, pressed into flat close carpets with the weight of winter snow. The lakelets, which a few miles down the valley were so richly broidered with meadows, had here, at an elevation of about 10,000 feet above the sea, only small mats of carex, leaving bare glaciated rocks around more than half their shores. Yet amidst all this alpine suppression the sturdy brown-barked mountain pine tossed his storm-beaten branches on ledges and buttresses of Red Mountain; some specimens over a hundred feet high and twenty-four feet in circumference, seemingly as fresh and vigorous as if made wholly of sunlight and snow.

Evening came on just as I got fairly within the portal of the grand fountain amphitheatre. I found it to be about a mile wide in the middle, and a little less than two miles long. Crumbling spurs and battlements of Red Mountain inclose it on the north, the sombre, rudely sculptured precipices of Black Mountain on the south, and a hacked and splintery *col* curves around from mountain to mountain at the head, shutting it in on the east.

I chose a camping ground for the night down on the brink of a glacier lake, where a thicket of Williamson spruce sheltered me from the night wind. After making a tin-cupful of tea, I sat by my camp fire, reflecting on the grandeur and significance of the glacial records I had seen, and speculating on the developments of the morrow. As the night advanced, the mighty rocks of my mountain mansion seemed to come nearer. The starry sky stretched across from wall to wall like a ceiling, and fitted closely down into all the spiky irregularities of the summits. After a long fireside rest and a glance at my field-notes, I cut a few pine tassels for a bed, and fell into the clear death-like sleep that always comes to the tired mountaineer.

Early next morning I set out to trace the ancient ice current back to its farthest recesses, filled with that inexpressible joy experienced by every explorer in nature's untrodden wilds. The mountain voices were still as in the hush of evening; the wind scarce stirred the branches of the mountain pine; the sun was up, but it was yet too cold for the birds and marmots— only the stream, cascading from pool to pool, seemed wholly awake and doing. Yet the spirit of the opening, blooming day called to action. The sunbeams came streaming gloriously through jagged openings of the *col*, glancing on ice-burnished pavements, and lighting the mirror surface of the lake, while every sunward rock and pinnacle burned white on the edges, like melting iron in a furnace. I passed round the north shore of the lake, and then followed the guidance of the stream back into the recesses of the amphitheatre. It led me past a chain of small lakelets set on bare granite benches, and connected by cascades and falls. The scenery became more rigidly arctic. The last dwarf pine was left far below, and the stream was bordered with icicles. As the sun advanced, rocks were loosened on shattered portions of the walls, and came bounding down gullies and *couloirs* in smoky, spattering avalanches, echoing wildly from crag to crag.

The main lateral moraines, that stretch so formally from the huge jaws of the amphitheatre out into the middle of the Illilouette basin, are continued upward in straggled masses along the amphitheatre walls, while separate stones, thousands of tons in weight, are left stranded here and there out in the middle of the main channel. Here, also, I observed a series of small, well-characterized, frontal moraines, ranged in regular order along the south wall of the amphitheatre, the shape and size of each moraine corresponding with the shapes and sizes of the daily shadows cast by different portions of the walls. This correspondence between moraines and shadows afterward became plain.

Tracing the stream back to the last of its chain of lakelets, I noticed a fine gray mud covering the stones on the bottom, excepting where the force of the entering and outflowing currents prevented its settling. On examination it proved to be wholly mineral in composition, and resembled the mud worn from a fine-grit grindstone. I at once suspected its glacial origin, for the stream which carried it came gurgling out of the base of a raw, fresh-looking moraine, which seemed to be in process of formation at that very moment. Not a plant, lichen, or weather-stain was any where visible upon its rough, unsettled surface. It is from sixty to over a hundred feet in height, and comes plunging down in front at an angle of thirty-eight degrees, which is the very steepest at which this moraine material will lie. Climbing the moraine in front was, therefore, no easy undertaking. The slightest touch loosened ponderous blocks, that went rumbling to the bottom, followed by a train of smaller stones and sand. Picking my way with the utmost caution, I at length gained the top, and beheld a small but well-characterized glacier swooping down from the sombre precipices of Black Mountain to the terminal moraine in a finely graduated curve. The solid ice appeared on all the lower portions of the glacier, though it was gray with dirt and stones imbedded in its surface. Farther up, the ice disappeared beneath coarsely granulated snow.

The surface of the glacier was still further characterized by dirt bands and the outcropping edges of blue veins that swept across from side to side in beautiful concentric curves, showing the laminated structure of the mass of the glacier ice. At the head of the glacier, where the *névé* joined the mountain, it was traversed by a huge yawning *Bergschrund*, in some places twelve or fourteen feet wide, and bridged at intervals by the remains of snow avalanches. Creeping along the edge of the *Schrund*, holding on with benumbed fingers, I discovered clear sections where the bedded and ribbon structure was beautifully illustrated. The surface snow, though every where sprinkled with stones shot down from the cliffs above, was in some places almost pure white, gradually becoming crystalline, and changing to porous whitish ice of different shades, and this again changing at a depth of twenty or thirty feet to bluer ice, some of the ribbon-like bands of which were nearly pure and solid, and blended with the paler bands in the most gradual and exquisite manner imaginable, reminding one of the way that color bands come together in a rainbow.

A series of rugged zigzags enabled me to make my way down into the weird ice world of the *Schrund*. Its chambered hollows were hung with a multitude of clustered icicles, amidst which thin subdued light pulsed and shimmered with indescribable loveliness. Water dripped and tinkled overhead, and from far below there came strange solemn murmurs from currents that were feeling their way among veins and fissures on the bottom.

Ice creations of this kind are perfectly enchanting, notwithstanding one feels so entirely out of place in their pure fountain beauty. I was soon uncomfortably cold in my shirt sleeves, and the leaning wall of the *Schrund* seemed ready to ingulph me. Yet it was hard to leave the delicious music of the water, and still more the intense loveliness of the light.

Coming again to the surface of the glacier, I noticed blocks of every size setting out on their downward journey to be built into the terminal moraine.

The noon sun gave birth to a multitude of sweet-voiced rills that ran gracefully down the glacier, curling and swirling in their shining channels, and cutting clear sections in which the structure of the ice was beautifully revealed.

The series of frontal moraines I had observed in the morning extending along the base of the south wall of the amphitheatre corresponds in every particular with the moraines of this active glacier; and the causes of all that is special in their forms and order of distribution with reference to shadows now plainly unfolded themselves. When those climatic changes came on that broke up the main glacier that once filled the amphitheatre from wall to wall, a series of residual glaciers was left in the cliff shadows, under whose protection they lingered until they formed the frontal moraines we are studying. But as the seasons became warmer, or the snow supply became less abundant, they died in succession, all excepting the one we have just examined, and the causes of its longer life are sufficiently apparent in the greater extent of snow basin it drains and in its more perfect shelter from the sun. How much longer this little glacier will live will, of course, depend upon climate and the changes slowly effected in the form and exposure of its basin.

Soon after this discovery I made excursions to the ice wombs situated on the head cañons of the Tuolumne and San Joaquin, and discovered that what at first sight and from a distance resemble extensive snow-fields are really active glaciers, still grinding the rocks over which they flow, and thus completing the sculpture of the summits so grandly blocked out by their giant predecessors.

That these residual glaciers are wearing the rocks on which they flow is shown by the fact that all the streams rushing out from beneath them are turbid with finely ground rock mud. They all present solid ice snouts creeping out from beneath their fountain snows, and all are carrying down stones that have fallen upon them, to be at length deposited in moraines.

All the specific crevasses of glaciers are also exhibited by them—marginal, transversal, and the jagged-edged *Bergschrund*.

In some transversal crevasses, as, for example, near the middle of the eastern branch of the Lyell Glacier, sections of blue ice eighty to a hundred feet deep occur, while the differential motion is manifested in the curves of the dirt bands and of the blue veins and moraines, not a single glacial attribute being either wanting or obscure. But notwithstanding the plainness and completeness of the proof, some of my friends who never take much trouble to investigate for themselves continued to regard my observations and deductions with distrust. I therefore determined to fix stakes in one of the more accessible of the glaciers, and measure their displacement, with a view to making the ordinary demonstration of true glacial movement, while subserving other desirable objects at the same time. The Maclure Glacier, situated on the north side of the mountain of that name, seemed best fitted for my purposes, and, with the assistance of my friend Galen Clark, I planted five stakes in it on the 21st of August, 1872, guarding against their being melted out by sinking them to a depth of five feet. Four of them were extended across the glacier in a straight line, beginning on the east side about halfway between the head and foot of the glacier, and terminating near the middle of the current. Stake No. 1 was placed about twenty-five yards from the side of the glacier; No. 2, ninety-four yards; No. 3, one hundred and fifty-two yards; No. 4, two hundred and twenty-five yards. No. 5 was placed up the glacier about midway between the *Bergschrund* and No. 4. On the 6th of October, or forty-six days after being planted, I found the displacement of stake No. 1 to be eleven inches, No. 2 to be eighteen inches, No. 3 to be thirty-four inches, No. 4 to be forty-seven inches, and No. 5 to be forty-six inches. As stake No. 4 was near the middle of the current, it was probably not far from the point of maximum velocity—forty-seven inches in forty-six days, or about one inch per twenty-four hours.

On setting out from Yosemite Valley to fix stakes in the Maclure Glacier, I invited Professor Joseph Leconte to accompany me. He had already given in his adhesion to my glacial theory for the formation of Yosemite Valley, and I was anxious to direct attention to other erosive effects of the ancient glaciers in the formation of mountains, ridges, lake basins, etc., as well as to point out some of the newly discovered glaciers.

Shortly after his return to Oakland he prepared a paper "On some of the Ancient Glaciers of the Sierra," which was read before the California Academy of Sciences, and afterward published in the *American Journal of Science and Arts*, in which he says, "Here, then" (on Mount Lyell), "we have *now existing not a true glacier*, perhaps, *certainly not a typical glacier* (since there is no true glacier ice *visible*, but only snow and *névé*, and certainly *no protrusion of an icy tongue* beyond the snow-field), yet nevertheless in some sense a glacier."

The above is an example of the rashness sometimes evinced by scientific observers in allowing themselves to decide upon imperfect data. Professor Leconte had never before seen a glacier of any kind, and did nothing more by way of investigation of this one than to spend a few minutes on the terminal moraine. Yet this, it seems, was deemed sufficient to enable him to decide "certainly" concerning it. Now the Lyell Glacier, which Professor Leconte approached, but did not set foot upon, was at the time of his visit (August 19) still covered with winter snow. Had his visit been delayed a few weeks he would have observed the required "icy tongue protruding from beneath the *névé*," because by this time the sun melted the covering of snow, and, according to his own chosen definition, the glacier suddenly became changed to a typical one.

As to the statement, "there is no true glacier ice visible," it is only necessary to observe that though there was none visible from the moraine where he was seated, there were many fine sections of "true glacier ice" visible in marginal and transversal crevasses, had he taken the pains to reach them.

Great vagueness prevails concerning the essential characteristics of glaciers. The icy snout creeping down out of the *névé* fountains is not available for all glaciers at all seasons, because in years of extraordinary snow-fall the whole surface of some slow-flowing glaciers remains covered during the whole year, and would accordingly be classified as true glaciers one season, *névé* fields another; and, as we have seen, the Lyell Glacier, though not typical in August, became typical in September.

A glacier is a current of ice derived from snow. Complete glaciers of the first order take their rise on the mountains, and descend into the sea, just as all complete rivers of the first order do. In North Greenland the snow supply and general climatic conditions are such that its glaciers pour directly into the ocean, and so undoubtedly did those of the Pacific slope during the flush times of the glacial epoch; but now the world is so warm and the snow crop so scanty, nearly all the glaciers left alive have melted to mere hints of their former selves. The Lyell Glacier is now less than a mile long; yet, setting out from the frontal moraine, we may trace its former course on grooved and polished surfaces and by immense cañons and moraines a distance of more than forty miles.

The glaciers of Switzerland are in a like decaying condition as compared with their former grandeur; so also are those of Norway, Asia, and South America. They have come to resemble the short rivers of the eastern slope of the Sierra that flow out into the hot plains and are dried up. According to the Schlagintweit brothers, the glaciers of Switzerland melt at an average elevation above the level of the sea of 7414 feet. The glacier of Grindelwald melts at less than 4000 feet; that of the Aar at about 6000. The Himalaya glacier, in which the Ganges takes its rise, does not, according to Captain Hodgson, descend below 12,914 feet. The average elevation at which the glaciers of the Sierra melt is not far from 11,000 feet above sea-level. The Whitney Glacier, discovered by Clarence King, is situated on the north side of Mount Shasta, and descends to 9500 feet above the sea, which is the lowest point reached by any glacier within the limits of California. Mount Shasta, however, is an isolated volcanic cone, and can not in any sense be regarded as a portion of the Sierra. Mount Whitney, situated near the southern extremity of the Sierra, although the highest mountain in the range (nearly 15,000 feet), does not give birth to a single glacier. Small patches of perpetual snow and ice occur on its northern slopes, but they are shallow, and give no evidence of glacial motion. Its sides, however, are still brilliantly polished by vanished glaciers that once descended into the main trunk glacier of Kern Valley on the west and to the Owens River on the east.

Mount Ritter, about 13,300 feet in height, still nourishes five glaciers, which, though small, are exceedingly well characterized, and differ in no particular from those of Switzerland excepting in degree. The finest of the five is on the north side, and flows at first in a northerly direction, then curves toward the west, and descends into a small blue glacier lake, whose banks around more than half its circumference are buried beneath perpetual snow. The outcropping edges of "the blue veins" are presented on the lower portion of this glacier, sweeping across the snout in fine concentric curves, scarcely marred by the rocky *débris* with which the glacier is laden. This beautiful glacier forms one of the highest sources of the North Fork of the San Joaquin.

Another of the Ritter glaciers, situated on the northeastern slopes of the mountain, is drained by a branch of Rush Creek, which flows into Mono Lake on the east side of the range. All the sixty-five Sierra glaciers that I have observed are a survival of the best fed and most favorably situated.

The Sierra granite is admirably fitted for the reception and preservation of glacial records, and from these it is plain that the Sierra ice once covered the whole range continuously as one sheet, which gradually broke up into individual glaciers, and these again into small residual glaciers arranged with reference to shadows. These last were very numerous; several thousand existed on the western flank alone, differing in no way from those that still linger in the highest and coolest fountains.

All the glaciers of California occur upon the north sides of mountains, and flow northward; or if they flow in an easterly or westerly direction, they are contained between protecting ridges trending in the same direction.

Furthermore, because the main axis of the Sierra extends in a north-northwesterly direction, the east side of the range is longer in shadow, and the greater number of the glaciers that occur along the immediate axis are on the east side.

The transformation of snow into glacier ice varies as to place and rapidity with the climate and with the form of the basin in which the fountain snow is collected. In the Sierra there is no definite snow-line, and therefore no fields of fountain snow extending to determinate elevations above the glaciers for the true glacier ice gradually to merge into. The change, therefore, of snow to flowing ice is more abrupt in the Sierra Nevada than in the Alps or in any mountain range possessed of perpetual snow not dependent upon shadows.

The whole number of active glaciers in the Alps is, according to the Schlagintweit brothers, 1100, of which one hundred may be regarded as primary. The total surface of snow, *névé*, and ice is estimated at 1177 square miles, or an average area of about one square mile per glacier. Some of the Sierra glaciers are as large; as, for example, the Lyell, North Ritter, and several that are nameless on the head of the South and Middle forks of the San Joaquin.

The main cause that has prevented the earlier discovery of Sierra Nevada glaciers is simply the want of explorations in the regions where they occur. The labors of the State Geological Survey in this connection amounted to a slight reconnaissance, while the common tourist, ascending the range only as far as Yosemite Valley, sees no portion of the true Alps containing the glaciers excepting a few peak clusters in the distance.

In the Swiss Alps carriage roads approach within a few hundred yards of some of the low-descending glaciers, while the comparative remoteness and inaccessibility of the Sierra glaciers may be inferred from the fact that, during the prosecution of my own explorations in five summers, I never met a single human being, not even an Indian or a hunter.

Harper's Monthly, November 1875

God's First Temples

E DS. RECORD-UNION: The forests of coniferous trees growing on our mountain ranges are by far the most destructible of the natural resources of California. Our gold, and silver,
and cinnabar are stored in the rocks, locked up in the safest of
all banks, so that notwithstanding the world has been making a
run upon them for the last twenty-five years, they still pay out
steadily, and will probably continue to do so centuries hence,
like rivers pouring from perennial mountain fountains. The
riches of our magnificent soil-beds are also comparatively safe,
because even the most barbarous methods of wildcat farming
cannot effect complete destruction, and however great the
impoverishment produced, full restoration of fertility is always
possible to the enlightened farmer. But our forest belts are being burned and cut down and wasted like a field of unprotected
grain, and once destroyed can never be wholly restored even
by centuries of persistent and painstaking cultivation.

The practical importance of the preservation of our forests
is augmented by their relations to climate, soil and streams.
Strip off the woods with their underbrush from the mountain
flanks, and the whole State, the lowlands as well as the high-
lands, would gradually change into a desert. During rainfalls,
and when the winter snow was melting, every stream would
become a destructive torrent, overflowing its banks, stripping
off and carrying away the fertile soils, filling up the lower river
channels, and overspreading the lowland fields with detritus
to a vastly more destructive degree than all the washings from
hydraulic mines concerning which we now hear so much.
Dripping forests give rise to moist sheets and currents of air,
and the sod of grasses and underbrush thus fostered, together
with the roots of trees themselves, absorb and hold back rains
and melting snow, yet allowing them to ooze and percolate
and flow gently in useful fertilizing streams. Indeed every pine
needle and rootlet, as well as fallen trunks and large clasping roots, may be regarded as dams, hoarding the bounty of
storm clouds, and dispensing it as blessings all through the

summer, instead of allowing it to gather and rush headlong in short-lived devastating floods. Streams taking their rise in deep woods flow unfailingly as those derived from the eternal ice and snow of the Alps. So constant indeed and apparent is the relationship between forests and never-failing springs, that effect is frequently mistaken for cause, it being often asserted that fine forests will grow only along streamsides where their roots are well watered, when in fact the forests themselves produce many of the streams flowing through them.

The main forest belt of the Sierra is restricted to the western flank, and extends unbrokenly from one end of the range to the other at an elevation of from three to eight thousand feet above sea level. The great master-existence of these noble woods is sequoia gigantea, or big tree. Only two species of sequoia are known to exist in the world. Both belong to California, one being found only in the Sierra, the other (sequoia sempervirens) in the Coast Ranges, although no less than five distinct fossil species have been discovered in the tertiary and cretaceous rocks of Greenland. I would like to call attention to this noble tree, with special reference to its preservation. The species extends from the well known Calaveras groves on the north, to the head of Deer creek on the south, near the big bend of the Kern river, a distance of about two hundred miles, at an elevation above sea level of from about five to eight thousand feet. From the Calaveras to the South Fork of King's river it occurs only in small isolated groves, and so sparsely and irregularly distributed that two gaps occur nearly forty miles in width, the one between the Calaveras and Tuolumne groves, the other between those of the Fresno and King's rivers. From King's river the belt extends across the broad, rugged basins of the Kaweah and Tule rivers to its southern boundary on Deer creek, interrupted only by deep, rocky canyons, the width of this portion of the belt being from three to ten miles.

In the northern groves few young trees or saplings are found ready to take the places of the failing old ones, and because these ancient, childless sequoias are the only ones known to botanists, the species has been generally regarded as doomed to speedy extinction, as being nothing more than an expiring remnant of an ancient flora, and that therefore there is no use trying to save it or to prolong its few dying days.

This, however, is in the main a mistaken notion, for the Sierra as it now exists never had an ancient flora. All the species now growing on the range have been planted since the close of the glacial period, and the Big Tree has never formed a greater part of these post-glacial forests than it does today, however widely it may have been distributed throughout pre-glacial forests.

In tracing the belt southward, all the phenomena bearing upon its history goes to show that the dominion of Sequoia Gigantea, as King of California trees, is not yet passing away. No tree in the woods seems more firmly established, or more safely settled in accordance with climate and soil. They fill the woods and form the principal tree, growing heartily on solid ledges, along water courses, in the deep, moist soil of meadows, and upon avalanche and glacial debris, with a multitude of thrifty seedlings and saplings crowding around the aged, ready to take their places and rule the woods.

Nevertheless Nature in her grandly deliberate way keeps up a rotation of forest crops. Species develop and die like individuals, animal as well as plant. Man himself will as surely become extinct as sequoia or mastodon, and be at length known only as a fossil. Changes of this kind are, however, exceedingly slow in their movements, and, as far as the lives of individuals are concerned, such changes have no appreciable effect. Sequoia seems scarcely further past prime as a species than its companion firs (*Picea amabilis* and *P. grandis*), and judging from its present condition and its ancient history, as far as I have been able to decipher it, our sequoia will live and flourish gloriously until A.D. 15,000 at least—probably for longer—that is, if it be allowed to remain in the hands of Nature.

But waste and pure destruction are already taking place at a terrible rate, and unless protective measures be speedily invented and enforced, in a few years this noblest tree-species in the world will present only a few hacked and scarred remnants. The great enemies of forests are fire and the ax. The destructive effects of these, as compared with those caused by the operations of nature, are instantaneous. Floods undermine and kill many a tree, storm winds bend and break, landslips and avalanches overwhelm whole groves, lightning shatters and burns, but the combined effects of all these amount only to a wholesome beauty-producing culture. Last summer I found some five saw mills located in or near the lower edge of the Sequoia belt, all of which saw more or less of the big tree into lumber. One of these (Hyde's), situated on the north fork of the Kaweah, cut no less than 2,000,000 feet of Sequoia lumber last season. Most of the Fresno big trees are doomed to feed the mills recently erected near them, and a company has been formed by Chas. Converse to cut the noble forest on the south fork of King's river. In these milling operations waste far exceeds use. After the choice young manageable trees have been felled, the woods are cleared of limbs and refuse by burning, and in these clearing fires, made with reference to further operations, all the young seedlings and saplings are destroyed, together with many valuable fallen trees and old trees, too large to be cut, thus effectually cutting off all hopes of a renewal of the forest.

These ravages, however, of mill-fires and mill-axes are small as compared with those of the "sheep-men's" fires. Incredible numbers of sheep are driven to the mountain pastures every summer, and in order to make easy paths and to improve the pastures, running fires are set everywhere to burn off the old logs and underbrush. These fires are far more universal and destructive than would be guessed. They sweep through nearly the entire forest belt of the range from one extremity to the other, and in the dry weather, before the coming on of winter storms, are very destructive to all kinds of young trees, and especially to sequoia, whose loose, fibrous bark catches and burns at once. Excepting the Calaveras, I, last summer, examined every sequoia grove in the range, together with the main belt extending across the basins of Kaweah and Tule, and found everywhere the most deplorable waste from this cause. Indians burn off underbrush to facilitate deer-hunting. Campers of all kinds often permit fires to run, so also do mill-men, but the fires of "sheep-men" probably form more than 90 per cent. of all destructive fires that sweep the woods.

Fire, then, is the arch destroyer of our forests, and sequoia forests suffer most of all. The young trees are most easily fire killed; the old are most easily burned, and the prostrate trunks, which *never rot* and would remain valuable until our tenth centennial, are reduced to ashes.

In European countries, especially in France, Germany, Italy and Austria, the economies of forestry have been carefully studied under the auspices of Government, with the most beneficial results. Whether our loose-jointed Government is really able or willing to do anything in the matter remains to be seen. If our law makers were to discover and enforce any method tending to lessen even in a small degree the destruction going on, they would thus cover a multitude of legislative sins in the eyes of every tree lover. I am satisfied, however, that the question can be intelligently discussed only after a careful survey of our forests has been made, together with studies of the forces now acting upon them.

A law was constructed some years ago making the cutting down of sequoias over sixteen feet in diameter illegal. A more absurd and shortsighted piece of legislation could not be conceived. All the young trees might be cut and burned, and all the old ones might be burned but not cut.

Sacramento Daily Union,
February 5, 1876

Snow-Storm on Mount Shasta

MOUNT SHASTA, situated near the northern extremity of the Sierra Nevada, rises in solitary grandeur from a lightly sculptured lava plain, and maintains a far more impressive and commanding individuality than any other mountain within the limits of California.

Go where you will within a radius of from fifty to a hundred miles, there stands the colossal cone of Shasta, clad in perpetual snow, the one grand landmark that never sets. While Mount Whitney, situated near the southern extremity of the Sierra, notwithstanding it lifts its granite summit some four or five hundred feet higher than Shasta, is yet almost entirely snowless during the summer months, and is so feebly individualized, the traveller often searches for it in vain amid the thickets of rival peaks by which it is surrounded.

The elevation of the highest point of Mount Shasta, as determined by the State Geological Survey, is in round numbers 14,400 feet above mean tide. That of Mount Whitney, computed from fewer and perhaps less reliable observations, is about 14,900 feet. But inasmuch as the average elevation of the common plain out of which Shasta rises is only about 4000 feet above the sea, while the actual base of Mount Whitney lies at an elevation of 11,000 feet, the individual stature of the former is nearly two and a half times that of the latter; and while the circumference of Mount Shasta around the base is nearly seventy miles, that of Whitney is less than five.

All that has been observed of the internal frame-work of Mount Shasta goes to show that its entire bulk originated in successive eruptions of ashes and lava, which, pouring over the lips of craters, layer upon layer, grew upward and outward like the trunk of an exogenous tree.

The Shasta lavas are chiefly trachytic and basaltic, varying greatly in color, density, and age. A few tufaceous and brecciated beds are visible in eroded sections near the summit, but pumice and obsidian, usually so abundant in other volcanic regions throughout the State, are here remarkably rare.

During the glacial period Mount Shasta was a centre of dispersal for the glaciers of the circumjacent region. The entire mountain was then loaded with ice, which, ever descending, grooved its sides and broke up its summit into a mass of ruins. But the whole quantity of denudation the mountain has undergone is not easily determined, its porous crumbling rocks being ill adapted for the reception and preservation of glacial inscriptions. All the finer striations have been effaced, while the extreme irregularity of its lavas, as regards erodibility, and the disturbances caused by inter and post glacial eruptions, have obscured or wholly obliterated those heavier characters of the glacial record found so clearly inscribed upon the granitic pages of the high Sierra between latitude 36° 30′ and 39°. This much, however, is plain, that when at length the ice period began to draw near a close, the Shasta ice cap was gradually melted off around the bottom, and, in receding and breaking up into its present condition, deposited the irregular heaps and rings of moraine soil upon which the Shasta forests are growing.

The Whitney glacier is the most important of the few fragmentary ice patches still remaining active. It takes its rise in extensive snow and *névé* fields on the summit, flows northward, and descends in a series of crevassed curves and cascades almost to the timber line—a distance of nearly three miles. Though not the very largest, this is perhaps the longest active glacier in the State. Glacial erosion of the Shasta lavas gives rise to light porous soils, largely made up of sandy detritus that yields very readily to the transporting power of running water. Several centuries ago immense quantities of this lighter material were washed down from the higher slopes by an extraordinary flood, giving rise to the simultaneous deposition of conspicuous delta-like beds, extending around the entire circumference of the base, their smooth gray surfaces offering a striking contrast to the rough scoriaceous lava flows that divide them. But notwithstanding the incalculable wear and tear and ruinous degradation that Shasta has undergone, the regularity and symmetry of its outlines remain unrivaled. The mountain begins to leave the plain in slopes scarcely perceptible, measuring from two to three degrees. These are continued by exquisitely drawn gradations, mile after mile, all the way to the truncated crater-like summit, where they attain a steepness of from twenty to thirty-five degrees. This grand simplicity is partially interrupted on the north by a subordinate cone that grows out of the side of the main cone about 3000 feet below the summit.

This side cone has been in a state of eruption subsequent to the breaking up of the main ice cap, as shown by the comparatively unwasted circular crater in which it terminates, and by numerous streams of fresh unglaciated lava that radiate from it as a centre.

The main summit is about one and a half miles in diameter from southwest to northeast, and consists mainly of two extensive snow and *névé* fields, bounded by crumbling peaks and ridges, among which we look in vain for any sure plan of an ancient crater. The extreme summit is situated upon the southern extremity of a narrow ridge that bounds the main summit on the east. As viewed from the north, it is an irregular blunt peaklet about ten feet high, fast disappearing before the stormy atmospheric erosion to which it is subjected. Hot sulphurous gases and vapors escape with a loud hissing noise from fissures in the lava near the base of the eastern ridge, opposite the highest peaklet. Several of the vents cast up a spray of clear bead-like drops of hot water, that rise repeatedly into the air and fall back until worn into vapor.

The steam and spray phenomena seem to be produced simply by melting snow coming in the way of the escaping gases, while the gases themselves are evidently derived from the heated interior, and may be regarded as the last feeble expression of that vast volcanic energy that builded the mountain.

Since the close of the ice period, nature has divided Mount Shasta into three distinct botanic zones. The first, which may be called the chaparral zone, has an average width of about four miles, and comprises the greater portion of the sandy flood beds noted above. They are densely overgrown with chaparral from three to six feet high, composed chiefly of manzanita, cherry, chincapin, and several species of ceanothus, forming when in full bloom one of the most glorious spectacles conceivable.

The continuity of these immense chaparral fields is grandly interrupted by wide swaths of coniferous trees, chiefly sugar and yellow pines, with Douglass spruce, silver-fir, and incense cedar, many specimens of which are over 200 feet high and six or seven feet in diameter at the base.

Golden-rods, asters, gilias, lilies, and lupines, with a multitude of less conspicuous herbaceous plants, occur in warm openings of the woods, with forms and colors in delightful accord, and enlivened with butterflies and bees.

The next higher is the fir zone, made up almost exclusively of the three silver-firs, viz., *Picea grandis*, *P. amabilis*, and *P. amabilis*, var. *nobilis*.

This zone is from two to three miles wide, has an average elevation above the sea on its lower edge of 6000 feet, on its upper of 8000, and is far the simplest and best defined of the three.

The Alpine zone is made up of dwarf pines, heath-worts, stiff wiry carices, lichens, and red snow.

The pines attain an elevation of 9500 feet, but at this height their summits rise only three or four feet into the frosty air, and are close-pressed and level, as if crushed by winter snow, and shorn off by the icy winds, yet flowering nevertheless, and sometimes producing cones and ripe nuts. Bryanthus, a beautiful flowering heath-wort, flourishes a few hundred feet higher, accompanied by kalmia and spiræa. Dwarf daisies and carices attain an elevation on favorable slopes of 11,000 feet, while beyond this a scanty growth of lichens and red snow composes the entire vegetation.

The following is a list of all the coniferous trees I have been able to find growing upon Mount Shasta, named downward in the order of their occurrence:

Pinus flexilis	Dwarf pine.
Pinus monticola	Mountain pine.
Pinus contorta	Tamarack pine.
Picea amabilis . . . . ⎫	
Picea amabilis, var. *nobilis* . . . . ⎬ Silver-fir.	
Picea grandis . . . . ⎭	
Pinus ponderosa	Yellow pine.
Pinus ponderosa, var. *jeffreyii* . . .	Jeffrey pine.
Pinus lambertiana	Sugar-pine
Abies douglassii	Douglass spruce.
Libocedrus decurrens	Incense cedar.
Pinus tuberculata.	
Juniperus occidentalis	Cedar.

The bulk of the forest is made up of the three silver-firs, Douglass spruce, the yellow and sugar pines, and incense cedar, and of these *Picea amabilis* is at once the most abundant and the most beautiful.

The ascent of Mount Shasta is usually made in July or August, from Strawberry Valley, on the Oregon and California stage-road. Storms are then less common and less violent, and the deep snows are melted from the lower slopes, and the beautiful Alpine vegetation is then coming into bloom. The ordinary plan is to ride from Strawberry Valley to the upper edge of the timber line, a distance of ten miles, the first day, and camp; then, rising early next morning, push to the summit, and return to the valley on the evening of the second day.

In journeying up the valley of the Upper Sacramento one obtains frequent views of Mount Shasta, through the pine-trees, from the tops of hills and ridges; but at Strawberry Valley there is a grand out-opening of the forests, and Shasta stands revealed at just the distance to be seen most comprehensively and impressively.

Looking at outlines, there, in the immediate foreground, is a smooth green meadow with its crooked stream; then a zone of dark forest, its countless spires of fir and pine rising above one another higher and higher in luxuriant ranks; and above all the great white cone sweeping far into the cloudless blue—meadow, forest, and mountain inseparably blended and framed in by the arching sky. My last ascent of Shasta was made on the 30th of April, 1875, accompanied by Jerome Fay, a hardy and competent mountaineer, for the purpose of making barometrical observations on the summit, while Captain A. F. Rodgers, of the United States Coast Survey, made simultaneous observations with a compared barometer at the base.

In the cooler portions of the woods winter snow was still lying five feet deep, and we had a tedious time breaking through it with the pack animals. It soon became apparent that we would not be able to reach the summer camping ground; and after floundering and breaking trail in the drifts until near sundown, we were glad to camp for the night as best we could upon a rough lava ridge that protruded through the snow. From here we carried blankets and one day's provision on our backs over the snow to the extreme edge of the timber line, and made a second camp in the lee of a block of red trachyte. This, of course, was done with a view to lessening as much as possible the labor of completing the ascent, to be undertaken next day. Here, on our trachyte bed, we obtained two hours of shallow sleep, mingled with fine glimpses of the keen starry night. We rose at 2 A.M., warmed a tin-cupful of coffee, broiled a slice of frozen venison on the coals, and started for the summit at 3.20 A.M.

The crisp icy sky was without a cloud, and the stars lighted us on our way. Deep silence brooded the mountain, broken only by the night wind and an occasional rock falling from crumbling buttresses to the snow slopes below. The wild beauty of the morning stirred our pulses in glad exhilaration, and we strode rapidly onward, seldom stopping to take breath—over the broad red apron of lava that descends from the west side of the smaller of the two cone summits, across the gorge that divides them, up the majestic snow curves sweeping to the top of the ancient crater, around the broad icy fountains of the Whitney glacier, past the hissing fumaroles, and at 7.30 A.M. we attained the utmost summit.

Up to this time there was nothing discernible either in the wind tones or in the sky that betokened the near approach of a storm; but on gaining the summit we observed several hundred square miles of white cumuli spread out on the lava plain toward Lassen's Peak, squirming dreamily in the sunshine far beneath, and exciting no alarm.

The slight weariness of the ascent was soon rested away. The sky was of the thinnest, purest azure; spiritual life filled every pore of rock and cloud; and we reveled in the marvelous abundance and beauty of the landscapes by which we were encircled.

At 9 A.M. the dry thermometer stood at 34° in shade, and rose steadily until 1 P.M., when it stood at 50°, although no doubt strongly influenced by sun heat radiated from the adjacent cliffs. A vigorous bumble-bee zigzagged around our heads, filling the air with a summery hay-field drone, as if wholly unconscious of the fact that the nearest honey flower was a mile beneath him.

Clouds the mean while were growing down in Shasta Valley—massive swelling cumuli, colored gray and purple and close pearly white. These, constantly extending around south-ward on both sides of Mount Shasta, at length united with the older field lying toward Lassen's Peak, thus circling the mountain in one continuous cloud zone. Rhett and Klamath lakes were eclipsed in clouds scarcely less bright than their own silvery disks. The black lava beds made famous by the Modoc war; many a snow-laden peak far north in Oregon; the Scott and Trinity mountains; the blue Coast Range; Shasta Valley, dotted with volcanoes; the dark coniferous forests filling the valleys of the Upper Sacramento—were all in turn obscured, leaving our own lofty cone solitary in the sunshine, and con-tained between two skies—a sky of spotless blue above, a sky of clouds beneath. The creative sun shone gloriously upon the white expanse, and rare cloud-lands, hill and dale, mountain and valley, rose responsive to his rays, and steadily developed to higher beauty and individuality.

One colossal master-cone, corresponding to Mount Shasta, rose close alongside with a visible motion, its firm polished bosses seemingly so near and substantial we fancied we might leap down upon them from where we stood, and reach the ground by scrambling down their sides.

Storm clouds on the mountains—how truly beautiful they are!—floating fountains bearing water for every well; the angels of streams and lakes; brooding in the deep pure azure, or sweeping along the ground, over ridge and dome, over meadow, over forest, over garden and grove; lingering with cooling shadows, refreshing every flower, and soothing rugged rock brows with a gentleness of touch and gesture no human hand can equal!

The weather of spring and summer throughout the middle region of the Sierra is usually well flecked with rain-storms and light dustings of snow, most of which are far too obviously joyous and life-giving to be regarded as storms. In the case of the smallest and most perfectly individualized specimens, a richly modeled cumulus cloud is seen rising above the dark forests, about 11 o'clock A.M., directly upward into the calm sky, to a height of about four or five thousand feet above the ground, or ten or twelve thousand feet above the sea; its pearly bosses finely relieved by gray and purple shadows, and exhibit-ing outlines as keen as those of a glacier-polished dome. In less than an hour it attains full development, and stands poised in the blazing sunshine like some colossal fungus. Presently a vigorous thunder-bolt crashes through the crisp sunny air, ringing like steel on steel, its startling detonation breaking into a spray of echoes among the rocky cañons below. Then down comes a cataract of rain to the wild gardens and groves. The big crystal drops tingle the pine needles, plash and spatter on granite pavements, and pour adown the sides of ridges and domes in a net-work of gray bubbling rills. In a few minutes the firm storm cloud withers to a mesh of dim filaments and disappears, leaving the sky more sunful than before. Every bird and plant is invigorated, a steam of fragrance rises from the ground, and the storm is finished—one cloud, one light-ning flash, one dash of rain. This is the California rain-storm reduced to its lowest terms. Snow-storms of the same tone and dimensions abound in the highest summits, but in spring they not unfrequently attain larger proportions, and assume a violence of expression scarcely surpassed by those bred in the depths of winter. Such was the storm now gathering close around us. It began to declare itself shortly after noon, and I entertained the idea of abandoning my purpose of making a 3 P.M. observation, as agreed on by Captain Rodgers and myself, and at once make a push down to our safe camp in the timber. Jerome peered at short intervals over the jagged ridge on which we stood, making anxious gestures in the rough wind, and becoming more and more emphatic in his remarks upon the weather, declaring that if we did not make a speedy escape, we should be compelled to pass the night on the summit. Anxiety, however, to complete my observations fixed me to the ridge. No inexperienced person was depending upon me, and I told Jerome that we two mountaineers could break down through any storm likely to fall. About half past 1 o'clock P.M. thin fibrous cloud films began to blow directly over the summit of the cone from north to south, drawn out in long fairy webs, like carded wool, forming and dissolving as if by magic. The wind twisted them into ringlets and whirled them in a succession of graceful convolutions, like the outside sprays of Yosemite falls; then sailing out in the pure azure over the precipitous brink of the cone, they were drifted together in light gray rolls, like foam wreaths on a river.

These higher cloud fabrics were evidently produced by the chilling of the air from its own expansion, caused by an upward deflection against the mountain slopes. They steadily increased on the north rim of the cone, forming a thick, opaque, ill-defined embankment, from whose icy meshes snow flowers began to fall, alternating with hail. The sky speedily darkened, and just after I had completed my observations and boxed the instruments, the storm broke in full vigor. The cliffs were covered with a remarkable net-work of hail rills that poured and rolled adown the gray and red lava slopes like cascades of rock-beaten water.

These hail-stones seemed to belong to an entirely distinct species from any I had before observed. They resembled small mushrooms both in texture and general form, their six straight sides widening upward from a narrow base to a wide domelike crown.

A few minutes after 3 P.M. we began to force our way down the eastern ridge, past the group of hissing fumaroles. The storm at once became inconceivably violent, with scarce a preliminary scowl. The thermometer fell twenty-two degrees, and soon sank below zero. Hail gave place to snow, and darkness came on like night. The wind, rising to the highest pitch of violence, boomed and surged like breakers on a rocky coast. The lightnings flashed amid the desolate crags in terrible accord, their tremendous muffled detonations unrelieved by a single echo, and seeming to come thudding passionately forth from out the very heart of the storm.

Could we have begun at once to descend the snow-filled grooves leading to the timber, we might have made good our escape, however dark or violent the storm. As it was, we had first to make our way along a dangerous snow ridge nearly a mile and a half in length, flanked by steep ice slopes on one side, and by shattered precipices on the other. Fortunately I had taken the precaution ere the storm began, while apprehensive of this very darkness, to make the most dangerous points clear to my mind, and to mark their relations with reference to the direction of the wind. When, therefore, the storm broke, I felt confident we could urge our way through the darkness and uproar with no other guidance. After passing the "Hot Springs," I halted in the shelter of a lava block to let Jerome, who had fallen a little behind, come up. Here he opened a council, in which, amid circumstances sufficiently exciting, but without evincing any bewilderment, he maintained, in opposition to my views, that it was impossible to proceed: the ridge was too dangerous, the snow was blinding, and the frost too intense to be borne; and finally, that, even supposing it possible for us to grope our way through the darkness, the wind was sufficiently violent to hurl us bodily over the cliffs, and that our only hope was in wearing away the afternoon and night among the fumaroles, where we should at least avoid freezing.

I urged that the wind was chiefly at our backs, and that, once arrived at the western edge of the cone, we had but to slide or wallow down steep inclines whose topographical leadings would insure our finding camp in any case, and that if need be we could creep along the more dangerous portions of the ridge, and clear the ice and precipices on hands and feet. He positively refused, however, to entertain any thought of venturing into the storm in that direction, while I, aware of the real dangers that would beset our efforts, and conscious of being the cause of his being thus imperiled, decided not to leave him.

Our discussions ended, Jerome made a dash from behind the lava block, and began forcing his way back some twenty or thirty yards to the Hot Springs against the wind flood, wavering and struggling as if caught in a torrent of water; and after watching in vain for any flaw in the storm that might be urged as a new argument for attempting the descent, I was compelled to follow. "Here," said Jerome, as we stood shivering in the midst of the hissing, sputtering fumaroles, "we shall be safe from frost." "Yes," said I, "we can lie in this mud and gravel, hot at least on one side; but how shall we protect our lungs from the acid gases? and how, after our clothing is saturated with melting snow, shall we be able to reach camp without freezing, even after the storm is over? We shall have to await the sunshine; and when will it come?"

The patch of volcanic climate to which we committed ourselves has an area of about one-fourth of an acre, but it was only about an eighth of an inch in thickness, because the scalding gas jets were shorn off close to the ground by the oversweeping flood of frost wind.

The marvelous lavishness of the snow can be conceived only by mountaineers. The crystal flowers seemed to touch one another and fairly to thicken the blast. This was the blooming time, the summer of the storm, and never before have I seen mountain cloud flowering so profusely. When the bloom of the Shasta chaparral is falling, the ground is covered for hundreds of square miles to the depth of half an inch; but the bloom of our Shasta cloud grew and matured and fell to a depth of two feet in less than a single day. Some crystals caught on my sleeve, and, examined under a lens, presented all their rays exquisitely perfect; but most were more or less bruised by striking against one another, or by falling and rolling over and over on the ground and rising again. The storm blast, laden with this fine-ground Alpine snow dust, can not long be braved with impunity, and the strongest mountaineer is glad to turn and flee.

I was in my shirt sleeves, and in less than half an hour was wet to the skin: Jerome fortunately had on a close-fitting coat, and his life was more deeply imbedded in flesh than mine. Yet we both trembled and shivered in a weak, nervous way, as much, I suppose, from exhaustion brought on by want of food and sleep as from the sifting of the icy wind through our wet clothing.

The snow fell with unabated lavishness until an hour or two after the coming on of what appeared to be the natural darkness of night. The whole quantity would probably measure about two feet. Up to the time the storm first fell upon the mountain, its development was gentle in the extreme—the deliberate growth of cumulus clouds beneath, the weaving of translucent tissue above, then the roar of the wind, the crash of thunder, and the darkening flight of snow flowers. Its decay was not less sudden—the clouds broke and vanished, not a snow-flake was left in the sky, and the stars shone out with pure and tranquil radiance.

As our experiences were somewhat exceptional during the long strange night that followed, it may perhaps be interesting to record them.

In the early stages of the night, while our sufferings were less severe, I tried to induce Jerome, who is a hunter, to break out in bear stories or Indian adventures to lessen our consciousness of the cold. But although meeting the storm bravely, he was not in talking condition. Occasionally he would indulge in calculations as to how long the fire of life would burn, whether the storm would last all the night and the next day, and if so, whether Sisson would be able to come to the rescue ere we succumbed to the cold. Then, with a view to cheering myself as well as him, I pictured the morning breaking all cloudless and sunful, assuring him that no storm ever lasted continuously from day to day at this season of the year; that out of all this frost and weariness we would yet escape to our friends and homes, and then all that would be left of the trying night would be a clump of unrelated memories he would tell to his children.

We lay flat on our backs, so as to present as little surface as possible to the wind. The mealy snow gathered on our breasts, and I did not rise again to my feet for seventeen hours. We were glad at first to see the snow drifting into the hollows of our clothing, hoping it would serve to deaden the force of the ice wind; but, though soft at first, it soon froze into a stiff, crusty heap, rather augmenting our novel misery. "Last year," said Jerome, "I guided a minister up here. I wish he were here now to try some prayers. What do you really think, Muir— would they help a fellow in a time like this?" Yet, after all, he seemed to recognize the unflinching fair play of Nature, and her essential kindliness, though making no jot of allowance for ignorance or mistakes. The snow fell on us not a whit more harshly than warm rain on the grass.

The night wind rushed in wild uproar across the shattered cliffs, piercing us through and through, and causing violent convulsive shivering, while those portions of our bodies in contact with the hot lava were being broiled.

When the heat became unendurable, we scraped snow and bits of trachyte beneath us, or shifted from place to place by shoving an inch or two at a time with heels and elbows; for to stand erect in blank exposure to the wind seemed like certain death.

The acrid incrustations sublimed from the escaping gases frequently gave way, opening new vents, over which we were scalded; and fearing that if at any time the wind should fall, carbonic acid, which usually forms so considerable a portion of the gaseous exhalations of volcanoes, might collect in sufficient quantities to cause sleep and death, I warned Jerome against forgetting himself for a single moment, even should his sufferings admit of such a thing. Accordingly, when, during the long dreary watches of the night, we roused suddenly from a state of half consciousness, we called each other excitedly by name, each fearing the other was benumbed or dead.

The ordinary sensations of cold give but faint conceptions of that which comes on after hard exercise, with want of food and sleep, combined with wetness in a high frost wind. Life is then seen to be a mere fire, that now smoulders, now brightens, showing how easily it may be quenched.

The weary hours wore away like a mass of unnumbered and half-forgotten years, in which all our other years and experiences were strangely interblended. Yet the pain we suffered was not of that bitter kind that precludes thought and takes away all capacity for enjoyment. A sort of stupefaction came on at times, in which we fancied we saw dry resiny pine logs suitable for camp fires, just as when, after going days without food, we fancy we see bread.

The extreme beauty of the sky at times beguiled our sense of suffering. Ursa Major, with its thousand home associations, circled in glorious brightness overhead; the mysterious star clouds of the Milky Way arched over with marvelous distinctness, and every planet glowed with long lance rays like lilies within reach. Then imagination, coming suddenly into play, would present the beauties of the warm zone beneath us, mingled with pictures of other lands. With unnatural vividness we saw fine secluded valleys, haunts of the deer and bear, and rich fir woods with their wealth of fern-like branches and orange lichens adorning their tall brown trunks. Then the bitter moaning wind and the drifting snow would break the blissful vision, and our dreary pains would cover us like clouds.

"Muir," Jerome would inquire, with pitiful faintness, "are you suffering much?" "Yes," I would reply, straining to keep my voice brave, "the pains of a Scandinavian hell, at once frozen and burned. But never mind, Jerome; the night will wear away at last, and to-morrow we go a-Maying, and what camp fires we will make, and what sun baths we will take!"

The frost became more and more intense, and we were covered with frozen snow and icicles, as if we had lain castaway beneath all the storms of winter. In about thirteen hours day began to dawn, but it was long ere the highest points of the cone were touched by the sun. No clouds were visible from where we lay, yet the morning was dull and blue and bitterly frosty, and never did the sun move so slowly to strip the shadows from the peaks. We watched the pale heatless light stealing toward us down the sparkling snow, but hour after hour passed by without a trace of that warm flushing sunrise splendor we were so eager to welcome. The extinction of a life seemed a simple thing after being so gradually drained of vitality, and as the time to make an effort to reach camp drew near, we became concerned to know what quantity of strength remained, and whether it would be sufficient to carry us through the miles of cold wind and snow that lay between us and the timber.

Healthy mountaineers always discover in themselves a reserve of power after great exhaustion. It is a kind of second life only available in emergencies like this, and having proved its existence, I had no great dread that either Jerome or myself would fail, though my left arm was already benumbed and hung powerless.

In our soaked and steamed condition we dared not attempt the descent until the temperature was somewhat mitigated. At length, about eight o'clock on this rare 1st of May, we rose to our feet, some seventeen hours after lying down, and began to struggle homeward. Our frozen trousers could scarce be made to bend; we therefore waded the snow with difficulty. The horizontal summit ridge was fortunately wind-swept and nearly bare, so that we were not compelled to lift our feet very high; and on reaching the long home slopes laden with fresh snow, we made rapid progress sliding and shuffling, our feebleness rather accelerating than diminishing our speed. After making a descent of 3000 feet, we felt the warm sun on our backs, and at once began to revive; and at 10 o'clock A.M. we reached camp and were safe. Half an hour afterward we heard Sisson shouting down in the fir woods on his way to camp with horses to take us to the hotel.

We had been so long without food, we cared but little about eating, but eagerly drank the hot coffee prepared by Sisson. Thawing our frozen toes was a painful task, but no permanent harm was done.

We learned from Sisson that when our terrific storm was in progress, only a calm, mild-looking cloud cap was observed on the mountain, that excited no solicitude for our safety. We estimated the snow-fall on the summit at two feet or more; at camp, some 5000 feet lower, we found only three inches, while down on the sloping base only a light shower had fallen, sufficient to freshen the grass.

We were soon mounted, and on our way down into the thick sunshine—to "God's country," as Sisson calls the chaparral zone. In two hours' ride the last snow bank was left behind. Violets appeared along the edges of the trail, and the chaparral was coming into bloom, with young lilies and larkspurs in rich profusion. How beautiful seemed the golden sunbeams streaming through the woods, and warming the brown furrowed boles of the cedar and pine! The birds observed us as we passed, and we felt like speaking to every flower.

At four in the afternoon we reached Strawberry Valley, and went to bed. Next morning we seemed to have risen from the dead. My bedroom was flooded with living sunshine, and from the window I saw the great white Shasta cone wearing its clouds and forests, and holding them loftily in the sky. How fresh and sunful and new-born our beautiful world appeared! Sisson's children came in with wild flowers and covered my bed, and the sufferings of our long freezing storm period on the mountain-top seemed all a dream.

Harper's Monthly, September 1877

Features of the Proposed
Yosemite National Park

THE upper Tuolumne Valley is the widest, smoothest, most serenely spacious, and in every way the most delightful summer pleasure park in all the high Sierra. And since it is connected with Yosemite by two good trails, and with the levels of civilization by a broad, well-graded carriage-road that passes between Yosemite and Mount Hoffman, it is also the most accessible. It lies in the heart of the high Sierra at a height of from 8500 to 9000 feet above the level of the sea, at a distance of less than ten miles from the northeastern boundary of the Yosemite reservation. It is bounded on the southwest by the gray, jagged, picturesque Cathedral range, which extends in a southeasterly direction from Cathedral Peak to Mount Lyell and Mount Ritter, the culminating peaks of the grand mass of icy mountains that form the "crown of the Sierra"; on the northeast, by a similar range or spur, the highest peak of which is Mount Conness; on the east, by the smooth, majestic masses of Mount Dana, Mount Gibbs, Mount Ord, and others, nameless as yet, on the axis of the main range; and on the west by a heaving, billowy mass of glacier-polished rocks, over which the towering masses of Mount Hoffman are seen. Down through the open sunny levels of the valley flows the bright Tuolumne River, fresh from many a glacial fountain in the wild recesses of the peaks, the highest of which are the glaciers that lie on the north sides of Mount Lyell and Mount McClure.

Along the river are a series of beautiful glacier meadows stretching, with but little interruption, from the lower end of the valley to its head, a distance of about twelve miles. These form charming sauntering grounds from which the glorious mountains may be enjoyed as they look down in divine serenity over the majestic swaths of forest that clothe their bases. Narrow strips of pine woods cross the meadow-carpet from side to side, and it is somewhat roughened here and there by groves, moraine boulders, and dead trees brought down from the heights by avalanches; but for miles and miles it is so smooth and level that a hundred horsemen may ride abreast over it.

The main lower portion of the meadow is about four miles long and from a quarter to half a mile wide; but the width of the valley is, on an average, about eight miles. Tracing the river we find that it forks a mile above the Soda Springs, which are situated on the north bank opposite the point where the Cathedral trail comes in—the main fork turning southward to Mount Lyell, the other eastward to Mount Dana and Mount Gibbs. Along both forks strips of meadow extend almost to their heads. The most beautiful portions of the meadows are spread over lake basins, which have been filled up by deposits from the river. A few of these river-lakes still exist, but they are now shallow and are rapidly approaching extinction. The sod in most places is exceedingly fine and silky and free from rough weeds and bushes; while charming flowers abound, especially gentians, dwarf daisies, ivesias, and the pink bells of dwarf vaccinium. On the banks of the river and its tributaries Cassiope and Bryanthus may be found where the sod curls over in bosses, and about piles of boulders. The principal grass of these meadows is a delicate Calamagrostis with very slender leaves, and when it is in flower the ground seems to be covered with a faint purple mist, the stems of the spikelets being so fine that they are almost invisible, and offer no appreciable resistance in walking through them. Along the edges of the meadows beneath the pines and throughout the greater part of the valley tall ribbon-leaved grasses grow in abundance, chiefly Bromus, Triticum, and Agrostis.

In October the nights are frosty, and then the meadows at sunrise, when every leaf is laden with crystals, are a fine sight. The days are warm and calm, and bees and butterflies continue to waver and hum about the late-blooming flowers until the coming of the snow, usually late in November. Storm then follows storm in close succession, burying the meadows to a depth of from ten to twenty feet, while magnificent avalanches descend through the forests from the laden heights, depositing huge piles of snow mixed with uprooted trees and boulders. In the open sunshine the snow lasts until June, but the new season's vegetation is not generally in bloom until late in July. Perhaps the best time to visit this valley is in August. The snow is then melted from the woods, and the meadows are dry and warm, while the weather is mostly sunshine, reviving and exhilarating in quality; and the few clouds that rise and the showers they yield are only enough for freshness, fragrance, and beauty.

The groves about the Soda Springs are favorite camping-grounds on account of the pleasant-tasting, ice-cold water of the springs, charged with carbonic acid, and because of the fine views of the mountains across the meadow—the Glacier Monument, Cathedral Peak, Cathedral Spires, Unicorn Peak, and their many nameless companions rising in grand beauty above a noble swath of forest that is growing on the left lateral moraine of the ancient Tuolumne Glacier, which, broad and deep and far-reaching, exerted vast influence on the scenery of this portion of the Sierra. But there are fine camping-grounds all along the meadows, and one may move from grove to grove every day all summer enjoying a fresh home and finding enough to satisfy every roving desire for change.

There are four capital excursions to be made from here—to the summits of Mounts Dana and Lyell; to Mono Lake and the volcanoes, through Bloody Cañon; and to the great Tuolumne Cañon as far as the foot of the main cascades. All of these are glorious, and sure to be crowded with joyful and exciting ex-periences; but perhaps none of them will be remembered with keener delight than the days spent in sauntering in the broad velvet lawns by the river, sharing the pure air and light with the trees and mountains, and gaining something of the peace of nature in the majestic solitude.

The excursion to the top of Mount Dana is a very easy one; for though the mountain is 13,000 feet high, the ascent from the west side is so gentle and smooth that one may ride a mule to the very summit. Across many a busy stream, from meadow to meadow, lies your flowery way, the views all sublime; and they are seldom hidden by irregular foregrounds. As you gradually ascend, new mountains come into sight, enrich-ing the landscape; peak rising above peak with its individual architecture, and its masses of fountain snow in endless variety of position and light and shade. Now your attention is turned to the moraines, sweeping in beautiful curves from the hollows and cañons of the mountains, regular in form as railroad embankments, or to the glossy waves and pavements of granite rising here and there from the flowery sod, polished a thousand years ago and still shining. Towards the base of the mountain you note the dwarfing of the trees, until at a height of about 11,000 feet you find patches of the tough white-barked pine pressed so flat by the ten or twenty feet of snow piled upon them every winter for centuries that you may walk over them as if walking on a shaggy rug. And, if curious about such things, you may discover specimens of this hardy mountaineer of a tree, not more than four feet high and about as many inches in diameter at the ground, that are from two hundred to four hundred years old, and are still holding on bravely to life, making the most of their short summers, shaking their tasseled needles in the breeze right cheerily, drinking the thin sunshine, and maturing their fine purple cones as if they meant to live forever. The general view from the summit is one of the most extensive and sublime to be found in all the range. To the eastward you gaze far out over the hot desert plains and mountains of the "Great Basin," range beyond range extending with soft outlines blue and purple in the distance. More than six thousand feet below you lies Lake Mono, overshadowed by the mountain on which you stand. It is ten miles in diameter from north to south and fourteen from east to west, but appears nearly circular, lying bare in the treeless desert like a disk of burnished metal, though at times it is swept by storm-winds from the mountains and streaked with foam. To the south of the lake there is a range of pale-gray volcanoes, now extinct, and though the highest of them rise nearly two thousand feet above the lake, you can look down into their well-defined circular, cup-like craters, from which, a comparatively short time ago, ashes and cinders were showered over the surrounding plains and glacier-laden mountains.

To the westward the landscape is made up of gray glaciated rocks and ridges, separated by a labyrinth of cañons and darkened with lines and broad fields of forest, while small lakes and meadows dot the foreground. Northward and southward the jagged peaks and towers that are marshaled along the axis of the range are seen in all their glory, crowded together in some places like trees in groves, making landscapes of wild, extravagant, bewildering magnificence, yet calm and silent as the scenery of the sky.

Some eight glaciers are in sight. One of these is the Dana Glacier on the northeast side of the mountain, lying at the foot of a precipice about a thousand feet high, with a lovely pale-green lake in the general basin a little below the glacier. This is one of the many small shrunken remnants of the vast glacial system of the Sierra that once filled all the hollows and valleys of the mountains and covered all the lower ridges below the immediate summit fountains, flowing to right and left away from the axis of the range, lavishly fed by the snows of the glacial period.

In the excursion to Mount Lyell the immediate base of the mountain is easily reached on horseback by following the meadows along the river. Turning to the southward above the forks of the river you enter the Lyell branch of the valley, which is narrow enough and deep enough to be called a cañon. It is about eight miles long and from 2000 to 3000 feet deep. The flat meadow bottom is from about 300 to 200 yards wide, with gently curved margins about 50 yards wide, from which rise the simple massive walls of gray granite at an angle of about thirty-three degrees, mostly timbered with a light growth of pine and streaked in many places with avalanche channels. Towards the upper end of the cañon the grand Sierra crown comes into sight, forming a sublime and finely balanced picture, framed by the massive cañon walls. In the foreground you have the purple meadow fringed with willows; in the middle distance, huge swelling bosses of granite that form the base of the general mass of the mountain, with fringing lines of dark woods marking the lower curves, but smoothly snow-clad except in the autumn.

There is a good camping-ground on the east side of the river about a mile above. A fine cascade comes down over the cañon wall in telling style and makes fine camp music. At one place near the top careful climbing is necessary, but it is not so dangerous or difficult as to deter any climber of ordinary strength and skill, while the views from the summit are glorious. To the northward are Mammoth Mountain, Mounts Gibbs, Dana, Warren, Conness, and many others, unnumbered and unnamed; to the southeast the indescribably wild and jagged range of Mount Ritter and the Minarets; southwestward stretches the dividing ridge between the North Fork of the San Joaquin and the Merced, uniting with the Obelisk or Merced group of peaks that form the main fountains of the Illilouette branch of the Merced River; and to the northwestward extends the Cathedral spur. All these spurs, like distinct ranges, meet at your feet. Therefore you look over them mostly in the direction of their extension, and their peaks seem to be massed and crowded together in bewildering combinations; while immense amphitheaters, cañons, and subordinate masses, with their wealth of lakes, glaciers, and snow-fields, maze and cluster between them. In making the ascent in June or October the glacier is easily crossed, for then its snow mantle is smooth or mostly melted off. But in midsummer the climbing is exceedingly tedious, because the snow is then weathered into curious and beautiful blades, sharp and slender, and set on edge in a leaning position. They lean towards the head of the glacier, and extend across from side to side in regular order in a direction at right angles to the direction of greatest declivity, the distance between the crests being about two or three feet, and the depth of the troughs between them about three feet. No more interesting problem is ever presented to the mountaineer than a walk over a glacier thus sculptured and adorned.

The Lyell Glacier is about a mile wide and less than a mile long, but presents, nevertheless, all the more characteristic features of large, river-like glaciers—moraines, earth-bands, blue-veins, crevasses, etc., while the streams that issue from it are turbid with rock-mud, showing its grinding action on its bed. And it is all the more interesting since it is the highest and most enduring remnant of the great Tuolumne Glacier, whose traces are still distinct fifty miles away, and whose influence on the landscape was so profound. The McClure Glacier, once a tributary of the Lyell, is much smaller. Eighteen years ago I set a series of stakes in it to determine its rate of motion, which towards the end of summer, in the middle of the glacier, I found to be a little over an inch in twenty-four hours.

The trip to Mono from the Soda Springs can be made in a day, but Bloody Cañon will be found rough for animals. The scenery of the cañon, however, is wild and rich, and many days may profitably be spent around the shores of the lake and out on its islands and about the volcanoes.

In making the trip down the Big Tuolumne Cañon animals may be led as far as a small, grassy, forested lake basin that lies below the crossing of the Virginia Creek trail. And from this point any one accustomed to walk on earthquake boulders, carpeted with cañon chaparral, can easily go down the cañon as far as the big cascades and return to camp in one day. Many, however, are not able to do this, and it is far better to go leisurely, prepared to camp anywhere, and enjoy the marvelous grandeur of the place.

The cañon begins near the lower end of the meadows and extends to the Hetch Hetchy Valley, a distance of about eighteen miles, though it will seem much longer to any one who scrambles through it. It is from 1200 to about 5000 feet deep, and is comparatively narrow, but there are several fine, roomy, park-like openings in it, and throughout its whole extent Yosemite features are displayed on a grand scale—domes, El Capitan rocks, gables, Sentinels, Royal Arches, glacier points, Cathedral Spires, etc. There is even a Half Dome among its wealth of rock forms, though less sublime and beautiful than the Yosemite Half Dome. It also contains falls and cascades innumerable. The sheer falls, except when the snow is melting in early spring, are quite small in volume as compared with those of Yosemite and Hetch Hetchy; but many of them are very beautiful, and in any other country would be regarded as great wonders. But it is the cascades or sloping falls on the main river that are the crowning glory of the cañon, and these in volume, extent, and variety surpass those of any other cañon in the Sierra. The most showy and interesting of the cascades are mostly in the upper part of the cañon, above the point where Cathedral Creek and Hoffman Creek enter. For miles the river is one wild, exulting, on-rushing mass of snowy purple bloom, spreading over glacial waves of granite without any definite channel, and through avalanche taluses, gliding in silver plumes, dashing and foaming through huge boulder-dams, leaping high into the air in glorious wheel-like whirls, tossing from side to side, doubling, glinting, singing in glorious exuberance of mountain energy.

Every one who is anything of a mountaineer should go on through the entire length of the cañon, coming out by Hetch Hetchy. There is not a dull step all the way. With wide variations it is a Yosemite Valley from end to end.

THE HETCH HETCHY VALLEY.

Most people who visit Yosemite are apt to regard it as an exceptional creation, the only valley of its kind in the world. But nothing in Nature stands alone. She is not so poor as to have only one of anything. The explorer in the Sierra and elsewhere finds many Yosemites, that differ not more than one tree differs from another of the same species. They occupy the same relative positions on the mountain flanks, were formed by the same forces in the same kind of granite, and have similar sculpture, waterfalls, and vegetation. The Hetch Hetchy Valley has long been known as the Tuolumne Yosemite. It is said to have been discovered by Joseph Screech, a hunter, in 1850, a year before the discovery of the great Merced Yosemite. It lies in a northwesterly direction from Yosemite, at a distance of about twenty miles, and is easily accessible to mounted travelers by a trail that leaves the Big Oak Flat road at Bronson's Meadows, a few miles below Crane Flat. But by far the best way to it for those who have useful limbs is across the divide direct from Yosemite. Leaving the valley by Indian Cañon or Fall Cañon, you cross the dome-paved basin of Yosemite Creek, then bear to the left around the head fountains of the South Fork of the Tuolumne to the summit of the Big Tuolumne Cañon, a few miles above the head of Hetch Hetchy. Here you will find a glorious view. Immediately beneath you, at a depth of more than 4000 feet, you see a beautiful ribbon of level ground, with a silver thread in the middle of it, and green or yellow according to the time of year. That ribbon is a strip of meadow, and the silver thread is the main Tuolumne River. The opposite wall of the cañon rises in precipices, steep and angular, or with rounded brows like those of Yosemite, and from this wall as a base extends a fine wilderness of mountains, rising dome above dome, ridge above ridge, to a group of snowy peaks on the summit of the range. Of all this sublime congregation of mountains Castle Peak is king: robed with snow and light, dipping unnumbered points and spires into the thin blue sky, it maintains amid noble companions a perfect and commanding individuality.

You will not encounter much difficulty in getting down into the cañon, for bear trails may readily be found leading from the upper feeding-grounds to the berry gardens and acorn orchards of Hetch Hetchy, and when you reach the river you have only to saunter by its side a mile or two down the cañon before you find yourself in the open valley. Looking about you, you cannot fail to discover that you are in a Yosemite valley. As the Merced flows through Yosemite, so does the Tuolumne through Hetch Hetchy. The bottom of Yosemite is about 4000 feet above sea level, the bottom of Hetch Hetchy is about 3800 feet, and in both the walls are of gray granite and rise abruptly in precipices from a level bottom, with but little debris along their bases. Furthermore it was a home and stronghold of the Tuolumne Indians, as Ahwahne was of the grizzlies. Standing boldly forward from the south wall near the lower end of the valley is the rock Kolana, the outermost of a picturesque group corresponding to the Cathedral Rocks of Yosemite, and about the same height. Facing Kolana on the north side of the valley is a rock about 1800 feet in height, which presents a bare, sheer front like El Capitan, and over its massive brow flows a stream that makes the most graceful fall I have ever seen. Its Indian name is Tu-ee-u-la-la, and no other, so far as I have heard, has yet been given it. From the brow of the cliff it makes a free descent of a thousand feet and then breaks up into a ragged, foaming web of cascades among the boulders of an earthquake talus. Towards the end of summer it vanishes, because its head streams do not reach back to the lasting snows of the summits of the range, but in May and June it is indescribably lovely. The only fall that I know with which it may fairly be compared is the Bridal Veil, but it excels even that fall in peaceful, floating, swaying gracefulness. For when we attentively observe the Bridal Veil, even towards the middle of summer when its waters begin to fail, we may discover, when the winds blow aside the outer folds of spray, dense comet-shaped masses shooting through the air with terrible energy; but from the top of the cliff, where the Hetch Hetchy veil first floats free, all the way to the bottom it is in perfect repose. Again, the Bridal Veil is in a shadow-haunted nook inaccessible to the main wind currents of the valley, and has to depend for many of its gestures on irregular, teasing side currents and whirls, while Tu-ee-u-la-la, being fully exposed on the open cliff, is sun drenched all day, and is ever ready to yield graceful compliance to every wind that blows. Most people unacquainted with the behavior of mountain streams fancy that when they escape the bounds of their rocky channels and launch into the air they at once lose all self-control and tumble in confusion. On the contrary, on no part of their travels do they manifest more calm self-possession. Imagine yourself in Hetch Hetchy. It is a sunny day in June, the pines sway dreamily, and you are shoulder-deep in grass and flowers. Looking across the valley through beautiful open groves you see a bare granite wall 1800 feet high rising abruptly out of the green and yellow vegetation and glowing with sunshine, and in front of it the fall, waving like a downy scarf, silver bright, burning with white sun-fire in every fiber. In coming forward to the edge of the tremendous precipice and taking flight a little hasty eagerness appears, but this is speedily hushed in divine repose. Now observe the marvelous distinctness and delicacy of the various kinds of sun-filled tissue into which the waters are woven. They fly and float and drowse down the face of that grand gray rock in so leisurely and unconfused a manner that you may examine their texture and patterns as you would a piece of embroidery held in the hand. It is a flood of singing air, water, and sunlight woven into cloth that spirits might wear.

The great Hetch Hetchy Fall, called Wa-páma by the Tuolumnes, is on the same side of the valley as the Veil, and so near it that both may be seen in one view. It is about 1800 feet in height, and seems to be nearly vertical when one is standing in front of it, though it is considerably inclined. Its location is similar to that of the Yosemite Fall, but the volume of water is much greater. No two falls could be more unlike than Wapáma and Tu-ee-u-la-la, the one thundering and beating in a shadowy gorge, the other chanting in deep, low tones, and with no other shadows about it than those of its own waters, pale-gray mostly, and violet and pink delicately graded. One whispers, "He dwells in peace," the other is the thunder of his chariot wheels in power. This noble pair are the main falls of the valley, though there are many small ones essential to the perfection of the general harmony.

The wall above Wa-páma corresponds, both in outlines and in details of sculpture, with the same relative portion of the Yosemite wall. Near the Yosemite Fall the cliff has two conspicuous benches extending in a horizontal direction 500 and 1500 feet above the valley. Two benches similarly situated, and timbered in the same way, occur on the same relative position on the Hetch Hetchy wall, and on no other portion. The upper end of Yosemite is closed by the great Half Dome, and the upper end of Hetch Hetchy is closed in the same way by a mountain rock. Both occupy angles formed by the confluence of two large glaciers that have long since vanished. In front of this head rock the river forks like the Merced in Yosemite. The right fork as you ascend is the main Tuolumne, which takes its rise in a glacier on the north side of Mount Lyell and flows through the Big Cañon. I have not traced the left fork to its highest source, but, judging from the general trend of the ridges, it must be near Castle Peak. Upon this left or North Fork there is a remarkably interesting series of cascades, five in number, ranged along a picturesque gorge, on the edges of which we may saunter safely and gain fine views of the dancing spray below. The first is a wide-spreading fan of white, crystal-covered water, half leaping half sliding over a steep polished pavement, at the foot of which it rests and sets forth clear and shining on its final flow to the main river. A short distance above the head of this cascade you discover the second, which is as impressively wild and beautiful as the first, and makes you sing with it as though you were a part of it. It is framed in deep rock walls that are colored yellow and red with lichens, and fringed on the jagged edges by live-oaks and sabine pines, and at the bottom in damp nooks you may see ferns, lilies, and azaleas.

Three or four hundred yards higher you come to the third of the choir, the largest of the five. It is formed of three smaller ones inseparably combined, which sing divinely, and make spray of the best quality for rainbows. A short distance beyond this the gorge comes to an end, and the bare stream, without any definite channel, spreads out in a thin, silvery sheet about 150 feet wide. Its waters are throughout almost its whole extent, drawn out in overlapping folds of lace, thick sown with diamond jets and sparks that give an exceedingly rich appearance. Still advancing, you hear a deep muffled booming, and you push eagerly on through flowery thickets until the last of the five appears through the foliage. The precipice down which

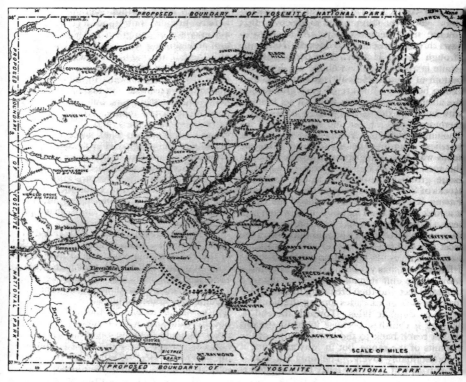

Map of the Yosemite region, showing present reservation, water-shed of the valley, and approximate limits of the proposed national park. *

it thunders is fretted with projecting knobs, forming polished keys upon which the wild waters play.

The bottom of the valley is divided by a low, glacier-polished bar of granite, the lower portion being mostly meadow land, the upper dry and sandy, and planted with fine Kellogg oaks,

*The above map represents the limits of the park as proposed by Mr. Muir and as advocated before the Committee on Public Lands of the House of Representatives. As we go to press, the Committee seems disposed to extend the north and south limits eastward to the Nevada line, thus adding an equal amount to the area here indicated. The honor of introducing the National Park bill belongs to General William Vandever of California.—EDITOR.

which frequently attain a diameter of six or seven feet. On the talus slopes the pines give place to the mountain live-oak, which forms the shadiest groves in the valley and the greatest in extent. Their glossy foliage, warm yellow-green and closely pressed, makes a kind of ceiling, supported by bare gray trunks and branches gnarled and picturesque. A few specimens of the sugar pine and tamarack pine are found in the valley, also the two silver firs. The Douglas spruce and the libocedrus attain noble dimensions in certain favorable spots, and a few specimens of the interesting *Torreya Californica* may be found on the south side. The brier-rose occurs in large patches, with tall, spiky mints and arching grasses. On the meadows lilies, larkspurs, and lupines of several species are abundant, and in some places reach above one's head. Rock-ferns of rare beauty fringe and rosette the walls from top to bottom—*Pellæa densa*, *P. mucronata* and *P. Bridgesii*, *Cheilanthes gracillima*, *Allosorus*, etc. *Adiantum pedatum* occurs in a few mossy corners that get spray from the falls. *Woodwardia radicans* and *Asplenium felix-fœmina* are the tallest ferns of the valley—six feet high, some of them. The whole valley was a charming garden when I last saw it, and the huts of the Indians and a lone cabin were the only improvements.

As will be seen by the map, I have thus briefly touched upon a number of the chief features of a region which it is proposed to reserve out of the public domain for the use and recreation of the people. A bill has already been introduced in Congress by Mr. Vandever creating a national park about the reservation which the State now holds in trust for the people. It is very desirable that the new reservation should at least extend to the limits indicated by the map, and the bill cannot too quickly become a law. Unless reserved or protected the whole region will soon or late be devastated by lumbermen and sheepmen, and so of course be made unfit for use as a pleasure ground. Already it is with great difficulty that campers, even in the most remote parts of the proposed reservation and in those difficult of access, can find grass enough to keep their animals from starving; the ground is already being gnawed and trampled into a desert condition, and when the region shall be stripped of its forests the ruin will be complete. Even the Yosemite will then suffer in the disturbance effected on the water-shed, the clear streams becoming muddy and much less regular in their flow. It is also devoutly to be hoped that the Hetch Hetchy will escape such ravages of man as one sees in Yosemite. Ax and plow, hogs and horses, have long been and are still busy in Yosemite's gardens and groves. All that is accessible and destructible is being rapidly destroyed—more rapidly than in any other Yosemite in the Sierra, though this is the only one that is under the special protection of the Government. And by far the greater part of this destruction of the fineness of wildness is of a kind that can claim no right relationship with that which necessarily follows use.

Century Magazine, September 1890

The American Forests

THE forests of America, however slighted by man, must have been a great delight to God; for they were the best he ever planted. The whole continent was a garden, and from the beginning it seemed to be favored above all the other wild parks and gardens of the globe. To prepare the ground, it was rolled and sifted in seas with infinite loving deliberation and forethought, lifted into the light, submerged and warmed over and over again, pressed and crumpled into folds and ridges, mountains, and hills, subsoiled with heaving volcanic fires, ploughed and ground and sculptured into scenery and soil with glaciers and rivers,—every feature growing and changing from beauty to beauty, higher and higher. And in the fullness of time it was planted in groves, and belts, and broad, exuberant, mantling forests, with the largest, most varied, most fruitful, and most beautiful trees in the world. Bright seas made its border, with wave embroidery and icebergs; gray deserts were outspread in the middle of it, mossy tundras on the north, savannas on the south, and blooming prairies and plains; while lakes and rivers shone through all the vast forests and openings, and happy birds and beasts gave delightful animation. Everywhere, everywhere over all the blessed continent, there were beauty and melody and kindly, wholesome, foodful abundance.

These forests were composed of about five hundred species of trees, all of them in some way useful to man, ranging in size from twenty-five feet in height and less than one foot in diameter at the ground to four hundred feet in height and more than twenty feet in diameter,—lordly monarchs proclaiming the gospel of beauty like apostles. For many a century after the ice-ploughs were melted, nature fed them and dressed them every day,—working like a man, a loving, devoted, painstaking gardener; fingering every leaf and flower and mossy furrowed bole; bending, trimming, modeling, balancing; painting them with the loveliest colors; bringing over them now clouds with cooling shadows and showers, now sunshine; fanning them with gentle winds and rustling their leaves; exercising them in every fibre with storms, and pruning them; loading them with flowers and fruit, loading them with snow, and ever making them more beautiful as the years rolled by. Wide-branching oak and elm in endless variety, walnut and maple, chestnut and beech, ilex and locust, touching limb to limb, spread a leafy translucent canopy along the coast of the Atlantic over the wrinkled folds and ridges of the Alleghanies,—a green billowy sea in summer, golden and purple in autumn, pearly gray like a steadfast frozen mist of interlacing branches and sprays in leafless, restful winter.

To the southward stretched dark, level-topped cypresses in knobby, tangled swamps, grassy savannas in the midst of them like lakes of light, groves of gay, sparkling spice-trees, magnolias and palms, glossy-leaved and blooming and shining continually. To the northward, over Maine and Ottawa, rose hosts of spiry, rosiny evergreens,—white pine and spruce, hemlock and cedar, shoulder to shoulder, laden with purple cones, their myriad needles sparkling and shimmering, covering hills and swamps, rocky headlands and domes, ever bravely aspiring and seeking the sky; the ground in their shade now snow-clad and frozen, now mossy and flowery; beaver meadows here and there, full of lilies and grass; lakes gleaming like eyes, and a silvery embroidery of rivers and creeks watering and brightening all the vast glad wilderness.

Thence westward were oak and elm, hickory and tupelo, gum and liriodendron, sassafras and ash, linden and laurel, spreading on ever wider in glorious exuberance over the great fertile basin of the Mississippi, over damp level bottoms, low dimpling hollows, and round dotting hills, embosoming sunny prairies and cheery park openings, half sunshine, half shade; while a dark wilderness of pines covered the region around the Great Lakes. Thence still westward swept the forests to right and left around grassy plains and deserts a thousand miles wide: irrepressible hosts of spruce and pine, aspen and willow, nut-pine and juniper, cactus and yucca, caring nothing for drought, extending undaunted from mountain to mountain, over mesa and desert, to join the darkening multitudes of pines that covered the high Rocky ranges and the glorious forests along the coast of the moist and balmy Pacific, where new species of pine, giant cedars and spruces, silver firs and Sequoias, kings of their race, growing close together like grass in a meadow, poised their brave domes and spires in the sky, three hundred feet above the ferns and the lilies that enameled the ground; towering serene through the long centuries, preaching God's forestry fresh from heaven.

Here the forests reached their highest development. Hence they went wavering northward over icy Alaska, brave spruce and fir, poplar and birch, by the coasts and the rivers, to within sight of the Arctic Ocean. American forests! the glory of the world! Surveyed thus from the east to the west, from the north to the south, they are rich beyond thought, immortal, immeasurable, enough and to spare for every feeding, sheltering beast and bird, insect and son of Adam; and nobody need have cared had there been no pines in Norway, no cedars and deodars on Lebanon and the Himalayas, no vine-clad selvas in the basin of the Amazon. With such variety, harmony, and triumphant exuberance, even nature, it would seem, might have rested content with the forests of North America, and planted no more.

So they appeared a few centuries ago when they were rejoicing in wildness. The Indians with stone axes could do them no more harm than could gnawing beavers and browsing moose. Even the fires of the Indians and the fierce shattering lightning seemed to work together only for good in clearing spots here and there for smooth garden prairies, and openings for sunflowers seeking the light. But when the steel axe of the white man rang out on the startled air their doom was sealed. Every tree heard the bodeful sound, and pillars of smoke gave the sign in the sky.

I suppose we need not go mourning the buffaloes. In the nature of things they had to give place to better cattle, though the change might have been made without barbarous wickedness. Likewise many of nature's five hundred kinds of wild trees had to make way for orchards and cornfields. In the settlement and civilization of the country, bread more than timber or beauty was wanted; and in the blindness of hunger, the early settlers, claiming Heaven as their guide, regarded God's trees as only a larger kind of pernicious weeds, extremely hard to get rid of. Accordingly, with no eye to the future, these pious destroyers waged interminable forest wars; chips flew thick and fast; trees in their beauty fell crashing by millions, smashed to confusion, and the smoke of their burning has been rising to heaven more than two hundred years. After the Atlantic coast from Maine to Georgia had been mostly cleared and scorched into melancholy ruins, the overflowing multitude of bread and money seekers poured over the Alleghanies into the fertile middle West, spreading ruthless devastation ever wider and farther over the rich valley of the Mississippi and the vast shadowy pine region about the Great Lakes. Thence still westward, the invading horde of destroyers called settlers made its fiery way over the broad Rocky Mountains, felling and burning more fiercely than ever, until at last it has reached the wild side of the continent, and entered the last of the great aboriginal forests on the shores of the Pacific.

Surely, then, it should not be wondered at that lovers of their country, bewailing its baldness, are now crying aloud, "Save what is left of the forests!" Clearing has surely now gone far enough; soon timber will be scarce, and not a grove will be left to rest in or pray in. The remnant protected will yield plenty of timber, a perennial harvest for every right use, without further diminution of its area, and will continue to cover the springs of the rivers that rise in the mountains and give irrigating waters to the dry valleys at their feet, prevent wasting floods and be a blessing to everybody forever.

Every other civilized nation in the world has been compelled to care for its forests, and so must we if waste and destruction are not to go on to the bitter end, leaving America as barren as Palestine or Spain. In its calmer moments, in the midst of bewildering hunger and war and restless over-industry, Prussia has learned that the forest plays an important part in human progress, and that the advance in civilization only makes it more indispensable. It has, therefore, as shown by Mr. Pinchot, refused to deliver its forests to more or less speedy destruction by permitting them to pass into private ownership. But the state woodlands are not allowed to lie idle. On the contrary, they are made to produce as much timber as is possible without spoiling them. In the administration of its forests, the state righteously considers itself bound to treat them as a trust for the nation as a whole, and to keep in view the common good of the people for all time.

In France no government forests have been sold since 1870. On the other hand, about one half of the fifty million francs spent on forestry has been given to engineering works, to make the replanting of denuded areas possible. The disappearance of the forests in the first place, it is claimed, may be traced in most cases directly to mountain pasturage. The provisions of the Code concerning private woodlands are substantially these: no private owner may clear his woodlands without giving notice to the government at least four months in advance, and the forest service may forbid the clearing on the following grounds,—to maintain the soil on mountains, to defend the soil against erosion and flooding by rivers or torrents, to insure the existence of springs and watercourses, to protect the dunes and seashore, etc. A proprietor who has cleared his forest without permission is subject to heavy fine, and in addition may be made to replant the cleared area.

In Switzerland, after many laws like our own had been found wanting, the Swiss forest school was established in 1865, and soon after the federal forest law was enacted, which is binding over nearly two thirds of the country. Under its provisions, the cantons must appoint and pay the number of suitably educated foresters required for the fulfillment of the forest law; and in the organization of a normally stocked forest, the object of first importance must be the cutting each year of an amount of timber equal to the total annual increase, and no more.

The Russian government passed a law in 1888, declaring that clearing is forbidden in protected forests, and is allowed in others "only when its effects will not be to disturb the suitable relations which should exist between forest and agricultural lands."

Even Japan is ahead of us in the management of her forests. They cover an area of about twenty-nine million acres. The feudal lords valued the woodlands, and enacted vigorous protective laws; and when, in the latest civil war, the Mikado government destroyed the feudal system, it declared the forests that had belonged to the feudal lords to be the property of the state, promulgated a forest law binding on the whole kingdom, and founded a school of forestry in Tokio. The forest service does not rest satisfied with the present proportion of woodland, but looks to planting the best forest trees it can find in any country, if likely to be useful and to thrive in Japan.

In India systematic forest management was begun about forty years ago, under difficulties—presented by the character of the country, the prevalence of running fires, opposition from lumbermen, settlers, etc.—not unlike those which confront us now. Of the total area of government forests, perhaps seventy million acres, fifty-five million acres have been brought under the control of the forestry department,—a larger area than that of all our national parks and reservations. The chief aims of the administration are effective protection of the forests from fire, an efficient system of regeneration, and cheap transportation of the forest products; the results so far have been most beneficial and encouraging.

It seems, therefore, that almost every civilized nation can give us a lesson on the management and care of forests. So far our government has done nothing effective with its forests, though the best in the world, but is like a rich and foolish spendthrift who has inherited a magnificent estate in perfect order, and then has left his rich fields and meadows, forests and parks, to be sold and plundered and wasted at will, depending on their inexhaustible abundance. Now it is plain that the forests are not inexhaustible, and that quick measures must be taken if ruin is to be avoided. Year by year the remnant is growing smaller before the axe and fire, while the laws in existence provide neither for the protection of the timber from destruction nor for its use where it is most needed.

As is shown by Mr. E. A. Bowers, formerly Inspector of the Public Land Service, the foundation of our protective policy, which has never protected, is an act passed March 1, 1817, which authorized the Secretary of the Navy to reserve lands producing live-oak and cedar, for the sole purpose of supplying timber for the navy of the United States. An extension of this law by the passage of the act of March 2, 1831, provided that if any person should cut live-oak or red cedar trees or *other timber* from the lands of the United States for any other purpose than the construction of the navy, such person should pay a fine not less than triple the value of the timber cut, and be imprisoned for a period not exceeding twelve months. Upon this old law, as Mr. Bowers points out, having the construction of a wooden navy in view, the United States government has to-day chiefly to rely in protecting its timber throughout the arid regions of the West, where none of the naval timber which the law had in mind is to be found.

By the act of June 3, 1878, timber can be taken from public lands not subject to entry under any existing laws except for minerals, by *bona fide* residents of the Rocky Mountain states and territories and the Dakotas. Under the timber and stone act, of the same date, land in the Pacific States and Nevada, valuable mainly for timber, and unfit for cultivation if the timber is removed, can be purchased for two dollars and a half an acre, under certain restrictions. By the act of March 3, 1875, all land-grant and right-of-way railroads are authorized to take timber from the public lands adjacent to their lines for construction purposes; and they have taken it with a vengeance, destroying a hundred times more than they have used, mostly by allowing fires to run into the woods. The settlement laws, under which a settler may enter lands valuable for timber as well as for agriculture, furnish another means of obtaining title to public timber.

With the exception of the timber culture act, under which, in consideration of planting a few acres of seedlings, settlers on the treeless plains got 160 acres each, the above is the only legislation aiming to protect and promote the planting of forests. In no other way than under some one of these laws can a citizen of the United States make any use of the public forests. To show the results of the timber-planting act, it need only be stated that of the thirty-eight million acres entered under it, less than one million acres have been patented. This means that less than fifty thousand acres have been planted with stunted, woebegone, almost hopeless sprouts of trees, while at the same time the government has allowed millions of acres of the grandest forest trees to be stolen or destroyed, or sold for nothing. Under the act of June 3, 1878, settlers in Colorado and the Territories were allowed to cut timber for mining and educational purposes from mineral land, which in the practical West means both cutting and burning anywhere and everywhere, for any purpose, on any sort of public land. Thus, the prospector, the miner, and mining and railroad companies are allowed by law to take all the timber they like for their mines and roads, and the forbidden settler, if there are no mineral lands near his farm or stock-ranch, or none that he knows of, can hardly be expected to forbear taking what he needs wherever he can find it. Timber is as necessary as bread, and no scheme of management failing to recognize and properly provide for this want can possibly be maintained. In any case, it will be hard to teach the pioneers that it is wrong to steal government timber. Taking from the government is with them the same as taking from nature, and their consciences flinch no more in cutting timber from the wild forests than in drawing water from a lake or river. As for reservation and protection of forests, it seems as silly and needless to them as protection and reservation of the ocean would be, both appearing to be boundless and inexhaustible.

The special land agents employed by the General Land Office to protect the public domain from timber depredations are supposed to collect testimony to sustain prosecution and to superintend such prosecution on behalf of the government, which is represented by the district attorneys. But timber thieves of the Western class are seldom convicted, for the good reason that most of the jurors who try such cases are themselves as guilty as those on trial. The effect of the present confused, discriminating, and unjust system has been to place almost the whole population in opposition to the government; and as conclusive of its futility, as shown by Mr. Bowers, we need only state that during the seven years from 1881 to 1887 inclusive, the value of the timber reported stolen from the government lands was $36,719,935, and the amount recovered was $478,073, while the cost of the services of special agents alone was $455,000, to which must be added the expense of the trials. Thus for nearly thirty-seven million dollars' worth of timber the government got less than nothing; and the value of that consumed by running fires during the same period, without benefit even to thieves, was probably over two hundred millions of dollars. Land commissioners and Secretaries of the Interior have repeatedly called attention to this ruinous state of affairs, and asked Congress to enact the requisite legislation for reasonable reform. But, busied with tariffs, etc., Congress has given no heed to these or other appeals, and our forests, the most valuable and the most destructible of all the natural resources of the country, are being robbed and burned more rapidly than ever. The annual appropriation for so-called "protection service" is hardly sufficient to keep twenty-five timber agents in the field, and as far as any efficient protection of timber is concerned these agents themselves might as well be timber.*

That a change from robbery and ruin to a permanent rational policy is urgently needed nobody with the slightest knowledge of American forests will deny. In the East and along the northern Pacific coast, where the rainfall is abundant, comparatively few care keenly what becomes of the trees as long as fuel and lumber are not noticeably dear. But in the Rocky Mountains and California and Arizona, where the forests are inflammable, and where the fertility of the lowlands depends upon irrigation, public opinion is growing stronger every year in favor of permanent protection by the federal government of all the forests that cover the sources of the streams. Even lumbermen in these regions, long accustomed to steal, are now willing and anxious to buy lumber for their mills under cover of law: some possibly from a late second growth of honesty, but most, especially the small mill-owners, simply because it no longer pays to steal where all may not only steal, but also destroy, and in particular because it costs about as much to steal timber for one mill as for ten, and, therefore, the ordinary lumberman can no longer compete with the large corporations. Many of the miners find that timber is already becoming scarce and dear on the denuded hills around their mills, and they, too, are asking for protection of forests, at least against fire. The slow-going, unthrifty farmers, also, are beginning to realize that when the timber is stripped from the mountains the irrigating streams dry up in summer, and are destructive in winter; that soil, scenery, and everything slips off with the trees: so of course they are coming into the ranks of tree-friends.

Of all the magnificent coniferous forests around the Great Lakes, once the property of the United States, scarcely any belong to it now. They have disappeared in lumber and smoke, mostly smoke, and the government got not one cent for them; only the land they were growing on was considered valuable,

---

*A change for the better, compelled by public opinion, is now going on,— 1901.

and two and a half dollars an acre was charged for it. Here and there in the Southern States there are still considerable areas of timbered government land, but these are comparatively unimportant. Only the forests of the West are significant in size and value, and these, although still great, are rapidly vanishing. Last summer, of the unrivaled redwood forests of the Pacific Coast Range, the United States Forestry Commission could not find a single quarter-section that remained in the hands of the government.*

Under the timber and stone act of 1878, which might well have been called the "dust and ashes act," any citizen of the United States could take up one hundred and sixty acres of timber land, and by paying two dollars and a half an acre for it obtain title. There was some virtuous effort made with a view to limit the operations of the act by requiring that the purchaser should make affidavit that he was entering the land exclusively for his own use, and by not allowing any association to enter more than one hundred and sixty acres. Nevertheless, under this act wealthy corporations have fraudulently obtained title to from ten thousand to twenty thousand acres or more. The plan was usually as follows: A mill company, desirous of getting title to a large body of redwood or sugar-pine land, first blurred the eyes and ears of the land agents, and then hired men to enter the land they wanted, and immediately deed it to the company after a nominal compliance with the law; false swearing in the wilderness against the government being held of no account. In one case which came under the observation of Mr. Bowers, it was the practice of a lumber company to hire the entire crew of every vessel which might happen to touch at any port in the redwood belt, to enter one hundred and sixty acres each and immediately deed the land to the company, in consideration of the company's paying all expenses and giving the jolly sailors fifty dollars apiece for their trouble.

By such methods have our magnificent redwoods and much of the sugar-pine forests of the Sierra Nevada been absorbed by foreign and resident capitalists. Uncle Sam is not often called

*The State of California recently appropriated two hundred and fifty thousand dollars to buy a block of redwood land near Santa Cruz for a state park. A much larger national park should be made in Humboldt or Mendocino county.

a fool in business matters, yet he has sold millions of acres
of timber land at two dollars and a half an acre on which a
single tree was worth more than a hundred dollars. But this
priceless land has been patented, and nothing can be done now
about the crazy bargain. According to the everlasting laws of
righteousness, even the fraudulent buyers at less than one per
cent of its value are making little or nothing, on account of
fierce competition. The trees are felled, and about half of each
giant is left on the ground to be converted into smoke and
ashes; the better half is sawed into choice lumber and sold to
citizens of the United States or to foreigners: thus robbing the
country of its glory and impoverishing it without right benefit
to anybody,—a bad, black business from beginning to end.

The redwood is one of the few conifers that sprout from
the stump and roots, and it declares itself willing to begin
immediately to repair the damage of the lumberman and also
that of the forest-burner. As soon as a redwood is cut down or
burned it sends up a crowd of eager, hopeful shoots, which, if
allowed to grow, would in a few decades attain a height of a
hundred feet, and the strongest of them would finally become
giants as great as the original tree. Gigantic second and third
growth trees are found in the redwoods, forming magnificent
temple-like circles around charred ruins more than a thousand
years old. But not one denuded acre in a hundred is allowed
to raise a new forest growth. On the contrary, all the brains,
religion, and superstition of the neighborhood are brought
into play to prevent a new growth. The sprouts from the roots
and stumps are cut off again and again, with zealous concern
as to the best time and method of making death sure. In the
clearings of one of the largest mills on the coast we found
thirty men at work, last summer, cutting off redwood shoots
"in the dark of the moon," claiming that all the stumps and
roots cleared at this auspicious time would send up no more
shoots. Anyhow, these vigorous, almost immortal trees are
killed at last, and black stumps are now their only monuments
over most of the chopped and burned areas.

The redwood is the glory of the Coast Range. It extends
along the western slope, in a nearly continuous belt about ten
miles wide, from beyond the Oregon boundary to the south

of Santa Cruz, a distance of nearly four hundred miles, and in massive, sustained grandeur and closeness of growth surpasses all the other timber woods of the world. Trees from ten to fifteen feet in diameter and three hundred feet high are not uncommon, and a few attain a height of three hundred and fifty feet or even four hundred, with a diameter at the base of fifteen to twenty feet or more, while the ground beneath them is a garden of fresh, exuberant ferns, lilies, gaultheria, and rhododendron. This grand tree, Sequoia sempervirens, is surpassed in size only by its near relative, Sequoia gigantea, or Big Tree, of the Sierra Nevada, if, indeed, it is surpassed. The sempervirens is certainly the taller of the two. The gigantea attains a greater girth, and is heavier, more noble in port, and more sublimely beautiful. These two Sequoias are all that are known to exist in the world, though in former geological times the genus was common and had many species. The redwood is restricted to the Coast Range, and the Big Tree to the Sierra.

As timber the redwood is too good to live. The largest sawmills ever built are busy along its seaward border, "with all the modern improvements," but so immense is the yield per acre it will be long ere the supply is exhausted. The Big Tree is also, to some extent, being made into lumber. It is far less abundant than the redwood, and is, fortunately, less accessible, extending along the western flank of the Sierra in a partially interrupted belt, about two hundred and fifty miles long, at a height of from four to eight thousand feet above the sea. The enormous logs, too heavy to handle, are blasted into manageable dimensions with gunpowder. A large portion of the best timber is thus shattered and destroyed, and, with the huge, knotty tops, is left in ruins for tremendous fires that kill every tree within their range, great and small. Still, the species is not in danger of extinction. It has been planted and is flourishing over a great part of Europe, and magnificent sections of the aboriginal forests have been reserved as national and State parks,—the Mariposa Sequoia Grove, near Yosemite, managed by the State of California, and the General Grant and Sequoia national parks on the Kings, Kaweah, and Tule rivers, efficiently guarded by a small troop of United States cavalry under the direction of the Secretary of the Interior. But there is not a single specimen of the redwood in any national park. Only by gift or purchase, so far as I know, can the government get back into its possession a single acre of this wonderful forest.

The legitimate demands on the forests that have passed into private ownership, as well as those in the hands of the government, are increasing every year with the rapid settlement and upbuilding of the country, but the methods of lumbering are as yet grossly wasteful. In most mills only the best portions of the best trees are used, while the ruins are left on the ground to feed great fires, which kill much of what is left of the less desirable timber, together with the seedlings, on which the permanence of the forest depends. Thus every mill is a centre of destruction far more severe from waste and fire than from use. The same thing is true of the mines, which consume and destroy indirectly immense quantities of timber with their innumerable fires, accidental or set to make open ways, and often without regard to how far they run. The prospector deliberately sets fires to clear off the woods just where they are densest, to lay the rocks bare and make the discovery of mines easier. Sheep-owners and their shepherds also set fires everywhere through the woods in the fall to facilitate the march of their countless flocks the next summer, and perhaps in some places to improve the pasturage. The axe is not yet at the root of every tree, but the sheep is, or was before the national parks were established and guarded by the military, the only effective and reliable arm of the government free from the blight of politics. Not only do the shepherds, at the driest time of the year, set fire to everything that will burn, but the sheep consume every green leaf, not sparing even the young conifers, when they are in a starving condition from crowding, and they rake and dibble the loose soil of the mountain sides for the spring floods to wash away, and thus at last leave the ground barren.

Of all the destroyers that infest the woods, the shake-maker seems the happiest. Twenty or thirty years ago, shakes, a kind of long, boardlike shingles split with a mallet and a frow, were in great demand for covering barns and sheds, and many are used still in preference to common shingles, especially those made from the sugar-pine, which do not warp or crack in the hottest sunshine. Drifting adventurers in California, after harvest and threshing are over, oftentimes meet to discuss their plans for the winter, and their talk is interesting. Once, in a company of this kind, I heard a man say, as he peacefully smoked his pipe: "Boys, as soon as this job's done I'm goin' into the duck business. There's big money in it, and your grub costs nothing. Tule Joe made five hundred dollars last winter on mallard and teal. Shot 'em on the Joaquin, tied 'em in dozens by the neck, and shipped 'em to San Francisco. And when he was tired wading in the sloughs and touched with rheumatiz, he just knocked off on ducks, and went to the Contra Costa hills for dove and quail. It's a mighty good business, and you're your own boss, and the whole thing's fun."

Another of the company, a bushy-bearded fellow, with a trace of brag in his voice, drawled out: "Bird business is well enough for some, but bear is my game, with a deer and a California lion thrown in now and then for change. There's always market for bear grease, and sometimes you can sell the hams. They're good as hog hams any day. And you are your own boss in my business, too, if the bears ain't too big and too many for you. Old grizzlies I despise,—they want cannon to kill 'em; but the blacks and browns are beauties for grease, and when once I get 'em just right, and draw a bead on 'em, I fetch 'em every time." Another said he was going to catch up a lot of mustangs as soon as the rains set in, hitch them to a gang-plough, and go to farming on the San Joaquin plains for wheat. But most preferred the shake business, until something more profitable and as sure could be found, with equal comfort and independence.

With a cheap mustang or mule to carry a pair of blankets, a sack of flour, a few pounds of coffee, and an axe, a frow, and a cross-cut saw, the shake-maker ascends the mountains to the pine belt where it is most accessible, usually by some mine or mill road. Then he strikes off into the virgin woods, where the sugar pine, king of all the hundred species of pines in the world in size and beauty, towers on the open sunny slopes of the Sierra in the fullness of its glory. Selecting a favorable spot for a cabin near a meadow with a stream, he unpacks his animal and stakes it out on the meadow. Then he chops into one after another of the pines, until he finds one that he feels sure will split freely, cuts this down, saws off a section four feet long, splits it, and from this first cut, perhaps seven feet in diameter, he gets shakes enough for a cabin and its furniture,—walls, roof, door, bedstead, table, and stool. Besides his labor, only a few pounds of nails are required. Sapling poles form the frame of the airy building, usually about six feet by eight in size, on which the shakes are nailed, with the edges overlapping. A few bolts from the same section that the shakes were made from are split into square sticks and built up to form a chimney, the inside and interspaces being plastered and filled in with mud. Thus, with abundance of fuel, shelter and comfort by his own fireside are secured. Then he goes to work sawing and splitting for the market, tying the shakes in bundles of fifty or a hundred. They are four feet long, four inches wide, and about one fourth of an inch thick. The first few thousands he sells or trades at the nearest mill or store, getting provisions in exchange. Then he advertises, in whatever way he can, that he has excellent sugar-pine shakes for sale, easy of access and cheap.

Only the lower, perfectly clear, free-splitting portions of the giant pines are used,—perhaps ten to twenty feet from a tree two hundred and fifty in height; all the rest is left a mass of ruins, to rot or to feed the forest fires, while thousands are hacked deeply and rejected in proving the grain. Over nearly all of the more accessible slopes of the Sierra and Cascade mountains in southern Oregon, at a height of from three to six thousand feet above the sea, and for a distance of about six hundred miles, this waste and confusion extends. Happy robbers! dwelling in the most beautiful woods, in the most salubrious climate, breathing delightful odors both day and night, drinking cool living water,—roses and lilies at their feet in the spring, shedding fragrance and ringing bells as if cheering them on in their desolating work. There is none to say them nay. They buy no land, pay no taxes, dwell in a paradise with no forbidding angel either from Washington or from heaven. Every one of the frail shake shanties is a centre of destruction, and the extent of the ravages wrought in this quiet way is in the aggregate enormous.

It is not generally known that, notwithstanding the immense quantities of timber cut every year for foreign and home markets and mines, from five to ten times as much is destroyed as is used, chiefly by running forest fires that only the federal government can stop. Travelers through the West in summer are not likely to forget the fire-work displayed along the various railway tracks. Thoreau, when contemplating the destruction of the forests on the east side of the continent, said that soon the country would be so bald that every man would have to grow whiskers to hide its nakedness, but he thanked God that at least the sky was safe. Had he gone West he would have found out that the sky was not safe; for all through the summer months, over most of the mountain regions, the smoke of mill and forest fires is so thick and black that no sunbeam can pierce it. The whole sky, with clouds, sun, moon, and stars, is simply blotted out. There is no real sky and no scenery. Not a mountain is left in the landscape. At least none is in sight from the lowlands, and they all might as well be on the moon, as far as scenery is concerned.

The half-dozen transcontinental railroad companies advertise the beauties of their lines in gorgeous many-colored folders, each claiming its as the "scenic route." "The route of superior desolation"—the smoke, dust, and ashes route—would be a more truthful description. Every train rolls on through dismal smoke and barbarous, melancholy ruins; and the companies might well cry in their advertisements: "Come! travel our way. Ours is the blackest. It is the only genuine Erebus route. The sky is black and the ground is black, and on either side there is a continuous border of black stumps and logs and blasted trees appealing to heaven for help as if still half alive, and their mute eloquence is most interestingly touching. The blackness is perfect. On account of the superior skill of our workmen, advantages of climate, and the kind of trees, the charring is generally deeper along our line, and the ashes are deeper, and the confusion and desolation displayed can never be rivaled. No other route on this continent so fully illustrates the abomination of desolation." Such a claim would be reasonable, as each seems the worst, whatever route you chance to take.

Of course a way had to be cleared through the woods. But the felled timber is not worked up into firewood for the engines and into lumber for the company's use; it is left lying in vulgar confusion, and is fired from time to time by sparks from locomotives or by the workmen camping along the line. The fires, whether accidental or set, are allowed to run into the woods as far as they may, thus assuring comprehensive destruction. The directors of a line that guarded against fires, and cleared a clean gap edged with living trees, and fringed and mantled with the grass and flowers and beautiful seedlings that are ever ready and willing to spring up, might justly boast of the beauty of their road; for nature is always ready to heal every scar. But there is no such road on the western side of the continent. Last summer, in the Rocky Mountains, I saw six fires started by sparks from a locomotive within a distance of three miles, and nobody was in sight to prevent them from spreading. They might run into the adjacent forests and burn the timber from hundreds of square miles; not a man in the State would care to spend an hour in fighting them, as long as his own fences and buildings were not threatened.

Notwithstanding all the waste and use which have been going on unchecked like a storm for more than two centuries, it is not yet too late—though it is high time—for the government to begin a rational administration of its forests. About seventy million acres it still owns,—enough for all the country, if wisely used. These residual forests are generally on mountain slopes, just where they are doing the most good, and where their removal would be followed by the greatest number of evils; the lands they cover are too rocky and high for agriculture, and can never be made as valuable for any other crop as for the present crop of trees. It has been shown over and over again that if these mountains were to be stripped of their trees and underbrush, and kept bare and sodless by hordes of sheep and the innumerable fires the shepherds set, besides those of the millmen, prospectors, shake-makers, and all sorts of adventurers, both lowlands and mountains would speedily become little better than deserts, compared with their present beneficent fertility. During heavy rainfalls and while the winter accumulations of snow were melting, the larger streams would swell into destructive torrents, cutting deep, rugged-edged gullies, carrying away the fertile humus and soil as well as sand and rocks, filling up and overflowing their lower channels, and covering the lowland fields with raw detritus. Drought and barrenness would follow.

In their natural condition, or under wise management, keeping out destructive sheep, preventing fires, selecting the trees that should be cut for lumber, and preserving the young ones and the shrubs and sod of herbaceous vegetation, these forests would be a never failing fountain of wealth and beauty. The cool shades of the forest give rise to moist beds and currents of air, and the sod of grasses and the various flowering plants and shrubs thus fostered, together with the network and sponge of tree roots, absorb and hold back the rain and the waters from melting snow, compelling them to ooze and percolate and flow gently through the soil in streams that never dry. All the pine needles and rootlets and blades of grass, and the fallen, decaying trunks of trees, are dams, storing the bounty of the clouds and dispensing it in perennial life-giving streams, instead of allowing it to gather suddenly and rush headlong in short-lived devastating floods. Everybody on the dry side of the continent is beginning to find this out, and, in view of the waste going on, is growing more and more anxious for government protection. The outcries we hear against forest reservations come mostly from thieves who are wealthy and steal timber by wholesale. They have so long been allowed to steal and destroy in peace that any impediment to forest robbery is denounced as a cruel and irreligious interference with "vested rights," likely to endanger the repose of all ungodly welfare.

Gold, gold, gold! How strong a voice that metal has!

"O wae for the siller, it is sae preva'lin'!"

Even in Congress a sizable chunk of gold, carefully concealed, will outtalk and outfight all the nation on a subject like forestry, well smothered in ignorance, and in which the money interests of only a few are conspicuously involved. Under these circumstances, the bawling, blethering oratorical stuff drowns the voice of God himself. Yet the dawn of a new day in forestry is breaking. Honest citizens see that only the rights of the government are being trampled, not those of the settlers. Only what belongs to all alike is reserved, and every acre that is left should be held together under the federal government as a basis for a general policy of administration for the public good. The people will not always be deceived by selfish opposition, whether from lumber and mining corporations or from sheepmen and prospectors, however cunningly brought forward underneath fables and gold.

Emerson says that things refuse to be mismanaged long. An exception would seem to be found in the case of our forests,

which have been mismanaged rather long, and now come desperately near being like smashed eggs and spilt milk. Still, in
the long run the world does not move backward. The wonderful advance made in the last few years, in creating four national
parks in the West, and thirty forest reservations, embracing
nearly forty million acres; and in the planting of the borders of
streets and highways and spacious parks in all the great cities,
to satisfy the natural taste and hunger for landscape beauty
and righteousness that God has put, in some measure, into
every human being and animal, shows the trend of awakening
public opinion. The making of the far-famed New York Central
Park was opposed by even good men, with misguided pluck,
perseverance, and ingenuity; but straight right won its way, and
now that park is appreciated. So we confidently believe it will
be with our great national parks and forest reservations. There
will be a period of indifference on the part of the rich, sleepy
with wealth, and of the toiling millions, sleepy with poverty,
most of whom never saw a forest; a period of screaming protest
and objection from the plunderers, who are as unconscionable
and enterprising as Satan. But light is surely coming, and the
friends of destruction will preach and bewail in vain.

The United States government has always been proud of
the welcome it has extended to good men of every nation,
seeking freedom and homes and bread. Let them be welcomed
still as nature welcomes them, to the woods as well as to the
prairies and plains. No place is too good for good men, and
still there is room. They are invited to heaven, and may well be
allowed in America. Every place is made better by them. Let
them be as free to pick gold and gems from the hills, to cut
and hew, dig and plant, for homes and bread, as the birds are
to pick berries from the wild bushes, and moss and leaves for
nests. The ground will be glad to feed them, and the pines will
come down from the mountains for their homes as willingly
as the cedars came from Lebanon for Solomon's temple. Nor
will the woods be the worse for this use, or their benign influences be diminished any more than the sun is diminished by
shining. Mere destroyers, however, tree-killers, wool and mutton men, spreading death and confusion in the fairest groves
and gardens ever planted,—let the government hasten to cast
them out and make an end of them. For it must be told again

and again, and be burningly borne in mind, that just now, while protective measures are being deliberated languidly, destruction and use are speeding on faster and farther every day. The axe and saw are insanely busy, chips are flying thick as snowflakes, and every summer thousands of acres of priceless forests, with their underbrush, soil, springs, climate, scenery, and religion, are vanishing away in clouds of smoke, while, except in the national parks, not one forest guard is employed.

All sorts of local laws and regulations have been tried and found wanting, and the costly lessons of our own experience, as well as that of every civilized nation, show conclusively that the fate of the remnant of our forests is in the hands of the federal government, and that if the remnant is to be saved at all, it must be saved quickly.

Any fool can destroy trees. They cannot run away; and if they could, they would still be destroyed,—chased and hunted down as long as fun or a dollar could be got out of their bark hides, branching horns, or magnificent bole backbones. Few that fell trees plant them; nor would planting avail much towards getting back anything like the noble primeval forests. During a man's life only saplings can be grown, in the place of the old trees—tens of centuries old—that have been destroyed. It took more than three thousand years to make some of the trees in these Western woods,—trees that are still standing in perfect strength and beauty, waving and singing in the mighty forests of the Sierra. Through all the wonderful, eventful centuries since Christ's time—and long before that—God has cared for these trees, saved them from drought, disease, avalanches, and a thousand straining, leveling tempests and floods; but he cannot save them from fools,—only Uncle Sam can do that.

from *Our National Parks*, 1901

The Wild Parks and Forest Reservations of the West

"Keep not standing fix'd and rooted,
    Briskly venture, briskly roam;
Head and hand, where'er thou foot it,
    And stout heart are still at home.
In each land the sun does visit
    We are gay, whate'er betide:
To give room for wandering is it
    That the world was made so wide."

THE tendency nowadays to wander in wildernesses is delightful to see. Thousands of tired, nerve-shaken, over-civilized people are beginning to find out that going to the mountains is going home; that wildness is a necessity; and that mountain parks and reservations are useful not only as fountains of timber and irrigating rivers, but as fountains of life. Awakening from the stupefying effects of the vice of over-industry and the deadly apathy of luxury, they are trying as best they can to mix and enrich their own little ongoings with those of Nature, and to get rid of rust and disease. Briskly venturing and roaming, some are washing off sins and cobweb cares of the devil's spinning in all-day storms on mountains; sauntering in rosiny pinewoods or in gentian meadows, brushing through chaparral, bending down and parting sweet, flowery sprays; tracing rivers to their sources, getting in touch with the nerves of Mother Earth; jumping from rock to rock, feeling the life of them, learning the songs of them, panting in whole-souled exercise, and rejoicing in deep, long-drawn breaths of pure wildness. This is fine and natural and full of promise. So also is the growing interest in the care and preservation of forests and wild places in general, and in the half wild parks and gardens of towns. Even the scenery habit in its most artificial forms, mixed with spectacles, silliness, and kodaks; its devotees arrayed more gorgeously than scarlet tanagers, frightening the wild game with red umbrellas,—even this is encouraging, and may well be regarded as a hopeful sign of the times.

All the Western mountains are still rich in wildness, and by means of good roads are being brought nearer civilization every year. To the sane and free it will hardly seem necessary to cross the continent in search of wild beauty, however easy the way, for they find it in abundance wherever they chance to be. Like Thoreau they see forests in orchards and patches of huckleberry brush, and oceans in ponds and drops of dew. Few in these hot, dim, strenuous times are quite sane or free; choked with care like clocks full of dust, laboriously doing so much good and making so much money,—or so little,—they are no longer good for themselves.

When, like a merchant taking a list of his goods, we take stock of our wildness, we are glad to see how much of even the most destructible kind is still unspoiled. Looking at our continent as scenery when it was all wild, lying between beautiful seas, the starry sky above it, the starry rocks beneath it, to compare its sides, the East and the West, would be like comparing the sides of a rainbow. But it is no longer equally beautiful. The rainbows of to-day are, I suppose, as bright as those that first spanned the sky; and some of our landscapes are growing more beautiful from year to year, notwithstanding the clearing, trampling work of civilization. New plants and animals are enriching woods and gardens, and many landscapes wholly new, with divine sculpture and architecture, are just now coming to the light of day as the mantling folds of creative glaciers are being withdrawn, and life in a thousand cheerful, beautiful forms is pushing into them, and new-born rivers are beginning to sing and shine in them. The old rivers, too, are growing longer, like healthy trees, gaining new branches and lakes as the residual glaciers at their highest sources on the mountains recede, while the rootlike branches in their flat deltas are at the same time spreading farther and wider into the seas and making new lands.

Under the control of the vast mysterious forces of the interior of the earth all the continents and islands are slowly rising or sinking. Most of the mountains are diminishing in size under the wearing action of the weather, though a few are increasing in height and girth, especially the volcanic ones, as fresh floods of molten rocks are piled on their summits and spread in successive layers, like the wood-rings of trees, on their sides. New mountains, also, are being created from time to time as islands in lakes and seas, or as subordinate cones on the slopes of old ones, thus in some measure balancing the waste of old beauty with new. Man, too, is making many far-reaching changes. This most influential half animal, half angel is rapidly multiplying and spreading, covering the seas and lakes with ships, the land with huts, hotels, cathedrals, and clustered city shops and homes, so that soon, it would seem, we may have to go farther than Nansen to find a good sound solitude. None of Nature's landscapes are ugly so long as they are wild; and much, we can say comfortingly, must always be in great part wild, particularly the sea and the sky, the floods of light from the stars, and the warm, unspoilable heart of the earth, infinitely beautiful, though only dimly visible to the eye of imagination. The geysers, too, spouting from the hot underworld; the steady, long-lasting glaciers on the mountains, obedient only to the sun; Yosemite domes and the tremendous grandeur of rocky cañons and mountains in general,—these must always be wild, for man can change them and mar them hardly more than can the butterflies that hover above them. But the continent's outer beauty is fast passing away, especially the plant part of it, the most destructible and most universally charming of all.

Only thirty years ago, the great Central Valley of California, five hundred miles long and fifty miles wide, was one bed of golden and purple flowers. Now it is ploughed and pastured out of existence, gone forever,—scarce a memory of it left in fence corners and along the bluffs of the streams. The gardens of the Sierra, also, and the noble forests in both the reserved and unreserved portions are sadly hacked and trampled, notwithstanding the ruggedness of the topography,—all excepting those of the parks guarded by a few soldiers. In the noblest forests of the world, the ground, once divinely beautiful, is desolate and repulsive, like a face ravaged by disease. This is true also of many other Pacific Coast and Rocky Mountain valleys and forests. The same fate, sooner or later, is awaiting them all, unless awakening public opinion comes forward to stop it. Even the great deserts in Arizona, Nevada, Utah, and New Mexico, which offer so little to attract settlers, and which a few years ago pioneers were afraid of, as places of desolation and death, are now taken as pastures at the rate of one or two square miles per cow, and of course their plant treasures are passing away,—the delicate abronias, phloxes, gilias, etc. Only a few of the bitter, thorny, unbitable shrubs are left, and the sturdy cactuses that defend themselves with bayonets and spears.

Most of the wild plant wealth of the East also has vanished,— gone into dusty history. Only vestiges of its glorious prairie and woodland wealth remain to bless humanity in boggy, rocky, unploughable places. Fortunately, some of these are purely wild, and go far to keep Nature's love visible. White water-lilies, with rootstocks deep and safe in mud, still send up every sum- mer a Milky Way of starry, fragrant flowers around a thousand lakes, and many a tuft of wild grass waves its panicles on mossy rocks, beyond reach of trampling feet, in company with saxi- frages, bluebells, and ferns. Even in the midst of farmers' fields, precious sphagnum bogs, too soft for the feet of cattle, are preserved with their charming plants unchanged,—chiogenes, Andromeda, Kalmia, Linnæa, Arethusa, etc. Calypso borealis still hides in the arbor vitæ swamps of Canada, and away to the southward there are a few unspoiled swamps, big ones, where miasma, snakes, and alligators, like guardian angels, defend their treasures and keep them as pure as paradise. And beside a' that and a' that, the East is blessed with good winters and blossoming clouds that shed white flowers over all the land, covering every scar and making the saddest landscape divine at least once a year.

The most extensive, least spoiled, and most unspoilable of the gardens of the continent are the vast tundras of Alaska. In summer they extend smooth, even, undulating, continuous beds of flowers and leaves from about lat. 62° to the shores of the Arctic Ocean; and in winter sheets of snowflowers make all the country shine, one mass of white radiance like a star. Nor are these Arctic plant people the pitiful frost-pinched unfortunates they are guessed to be by those who have never seen them. Though lowly in stature, keeping near the frozen ground as if loving it, they are bright and cheery, and speak Nature's love as plainly as their big relatives of the South. Tenderly happed and tucked in beneath downy snow to sleep through the long, white winter, they make haste to bloom in the spring without trying to grow tall, though some rise high enough to ripple and wave in the wind, and display masses of color,—yellow, purple, and blue,—so rich that they look like beds of rainbows, and are visible miles and miles away.

As early as June one may find the showy Geum glaciale in flower, and the dwarf willows putting forth myriads of fuzzy catkins, to be followed quickly, especially on the dryer ground, by mertensia, eritrichium, polemonium, oxytropis, astragalus, lathyrus, lupinus, myosotis, dodecatheon, arnica, chrysanthemum, nardosmia, saussurea, senecio, erigeron, matrecaria, caltha, valeriana, stellaria, Tofieldia, polygonum, papaver, phlox, lychnis, cheiranthus, Linnæa, and a host of drabas, saxifrages, and heathworts, with bright stars and bells in glorious profusion, particularly Cassiope, Andromeda, ledum, pyrola, and vaccinium,—Cassiope the most abundant and beautiful of them all. Many grasses also grow here, and wave fine purple spikes and panicles over the other flowers,— poa, aira, calamagrostis, alopecurus, trisetum, elymus, festuca, glyceria, etc. Even ferns are found thus far north, carefully and comfortably unrolling their precious fronds,—aspidium, cystopteris, and woodsia, all growing on a sumptuous bed of mosses and lichens; not the scaly lichens seen on rails and trees and fallen logs to the southward, but massive, round-headed, finely colored plants like corals, wonderfully beautiful, worth going round the world to see. I should like to mention all the plant friends I found in a summer's wanderings in this cool re-serve, but I fear few would care to read their names, although everybody, I am sure, would love them could they see them blooming and rejoicing at home.

On my last visit to the region about Kotzebue Sound, near the middle of September, 1881 the weather was so fine and mellow that it suggested the Indian summer of the Eastern States. The winds were hushed, the tundra glowed in creamy golden sunshine, and the colors of the ripe foliage of the heath-worts, willows, and birch—red, purple, and yellow, in pure bright tones—were enriched with those of berries which were scattered everywhere, as if they had been showered from the clouds like hail. When I was back a mile or two from the shore, reveling in this color-glory, and thinking how fine it would be could I cut a square of the tundra sod of conventional picture size, frame it, and hang it among the paintings on my study walls at home, saying to myself, "Such a Nature painting taken at random from any part of the thousand-mile bog would make the other pictures look dim and coarse," I heard merry shouting, and, looking round, saw a band of Eskimos—men, women, and children, loose and hairy like wild animals—running towards me. I could not guess at first what they were seeking, for they seldom leave the shore; but soon they told me, as they threw themselves down, sprawling and laughing, on the mellow bog, and began to feast on the berries. A lively picture they made, and a pleasant one, as they frightened the whirring ptarmigans, and surprised their oily stomachs with the beautiful acid berries of many kinds, and filled sealskin bags with them to carry away for festive days in winter.

Nowhere else on my travels have I seen so much warm-blooded, rejoicing life as in this grand Arctic reservation, by so many regarded as desolate. Not only are there whales in abundance along the shores, and innumerable seals, walruses, and white bears, but on the tundras great herds of fat reindeer and wild sheep, foxes, hares, mice, piping marmots, and birds. Perhaps more birds are born here than in any other region of equal extent on the continent. Not only do strong-winged hawks, eagles, and water-fowl, to whom the length of the continent is merely a pleasant excursion, come up here every summer in great numbers, but also many short-winged warblers, thrushes, and finches, repairing hither to rear their young in safety, reinforce the plant bloom with their plumage, and sweeten the wilderness with song; flying all the way, some of them, from Florida, Mexico, and Central America. In coming north they are coming home, for they were born here, and they go south only to spend the winter months, as New Englanders go to Florida. Sweet-voiced troubadours, they sing in orange groves and vine-clad magnolia woods in winter, in thickets of dwarf birch and alder in summer, and sing and chatter more or less all the way back and forth, keeping the whole country glad. Oftentimes, in New England, just as the last snow-patches are melting and the sap in the maples begins to flow, the blessed wanderers may be heard about orchards and the edges of fields where they have stopped to glean a scanty meal, not tarrying long, knowing they have far to go. Tracing the footsteps of spring, they arrive in their tundra homes in June or July, and set out on the return journey in September, or as soon as their families are able to fly well.

This is Nature's own reservation, and every lover of wildness will rejoice with me that by kindly frost it is so well defended. The discovery lately made that it is sprinkled with gold may cause some alarm; for the strangely exciting stuff makes the timid bold enough for anything, and the lazy destructively industrious. Thousands at least half insane are now pushing their way into it, some by the southern passes over the mountains, perchance the first mountains they have ever seen,—sprawling, struggling, gasping for breath, as, laden with awkward, merciless burdens of provisions and tools, they climb over rough-angled boulders and cross thin miry bogs. Some are going by the mountains and rivers to the eastward through Canada, tracing the old romantic ways of the Hudson Bay traders; others by Bering Sea and the Yukon, sailing all the way, getting glimpses perhaps of the famous fur-seals, the ice-floes, and the innumerable islands and bars of the great Alaska river. In spite of frowning hardships and the frozen ground, the Klondike gold will increase the crusading crowds for years to come, but comparatively little harm will be done. Holes will be burned and dug into the hard ground here and there, and into the quartz-ribbed mountains and hills; ragged towns like beaver and muskrat villages will be built, and mills and locomotives will make rumbling, screeching, disenchanting noises; but the miner's pick will not be followed far by the plough, at least not until Nature is ready to unlock the frozen soil-beds with her slow-turning climate key. On the other hand, the roads of the pioneer miners will lead many a lover of wildness into the heart of the reserve, who without them would never see it.

In the meantime, the wildest health and pleasure grounds accessible and available to tourists seeking escape from care and dust and early death are the parks and reservations of the West. There are four national parks,*—the Yellowstone, Yosemite, General Grant, and Sequoia,—all within easy reach, and thirty forest reservations, a magnificent realm of woods, most of which, by railroads and trails and open ridges, is also

---

*There are now five parks and thirty-eight reservations.

fairly accessible, not only to the determined traveler rejoicing in difficulties, but to those (may their tribe increase) who, not tired, not sick, just naturally take wing every summer in search of wildness. The forty million acres of these reserves are in the main unspoiled as yet, though sadly wasted and threatened on their more open margins by the axe and fire of the lumberman and prospector, and by hoofed locusts, which, like the winged ones, devour every leaf within reach, while the shepherds and owners set fires with the intention of making a blade of grass grow in the place of every tree, but with the result of killing both the grass and the trees.

In the million acre Black Hills Reserve of South Dakota, the easternmost of the great forest reserves, made for the sake of the farmers and miners, there are delightful, reviving sauntering-grounds in open parks of yellow pine, planted well apart, allowing plenty of sunshine to warm the ground. This tree is one of the most variable and most widely distributed of American pines. It grows sturdily on all kinds of soil and rocks, and, protected by a mail of thick bark, defies frost and fire and disease alike, daring every danger in firm, calm beauty and strength. It occurs here mostly on the outer hills and slopes where no other tree can grow. The ground beneath it is yellow most of the summer with showy Wythia, arnica, applopappus, solidago, and other sun-loving plants, which, though they form no heavy entangling growth, yet give abundance of color and make all the woods a garden. Beyond the yellow pine woods there lies a world of rocks of wildest architecture, broken, splintery, and spiky, not very high, but the strangest in form and style of grouping imaginable. Countless towers and spires, pinnacles and slender domed columns, are crowded together, and feathered with sharp-pointed Engelmann spruces, making curiously mixed forests,—half trees, half rocks. Level gardens here and there in the midst of them offer charming surprises, and so do the many small lakes with lilies on their meadowy borders, and bluebells, anemones, daisies, castilleias, comandras, etc., together forming landscapes delightfully novel, and made still wilder by many interesting animals,—elk, deer, beavers, wolves, squirrels, and birds. Not very long ago this was the richest of all the red man's hunting-grounds hereabout. After the season's buffalo hunts were over,—as described by

Parkman, who, with a picturesque cavalcade of Sioux savages, passed through these famous hills in 1846,—every winter deficiency was here made good, and hunger was unknown until, in spite of most determined, fighting, killing opposition, the white gold-hunters entered the fat game reserve and spoiled it. The Indians are dead now, and so are most of the hardly less striking free trappers of the early romantic Rocky Mountain times. Arrows, bullets, scalping-knives, need no longer be feared; and all the wilderness is peacefully open.

The Rocky Mountain reserves are the Teton, Yellowstone, Lewis and Clark, Bitter Root, Priest River and Flathead, comprehending more than twelve million acres of mostly unclaimed, rough, forest-covered mountains in which the great rivers of the country take their rise. The commonest tree in most of them is the brave, indomitable, and altogether admirable Pinus contorta, widely distributed in all kinds of climate and soil, growing cheerily in frosty Alaska, breathing the damp salt air of the sea as well as the dry biting blasts of the Arctic interior, and making itself at home on the most dangerous flame-swept slopes and ridges of the Rocky Mountains in immeasurable abundance and variety of forms. Thousands of acres of this species are destroyed by running fires nearly every summer, but a new growth springs quickly from the ashes. It is generally small, and yields few sawlogs of commercial value, but is of incalculable importance to the farmer and miner; supplying fencing, mine timbers, and firewood, holding the porous soil on steep slopes, preventing landslips and avalanches, and giving kindly, nourishing shelter to animals and the widely outspread sources of the life-giving rivers. The other trees are mostly spruce, mountain pine, cedar, juniper, larch, and balsam fir; some of them, especially on the western slopes of the mountains, attaining grand size and furnishing abundance of fine timber.

Perhaps the least known of all this grand group of reserves is the Bitter Root, of more than four million acres. It is the wildest, shaggiest block of forest wildness in the Rocky Mountains, full of happy, healthy, storm-loving trees, full of streams that dance and sing in glorious array, and full of Nature's animals,—elk, deer, wild sheep, bears, cats, and innumerable smaller people.

In calm Indian summer, when the heavy winds are hushed, the vast forests covering hill and dale, rising and falling over the rough topography and vanishing in the distance, seem lifeless. No moving thing is seen as we climb the peaks, and only the low, mellow murmur of falling water is heard, which seems to thicken the silence. Nevertheless, how many hearts with warm red blood in them are beating under cover of the woods, and how many teeth and eyes are shining! A multitude of animal people, intimately related to us, but of whose lives we know almost nothing, are as busy about their own affairs as we are about ours: beavers are building and mending dams and huts for winter, and storing them with food; bears are studying winter quarters as they stand thoughtful in open spaces, while the gentle breeze ruffles the long hair on their backs; elk and deer, assembling on the heights, are considering cold pastures where they will be farthest away from the wolves; squirrels and marmots are busily laying up provisions and lining their nests against coming frost and snow foreseen; and countless thousands of birds are forming parties and gathering their young about them for flight to the southlands; while butterflies and bees, apparently with no thought of hard times to come, are hovering above the late-blooming goldenrods, and, with countless other insect folk, are dancing and humming right merrily in the sunbeams and shaking all the air into music.

Wander here a whole summer, if you can. Thousands of God's wild blessings will search you and soak you as if you were a sponge, and the big days will go by uncounted. If you are business-tangled, and so burdened with duty that only weeks can be got out of the heavy-laden year, then go to the Flathead Reserve; for it is easily and quickly reached by the Great Northern Railroad. Get off the track at Belton Station, and in a few minutes you will find yourself in the midst of what you are sure to say is the best care-killing scenery on the continent,—beautiful lakes derived straight from glaciers, lofty mountains steeped in lovely nemophila-blue skies and clad with forests and glaciers, mossy, ferny waterfalls in their hollows, nameless and numberless, and meadowy gardens abounding in the best of everything. When you are calm enough for discriminating observation, you will find the king of the larches, one of the best of the Western giants, beautiful, picturesque, and regal in port, easily the grandest of all the larches in the world. It grows to a height of one hundred and fifty to two hundred feet, with a diameter at the ground of five to eight feet, throwing out its branches into the light as no other tree does. To those who before have seen only the European larch or the Lyall species of the eastern Rocky Mountains, or the little tamarack or hackmatack of the Eastern States and Canada, this Western king must be a revelation.

Associated with this grand tree in the making of the Flathead forests is the large and beautiful mountain pine, or Western white pine (Pinus monticola), the invincible contorta or lodgepole pine, and spruce and cedar. The forest floor is covered with the richest beds of Linnæa borealis I ever saw, thick fragrant carpets, enriched with shining mosses here and there, and with Clintonia, pyrola, moneses, and vaccinium, weaving hundred-mile beds of bloom that would have made blessed old Linnæus weep for joy.

Lake McDonald, full of brisk trout, is in the heart of this forest, and Avalanche Lake is ten miles above McDonald, at the feet of a group of glacier-laden mountains. Give a month at least to this precious reserve. The time will not be taken from the sum of your life. Instead of shortening, it will indefinitely lengthen it and make you truly immortal. Nevermore will time seem short or long, and cares will never again fall heavily on you, but gently and kindly as gifts from heaven.

The vast Pacific Coast reserves in Washington and Oregon—the Cascade, Washington, Mount Rainier, Olympic, Bull Run, and Ashland, named in order of size—include more than 12,500,000 acres of magnificent forests of beautiful and gigantic trees. They extend over the wild, unexplored Olympic Mountains and both flanks of the Cascade Range, the wet and the dry. On the east side of the Cascades the woods are sunny and open, and contain principally yellow pine, of moderate size, but of great value as a cover for the irrigating streams that flow into the dry interior, where agriculture on a grand scale is being carried on. Along the moist, balmy, foggy, west flank of the mountains, facing the sea, the woods reach their highest development, and, excepting the California redwoods, are the heaviest on the continent. They are made up mostly of the Douglas spruce (Pseudotsuga taxifolia), with the giant arbor vitæ, or cedar, and several species of fir and hemlock in varying abundance, forming a forest kingdom unlike any other, in which limb meets limb, touching and overlapping in bright, lively, triumphant exuberance, two hundred and fifty, three hundred, and even four hundred feet above the shady, mossy ground. Over all the other species the Douglas spruce reigns supreme. It is not only a large tree, the tallest in America next to the redwood, but a very beautiful one, with bright green drooping foliage, handsome pendent cones, and a shaft exquisitely straight and round and regular. Forming extensive forests by itself in many places, it lifts its spiry tops into the sky close together with as even a growth as a well-tilled field of grain. No ground has been better tilled for wheat than these Cascade Mountains for trees: they were ploughed by mighty glaciers, and harrowed and mellowed and outspread by the broad streams that flowed from the ice-ploughs as they were withdrawn at the close of the glacial period.

In proportion to its weight when dry, Douglas spruce timber is perhaps stronger than that of any other large conifer in the country, and being tough, durable, and elastic, it is admirably suited for ship-building, piles, and heavy timbers in general; but its hardness and liability to warp when it is cut into boards render it unfit for fine work. In the lumber markets of California it is called "Oregon pine." When lumbering is going on in the best Douglas woods, especially about Puget Sound, many of the long, slender boles are saved for spars; and so superior is their quality that they are called for in almost every shipyard in the world, and it is interesting to follow their fortunes. Felled and peeled and dragged to tide-water, they are raised again as yards and masts for ships, given iron roots and canvas foliage, decorated with flags, and sent to sea, where in glad motion they go cheerily over the ocean prairie in every latitude and longitude, singing and bowing responsive to the same winds that waved them when they were in the woods. After standing in one place for centuries they thus go round the world like tourists, meeting many a friend from the old home forest; some traveling like themselves, some standing head downward in muddy harbors, holding up the platforms of wharves, and others doing all kinds of hard timber work, showy or hidden.

This wonderful tree also grows far northward in British Columbia, and southward along the coast and middle regions of Oregon and California; flourishing with the redwood wherever it can find an opening, and with the sugar pine, yellow pine, and libocedrus in the Sierra. It extends into the San Gabriel, San Bernardino, and San Jacinto Mountains of southern California. It also grows well on the Wasatch Mountains, where it is called "red pine," and on many parts of the Rocky Mountains and short interior ranges of the Great Basin. But though thus widely distributed, only in Oregon, Washington, and some parts of British Columbia does it reach perfect development.

To one who looks from some high standpoint over its vast breadth, the forest on the west side of the Cascades seems all one dim, dark, monotonous field, broken only by the white volcanic cones along the summit of the range. Back in the untrodden wilderness a deep furred carpet of brown and yellow mosses covers the ground like a garment, pressing about the feet of the trees, and rising in rich bosses softly and kindly over every rock and mouldering trunk, leaving no spot uncared for; and dotting small prairies, and fringing the meadows and the banks of streams not seen in general views, we find, besides the great conifers, a considerable number of hardwood trees,—oak, ash, maple, alder, wild apple, cherry, arbutus, Nuttall's flowering dogwood, and in some places chestnut. In a few favored spots the broad-leaved maple grows to a height of a hundred feet in forests by itself, sending out large limbs in magnificent interlacing arches covered with mosses and ferns, thus forming lofty sky-gardens, and rendering the underwoods delightfully cool. No finer forest ceiling is to be found than these maple arches, while the floor, ornamented with tall ferns and rubus vines, and cast into hillocks by the bulging, moss-covered roots of the trees, matches it well.

Passing from beneath the heavy shadows of the woods, almost anywhere one steps into lovely gardens of lilies, orchids, heathworts, and wild roses. Along the lower slopes, especially in Oregon, where the woods are less dense, there are miles of rhododendron, making glorious masses of purple in the spring, while all about the streams and the lakes and the beaver meadows there is a rich tangle of hazel, plum, cherry, crabapple, cornel, gaultheria, and rubus, with myriads of flowers and abundance of other more delicate bloomers, such as erythronium, brodiæa, fritillaria, calochortus, Clintonia, and the lovely hider of the north, Calypso. Beside all these bloomers there are wonderful ferneries about the many misty waterfalls, some of the fronds ten feet high, others the most delicate of their tribe, the maidenhair fringing the rocks within reach of the lightest dust of the spray, while the shading trees on the cliffs above them, leaning over, look like eager listeners anxious to catch every tone of the restless waters. In the autumn berries of every color and flavor abound, enough for birds, bears, and everybody, particularly about the stream-sides and meadows where sunshine reaches the ground: huckleberries, red, blue, and black, some growing close to the ground, others on bushes ten feet high; gaultheria berries, called "sal-al" by the Indians; salmon berries, an inch in diameter, growing in dense prickly tangles, the flowers, like wild roses, still more beautiful than the fruit; raspberries, gooseberries, currants, blackberries, and strawberries. The underbrush and meadow fringes are in great part made up of these berry bushes and vines; but in the depths of the woods there is not much underbrush of any kind,—only a thin growth of rubus, huckleberry, and vine-maple.

Notwithstanding the outcry against the reservations last winter in Washington, that uncounted farms, towns, and villages were included in them, and that all business was threatened or blocked, nearly all the mountains in which the reserves lie are still covered with virgin forests. Though lumbering has long been carried on with tremendous energy along their boundaries, and home-seekers have explored the woods for openings available for farms, however small, one may wander in the heart of the reserves for weeks without meeting a human being, Indian or white man, or any conspicuous trace of one. Indians used to ascend the main streams on their way to the mountains for wild goats, whose wool furnished them clothing. But with food in abundance on the coast there was little to draw them into the woods, and the monuments they have left there are scarcely more conspicuous than those of birds and squirrels; far less so than those of the beavers, which have dammed streams and made clearings that will endure for centuries. Nor is there much in these woods to attract cattle-keepers. Some of the first settlers made farms on the small bits of prairie and in the comparatively open Cowlitz and Chehalis valleys of Washington; but before the gold period most of the immigrants from the Eastern States settled in the fertile and open Willamette Valley of Oregon. Even now, when the search for tillable land is so keen, excepting the bottom-lands of the rivers around Puget Sound, there are few cleared spots in all western Washington. On every meadow or opening of any sort some one will be found keeping cattle, raising hops, or cultivating patches of grain, but these spots are few and far between. All the larger spaces were taken long ago; therefore most of the newcomers build their cabins where the beavers built theirs. They keep a few cows, laboriously widen their little meadow openings by hacking, girdling, and burning the rim of the close-pressing forest, and scratch and plant among the huge blackened logs and stumps, girdling and killing themselves in killing the trees.

Most of the farm lands of Washington and Oregon, excepting the valleys of the Willamette and Rogue rivers, lie on the east side of the mountains. The forests on the eastern slopes of the Cascades fail altogether ere the foot of the range is reached, stayed by drought as suddenly as on the west side they are stopped by the sea; showing strikingly how dependent are these forest giants on the generous rains and fogs so often complained of in the coast climate. The lower portions of the reserves are solemnly soaked and poulticed in rain and fog during the winter months, and there is a sad dearth of sunshine, but with a little knowledge of woodcraft any one may enjoy an excursion into these woods even in the rainy season. The big, gray days are exhilarating, and the colors of leaf and branch and mossy bole are then at their best. The mighty trees getting their food are seen to be wide-awake, every needle thrilling in the welcome nourishing storms, chanting and bowing low in glorious harmony, while every raindrop and snowflake is seen as a beneficent messenger from the sky. The snow that falls on the lower woods is mostly soft, coming through the trees in downy tufts, loading their branches, and bending them down against the trunks until they look like arrows, while a strange muffled silence prevails, making everything impressively solemn. But these lowland snowstorms and their effects quickly vanish. The snow melts in a day or two, sometimes in a few hours, the bent branches spring up again, and all the forest work is left to the fog and the rain. At the same time, dry snow is falling on the upper forests and mountain tops. Day after day, often for weeks, the big clouds give their flowers without ceasing, as if knowing how important is the work they have to do. The glinting, swirling swarms thicken the blast, and the trees and rocks are covered to a depth of ten to twenty feet. Then the mountaineer, snug in a grove with bread and fire, has nothing to do but gaze and listen and enjoy. Ever and anon the deep, low roar of the storm is broken by the booming of avalanches, as the snow slips from the overladen heights and rushes down the long white slopes to fill the fountain hollows. All the smaller streams are hushed and buried, and the young groves of spruce and fir near the edge of the timber-line are gently bowed to the ground and put to sleep, not again to see the light of day or stir branch or leaf until the spring.

These grand reservations should draw thousands of admiring visitors at least in summer, yet they are neglected as if of no account, and spoilers are allowed to ruin them as fast as they like.* A few peeled spars cut here were set up in London, Philadelphia, and Chicago, where they excited wondering attention; but the countless hosts of living trees rejoicing at home on the mountains are scarce considered at all. Most travelers here are content with what they can see from car windows or the verandas of hotels, and in going from place to place cling to their precious trains and stages like wrecked sailors to rafts. When an excursion into the woods is proposed, all sorts of dangers are imagined,—snakes, bears, Indians. Yet it is far safer to wander in God's woods than to travel on black highways or to stay at home. The snake danger is so slight it is hardly worth mentioning. Bears are a peaceable people, and mind their own business, instead of going about like the devil seeking whom they may devour. Poor fellows, they have been poisoned, trapped, and shot at until they have lost confidence in brother man, and it is not now easy to make their acquaintance. As to Indians, most of them are dead or civilized into useless innocence. No American wilderness that I know of is so dangerous as a city home "with all the modern improvements." One should go

*The outlook over forest affairs is now encouraging. Popular interest, more practical than sentimental in whatever touches the welfare of the country's forests, is growing rapidly, and a hopeful beginning has been made by the Government in real protection for the reservations as well as for the parks. From July 1, 1900, there have been 9 superintendents, 39 supervisors, and from 330 to 445 rangers of reservations.

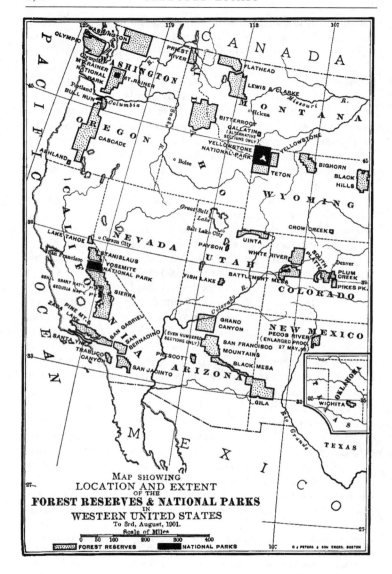

MAP SHOWING
LOCATION AND EXTENT
OF THE
FOREST RESERVES & NATIONAL PARKS
IN
WESTERN UNITED STATES
To 3rd, August, 1901.
Scale of Miles
FOREST RESERVES   NATIONAL PARKS

to the woods for safety, if for nothing else. Lewis and Clark, in their famous trip across the continent in 1804–1805, did not lose a single man by Indians or animals, though all the West was then wild. Captain Clark was bitten on the hand as he lay asleep. That was one bite among more than a hundred men while traveling nine thousand miles. Loggers are far more likely to be met than Indians or bears in the reserves or about their boundaries, brown weather-tanned men with faces furrowed like bark, tired-looking, moving slowly, swaying like the trees they chop. A little of everything in the woods is fastened to their clothing, rosiny and smeared with balsam, and rubbed into it, so that their scanty outer garments grow thicker with use and never wear out. Many a forest giant have these old woodmen felled, but, round-shouldered and stooping, they too are leaning over and tottering to their fall. Others, however, stand ready to take their places, stout young fellows, erect as saplings; and always the foes of trees outnumber their friends. Far up the white peaks one can hardly fail to meet the wild goat, or American chamois,—an admirable mountaineer, familiar with woods and glaciers as well as rocks,—and in leafy thickets deer will be found; while gliding about unseen there are many sleek furred animals enjoying their beautiful lives, and birds also, notwithstanding few are noticed in hasty walks. The ousel sweetens the glens and gorges where the streams flow fastest, and every grove has its singers, however silent it seems,—thrushes, linnets, warblers; humming-birds glint about the fringing bloom of the meadows and peaks, and the lakes are stirred into lively pictures by water-fowl.

The Mount Rainier Forest Reserve should be made a national park and guarded while yet its bloom is on;* for if in the making of the West Nature had what we call parks in mind,—places for rest, inspiration, and prayers,—this Rainier region must surely be one of them. In the centre of it there is

---

*This was done shortly after the above was written. "One of the most important measures taken during the past year in connection with forest reservations was the action of Congress in withdrawing from the Mount Rainier Forest Reserve a portion of the region immediately surrounding Mount Rainier and setting it apart as a national park." (*Report of Commissioner of General Land Office*, for the year ended June, 1899.) But the park as it now stands is far too small.

a lonely mountain capped with ice; from the ice-cap glaciers radiate in every direction, and young rivers from the glaciers; while its flanks, sweeping down in beautiful curves, are clad with forests and gardens, and filled with birds and animals. Specimens of the best of Nature's treasures have been lovingly gathered here and arranged in simple symmetrical beauty within regular bounds.

Of all the fire-mountains which, like beacons, once blazed along the Pacific Coast, Mount Rainier is the noblest in form, has the most interesting forest cover, and, with perhaps the exception of Shasta, is the highest and most flowery. Its massive white dome rises out of its forests, like a world by itself, to a height of fourteen thousand to fifteen thousand feet. The forests reach to a height of a little over six thousand feet, and above the forests there is a zone of the loveliest flowers, fifty miles in circuit and nearly two miles wide, so closely planted and luxuriant that it seems as if Nature, glad to make an open space between woods so dense and ice so deep, were economizing the precious ground, and trying to see how many of her darlings she can get together in one mountain wreath,—daisies, anemones, geraniums, columbines, erythroniums, larkspurs, etc., among which we wade knee-deep and waist-deep, the bright corollas in myriads touching petal to petal. Picturesque detached groups of the spiry Abies lasiocarpa stand like islands along the lower margin of the garden zone, while on the upper margin there are extensive beds of bryanthus, Cassiope, Kalmia, and other heathworts, and higher still saxifrages and drabas, more and more lowly, reach up to the edge of the ice. Altogether this is the richest subalpine garden I ever found, a perfect floral elysium. The icy dome needs none of man's care, but unless the reserve is guarded the flower bloom will soon be killed, and nothing of the forests will be left but black stump monuments.

The Sierra of California is the most openly beautiful and useful of all the forest reserves, and the largest, excepting the Cascade Reserve of Oregon and the Bitter Root of Montana and Idaho. It embraces over four million acres of the grandest scenery and grandest trees on the continent, and its forests are planted just where they do the most good, not only for beauty, but for farming in the great San Joaquin Valley beneath them.

It extends southward from the Yosemite National Park to the end of the range, a distance of nearly two hundred miles. No other coniferous forest in the world contains so many species or so many large and beautiful trees,—Sequoia gigantea, king of conifers, "the noblest of a noble race," as Sir Joseph Hooker well says; the sugar pine, king of all the world's pines, living or extinct; the yellow pine, next in rank, which here reaches most perfect development, forming noble towers of verdure two hundred feet high; the mountain pine, which braves the coldest blasts far up the mountains on grim, rocky slopes; and five others, flourishing each in its place, making eight species of pine in one forest, which is still further enriched by the great Douglas spruce, libocedrus, two species of silver fir, large trees and exquisitely beautiful, the Paton hemlock, the most graceful of evergreens, the curious tumion, oaks of many species, maples, alders, poplars, and flowering dogwood, all fringed with flowery underbrush, manzanita, ceanothus, wild rose, cherry, chestnut, and rhododendron. Wandering at random through these friendly, approachable woods, one comes here and there to the loveliest lily gardens, some of the lilies ten feet high, and the smoothest gentian meadows, and Yosemite valleys known only to mountaineers. Once I spent a night by a camp-fire on Mount Shasta with Asa Gray and Sir Joseph Hooker, and, knowing that they were acquainted with all the great forests of the world, I asked whether they knew any coniferous forest that rivaled that of the Sierra. They unhesitatingly said: "No. In the beauty and grandeur of individual trees, and in number and variety of species, the Sierra forests surpass all others."

This Sierra Reserve, proclaimed by the President of the United States in September, 1893, is worth the most thoughtful care of the government for its own sake, without considering its value as the fountain of the rivers on which the fertility of the great San Joaquin Valley depends. Yet it gets no care at all. In the fog of tariff, silver, and annexation politics it is left wholly unguarded, though the management of the adjacent national parks by a few soldiers shows how well and how easily it can be preserved. In the meantime, lumbermen are allowed to spoil it at their will, and sheep in uncountable ravenous hordes to trample it and devour every green leaf within reach; while the shepherds, like destroying angels, set innumerable fires, which burn not only the undergrowth of seedlings on which the permanence of the forest depends, but countless thousands of the venerable giants. If every citizen could take one walk through this reserve, there would be no more trouble about its care; for only in darkness does vandalism flourish.*

The reserves of southern California,—the San Gabriel, San Bernardino, San Jacinto, and Trabuco,—though not large, only about two million acres altogether, are perhaps the best appreciated. Their slopes are covered with a close, almost impenetrable growth of flowery bushes, beginning on the sides of the fertile coast valleys and the dry interior plains. Their higher ridges, however, and mountains are open, and fairly well forested with sugar pine, yellow pine, Douglas spruce, libocedrus, and white fir. As timber fountains they amount to little, but as bird and bee pastures, cover for the precious streams that irrigate the lowlands, and quickly available retreats from dust and heat and care, their value is incalculable. Good roads have been graded into them, by which in a few hours lowlanders can get well up into the sky and find refuge in hospitable camps and club-houses, where, while breathing reviving ozone, they may absorb the beauty about them, and look comfortably down on the busy towns and the most beautiful orange groves ever planted since gardening began.

The Grand Cañon Reserve of Arizona, of nearly two million acres, or the most interesting part of it, as well as the Rainier region, should be made into a national park, on account of their supreme grandeur and beauty. Setting out from Flagstaff, a station on the Atchison, Topeka, and Santa Fé Railroad, on the way to the cañon you pass through beautiful forests of yellow pine,—like those of the Black Hills, but more extensive,—and curious dwarf forests of nut pine and juniper, the spaces between the miniature trees planted with many interesting species of eriogonum, yucca, and cactus. After riding or walking seventy-five miles through these pleasure-grounds, the San Francisco and other mountains, abounding in flowery parklike openings and smooth shallow valleys with long vistas which in fineness of finish and arrangement suggest the work of a consummate landscape artist, watching you all the way, you come

*See note, p. 277.

to the most tremendous cañon in the world. It is abruptly countersunk in the forest plateau, so that you see nothing of it until you are suddenly stopped on its brink, with its immeasurable wealth of divinely colored and sculptured buildings before you and beneath you. No matter how far you have wandered hitherto, or how many famous gorges and valleys you have seen, this one, the Grand Cañon of the Colorado, will seem as novel to you, as unearthly in the color and grandeur and quantity of its architecture, as if you had found it after death, on some other star; so incomparably lovely and grand and supreme is it above all the other cañons in our fire-moulded, earthquake-shaken, rain-washed, wave-washed, river and glacier sculptured world. It is about six thousand feet deep where you first see it, and from rim to rim ten to fifteen miles wide. Instead of being dependent for interest upon waterfalls, depth, wall sculpture, and beauty of parklike floor, like most other great cañons, it has no waterfalls in sight, and no appreciable floor spaces. The big river has just room enough to flow and roar obscurely, here and there groping its way as best it can, like a weary, murmuring, overladen traveler trying to escape from the tremendous, bewildering labyrinthic abyss, while its roar serves only to deepen the silence. Instead of being filled with air, the vast space between the walls is crowded with Nature's grandest buildings,—a sublime city of them, painted in every color, and adorned with richly fretted cornice and battlement spire and tower in endless variety of style and architecture. Every architectural invention of man has been anticipated, and far more, in this grandest of God's terrestrial cities.

from *Our National Parks*, 1901

The Forests of the Yosemite Park

THE coniferous forests of the Yosemite Park, and of the Sierra in general, surpass all others of their kind in America or indeed in the world, not only in the size and beauty of the trees, but in the number of species assembled together, and the grandeur of the mountains they are growing on. Leaving the workaday lowlands, and wandering into the heart of the mountains, we find a new world, and stand beside the majestic pines and firs and sequoias silent and awestricken, as if in the presence of superior beings new arrived from some other star, so calm and bright and godlike they are.

Going to the woods is going home; for I suppose we came from the woods originally. But in some of nature's forests the adventurous traveler seems a feeble, unwelcome creature; wild beasts and the weather trying to kill him, the rank, tangled vegetation, armed with spears and stinging needles, barring his way and making life a hard struggle. Here everything is hospitable and kind, as if planned for your pleasure, ministering to every want of body and soul. Even the storms are friendly and seem to regard you as a brother, their beauty and tremendous fateful earnestness charming alike. But the weather is mostly sunshine, both winter and summer, and the clear sunny brightness of the park is one of its most striking characteristics. Even the heaviest portions of the main forest belt, where the trees are tallest and stand closest, are not in the least gloomy. The sunshine falls in glory through the colossal spires and crowns, each a symbol of health and strength, the noble shafts faithfully upright like the pillars of temples, upholding a roof of infinite leafy interlacing arches and fretted skylights. The more open portions are like spacious parks, carpeted with small shrubs, or only with the fallen needles sprinkled here and there with flowers. In some places, where the ground is level or slopes gently, the trees are assembled in groves, and the flowers and underbrush in trim beds and thickets as in landscape gardens or the lovingly planted grounds of homes; or they are drawn up in orderly rows around meadows and lakes and along the brows of cañons. But in general the forests are distributed in wide belts in accordance with climate and the comparative strength of each kind in gaining and holding possession of the ground, while anything like monotonous uniformity is prevented by the grandly varied topography, and by the arrangement of the best soilbeds in intricate patterns like embroidery; for these soilbeds are the moraines of ancient glaciers more or less modified by weathering and stream action, and the trees trace them over the hills and ridges, and far up the sides of the mountains, rising with even growth on levels, and towering above one another on the long rich slopes prepared for them by the vanished glaciers.

Had the Sierra forests been cheaply accessible, the most valuable of them commercially would ere this have fallen a prey to the lumberman. Thus far the redwood of the Coast Mountains and the Douglas spruce of Oregon and Washington have been more available for lumber than the pine of the Sierra. It cost less to go a thousand miles up the coast for timber, where the trees came down to the shores of navigable rivers and bays, than fifty miles up the mountains. Nevertheless, the superior value of the sugar pine for many purposes has tempted capitalists to expend large sums on flumes and railroads to reach the best forests, though perhaps none of these enterprises has paid. Fortunately, the lately established system of parks and reservations has put a stop to any great extension of the business hereabouts in its most destructive forms. And as the Yosemite Park region has escaped the millmen, and the all-devouring hordes of hoofed locusts have been banished, it is still in the main a pure wilderness, unbroken by axe clearings except on the lower margin, where a few settlers have opened spots beside hay meadows for their cabins and gardens. But these are mere dots of cultivation, in no appreciable degree disturbing the grand solitude. Twenty or thirty years ago a good many trees were felled for their seeds; traces of this destructive method of seed-collecting are still visible along the trails; but these as well as the shingle-makers' ruins are being rapidly overgrown, the gardens and beds of underbrush once devastated by sheep are blooming again in all their wild glory, and the park is a paradise that makes even the loss of Eden seem insignificant.

On the way to Yosemite Valley, you get some grand views over the forests of the Merced and Tuolumne basins and glimpses of some of the finest trees by the roadside without leaving your seat in the stage. But to learn how they live and behave in pure wildness, to see them in their varying aspects through the seasons and weather, rejoicing in the great storms, in the spiritual mountain light, putting forth their new leaves and flowers when all the streams are in flood and the birds are singing, and sending away their seeds in the thoughtful Indian summer when all the landscape is glowing in deep calm enthusiasm,—for this you must love them and live with them, as free from schemes and cares and time as the trees themselves.

And surely nobody will find anything hard in this. Even the blind must enjoy these woods, drinking their fragrance, listening to the music of the winds in their groves, and fingering their flowers and plumes and cones and richly furrowed boles. The kind of study required is as easy and natural as breathing. Without any great knowledge of botany or wood-craft, in a single season you may learn the name and something more of nearly every kind of tree in the park.

With few exceptions all the Sierra trees are growing in the park,—nine species of pine, two of silver fir, one each of Douglas spruce, libocedrus, hemlock, juniper, and sequoia,—sixteen conifers in all, and about the same number of round-headed trees, oaks, maples, poplars, laurel, alder, dogwood, tumion, etc.

The first of the conifers you meet in going up the range from the west is the digger nut-pine (*Pinus Sabiniana*), a remarkably open, airy, wide-branched tree, forty to sixty feet high, with long, sparse, grayish green foliage and large cones. At a height of fifteen to thirty feet from the ground the trunk usually divides into several main branches, which, after bearing away from one another, shoot straight up and form separate heads as if the axis of the tree had been broken, while the secondary branches divide again and again into rather slender sprays loosely tasseled, with leaves eight to twelve inches long. The yellow and purple flowers are about an inch long, the staminate in showy clusters. The big, rough, burly cones, five to eight or ten inches in length and five or six in diameter, are rich brown in color when ripe, and full of hard-shelled nuts that are greatly prized by Indians and squirrels. This strange-looking pine, enjoying hot sunshine like a palm, is sparsely distributed along the driest part of the Sierra among small oaks and chaparral, and with its gray mist of foliage, strong trunk and branches, and big cones seen in relief on the glowing sky, forms the most striking feature of the foothill vegetation.

Pinus attenuata is a small, slender, arrowy tree, with pale green leaves in threes, clustered flowers half an inch long, brownish yellow and crimson, and cones whorled in conspicuous clusters around the branches and also around the trunk. The cones never fall off or open until the tree dies. They are about four inches long, exceedingly strong and solid, and varnished with hard resin forming a waterproof and almost worm and squirrel proof package, in which the seeds are kept fresh and safe during the lifetime of the tree. Sometimes one of the trunk cones is overgrown and imbedded in the heart wood like a knot, but nearly all are pushed out and kept on the surface by the pressure of the successive layers of wood against the base.

This admirable little tree grows on brushy, sunbeaten slopes, which from their position and the inflammable character of the vegetation are most frequently fire-swept. These grounds it is able to hold against all comers, however big and strong, by saving its seeds until death, when all it has produced are scattered over the bare cleared ground, and a new generation quickly springs out of the ashes. Thus the curious fact that all the trees of extensive groves and belts are of the same age is accounted for, and their slender habit; for the lavish abundance of seed sown at the same time makes a crowded growth, and the seedlings with an even start rush up in a hurried race for light and life.

Only a few of the attenuata and Sabiniana pines are within the boundaries of the park, the former on the side of the Merced Cañon, the latter on the walls of Hetch-Hetchy Valley and in the cañon below it.

The nut-pine (*Pinus monophylla*) is a small, hardy, contented-looking tree, about fifteen or twenty feet high and a foot in diameter. In its youth the close radiating and aspiring branches form a handsome broad-based pyramid, but when fully grown it becomes round-topped, knotty, and irregular, throwing out crooked divergent limbs like an apple tree. The leaves are pale grayish green, about an inch and a half long, and instead of being divided into clusters they are single, round, sharp-pointed, and rigid like spikes, amid which in the spring the red flowers glow brightly. The cones are only about two inches in length and breadth, but nearly half of their bulk is made up of sweet nuts.

This fruitful little pine grows on the dry east side of the park, along the margin of the Mono sage plain, and is the commonest tree of the short mountain ranges of the Great Basin. Tens of thousands of acres are covered with it, forming bountiful orchards for the Red-man. Being so low and accessible, the cones are easily beaten off with poles, and the nuts procured by roasting until the scales open. To the tribes of the desert and sage plains these seeds are the staff of life. They are eaten either raw or parched, or in the form of mush or cakes after being pounded into meal. The time of nut harvest in the autumn is the Indian's merriest time of all the year. An industrious squirrelish family can gather fifty or sixty bushels in a single month before the snow comes, and then their bread for the winter is sure.

The white pine (*Pinus flexilis*) is widely distributed through the Rocky Mountains and the ranges of the Great Basin, where in many places it grows to a good size, and is an important timber tree where none better is to be found. In the park it is sparsely scattered along the eastern flank of the range from Mono Pass southward, above the nut-pine, at an elevation of from eight to ten thousand feet, dwarfing to a tangled bush near the timber-line, but under favorable conditions attaining a height of forty or fifty feet, with a diameter of three to five. The long branches show a tendency to sweep out in bold curves, like those of the mountain and sugar pines to which it is closely related. The needles are in clusters of five, closely packed on the ends of the branchlets. The cones are about five inches long,—the smaller ones nearly oval, the larger cylindrical. But the most interesting feature of the tree is its bloom, the vivid red pistillate flowers glowing among the leaves like coals of fire.

The dwarfed pine or white-barked pine (*Pinus albicaulis*) is sure to interest every observer on account of its curious low matted habit, and the great height on the snowy mountains at which it bravely grows. It forms the extreme edge of the timber-line on both flanks of the summit mountains—if so lowly a tree can be called timber—at an elevation of ten to twelve thousand feet above the level of the sea. Where it is first met on the lower limit of its range it may be thirty or forty feet high, but farther up the rocky wind-swept slopes, where the snow lies deep and heavy for six months of the year, it makes shaggy clumps and beds, crinkled and pressed flat, over which you can easily walk. Nevertheless in this crushed, down-pressed, felted condition it clings hardily to life, puts forth fresh leaves every spring on the ends of its tasseled branchlets, blooms bravely in the lashing blasts with abundance of gay red and purple flowers, matures its seeds in the short summers, and often outlives the favored giants of the sun lands far below. One of the trees that I examined was only about three feet high, with a stem six inches in diameter at the ground, and branches that spread out horizontally as if they had grown up against a ceiling; yet it was four hundred and twenty-six years old, and one of its supple branchlets, about an eighth of an inch in diameter inside the bark, was seventy-five years old, and so tough that I tied it into knots. At the age of this dwarf many of the sugar and yellow pines and sequoias are seven feet in diameter and over two hundred feet high.

In detached clumps never touched by fire the fallen needles of centuries of growth make fine elastic mattresses for the weary mountaineer, while the tasseled branchlets spread a roof over him, and the dead roots, half resin, usually found in abundance, make capital camp-fires, unquenchable in thickest storms of rain or snow. Seen from a distance the belts and patches darkening the mountain sides look like mosses on a roof, and bring to mind Dr. Johnson's remarks on the trees of Scotland. His guide, anxious for the honor of Mull, was still talking of its woods and pointing them out. "Sir," said Johnson, "I saw at Tobermory what they called a wood, which I unluckily took for heath. If you show me what I shall take for furze, it will be something."

The mountain pine (*Pinus monticola*) is far the largest of the Sierra tree mountaineers. Climbing nearly as high as the dwarf albicaulis, it is still a giant in size, bold and strong, standing erect on the storm-beaten peaks and ridges, tossing its cone-laden branches in the rough winds, living a thousand years, and reaching its greatest size—ninety to a hundred feet in height, six to eight in diameter—just where other trees, its companions, are dwarfed. But it is not able to endure burial in snow so long as the albicaulis and flexilis. Therefore, on the upper limit of its range it is found on slopes which, from their steepness or exposure, are least snowy. Its soft graceful beauty in youth, and its leaves, cones, and outsweeping feathery branches constantly remind you of the sugar pine, to which it is closely allied. An admirable tree, growing nobler in form and size the colder and balder the mountains about it.

The giants of the main forest in the favored middle region are the sequoia, sugar pine, yellow pine, libocedrus, Douglas spruce, and the two silver firs. The park sequoias are restricted to two small groves, a few miles apart, on the Tuolumne and Merced divide, about seventeen miles from Yosemite Valley. The Big Oak Flat road to the valley runs through the Tuolumne Grove, the Coulterville through the Merced. The more famous and better known Mariposa Grove, belonging to the state, lies near the southwest corner of the park, a few miles above Wawona.

The sugar pine (*Pinus Lambertiana*) is first met in the park in open, sunny, flowery woods, at an elevation of about thirty-five hundred feet above the sea, attains full development at a height between five and six thousand feet, and vanishes at the level of eight thousand feet. In many places, especially on the northern slopes of the main ridges between the rivers, it forms the bulk of the forest, but mostly it is intimately associated with its noble companions, above which it towers in glorious majesty on every hill, ridge, and plateau from one extremity of the range to the other, a distance of five hundred miles,—the largest, noblest, and most beautiful of all the seventy or eighty species of pine trees in the world, and of all the conifers second only to King Sequoia.

A good many are from two hundred to two hundred and twenty feet in height, with a diameter at four feet from the ground of six to eight feet, and occasionally a grand patriarch, seven or eight hundred years old, is found that is ten or even twelve feet in diameter and two hundred and forty feet high, with a magnificent crown seventy feet wide. David Douglas, who discovered "this most beautiful and immensely grand tree" in the fall of 1826 in southern Oregon, says that the largest of several that had been blown down, "at three feet from the ground was fifty-seven feet nine inches in circumference" (or fully eighteen feet in diameter); "at one hundred and thirty-four feet, seventeen feet five inches; extreme length, two hundred and forty-five feet." Probably for *fifty-seven* we should read *thirty-seven* for the base measurement, which would make it correspond with the other dimensions; for none of this species with anything like so great a girth has since been seen. A girth of even thirty feet is uncommon. A fallen specimen that I measured was nine feet three inches in diameter inside the bark at four feet from the ground, and six feet in diameter at a hundred feet from the ground. A comparatively young tree, three hundred and thirty years old, that had been cut down, measured seven feet across the stump, was three feet three inches in diameter at a height of one hundred and fifty feet, and two hundred and ten feet in length.

The trunk is a round, delicately tapered shaft with finely furrowed purplish-brown bark, usually free of limbs for a hundred feet or more. The top is furnished with long and comparatively slender branches, which sweep gracefully downward and outward, feathered with short tasseled branchlets, and divided only at the ends, forming a palmlike crown fifty to seventy-five feet wide, but without the monotonous uniformity of palm crowns or of the spires of most conifers. The old trees are as tellingly varied and picturesque as oaks. No two are alike, and we are tempted to stop and admire every one we come to, whether as it stands silent in the calm balsam-scented sunshine or waving in accord with enthusiastic storms. The leaves are about three or four inches long, in clusters of five, finely tempered, bright lively green, and radiant. The flowers are but little larger than those of the dwarf pine, and far less showy. The immense cylindrical cones, fifteen to twenty or even twenty-four inches long and three in diameter, hang singly or in clusters, like ornamental tassels, at the ends of the long branches, green, flushed with purple on the sunward side. Like those of almost all the pines they ripen in the autumn of the second season from the flower, and the seeds of all that have escaped the Indians, bears, and squirrels take wing and fly to their places. Then the cones become still more effective as ornaments, for by the spreading of the scales the diameter is nearly doubled, and the color changes to a rich brown. They remain on the tree the following winter and summer; therefore few fertile trees are ever found without them. Nor even after they fall is the beauty work of these grand cones done, for they make a fine show on the flowery, needle-strewn ground. The wood is pale yellow, fine in texture, and deliciously fragrant. The sugar, which gives name to the tree, exudes from the heart wood on wounds made by fire or the axe, and forms irregular crisp white candy-like masses. To the taste of most people it is as good as maple sugar, though it cannot be eaten in large quantities.

No traveler, whether a tree lover or not, will ever forget his first walk in a sugar-pine forest. The majestic crowns approaching one another make a glorious canopy, through the feathery arches of which the sunbeams pour, silvering the needles and gilding the stately columns and the ground into a scene of enchantment.

The yellow pine (*Pinus ponderosa*) is surpassed in size and nobleness of port only by its kingly companion. Full-grown trees in the main forest, where it is associated with the sugar pine, are about one hundred and seventy-five feet high, with a diameter of five to six feet, though much larger specimens may easily be found. The largest I ever measured was a little over eight feet in diameter four feet above the ground, and two hundred and twenty feet high. Where there is plenty of sunshine and other conditions are favorable, it is a massive symmetrical spire, formed of a strong straight shaft clad with innumerable branches, which are divided again and again into stout branchlets laden with bright shining needles and green or purple cones. Where the growth is at all close half or more of the trunk is branchless. The species attains its greatest size and most majestic form in open groves on the deep, well-drained soil of lake basins at an elevation of about four thousand feet. There nearly all the old trees are over two hundred feet high, and the heavy, leafy, much-divided branches sumptuously clothe the trunk almost to the ground. Such trees are easily climbed, and in going up the winding stairs of knotty limbs to the top you will gain a most telling and memorable idea of the height, the richness and intricacy of the branches, and the marvelous abundance and beauty of the long shining elastic foliage. In tranquil weather, you will see the firm outstanding needles in calm content, shimmering and throwing off keen minute rays of light like lances of ice; but when heavy winds are blowing, the strong towers bend and wave in the blast with eager wide-awake enthusiasm, and every tree in the grove glows and flashes in one mass of white sunfire.

Both the yellow and sugar pines grow rapidly on good soil where they are not crowded. At the age of a hundred years they are about two feet in diameter and a hundred feet or more high. They are then very handsome, though very unlike: the sugar pine, lithe, feathery, closely clad with ascending branches; the yellow, open, showing its axis from the ground to the top, its whorled branches but little divided as yet, spreading and turning up at the ends with magnificent tassels of long stout bright needles, the terminal shoot with its leaves being often three or four feet long and a foot and a half wide, the most hopeful looking and the handsomest treetop in the woods. But instead of increasing, like its companion, in wildness and individuality of form with age, it becomes more evenly and compactly spiry. The bark is usually very thick, four to six inches at the ground, and arranged in large plates, some of them on the lower part of the trunk four or five feet long and twelve to eighteen inches wide, forming a strong defense against fire. The leaves are in threes, and from three inches to a foot long. The flowers appear in May: the staminate pink or brown, in conspicuous clusters two or three inches wide; the pistillate crimson, a fourth of an inch wide, and mostly hidden among the leaves on the tips of the branchlets. The cones vary from about three to ten inches in length, two to five in width, and grow in sessile outstanding clusters near the ends of the upturned branchlets.

Being able to endure fire and hunger and many climates this grand tree is widely distributed: eastward from the coast across the broad Rocky Mountain ranges to the Black Hills of Dakota, a distance of more than a thousand miles, and southward from British Columbia, near latitude 51°, to Mexico, about fifteen hundred miles. South of the Columbia River it meets the sugar pine, and accompanies it all the way down along the Coast and Cascade mountains and the Sierra and southern ranges to the mountains of the peninsula of Lower California, where they find their southmost homes together. Pinus ponderosa is extremely variable, and much bother it gives botanists who try to catch and confine the unmanageable proteus in two or a dozen species,—Jeffreyi, deflexa, Apacheca latifolia, etc. But in all its wanderings, in every form, it manifests noble strength. Clad in thick bark like a warrior in mail, it extends its bright ranks over all the high ranges of the wild side of the continent: flourishes in the drenching fog and rain of the northern coast at the level of the sea, in the snow-laden blasts of the mountains, and the white glaring sunshine of the interior plateaus and plains, on the borders of mirage-haunted deserts, volcanoes, and lava beds, waving its bright plumes in the hot winds undaunted, blooming every year for centuries, and tossing big ripe cones among the cinders and ashes of nature's hearths.

The Douglas spruce grows with the great pines, especially on the cool north sides of ridges and cañons, and is here nearly as large as the yellow pine, but less abundant. The wood is strong and tough, the bark thick and deeply furrowed, and on vigorous, quick-growing trees the stout, spreading branches are covered with innumerable slender, swaying sprays, handsomely clothed with short leaves. The flowers are about three fourths of an inch in length, red or greenish, not so showy as the pendulous bracted cones. But in June and July, when the young bright yellow leaves appear, the entire tree seems to be covered with bloom.

It is this grand tree that forms the famous forests of western Oregon, Washington, and the adjacent coast regions of British Columbia, where it attains its greatest size and is most abundant, making almost pure forests over thousands of square miles, dark and close and almost inaccessible, many of the trees towering with straight, imperceptibly tapered shafts to a height of three hundred feet, their heads together shutting out the light,—one of the largest, most widely distributed, and most important of all the Western giants.

The incense cedar (*Libocedrus decurrens*), when full grown, is a magnificent tree, one hundred and twenty to nearly two hundred feet high, five to eight and occasionally twelve feet in diameter, with cinnamon-colored bark and warm yellow-green foliage, and in general appearance like an arbor vitæ. It is distributed through the main forest from an elevation of three to six thousand feet, and in sheltered portions of cañons on the warm sides to seven thousand five hundred. In midwinter, when most trees are asleep, it puts forth its flowers. The pistillate are pale green and inconspicuous; but the staminate are yellow, about one fourth of an inch long, and are produced in myriads, tingeing all the branches with gold, and making the tree as it stands in the snow look like a gigantic goldenrod. Though scattered rather sparsely amongst its companions in the open woods, it is seldom out of sight, and its bright brown shafts and warm masses of plumy foliage make a striking feature of the landscape. While young and growing fast in an open situation no other tree of its size in the park forms so exactly tapered a pyramid. The branches, outspread in flat plumes and beautifully fronded, sweep gracefully downward and outward, except those near the top, which aspire; the lowest droop to the ground, overlapping one another, shedding off rain and snow, and making fine tents for storm-bound mountaineers and birds. In old age it becomes irregular and picturesque, mostly from accidents: running fires, heavy wet snow breaking the branches, lightning shattering the top, compelling it to try to make new summits out of side branches, etc. Still it frequently lives more than a thousand years, invincibly beautiful, and worthy its place beside the Douglas spruce and the great pines.

This unrivaled forest is still further enriched by two majestic silver firs, Abies magnifica and Abies concolor, bands of which come down from the main fir belt by cool shady ridges and glens. Abies magnifica is the noblest of its race, growing on moraines, at an elevation of seven thousand to eight thousand five hundred feet above the sea, to a height of two hundred or two hundred and fifty feet, and five to seven in diameter; and with these noble dimensions there is a richness and symmetry and perfection of finish not to be found in any other tree in the Sierra. The branches are whorled, in fives mostly, and stand out from the straight red purple bole in level or, on old trees, in drooping collars, every branch regularly pinnated like fern fronds, and clad with silvery needles, making broad plumes singularly rich and sumptuous.

The flowers are in their prime about the middle of June: the staminate red, growing on the underside of the branchlets in crowded profusion, giving a rich color to nearly all the tree; the pistillate greenish yellow tinged with pink, standing erect on the upper side of the topmost branches; while the tufts of young leaves, about as brightly colored as those of the Douglas spruce, push out of their fragrant brown buds a few weeks later, making another grand show.

The cones mature in a single season from the flowers. When full grown they are about six to eight inches long, three or four in diameter, blunt, massive, cylindrical, greenish gray in color, covered with a fine silvery down, and beaded with transparent balsam, very rich and precious-looking, standing erect like casks on the topmost branches. If possible, the inside of the cone is still more beautiful. The scales and bracts are tinged with red, and the seed wings are purple with bright iridescence.

Abies concolor, the white silver fir, grows best about two thousand feet lower than the magnifica. It is nearly as large, but the branches are less regularly pinnated and whorled, the leaves are longer, and instead of standing out around the branchlets or turning up and clasping them they are mostly arranged in two horizontal or ascending rows, and the cones are less than half as large. The bark of the magnifica is reddish purple and closely furrowed, that of the concolor is gray and widely furrowed,—a noble pair, rivaled only by the Abies grandis, amabilis, and nobilis of the forests of Oregon, Washington, and the Northern California Coast Range. But none of these northern species form pure forests that in extent and beauty approach those of the Sierra.

The seeds of the conifers are curiously formed and colored, white, brown, purple, plain or spotted like birds' eggs, and excepting the juniper they are all handsomely and ingeniously winged with reference to their distribution. They are a sort of cunningly devised flying machines,—one-winged birds, birds with but one feather,—and they take but one flight, all save those which, after flying from the cone-nest in calm weather, chance to alight on branches where they have to wait for a wind. And though these seed wings are intended for only a moment's use, they are as thoughtfully colored and fashioned as the wings of birds, and require from one to two seasons to grow. Those of the pine, fir, hemlock, and spruce are curved in such manner that, in being dragged through the air by the seeds, they are made to revolve, whirling the seeds in a close spiral, and sustaining them long enough to allow the winds to carry them to considerable distances,—a style of flying full of quick merry motion, strikingly contrasted to the sober dignified sailing of seeds on tufts of feathery pappus. Surely no merrier adventurers ever set out to seek their fortunes. Only in the fir woods are large flocks seen; for, unlike the cones of the pine, spruce, hemlock, etc., which let the seeds escape slowly, one or two at a time, by spreading the scales, the fir cones when ripe fall to pieces, and let nearly all go at once in favorable weather. All along the Sierra for hundreds of miles, on dry breezy autumn days, the sunny spaces in the woods among the colossal spires are in a whirl with these shining purple-winged wanderers, notwithstanding the harvesting squirrels have been working at the top of their speed for weeks trying to cut off every cone before the seeds were ready to swarm and fly. Sequoia seeds have flat wings, and glint and glance in their flight like a boy's kite. The dispersal of juniper seeds is effected by the plum and cherry plan of hiring birds at the cost of their board, and thus obtaining the use of a pair of extra good wings.

Above the great fir belt, and below the ragged beds and fringes of the dwarf pine, stretch the broad dark forests of Pinus contorta, var. Murrayana, usually called tamarack pine. On broad fields of moraine material it forms nearly pure forests at an elevation of about eight or nine thousand feet above the sea, where it is a small, well proportioned tree, fifty or sixty feet high and one or two in diameter, with thin gray bark, crooked much-divided straggling branches, short needles in clusters of two, bright yellow and crimson flowers, and small prickly cones. The very largest I ever measured was ninety feet in height, and a little over six feet in diameter four feet above the ground. On moist well-drained soil in sheltered hollows along streamsides it grows tall and slender with ascending branches, making graceful arrowy spires fifty to seventy-five feet high, with stems only five or six inches thick.

The most extensive forest of this pine in the park lies to the north of the Big Tuolumne Meadows,—a famous deer pasture and hunting ground of the Mono Indians. For miles over wide moraine beds there is an even, nearly pure growth, broken only by glacier meadows, around which the trees stand in trim array, their sharp spires showing to fine advantage both in green flowery summer and white winter. On account of the closeness of its growth in many places, and the thinness and gumminess of its bark, it is easily killed by running fires, which work widespread destruction in its ranks; but a new generation rises quickly from the ashes, for all or a part of its seeds are held in reserve for a year or two or many years, and when the tree is killed the cones open and the seeds are scattered over the burned ground like those of the attenuata.

Next to the mountain hemlock and the dwarf pine this species best endures burial in heavy snow, while in braving hunger and cold on rocky ridgetops it is not surpassed by any. It is distributed from Alaska to Southern California, and inland across the Rocky Mountains, taking many forms in accordance with demands of climate, soil, rivals, and enemies; growing patiently in bogs and on sand dunes beside the sea where it is pelted with salt scud, on high snowy mountains and down in the throats of extinct volcanoes; springing up with invincible vigor after every devastating fire and extending its conquests farther.

The sturdy storm-enduring red cedar (*Juniperus occidentalis*) delights to dwell on the tops of granite domes and ridges and glacier pavements of the upper pine belt, at an elevation of seven to ten thousand feet, where it can get plenty of sunshine and snow and elbow-room without encountering quick-growing overshadowing rivals. They never make anything like a forest, seldom come together even in groves, but stand out separate and independent in the wind, clinging by slight joints to the rock, living chiefly on snow and thin air, and maintaining tough health on this diet for two thousand years or more, every feature and gesture expressing steadfast dogged endurance. The largest are usually about six or eight feet in diameter, and fifteen or twenty in height. A very few are ten feet in diameter, and on isolated moraine heaps forty to sixty feet in height. Many are mere stumps, as broad as high, broken by avalanches and lightning, picturesquely tufted with dense gray scalelike foliage, and giving no hint of dying. The staminate flowers are like those of the libocedrus, but smaller; the pistillate are inconspicuous. The wood is red, fine-grained, and fragrant; the bark bright cinnamon and red, and in thrifty trees is strikingly braided and reticulated, flaking off in thin lustrous ribbons, which the Indians used to weave into matting and coarse cloth. These brown unshakable pillars, standing solitary on polished pavements with bossy masses of foliage in their arms, are exceedingly picturesque, and never fail to catch the eye of the artist. They seem sole survivors of some ancient race, wholly unacquainted with their neighbors.

I have spent a good deal of time, trying to determine their age, but on account of dry rot which honeycombs most of the old ones, I never got a complete count of the largest. Some are undoubtedly more than two thousand years old; for though on good moraine soil they grow about as fast as oaks, on bare pavements and smoothly glaciated overswept granite ridges in the dome region they grow extremely slowly. One on the Starr King ridge, only two feet eleven inches in diameter, was eleven hundred and forty years old. Another on the same ridge, only one foot seven and a half inches in diameter, had reached the age of eight hundred and thirty-four years. The first fifteen inches from the bark of a medium-sized tree—six feet in diameter—on the north Tenaya pavement had eight hundred and fifty-nine layers of wood, or fifty-seven to the inch. Beyond this the count was stopped by dry rot and scars of old wounds. The largest I examined was thirty-three feet in girth, or nearly ten in diameter; and though I failed to get anything like a complete count, I learned enough from this and many other specimens to convince me that most of the trees eight to ten feet thick standing on pavements are more than twenty centuries of age rather than less. Barring accidents, for all I can see, they would live forever. When killed, they waste out of existence about as slowly as granite. Even when overthrown by avalanches, after standing so long, they refuse to lie at rest, leaning stubbornly on their big elbows as if anxious to rise, and while a single root holds to the rock putting forth fresh leaves with a grim never-say-die and never-lie-down expression.

As the juniper is the most stubborn and unshakable of trees, the mountain hemlock (*Tsuga Mertensiana*) is the most graceful and pliant and sensitive, responding to the slightest touches of the wind. Until it reaches a height of fifty or sixty feet it is sumptuously clothed down to the ground with drooping branches, which are divided into countless delicate waving sprays, grouped and arranged in most indescribably beautiful ways, and profusely sprinkled with handsome brown cones. The flowers also are peculiarly beautiful and effective: the pistillate very dark rich purple; the staminate blue of so fine and pure a tone that the best azure of the high sky seems to be condensed in them.

Though apparently the most delicate and feminine of all the mountain trees, it grows best where the snow lies deepest, at an elevation of from nine thousand to nine thousand five hundred feet, in hollows on the northern slopes of mountains and ridges. But under all circumstances and conditions of weather and soil, sheltered from the main currents of the winds or in blank exposure to them, well fed or starved, it is always singularly graceful in habit. Even at its highest limit in the park, ten thousand five hundred feet above the sea on exposed ridgetops, where it crouches and huddles close together in low thickets like those of the dwarf pine, it still contrives to put forth its sprays and branches in forms of irrepressible beauty, while on moist well-drained moraines it displays a perfectly tropical luxuriance of foliage, flower, and fruit.

In the first winter storms the snow is oftentimes soft, and lodges in the dense leafy branches, pressing them down against the trunk, and the slender drooping axis bends lower and lower as the load increases, until the top touches the ground and an ornamental arch is made. Then, as storm succeeds storm and snow is heaped on snow, the whole tree is at last buried, not again to see the light or move leaf or limb until set free by the spring thaws in June or July. Not the young saplings only are thus carefully covered and put to sleep in the whitest of white beds for five or six months of the year, but trees thirty and forty feet high. From April to May, when the snow is compacted, you may ride over the prostrate groves without seeing a single branch or leaf of them. In the autumn they are full of merry life, when Clark crows, squirrels, and chipmunks are gathering the abundant crop of seeds while the deer rest beneath the thick concealing branches. The finest grove in the park is near Mount Conness, and the trail from the Tuolumne soda springs to the mountain runs through it. Many of the trees in this grove are three to four or five feet in diameter and about a hundred feet high.

The mountain hemlock is widely distributed from near the south extremity of the high Sierra northward along the Cascade Mountains of Oregon and Washington and the coast ranges of British Columbia to Alaska, where it was first discovered in

1827. Its northmost limit, so far as I have observed, is in the icy fiords of Prince William's Sound in latitude 61°, where it forms pure forests at the level of the sea, growing tall and majestic on the banks of the great glaciers, waving in accord with the mountain winds and the thunder of the falling icebergs. Here as in the Sierra it is ineffably beautiful, the very loveliest evergreen in America.

Of the round-headed dicotyledonous trees in the park the most influential are the black and goldcup oaks. They occur in some parts of the main forest belt, scattered among the big pines like a heavier chaparral, but form extensive groves and reach perfect development only in the Yosemite valleys and flats of the main cañons. The California black oak (*Quercus Californica*) is one of the largest and most beautiful of the Western oaks, attaining under favorable conditions a height of sixty to a hundred feet, with a trunk three to seven feet in diameter, wide-spreading picturesque branches, and smooth lively green foliage handsomely scalloped, purple in the spring, yellow and red in autumn. It grows best in sunny open groves on ground covered with ferns, chokecherry, brier rose, rubus, mints, goldenrods, etc. Few, if any, of the famous oak groves of Europe, however extensive, surpass these in the size and strength and bright, airy beauty of the trees, the color and fragrance of the vegetation beneath them, the quality of the light that fills their leafy arches, and in the grandeur of the surrounding scenery. The finest grove in the park is in one of the little Yosemite valleys of the Tuolumne Cañon, a few miles above Hetch-Hetchy.

The mountain live-oak, or goldcup oak (*Quercus chrysolepis*), forms extensive groves on earthquake and avalanche taluses and terraces in cañons and Yosemite valleys, from about three to five thousand feet above the sea. In tough, sturdy, unwedgeable strength this is the oak of oaks. In general appearance it resembles the great live-oak of the Southern states. It has pale gray bark, a short, uneven, heavily buttressed trunk which usually divides a few feet above the ground into strong wide-reaching limbs, forming noble arches, and ending in an intricate maze of small branches and sprays, the outer ones frequently drooping in long tresses to the ground like those of the weeping willow, covered with small simple polished leaves, making a canopy broad and bossy, on which the sunshine falls in glorious brightness. The acorn cups are shallow, thick-walled, and covered with yellow fuzzy dust. The flowers appear in May and June with a profusion of pollened tresses, followed by the bronze-colored young leaves.

No tree in the park is a better measure of altitude. In cañons, at an elevation of four thousand feet, you may easily find a tree six or eight feet in diameter; and at the head of a side cañon, three thousand feet higher, up which you can climb in less than two hours, you find the knotty giant dwarfed to a slender shrub, with leaves like those of huckleberry bushes, still bear-ing acorns, and seemingly contented, forming dense patches of chaparral, on the top of which you may make your bed and sleep softly like a Highlander in heather. About a thousand feet higher it is still smaller, making fringes about a foot high around boulders and along seams in pavements and the brows of cañons, giving hand-holds here and there on cliffs hard to climb. The largest I have measured were from twenty-five to twenty-seven feet in girth, fifty to sixty feet high, and the spread of the limbs was about double the height.

The principal riverside trees are poplar, alder, willow, broad-leaved maple, and Nuttall's flowering dogwood. The poplar (*Populus trichocarpa*), often called balm of Gilead from the gum on its buds, is a tall, stately tree, towering above its companions and gracefully embowering the banks of the main streams at an elevation of about four thousand feet. Its abundant foliage turns bright yellow in the fall, and the Indian-summer sunshine sifts through it in delightful tones over the slow-gliding waters when they are at their lowest ebb.

The flowering dogwood is brighter still in these brooding days, for every branch of its broad head is then a brilliant crim-son flame. In the spring, when the streams are in flood, it is the whitest of trees, white as a snow bank with its magnificent flowers four to eight inches in width, making a wonderful show, and drawing swarms of moths and butterflies.

The broad-leaved maple is usually found in the coolest boulder-choked cañons, where the streams are gray and white with foam, over which it spreads its branches in beautiful arches from bank to bank, forming leafy tunnels full of soft green light and spray,—favorite homes of the water ousel.

Around the glacier lakes, two or three thousand feet higher, the common aspen grows in fringing lines and groves which are brilliantly colored in autumn, reminding you of the color glory of the Eastern woods.

Scattered here and there or in groves the botanist will find a few other trees, mostly small,—the mountain mahogany, cherry, chestnut-oak, laurel, and nutmeg. The California nutmeg (*Tumion Californicum*) is a handsome evergreen, belonging to the yew family, with pale bark, prickly leaves, fruit like a green-gage plum, and seed like a nutmeg. One of the best groves of it in the park is at the Cascades below Yosemite.

But the noble oaks and all these rock-shading, stream-embowering trees are as nothing amid the vast abounding billowy forests of conifers. During my first years in the Sierra I was ever calling on everybody within reach to admire them, but I found no one half warm enough until Emerson came. I had read his essays, and felt sure that of all men he would best interpret the sayings of these noble mountains and trees. Nor was my faith weakened when I met him in Yosemite. He seemed as serene as a sequoia, his head in the empyrean; and forgetting his age, plans, duties, ties of every sort, I proposed an immeasurable camping trip back in the heart of the mountains. He seemed anxious to go, but considerately mentioned his party. I said: "Never mind. The mountains are calling; run away, and let plans and parties and dragging lowland duties all 'gang tapsal-teerie.' We'll go up a cañon singing your own song, 'Good-by, proud world! I'm going home,' in divine earnest. Up there lies a new heaven and a new earth; let us go to the show." But alas, it was too late,—too near the sundown of his life. The shadows were growing long, and he leaned on his friends. His party, full of indoor philosophy, failed to see the natural beauty and fullness of promise of my wild plan, and laughed at it in good-natured ignorance, as if it were necessarily amusing to imagine that Boston people might be led to accept Sierra manifestations of God at the price of rough camping. Anyhow, they would have none of it, and held Mr. Emerson to the hotels and trails.

After spending only five tourist days in Yosemite he was led away, but I saw him two days more; for I was kindly invited to go with the party as far as the Mariposa big trees. I told Mr.

Emerson that I would gladly go to the sequoias with him, if he would camp in the grove. He consented heartily, and I felt sure that we would have at least one good wild memorable night round a sequoia camp-fire. Next day we rode through the magnificent forests of the Merced basin, and I kept calling his attention to the sugar pines, quoting his wood-notes, "Come listen what the pine tree saith," etc., pointing out the noblest as kings and high priests, the most eloquent and commanding preachers of all the mountain forests, stretching forth their century-old arms in benediction over the worshiping congregations crowded about them. He gazed in devout admiration, saying but little, while his fine smile faded away.

Early in the afternoon, when we reached Clark's Station, I was surprised to see the party dismount. And when I asked if we were not going up into the grove to camp they said: "No; it would never do to lie out in the night air. Mr. Emerson might take cold; and you know, Mr. Muir, that would be a dreadful thing." In vain I urged, that only in homes and hotels were colds caught, that nobody ever was known to take cold camping in these woods, that there was not a single cough or sneeze in all the Sierra. Then I pictured the big climate-changing, inspiring fire I would make, praised the beauty and fragrance of sequoia flame, told how the great trees would stand about us transfigured in the purple light, while the stars looked down between the great domes; ending by urging them to come on and make an immortal Emerson night of it. But the house habit was not to be overcome, nor the strange dread of night air, though it is only cooled day air with a little dew in it. So the carpet dust and unknowable reeks were preferred. And to think of this being a Boston choice! Sad commentary on culture and the glorious transcendentalism.

Accustomed to reach whatever place I started for, I was going up the mountain alone to camp, and wait the coming of the party next day. But since Emerson was so soon to vanish, I concluded to stop with him. He hardly spoke a word all the evening, yet it was a great pleasure simply to be near him, warming in the light of his face as at a fire. In the morning we rode up the trail through a noble forest of pine and fir into the famous Mariposa Grove, and stayed an hour or two, mostly in ordinary tourist fashion,—looking at the biggest

giants, measuring them with a tape line, riding through prostrate fire-bored trunks, etc., though Mr. Emerson was alone
occasionally, sauntering about as if under a spell. As we walked
through a fine group, he quoted, "There were giants in those
days," recognizing the antiquity of the race. To commemorate
his visit, Mr. Galen Clark, the guardian of the grove, selected
the finest of the unnamed trees and requested him to give it a
name. He named it Samoset, after the New England sachem,
as the best that occurred to him.

The poor bit of measured time was soon spent, and while
the saddles were being adjusted I again urged Emerson to stay.
"You are yourself a sequoia," I said. "Stop and get acquainted
with your big brethren." But he was past his prime, and was
now as a child in the hands of his affectionate but sadly civilized
friends, who seemed as full of old-fashioned conformity as of
bold intellectual independence. It was the afternoon of the day
and the afternoon of his life, and his course was now westward
down all the mountains into the sunset. The party mounted
and rode away in wondrous contentment, apparently, tracing
the trail through ceanothus and dogwood bushes, around the
bases of the big trees, up the slope of the sequoia basin, and
over the divide. I followed to the edge of the grove. Emerson
lingered in the rear of the train, and when he reached the top
of the ridge, after all the rest of the party were over and out of
sight, he turned his horse, took off his hat and waved me a last
good-by. I felt lonely, so sure had I been that Emerson of all
men would be the quickest to see the mountains and sing them.
Gazing awhile on the spot where he vanished, I sauntered back
into the heart of the grove, made a bed of sequoia plumes and
ferns by the side of a stream, gathered a store of firewood, and
then walked about until sundown. The birds, robins, thrushes,
warblers, etc., that had kept out of sight, came about me, now
that all was quiet, and made cheer. After sundown I built a
great fire, and as usual had it all to myself. And though lone-
some for the first time in these forests, I quickly took heart
again,—the trees had not gone to Boston, nor the birds; and
as I sat by the fire, Emerson was still with me in spirit, though
I never again saw him in the flesh. He sent books and wrote,
cheering me on; advised me not to stay too long in solitude.
Soon he hoped that my guardian angel would intimate that my

probation was at a close. Then I was to roll up my herbariums, sketches, and poems (though I never knew I had any poems), and come to his house; and when I tired of him and his humble surroundings, he would show me to better people.

But there remained many a forest to wander through, many a mountain and glacier to cross, before I was to see his Wachusett and Monadnock, Boston and Concord. It was seventeen years after our parting on the Wawona ridge that I stood beside his grave under a pine tree on the hill above Sleepy Hollow. He had gone to higher Sierras, and, as I fancied, was again waving his hand in friendly recognition.

from *Our National Parks*, 1901

Hetch Hetchy Valley

YOSEMITE is so wonderful that we are apt to regard it as an exceptional creation, the only valley of its kind in the world; but Nature is not so poor as to have only one of anything. Several other yosemites have been discovered in the Sierra that occupy the same relative positions on the Range and were formed by the same forces in the same kind of granite. One of these, the Hetch Hetchy Valley, is in the Yosemite National Park about twenty miles from Yosemite and is easily accessible to all sorts of travelers by a road and trail that leaves the Big Oak Flat road at Bronson Meadows a few miles below Crane Flat, and to mountaineers by way of Yosemite Creek basin and the head of the middle fork of the Tuolumne.

It is said to have been discovered by Joseph Screech, a hunter, in 1850, a year before the discovery of the great Yosemite. After my first visit to it in the autumn of 1871, I have always called it the "Tuolumne Yosemite," for it is a wonderfully exact counterpart of the Merced Yosemite, not only in its sublime rocks and waterfalls but in the gardens, groves and meadows of its flowery park-like floor. The floor of Yosemite is about 4000 feet above the sea; the Hetch Hetchy floor about 3700 feet. And as the Merced River flows through Yosemite, so does the Tuolumne through Hetch Hetchy. The walls of both are of gray granite, rise abruptly from the floor, are sculptured in the same style and in both every rock is a glacier monument.

Standing boldly out from the south wall is a strikingly picturesque rock called by the Indians, Kolana, the outermost of a group 2300 feet high, corresponding with the Cathedral Rocks of Yosemite both in relative position and form. On the opposite side of the Valley, facing Kolana, there is a counterpart of the El Capitan that rises sheer and plain to a height of 1800 feet, and over its massive brow flows a stream which makes the most graceful fall I have ever seen. From the edge of the cliff to the top of an earthquake talus it is perfectly free in the air for a thousand feet before it is broken into cascades among talus boulders. It is in all its glory in June, when the snow is melting fast, but fades and vanishes toward the end of summer. The only fall I know with which it may fairly be compared is the Yosemite Bridal Veil; but it excels even that favorite fall both in height and airy-fairy beauty and behavior. Lowlanders are apt to suppose that mountain streams in their wild career over cliffs lose control of themselves and tumble in a noisy chaos of mist and spray. On the contrary, on no part of their travels are they more harmonious and self-controlled. Imagine yourself in Hetch Hetchy on a sunny day in June, standing waist-deep in grass and flowers (as I have often stood), while the great pines sway dreamily with scarcely perceptible motion. Looking northward across the Valley you see a plain, gray granite cliff rising abruptly out of the gardens and groves to a height of 1800 feet, and in front of it Tueeulala's silvery scarf burning with irised sun-fire. In the first white outburst at the head there is abundance of visible energy, but it is speedily hushed and concealed in divine repose, and its tranquil progress to the base of the cliff is like that of a downy feather in a still room. Now observe the fineness and marvelous distinctness of the various sun-illumined fabrics into which the water is woven; they sift and float from form to form down the face of that grand gray rock in so leisurely and unconfused a manner that you can examine their texture, and patterns and tones of color as you would a piece of embroidery held in the hand. Toward the top of the fall you see groups of booming, comet-like masses, their solid, white heads separate, their tails like combed silk interlacing among delicate gray and purple shadows, ever forming and dissolving, worn out by friction in their rush through the air. Most of these vanish a few hundred feet below the summit, changing to varied forms of cloud-like drapery. Near the bottom the width of the fall has increased from about twenty-five feet to a hundred feet. Here it is composed of yet finer tissues, and is still without a trace of disorder—air, water and sunlight woven into stuff that spirits might wear.

So fine a fall might well seem sufficient to glorify any valley; but here, as in Yosemite, Nature seems in nowise moderate, for a short distance to the eastward of Tueeulala booms and thunders the great Hetch Hetchy Fall, Wapama, so near that you have both of them in full view from the same standpoint. It is the counterpart of the Yosemite Fall, but has a much greater volume of water, is about 1700 feet in height, and appears to be nearly vertical, though considerably inclined, and is dashed into huge outbounding bosses of foam on projecting shelves and knobs. No two falls could be more unlike—Tueeulala out in the open sunshine descending like thistledown; Wapama in a jagged, shadowy gorge roaring and thundering, pounding its way like an earthquake avalanche.

Besides this glorious pair there is a broad, massive fall on the main river a short distance above the head of the Valley. Its position is something like that of the Vernal in Yosemite, and its roar as it plunges into a surging trout-pool may be heard a long way, though it is only about twenty feet high. On Rancheria Creek, a large stream, corresponding in position with the Yosemite Tenaya Creek, there is a chain of cascades joined here and there with swift flashing plumes like the one between the Vernal and Nevada Falls, making magnificent shows as they go their glacier-sculptured way, sliding, leaping, hurrahing, covered with crisp clashing spray made glorious with sifting sunshine. And besides all these a few small streams come over the walls at wide intervals, leaping from ledge to ledge with birdlike song and watering many a hidden cliff-garden and fernery, but they are too unshowy to be noticed in so grand a place.

The correspondence between the Hetch Hetchy walls in their trends, sculpture, physical structure, and general arrangement of the main rock-masses and those of the Yosemite Valley has excited the wondering admiration of every observer. We have seen that the El Capitan and Cathedral rocks occupy the same relative positions in both valleys; so also do their Yosemite points and North Domes. Again, that part of the Yosemite north wall immediately to the east of the Yosemite Fall has two horizontal benches, about 500 and 1500 feet above the floor, timbered with golden-cup oak. Two benches similarly situated and timbered occur on the same relative portion of the Hetch Hetchy north wall, to the east of Wapama Fall, and on no other. The Yosemite is bounded at the head by the great Half Dome. Hetch Hetchy is bounded in the same way, though its head rock is incomparably less wonderful and sublime in form.

The floor of the Valley is about three and a half miles long, and from a fourth to half a mile wide. The lower portion is mostly a level meadow about a mile long, with the trees restricted to the sides and the river banks, and partially separated from the main, upper, forested portion by a low bar of glacier-polished granite across which the river breaks in rapids.

The principal trees are the yellow and sugar pines, digger pine, incense cedar, Douglas spruce, silver fir, the California and golden-cup oaks, balsam cottonwood, Nuttall's flowering dogwood, alder, maple, laurel, tumion, etc. The most abundant and influential are the great yellow or silver pines like those of Yosemite, the tallest over two hundred feet in height, and the oaks assembled in magnificent groves with massive rugged trunks four to six feet in diameter, and broad, shady, wide-spreading heads. The shrubs forming conspicuous flowery clumps and tangles are manzanita, azalea, spiræa, brier-rose, several species of ceanothus, calycanthus, philadelphus, wild cherry, etc.; with abundance of showy and fragrant herbaceous plants growing about them or out in the open in beds by themselves—lilies, Mariposa tulips, brodiaeas, orchids, iris, spraguea, draperia, collomia, collinsia, castilleja, nemophila, larkspur, columbine, goldenrods, sunflowers, mints of many species, honeysuckle, etc. Many fine ferns dwell here also, especially the beautiful and interesting rock-ferns—pellaea, and cheilanthes of several species—fringing and rosetting dry rock-piles and ledges; woodwardia and asplenium on damp spots with fronds six or seven feet high; the delicate maiden-hair in mossy nooks by the falls, and the sturdy, broad-shouldered pteris covering nearly all the dry ground beneath the oaks and pines.

It appears, therefore, that Hetch Hetchy Valley, far from being a plain, common, rock-bound meadow, as many who have not seen it seem to suppose, is a grand landscape garden, one of Nature's rarest and most precious mountain temples. As in Yosemite, the sublime rocks of its walls seem to glow with life, whether leaning back in repose or standing erect in thoughtful attitudes, giving welcome to storms and calms alike, their brows in the sky, their feet set in the groves and gay flowery meadows, while birds, bees, and butterflies help the river and waterfalls to stir all the air into music—things frail and fleeting and types of permanence meeting here and blending, just as they do in Yosemite, to draw her lovers into close and confiding communion with her.

Sad to say, this most precious and sublime feature of the Yosemite National Park, one of the greatest of all our natural resources for the uplifting joy and peace and health of the people, is in danger of being dammed and made into a reservoir to help supply San Francisco with water and light, thus flooding it from wall to wall and burying its gardens and groves one or two hundred feet deep. This grossly destructive commercial scheme has long been planned and urged (though water as pure and abundant can be got from sources outside of the people's park, in a dozen different places), because of the comparative cheapness of the dam and of the territory which it is sought to divert from the great uses to which it was dedicated in the Act of 1890 establishing the Yosemite National Park.

The making of gardens and parks goes on with civilization all over the world, and they increase both in size and number as their value is recognized. Everybody needs beauty as well as bread, places to play in and pray in, where Nature may heal and cheer and give strength to body and soul alike. This natural beauty-hunger is made manifest in the little window-sill gardens of the poor, though perhaps only a geranium slip in a broken cup, as well as in the carefully tended rose and lily gardens of the rich, the thousands of spacious city parks and botanical gardens, and in our magnificent National parks—the Yellowstone, Yosemite, Sequoia, etc.—Nature's sublime wonderlands, the admiration and joy of the world. Nevertheless, like anything else worth while, from the very beginning, however well guarded, they have always been subject to attack by despoiling gain-seekers and mischief-makers of every degree from Satan to Senators, eagerly trying to make everything immediately and selfishly commercial, with schemes disguised in smug-smiling philanthropy, industriously, sham-piously crying, "Conservation, conservation, panutilization," that man and beast may be fed and the dear Nation made great. Thus long ago a few enterprising merchants utilized the Jerusalem temple as a place of business instead of a place of prayer, changing money, buying and selling cattle and sheep and doves; and earlier still, the first forest reservation, including only one tree, was likewise despoiled. Ever since the establishment of the Yosemite National Park, strife has been going on around its borders and I suppose this will go on as part of the universal battle between right and wrong, however much its boundaries may be shorn, or its wild beauty destroyed.

The first application to the Government by the San Francisco Supervisors for the commercial use of Lake Eleanor and the Hetch Hetchy Valley was made in 1903, and on December 22nd of that year it was denied by the Secretary of the Interior, Mr. Hitchcock, who truthfully said:

> Presumably the Yosemite National Park was created such by law because of the natural objects of varying degrees of scenic importance located within its boundaries, inclusive alike of its beautiful small lakes, like Eleanor, and its majestic wonders, like Hetch Hetchy and Yosemite Valley. It is the aggregation of such natural scenic features that makes the Yosemite Park a wonderland which the Congress of the United States sought by law to reserve for all coming time as nearly as practicable in the condition fashioned by the hand of the Creator—a worthy object of National pride and a source of healthful pleasure and rest for the thousands of people who may annually sojourn there during the heated months.

In 1907 when Mr. Garfield became Secretary of the Interior the application was renewed and granted; but under his successor, Mr. Fisher, the matter has been referred to a Commission, which as this volume goes to press still has it under consideration.

The most delightful and wonderful camp grounds in the Park are its three great valleys—Yosemite, Hetch Hetchy, and Upper Tuolumne; and they are also the most important places with reference to their positions relative to the other great features—the Merced and Tuolumne Cañons, and the High Sierra peaks and glaciers, etc., at the head of the rivers. The main part of the Tuolumne Valley is a spacious flowery lawn four or five miles long, surrounded by magnificent snowy mountains, slightly separated from other beautiful meadows, which together make a series about twelve miles in length, the highest reaching to the feet of Mount Dana, Mount Gibbs, Mount Lyell and Mount McClure. It is about 8500 feet above the sea, and forms the grand central High Sierra camp ground from which excursions are made to the noble mountains, domes, glaciers, etc.; across the Range to the Mono Lake and volcanoes and down the Tuolumne Cañon to Hetch Hetchy. Should Hetch Hetchy be submerged for a reservoir, as proposed, not only would it be utterly destroyed, but the sublime cañon way to the heart of the High Sierra would be hopelessly blocked and the great camping ground, as the watershed of a city drinking system, virtually would be closed to the public. So far as I have learned, few of all the thousands who have seen the park and seek rest and peace in it are in favor of this outrageous scheme.

One of my later visits to the Valley was made in the autumn of 1907 with the late William Keith, the artist. The leaf-colors were then ripe, and the great godlike rocks in repose seemed to glow with life. The artist, under their spell, wandered day after day along the river and through the groves and gardens, studying the wonderful scenery; and, after making about forty sketches, declared with enthusiasm that although its walls were less sublime in height, in picturesque beauty and charm Hetch Hetchy surpassed even Yosemite.

That any one would try to destroy such a place seems incredible; but sad experience shows that there are people good enough and bad enough for anything. The proponents of the dam scheme bring forward a lot of bad arguments to prove that the only righteous thing to do with the people's parks is to destroy them bit by bit as they are able. Their arguments are curiously like those of the devil, devised for the destruction of the first garden—so much of the very best Eden fruit going to waste; so much of the best Tuolumne water and Tuolumne scenery going to waste. Few of their statements are even partly true, and all are misleading.

Thus, Hetch Hetchy, they say, is a "low-lying meadow." On the contrary, it is a high-lying natural landscape garden, as the photographic illustrations show.

"It is a common minor feature, like thousands of others." On the contrary it is a very uncommon feature; after Yosemite, the rarest and in many ways the most important in the National Park.

"Damming and submerging it 175 feet deep would enhance its beauty by forming a crystal-clear lake." Landscape gardens, places of recreation and worship, are never made beautiful by destroying and burying them. The beautiful sham lake, forsooth, would be only an eyesore, a dismal blot on the landscape, like many others to be seen in the Sierra. For, instead of keeping it at the same level all the year, allowing Nature centuries of time to make new shores, it would, of course, be full only a month or two in the spring, when the snow is melting fast; then it would be gradually drained, exposing the slimy sides of the basin and shallower parts of the bottom, with the gathered drift and waste, death and decay of the upper basins, caught here instead of being swept on to decent natural burial along the banks of the river or in the sea. Thus the Hetch Hetchy dam-lake would be only a rough imitation of a natural lake for a few of the spring months, an open sepulcher for the others.

"Hetch Hetchy water is the purest of all to be found in the Sierra, unpolluted, and forever unpollutable." On the contrary, excepting that of the Merced below Yosemite, it is less pure than that of most of the other Sierra streams, because of the sewerage of camp grounds draining into it, especially of the Big Tuolumne Meadows camp ground, occupied by hundreds of tourists and mountaineers, with their animals, for months every summer, soon to be followed by thousands from all the world.

These temple destroyers, devotees of ravaging commercialism, seem to have a perfect contempt for Nature, and, instead of lifting their eyes to the God of the mountains, lift them to the Almighty Dollar.

Dam Hetch Hetchy! As well dam for water-tanks the people's cathedrals and churches, for no holier temple has ever been consecrated by the heart of man.

from *The Yosemite*, 1912

Save the Redwoods

WE ARE often told that the world is going from bad to worse, sacrificing everything to mammon. But this righteous uprising in defense of God's trees in the midst of exciting politics and wars is telling a different story, and every Sequoia, I fancy, has heard the good news and is waving its branches for joy. The wrongs done to trees, wrongs of every sort, are done in the darkness of ignorance and unbelief, for when light comes the heart of the people is always right. Forty-seven years ago one of these Calaveras King Sequoias was laboriously cut down, that the stump might be had for a dancing-floor. Another, one of the finest in the grove, more than three hundred feet high, was skinned alive to a height of one hundred and sixteen feet from the ground and the bark sent to London to show how fine and big that Calaveras tree was—as sensible a scheme as skinning our great men would be to prove their greatness. This grand tree is of course dead, a ghastly disfigured ruin, but it still stands erect and holds forth its majestic arms as if alive and saying, "Forgive them; they know not what they do." Now some millmen want to cut all the Calaveras trees into lumber and money. But we have found a better use for them. No doubt these trees would make good lumber after passing through a sawmill, as George Washington after passing through the hands of a French cook would have made good food. But both for Washington and the tree that bears his name higher uses have been found.

Could one of these Sequoia kings come to town in all its god-like majesty so as to be strikingly seen and allowed to plead its own cause, there would never again be any lack of defenders. And the same may be said of all the other Sequoia groves and forests of the Sierra with their companions and the noble *Sequoia sempervirens*, or redwood, of the coast mountains.

In a general view we find that the *Sequoia gigantea*, or Big Tree, is distributed in a widely interrupted belt along the west flank of the Sierra, from a small grove on the middle fork of the American River to the head of Deer Creek, a distance of about two hundred and sixty miles, at an elevation of about five thousand to a little over eight thousand feet above the sea. From the American River grove to the forest on Kings River the species occurs only in comparatively small isolated patches or groves so sparsely distributed along the belt that three of the gaps in it are from forty to sixty miles wide. From Kings River southward the Sequoia is not restricted to mere groves, but extends across the broad rugged basins of the Kaweah and Tule rivers in majestic forests a distance of nearly seventy miles, the continuity of this portion of the belt being but slightly broken save by the deep cañons.

In these noble groves and forests to the southward of the Calaveras Grove the axe and saw have long been busy, and thousands of the finest Sequoias have been felled, blasted into manageable dimensions, and sawed into lumber by methods destructive almost beyond belief, while fires have spread still wider and more lamentable ruin. In the course of my explorations twenty-five years ago, I found five sawmills located on or near the lower margin of the Sequoia belt, all of which were cutting more or less Big Tree lumber, which looks like the redwood of the coast, and was sold as redwood. One of the smallest of these mills in the season of 1874 sawed two million feet of Sequoia lumber. Since that time other mills have been built among the Sequoias, notably the large ones on Kings River and the head of the Fresno. The destruction of these grand trees is still going on.

On the other hand, the Calaveras Grove for forty years has been faithfully protected by Mr. Sperry, and with the exception of the two trees mentioned above is still in primeval beauty. The Tuolumne and Merced groves near Yosemite, the Dinky Creek grove, those of the General Grant National Park and the Sequoia National Park, with several outstanding groves that are nameless on the Kings, Kaweah, and Tule river basins, and included in the Sierra forest reservation, have of late years been partially protected by the Federal Government; while the well-known Mariposa Grove has long been guarded by the State.

For the thousands of acres of Sequoia forest outside of the reservation and national parks, and in the hands of lumbermen, no help is in sight. Probably more than three times as many Sequoias as are contained in the whole Calaveras Grove have been cut into lumber every year for the last twenty-six years without let or hindrance, and with scarce a word of protest on the part of the public, while at the first whisper of the bonding of the Calaveras Grove to lumbermen most everybody rose in alarm. This righteous and lively indignation on the part of Californians after the long period of deathlike apathy, in which they have witnessed the destruction of other groves unmoved, seems strange until the rapid growth that right public opinion has made during the last few years is considered and the peculiar interest that attaches to the Calaveras giants. They were the first discovered and are best known. Thousands of travelers from every country have come to pay them tribute of admiration and praise, their reputation is world-wide, and the names of great men have long been associated with them— Washington, Humboldt, Torrey and Gray, Sir Joseph Hooker, and others. These kings of the forest, the noblest of a noble race, rightly belong to the world, but as they are in California we cannot escape responsibility as their guardians. Fortunately the American people are equal to this trust, or any other that may arise, as soon as they see it and understand it.

Any fool can destroy trees. They cannot defend themselves or run away. And few destroyers of trees ever plant any; nor can planting avail much toward restoring our grand aboriginal giants. It took more than three thousand years to make some of the oldest of the Sequoias, trees that are still standing in perfect strength and beauty, waving and singing in the mighty forests of the Sierra. Through all the eventful centuries since Christ's time, and long before that, God has cared for these trees, saved them from drought, disease, avalanches, and a thousand storms; but he cannot save them from sawmills and fools; this is left to the American people. The news from Washington is encouraging. On March third [1905?] the House passed a bill providing for the Government acquisition of the Calaveras giants. The danger these Sequoias have been in will do good far beyond the boundaries of the Calaveras Grove, in saving other groves and forests, and quickening interest in forest affairs in general. While the iron of public sentiment is hot let us strike hard. In particular, a reservation or national park of the only other species of Sequoia, the *sempervirens*, or redwood, hardly less wonderful than the *gigantea*, should be quickly secured. It will have to be acquired by gift or purchase, for the Government has sold every section of the entire redwood belt from the Oregon boundary to below Santa Cruz.

Sierra Club Bulletin, January 1920

Chronology

1838   Born John Muir on April 21 in Dunbar, Scotland, to Ann
        Gilrye Muir (b. 1813) and Daniel Muir (b. 1804). Siblings
        are Margaret (b. 1834) and Sarah (b. 1836). Father runs
        a grain and feed store that he inherited from his first
        wife and has a reputation for honesty and stern religious
        convictions. Grandparents Margaret Hay Gilrye and David
        Gilrye, a retired meat merchant originally of Northumber-
        land, both members of the Church of Scotland, live near
        the Muirs. (Grandfather John Muir, the son of tenant
        farmers of Lanarkshire, Scotland, joined the British army
        and married Sarah Higgs, an Englishwoman. After their
        deaths within a few months of each other around 1804–5,
        father was raised by relatives in Lanarkshire; he worked on
        their farms throughout his youth and was converted to an
        evangelical type of Presbyterianism. He joined the British
        army at the age of 21 and while serving as a recruiting
        sergeant in Dunbar met his first wife. Around this time,
        father left the Church of Scotland and subsequently joined
        a series of denominations. Some months after the death of
        his first wife, he began courting Ann Gilrye; they married
        in 1833.)

1840–48 Brother David is born in 1840. Muir goes on walks and
        outings with grandfather, who teaches him letters and
        numbers; throughout childhood often visits grandparents.
        Begins primary school at age three and quickly moves on
        to second reader. Enjoys singing ballads and hymns at
        school and at home. Moves with family into three-story
        house that father buys for cash in January 1842. Brother
        Daniel born in 1843. Muir enters grammar school at age
        seven or eight; studies Latin, French, English, spelling,
        history, mathematics, and geography. Students learn by
        rote, and are beaten with a leather strap for failures or mis-
        behavior. Muir is required by father to memorize verses
        from the Bible daily (by 1849 memorizes all of the New
        Testament and much of the Old) and is beaten by father
        for any deviation from his inflexible code of Christian

behavior. Is impressed by natural history accounts in school reader, especially of America's fauna as described by John Audubon and Alexander Wilson, and fascinated with the natural world; spends much time wandering the local shore and countryside, exploring caves and Dunbar Castle, and playing war with friends. Twin sisters Mary and Annie are born in 1846. Father joins Campbellite Disciples of Christ and around the end of 1848 plans to migrate to Canada.

1849   Parents sell their house and property. Muir leaves with father, David, and Sarah for America on February 19 (mother remains in Scotland until new home is established). Father learns of a proposed canal in southern Wisconsin that would link the St. Lawrence Seaway with the Gulf of Mexico, providing wide markets for farmers, and decides to settle there. Buys 80-acre tract of isolated land by a small lake in Marquette County, Wisconsin, near the Fox River; names it Fountain Lake Farm and constructs a shanty as temporary housing. Muir spends much of the summer stalking local wildlife and roaming the nearby forest, meadows, streams, and lake; later writes: "I was set down in the midst of pure wildness where every object excited endless admiration and wonder." With hired help, father clears the area, plants crops, and by the end of October completes eight-room, two-and-a-half-story house. Mother arrives in November with Margaret, Dan, Mary, and Annie.

1850–54   Sister Joanna is born in 1850. Required by father to work on the farm up to 16 hours a day, Muir labors nearly every day of the year but the Sabbath, and except for brief periods his formal schooling ends. Leaves the farm only rarely, traveling occasionally to Portage, 16 miles away, to help get supplies. Feels increasingly trapped by father's cruel discipline and constant religious discourse, finding relief only when father is away distributing religious books or delivering sermons as an itinerant preacher. Chosen in autumn of 1854 to help build a corduroy road through the township along with young Scots immigrants David Gray and David Taylor, Muir comes to share their taste for poetry. "I remember as a great and sudden discovery that the poetry of the Bible, Shakespeare, and Milton was a source of inspiring, exhilarating, uplifting pleasure," he later writes, "and I became anxious to know all the poets, and saved up small sums to buy as many of their books as possible." Reads voraciously in his spare time, including histories, ancient classics, the works of Scott, Burns, Cowper, and others, borrowing some of the books from neighbors. Father disapproves of most non-religious books, and mother and siblings help Muir to conceal this reading from him.

1855–59 Finds little time to read before his prescribed bedtime and gains father's permission to rise early; begins getting up at I A.M. to study until dawn. With soil fertility at Fountain Lake Farm rapidly diminishing, father buys a new tract of land nearby that he calls Hickory Hill. Work of clearing the land, plowing, planting crops, and establishing a new home falls primarily upon Muir. Without water nearby, Muir is also assigned to dig a well and spends months chiseling away at a vein of sandstone. When the well reaches 80 feet, he is overcome by carbon dioxide and pulled unconscious from the hole; soon recovers and returns to digging, but the incident leaves him with a permanent throat irritation. In winter, when it is too cold to read in early hours without the use of firewood, Muir tinkers in cellar with father's tools and some of his own design. Having constructed miniature waterwheels and windmills at Fountain Lake Farm, he turns to more elaborate designs; creates numerous devices including a self-setting sawmill, complex clocks, thermometers, an "early-rising machine" (a bed balanced on a fulcrum and connected to a clock that tilts to a 45-degree angle at a given hour, tipping the sleeper to his feet), and a "field thermometer" large enough to be read from the surrounding hills and able to measure the increase in temperature caused by a person approaching within about five feet of it.

1860 At urging of neighbor William Duncan, Muir decides (against his father's wishes) to exhibit at the State Agricultural Fair in Madison in September; exhibits clocks and a thermometer fashioned from a washboard whose sensitivity is equal to that of his larger field thermometer, and demonstrates his early-rising machine. Meets Jeanne Smith Carr, a judge of the exhibits, whose husband teaches science at the nearby University of Wisconsin. Receives honorarium of $15 and is commended as "a genius" by the judges. Accepts offer of employment from fellow exhibitor Norman Wiard, who claims to have invented a steam-powered iceboat capable of operating on a frozen river. Travels with Wiard to Prairie du Chien in fall; while caring for the boat, supports himself by tending livestock and doing chores in return for board at a local hotel. Wiard's boat proves a failure, and Muir receives little of the formal training in mechanical drawing he had been promised.

1861   Returns to Madison in January hoping to enroll at the University of Wisconsin. Finds only small jobs as a coach-man and assistant to an insurance agent. Learning that it is possible to attend classes with little money by boarding oneself, Muir quits jobs and gains admission during spring semester. Takes geology and chemistry classes with Ezra Slocum Carr, Jeanne Carr's husband, and is exposed for the first time to precepts and empirical methods of science. Studies Latin and Greek with James Davie Butler. Invents a study desk that retrieves a book, holds it in place for reading for a period of time, and then automatically replaces it with another. Subsists on a sparse diet, some-times only graham mush and an occasional potato. Walks the 35 miles home to work on family farm during summer. Returns to classes in fall, but lack of money soon forces him to suspend his education. Takes job during winter as a district school teacher 10 miles south of Madison.

1862   Returns to classes in spring with new confidence, having won local renown as lecturer and science teacher. Intro-duced by fellow student Milton S. Griswold to botany, in which he becomes keenly interested. During summer vacation works at Fountain Lake Farm, now owned by sister Sarah and husband David Galloway. Uses free time to collect, catalog, and classify specimens of local plant life. With his acceptance of scientific methodology, Muir grows further away from father's religious beliefs and the two find it increasingly difficult to get along.

1863   Depressed by the Civil War, wants nothing to do with the conflict; makes plans to attend medical school and become a doctor, but by spring the war threatens to disrupt them. "This war seems farther from a close than ever," he writes. "How strange that a country with so many schools and churches should be desolated by so unsightly a monster."

Takes extended botanical trip in summer, traveling down the Wisconsin River, across the Mississippi, and roaming along the Iowa Bluffs before returning home. Lives with Sarah and David Galloway over fall and winter.

1864   A new draft order is signed by President Lincoln, to become effective in March. Muir takes a train heading north on March 1; walks through part of Michigan and crosses Canadian border, seeking to lose himself in the forests and swamps surrounding Lake Huron. Spends summer tramping along an unplanned, zigzagging route through the islands and inland swamps near Lake Huron and Georgian Bay; collects botanical samples. Lives for a time with a family of Scots immigrants, doing chores in return for board; at other times camps outdoors. In June, deeply moved when he comes upon the rare white orchid *Calypso borealis* alone next to a stream in deep woods: "I never before saw a plant so full of life; so perfectly spiritual," he later writes, "it seemed pure enough for the throne of its Creator. I felt as if I were in the presence of superior beings who loved me and beckoned me to come. I sat down beside them and wept for joy." Travels to Niagara Falls in September to meet brother Dan, who had fled to Canada in 1862. Continues traveling, eventually stopping at Meaford on the southern end of Georgian Bay where he and Dan take jobs at Trout and Jay woodworking factory for winter.

1865   Works as machinist at the factory. In free time continues collecting and naming plant species. When asked to teach a Sunday school class in the community, offers his students instruction in botany instead of the Bible as a means of understanding creation. With few people to talk to about nature, writes to Ezra Carr, his former professor; Carr's wife, Jeanne, responds and the two begin a correspondence that will last for the next decade. Brother Dan returns to the United States in May after the war ends, and Muir's loneliness deepens. Without money and uncertain of his future direction, signs contract in September to use his inventing talents to increase Trout and Jay's productivity; agrees to produce 30,000 broom handles and 12,000 rakes, in return for half the profits. Working 18-hour days, Muir succeeds in increasing output; invents a self-feeding lathe and other automatic devices to improve production of rakes.

1866   Has completed broom handles and 6,000 rakes, but not
              yet been paid, when the factory is destroyed by a fire in
              March. Declining offer of a partnership in return for help-
              ing to rebuild the plant, accepts a note for $200 and a
              small amount of cash and returns to the United States.
              Wanders through New York, Ohio, Indiana, and Illinois
              before stopping in Indianapolis, where he finds work as a
              sawyer at Osgood, Smith & Co., a factory making wagon
              parts. Is quickly promoted to supervisor and spends long
              hours tinkering with gadgets and machines, but regrets
              suspending his studies of nature and botany.

1867   Working late at night on the factory's belt system in early
              March, Muir loses his grip on a file, which flies up and
              pierces his right eye, temporarily blinding it; loses sight in
              left eye from sympathetic nervous shock. Although vision
              in the left eye returns quickly and vision is restored in the
              right eye over the next several weeks, the incident causes
              Muir to reconsider his priorities. While recuperating with
              family during summer, decides "to make and take one
              more grand sabbath day three years long," a trip "sufficient
              to lighten and brighten my after life in the gloom and
              hunger of civilization's defrauding duties." Intending to
              go to South America to botanize, takes train from India-
              napolis to Louisville in September and from there walks to
              the Gulf of Mexico; carries with him in a waterproof bag
              the New Testament, Milton's *Paradise Lost*, a collection of
              Robert Burns' poems, and a journal he will keep on the
              trip (posthumously published in 1916 as *A Thousand-Mile
              Walk to the Gulf*). Tramps through Kentucky into the
              Cumberland Mountains of Tennessee, then continues into
              Georgia. Arrives in Savannah and camps for nearly a week
              in a cemetery in nearby Bonneville, subsisting on crackers
              and stale water. Travels by boat for Fernandina, Florida,
              then walks from the Atlantic Coast southwest across the
              state to the Gulf. In Cedar Keys, while waiting for a boat
              to Galveston, Texas, takes a job at a local sawmill. Several
              days later, is stricken with fever and remains bedridden
              for several weeks, desperately ill, at the home of the mill's
              owner.

1868   Altering his plans, takes a schooner to Havana in Janu-
              ary and spends nearly a month exploring the harbor and
              coastline surrounding the city; still too weak to investigate

mountains of the interior, decides to return to a more northerly climate. Takes an orange boat to New York in February, but feels overwhelmed by the size of the city and its crowds. Travels to California by steamer in March by way of the Isthmus of Panama, arriving in San Francisco at the end of the month; decides to remain in California for a few months before re-embarking for South America. Spends summer wandering through the Central Valley region; investigates local plant life and works at odd jobs, including breaking horses, shearing sheep, and serving as a farm laborer. In autumn, takes a job as a shepherd for 1,800 sheep.

1869   Returns to the valley in spring and contracts as chief shepherd with Patrick Delaney; follows his flock into the Sierra Nevada mountains in search of good grazing. Continues into the high country and eventually into the Yosemite Valley, where he explores the region thoroughly for the first time. Returns to the low country as fall approaches and works on Delaney's ranch; goes back to Yosemite in November. Contracts with James Hutchings, one of the valley's original white settlers, to build and operate a sawmill on condition that no living trees will be cut. Becomes a good friend of Hutchings' wife, Elvira Sproat Hutchings, who shares an interest in botany.

1870   Muir continues to operate the sawmill, using Sundays to explore the valley. Maintains correspondence with Jeanne Carr, now living in Oakland where Ezra is teaching at University of California. When she begins directing important persons to the Yosemite with notes to Muir requesting that he guide them through the valley, he becomes known to a wider circle. Finds himself embroiled in scientific controversy over the geologic origins of the Yosemite area when his theory that glaciers were responsible for carving out the area's landscape is contradicted by California state geologist Josiah D. Whitney, who holds random catastrophic forces responsible; wins many converts to his theory while leading tours of the region.

1871   Ralph Waldo Emerson arrives in Yosemite on vacation in May. Initially too timid to approach him, Muir leaves a note at Emerson's hotel: "I invite you to join me in a month's worship with Nature in the high temples of the great Sierra Crown beyond our holy Yosemite." Emerson declines Muir's repeated offers to join him on a camping trip but does meet Muir at his cabin near Yosemite Falls and tours parts of the valley with him. In late summer Muir quits his job at the mill in order to devote more time to his search for evidence of glacial activity (he eventually succeeds in finding a small living glacier high in the mountains). Urged to publish the results by Clinton L. Merriam (a New York congressman interested in geology) and John Daniel Runkle (president of Massachusetts Institute of Technology), he adapts several of his letters about glaciers into article form. His first published essay, "Yosemite Glaciers," appears in the *New-York Tribune* in December.

1872   Spends winter working on his writing, putting together accounts of life and nature in the Yosemite. *The Overland Monthly*, a California literary magazine, publishes "Yosemite Valley in Flood" (April), "Twenty Hill Hollow" (July), and "Living Glaciers of California" (December). Despite his accomplishment, Muir confronts a growing loneliness. "In all God's mountain mansions," he writes, "I find no human sympathy, and I hunger." Through Jeanne Carr, in October meets artist William Keith, with whom he forms close friendship. Travels to San Francisco near the end of the year; spends two weeks visiting the Carrs and other friends, and meets a host of celebrated literary figures. Returning to Yosemite, goes into the mountains and embarks on extended exploration of Tenaya Canyon.

1873   By April is working on 15 different articles; becomes a regular contributor to *The Overland Monthly*, which publishes an article on his Tenaya trip in April, a piece on Hetch Hetchy Valley in July, and another on the Tuolumne Canyon in August. He embarks on another extended exploration, this time intending to investigate the entire length of the Sierra. On returning late in the year, he leaves again for Oakland to pursue his writing during the winter.

1874   Resides at the home of friend J. B. McChesney, Oakland superintendent of schools, whom he met through Jeanne Carr. Grows more accustomed to life in civilization, delighting in old friendships and attending occasional social affairs. At the Carrs', meets Louie Wanda Strentzel,

27-year-old daughter of Louisiana Irwin Strentzel and Dr. John Theophil Strentzel, a Polish immigrant who owns a prosperous fruit farm near Martinez; she shares Muir's interest in botany. Also forms close friendship with State Superintendent of Schools John Swett and his wife, Mary Tracy Swett. Muir completes the last of his glacier articles for *The Overland Monthly* in September and returns briefly to Yosemite. Although pleased to be in the wild again, finds that he no longer feels at home: "No one of the rocks seems to call me now," he writes to Jeanne Carr, "nor any of the distant mountains. Surely this Merced and Tuolumne chapter of my life is done."

1875–79   Moves in with the Swetts; enjoys company of the couple and their four children and feels less lonely. In "God's First Temples: How Shall We Preserve Our Forests?" (published in the *Sacramento Record-Union*, February 1876), urges that the government take responsibility for the forests. Becomes a popular local lecturer, overcoming stage fright in order to preach the spiritual value of wilderness. Extends his wanderings farther during summer and fall of 1877, traveling to Utah and the mountains surrounding the Great Salt Lake, and later exploring the San Gabriel Mountains in the southern part of the state. Takes a river journey in fall, traveling down the Merced and the San Joaquin to the Sacramento; visits Strentzel household in Martinez. Sees them more frequently in spring of 1878 and considers marrying Louie. Travels to Nevada during summer; spends winter writing in San Francisco. In June 1879, shortly before he leaves on his first voyage to Alaska, Muir and Louie agree to marry upon his return. Spends six months in Alaska.

1880   On return journey, arrives in Portland in early January. Explores the Columbia and delivers several lectures in Portland, then spends two weeks in San Francisco before visiting the Strentzels in mid-February. Muir and Louie Strentzel marry on April 14 (her parents give them their house as a wedding gift and build another for themselves). Muir spends three months working on the farm, and in July departs again for Alaska; Louie, who is one month pregnant, remains at home. On the journey, Muir explores glaciers with missionary S. Hall Young; Young's dog, Stickeen, accompanies them, displaying intelligence and stubborn will that Muir admires despite his usual disdain for domesticated animals. On August 30, Muir and Stickeen find themselves trapped while exploring Taylor Glacier; they make a narrow escape on a thin band of ice stretching across a 70-foot chasm. Returns to Martinez to await the birth of his child.

1881–88   Daughter Anna Wanda (called Wanda) Muir is born on March 25, 1881. Muir leaves again for Alaska in May. On returning to Martinez in October, takes over responsibility for the farm and settles into a comfortable family life. Sharply curtails wilderness trips for several years, visiting Yosemite only briefly in 1884 and 1885, and does little writing. Father, who has lived apart from mother since 1874, dies in October 1885 with Muir at his bedside. Daughter Helen Muir is born on January 23, 1886; concerned about her fragile health, Muir rarely leaves the ranch for 18 months after her birth. Prodded by wife and friends to take up writing again, accepts offer to edit and contribute to proposed collection of California nature studies (published by the J. Dewing Co. as *Picturesque California* in 1888). Travels with William Keith to the Cascade Mountains in Washington in summer of 1888 and finds that forest destruction caused by commercial logging has grown more severe. Agrees with Louie to shed some of his responsibilities by selling and leasing portions of their land.

1889   Meets Robert Underwood Johnson, associate editor of the prestigious *Century* magazine, when he visits California in the spring. Travels with Johnson to Yosemite in early June to explore the valley and the high country along the Tuolumne River; they find substantial damage caused by lumbering, tourists, and grazing sheep. Johnson proposes creation of a national park to incorporate both the Yosemite Valley and the surrounding region. Muir agrees to write two articles for *The Century Magazine*, while Johnson undertakes to lobby for the park in Washington.

1890–91   Completes "The Treasures of the Yosemite" and "Features of the Proposed Yosemite National Park" for *The Century Magazine* by the early summer and embarks on another trip to Alaska. Articles (published in August and September 1890) help precipitate debate in Congress over the proposed park. Muir returns from Alaska in September in time to see Congress pass a bill creating a national park even larger than he himself had outlined (law goes into effect October 1). Muir's role in publicizing the park reinvigorates his literary career, and he continues to write and lobby for government protection of wilderness. Father-in-law John Strentzel dies in October 1890; Muir moves with family into the Strentzel home so mother-in-law will not be alone. Sister Margaret and husband John Reid settle in Martinez in 1891 and Reid takes over supervision of Muir's land.

1892   Approached by Henry Senger, a professor of philology at Berkeley, with the idea of forming a local club for mountain lovers, Muir agrees to meet with a small group of enthusiasts in late May, and they form the Sierra Club. Muir is elected president, a post he will hold for the rest of his life. With Muir granting newspaper interviews and sending telegrams to Washington, the club helps prevent passage of a bill in the Senate aimed at reducing Yosemite's boundaries.

1893–94   Plans trip to Europe with William Keith. Goes to New York in May and is introduced by Robert Underwood Johnson to New York society, meeting Mark Twain, Rudyard Kipling, Nicola Tesla, and John Burroughs, among others. During brief trip to Boston, Cambridge, and Concord, lays flowers on Thoreau's and Emerson's graves, visits Walden Pond, and meets Sarah Orne Jewett, Francis Parkman, and Josiah Royce. Embarks for Europe in late June; returns to Dunbar, his boyhood home in Scotland, then visits Norway, England, Switzerland, and Italy. After returning in fall goes to Washington, D.C., at his wife's suggestion to assess the new political situation. Accompanied by Johnson, visits Interior Secretary Hoke Smith and other persons influential in conservation policy. Back home, reworks essays first published 1875–81 for his first book (published in 1894 by Century Company as *The Mountains of California*). Sends first of what will become annual Christmas donations to cousin in Dunbar for distribution to the poor.

1896   Johnson, botanist Charles Sprague Sargent, and forester Gifford Pinchot persuade Hoke Smith to help create a public forest commission through the National Academy of Sciences, thus bypassing Congressional opposition. The six-man commission, including both Sargent and Pinchot, plans a tour of the nation's forest reserves during summer and asks Muir to join them as adviser. Muir visits mother in Portage in June, then goes to Cambridge to accept honorary degree from Harvard (will also receive honorary degrees from University of Wisconsin in 1897, Yale, 1911, and University of California, 1913). Mother dies on June 23. Joining the forest commission in Chicago, Muir travels with them through South Dakota, Wyoming, Montana, Washington, Oregon, and California, and to the Grand Canyon in Arizona and the forest reserves of Colorado. Having observed the poor condition of many forests, commission members agree that more formal protection is necessary, but differ on the means to use. Muir follows Sargent in arguing that forest reserves should be inviolate, and that their protection should be under the control of the Army, and thus outside the corrupting influence of politics; Pinchot favors less severe restrictions, arguing for regulated use along guidelines established by a professional forest service.

1897   The forestry commission releases a preliminary version of its report to President Grover Cleveland in February, calling for the creation of 13 new reserves. Just prior to leaving office, Cleveland approves these reserves and places more than 21 million acres under federal protection. Outraged western politicians attempt to reverse the action in Congress, but their effort stalls and the debate continues. Muir campaigns for wilderness protection; sends letters to politicians and helps organize the Sierra Club to lobby for the reserves. Writes story about Stickeen for *The Century Magazine* (published in September as "An Adventure With a Dog and a Glacier"). Annoyed that Robert Johnson has abridged the piece, Muir agrees to write articles for *The Atlantic Monthly*; the first, "The American Forests" (August), is an impassioned plea for the protection of America's wilderness. Congress suspends all but two of the new reserves in June. With Sargent and botanist William Canby, Muir takes brief trip to Alaska in August. Later that summer, on Pinchot's recommendation, the new Secretary of the Interior, Cornelius Bliss, allows the grazing of sheep in the Oregon and Washington reserves; Muir and Sargent, who had helped to launch Pinchot's career, feel betrayed. Mother-in-law Louisiana Strentzel dies.

1898   Second *Atlantic Monthly* article, "Wild Parks and For-
        est Reservations of the West" (January), helps to ignite
        public sympathy for the forest reserves; a renewed effort
        to abolish President Cleveland's reserves in March fails
        in Congress. Muir travels with Sargent through North
        Carolina and Tennessee, revisiting part of the route he had
        traveled on his 1867 walk to the Gulf of Mexico. Spends
        late fall roaming about New England and parts of Canada.
        Tours Washington, D.C., and travels to Florida, where he
        visits several friends.

1899   Participates in summer expedition to Alaska organized
        by New York financier and railroad magnate Edward H.
        Harriman. At first mistrustful of Harriman, Muir comes to
        admire him during the voyage and the two become friends.
        The expedition, which includes more than 20 scientists,
        travels along the Alaska coastline, stopping occasionally to
        explore glaciers and conduct experiments.

1900–2 Enjoys visits from friends made on Alaska expedition, in-
        cluding biologist C. Hart Merriam and geographer Henry
        Gannett. Finishes last of ten articles for *Atlantic Monthly*
        and prepares them for book version (published 1901 by
        Houghton Mifflin as *Our National Parks*). Leads first of
        annual trips to the mountains sponsored by the Sierra
        Club, guiding nearly 100 club members around Yosemite
        for a month.

1903–4 Agrees to guide President Theodore Roosevelt on a
        trip through the Sierra high country; joins Roosevelt in
        May in San Francisco and travels with him to Yosemite.
        Spurning a banquet organized by local politicians and
        park officials, Roosevelt instead spends three nights
        camping alone with Muir; they explore Glacier Point, the
        head of Nevada Falls, and other points. Roosevelt departs
        Yosemite persuaded that the federal government should
        assume full control of the park. Muir accompanies Sar-
        gent in summer 1903 on a trip to Europe and Asia; they
        travel through Paris and on to Finland and Russia. After
        exploring Siberia and then sailing to Shanghai, Muir parts
        company with Sargent in order to visit India; from there,
        takes a steamship to Egypt where he sees the pyramids
        and journeys up the Nile. Takes a southerly route home

through the Far East, stopping along the way to visit Australia, New Zealand, the Philippines, China, Japan, and Hawaii. Arrives in San Francisco near the end of May 1904.

1905–6   At Muir's request, William Colby, a lawyer belonging to the Sierra Club, drafts a bill to cede the Yosemite Valley back to federal control. Introduced in the state legislature in January 1905, the bill unleashes another round of debate. Muir makes several trips to Sacramento campaigning for the bill; appeals to Edward H. Harriman for help. With the aid of Harriman's railroad lobby, the bill passes in February. The struggle then moves to Congress, where its passage is delayed for another year. Muir again appeals to Harriman, who plays a critical role in ensuring the measure's success (Yosemite Valley is added officially to the national park in June 1906). Daughter Helen is stricken with pneumonia and on doctor's advice in May 1905 Muir takes her to Arizona to aid her recovery. Learns in late June that Louie is seriously ill and returns home; she dies on August 6, 1905, from a lung tumor. Grief-stricken, Muir is unable to write for the next year. Daughter Wanda marries Thomas Rae Hanna, a civil engineer who studied with her at Berkeley, in June 1906. Helen returns home in August.

1907–9   Learns that the city of San Francisco (with assistance from Gifford Pinchot and the new Secretary of the Interior, James Garfield) may succeed in an application to dam the Hetch Hetchy Valley (which lies within Yosemite National Park) in order to obtain water for the city. Muir and the Sierra Club launch a campaign to arouse public opinion against the dam, but fail to rally enough support. In May 1908, Garfield grants permission to dam the valley, subject to Congressional approval. Hetch Hetchy dam approval stalls in Congress due to adverse public opinion; new president William Howard Taft and Secretary of the Interior Richard A. Ballinger also help to delay the project. Taft and Ballinger visit Yosemite in October 1909; Muir, serving as presidential guide, takes the opportunity to argue that San Francisco could find alternative water supplies without violating the park's boundaries. *Stickeen*, published by Houghton Mifflin in March, becomes Muir's most popular book.

1910–12   Daughter Helen is married to Buell A. Funk, son of a cattle rancher. Muir stays for long visits with friends Katharine and John D. Hooker of Los Angeles and Henry F. Osborne and his family at Garrison's-on-the-Hudson. Revises his early Sierra journals (published by Houghton Mifflin in 1911 as *My First Summer in the Sierra*); completes the manuscripts for *The Yosemite* (published by Century Company in 1912) and *The Story of My Boyhood and Youth* (Houghton Mifflin, 1913). Saddened by death of close friend William Keith in April 1911. Decides to fulfill a lifelong dream by exploring the Amazon River. Ignoring protests of family and friends, he departs in August. Sails up the Amazon and investigates the surrounding forests, exploring lagoon at Rio Negro before returning to the mouth of the river. Sails down coast to Buenos Aires and takes train across continent to Santiago, Chile. Treks to Montevideo and boards ship bound for Africa, intent on locating and examining a baobab tree. Finds the trees near Victoria Falls ("one of the greatest of the great tree days of my lucky life"); journeys on to explore the Nile valley. Arrives back in New York in late March 1912.

1913   Muir once again campaigns to save Hetch Hetchy after President Woodrow Wilson appoints dam supporter Franklin K. Lane as Secretary of the Interior. Writes letters and newspaper articles and rallies Sierra Club to defeat the proposal; the effort begins to take a toll on Muir, and he falls ill several times. With the new administration backing the proposal, a bill granting San Francisco permission to dam Hetch Hetchy passes Congress in December (Muir later writes to a friend: "it is a monumental mistake, but it is more, it is a monumental crime").

1914   Hampered by failing health, attempts to finish account of his Alaska journeys (published posthumously by Houghton Mifflin as *Travels in Alaska* in 1915). Visits daughter Helen in Daggett in December; develops pneumonia and on December 23 is admitted to California Hospital in Los Angeles. Dies December 24. Buried in family plot on the Martinez ranch.

Note on the Texts

Drawn from *John Muir: Nature Writings* (William Cronon, editor), volume number 92 in the Library of America series, this volume presents *My First Summer in the Sierra* (1911), followed by a selection of thirteen essays, twelve of which were published between 1871 and 1912 and one of which was published posthumously.

My First Summer in the Sierra is an account of Muir's 1869 stay in the Yosemite and its environs. Muir used part of his 1869 journal as the basis for the book, but he significantly revised and rearranged it, adding episodes that occurred in later years. It was published by Houghton Mifflin Company in 1911. The text printed here is of the Houghton Mifflin first edition.

The texts of the thirteen essays included in this volume are arranged in the order of their initial appearances and are taken from their first publications, with the exceptions noted below. The following is a list of the sources:

"Yosemite Glaciers," *New-York Tribune*, December 5, 1871.

"Yosemite Valley in Flood," *The Overland Monthly*, April 1872.

"A Geologist's Winter Walk," *The Overland Monthly*, April 1873. (This was an excerpt from a letter to Jeanne Carr that she submitted for publication without Muir's knowledge.)

"Flood-Storm in the Sierra," *The Overland Monthly*, June 1875 (later published in substantially revised form as Chapter XI, "The River Floods," in *The Mountains of California*).

"Living Glaciers of California," *Harper's Monthly Magazine*, November 1875 (later published in substantially revised form as Chapter II, "The Glaciers," in *The Mountains of California*).

"God's First Temples: How Shall We Preserve Our Forests?," *Sacramento Daily Union*, February 5, 1876. Courtesy of the John Muir Papers, Holt-Atherton Department of Special Collections, University of the Pacific Libraries.

"Snow-Storm on Mount Shasta," *Harper's Monthly Magazine*, September 1877.

"Features of the Proposed Yosemite National Park," *The Century Magazine*, September 1890.

"The American Forests" first appeared in *The Atlantic Monthly*, August 1897, and was revised by Muir for Chapter X of *Our National Parks* (Boston: Houghton Mifflin Company, 1901), a collection of his essays. The text presented in this volume is taken from *Our National Parks*.

"The Wild Parks and Forest Reservations of the West" first appeared in *The Atlantic Monthly*, January 1898, and was revised by Muir for Chapter I of *Our National Parks*. The text presented in this volume is taken from *Our National Parks*.

"The Forests of the Yosemite Park" first appeared in *The Atlantic Monthly*, April 1900, and was revised by Muir for Chapter IV of *Our National Parks*. The text presented in this volume is taken from *Our National Parks*.

"Hetch Hetchy Valley" appeared as Chapter XV of *The Yosemite* (New York: The Century Co., 1912), a collection of otherwise previously published essays by Muir. In writing "Hetch Hetchy Valley," a plea for the preservation of the valley, Muir drew on the closing section of his 1890 essay, "Features of the Proposed Yosemite National Park" (see above).

"Save the Redwoods" was first published in the *Sierra Club Bulletin*, January 1920. The passage was found among Muir's papers after his death.

This volume presents the texts of the printings chosen for inclusion here but does not attempt to reproduce features of their typographic design. Spelling, punctuation, and capitalization often are expressive features and they are not altered, even when inconsistent or irregular. The following is a list of typographical errors corrected, cited by page and line number: 48.9, plant; 55.16, others; 95.34, Cathderal; 101.30, currus; 109.30, though; 166.22, hight; 170.27, as the; 174.9, of all; 174.22, death,; 183.17, "benmost bore"; 200.11, *coulairs*; 211.18, sheepmens'; 275.9, ground; 292.18, forest where; 311.31, shampiously.

Notes

In the notes below, the reference numbers denote page and line of this volume (the line count includes titles, headings, and captions). No note is made for material included in standard desk-reference books such as Webster's *Collegiate*, *Biographical*, and *Geographical* dictionaries. Biblical references are keyed to the King James Version. Footnotes in the text were in the originals. For further background and references to other studies, see: William Frederic Badè, *The Life and Letters of John Muir* (Boston: Houghton Mifflin Company, 1924); *John of the Mountains: The Unpublished Journals of John Muir*, ed. Linnie Marsh Wolfe (Boston: Houghton Mifflin Company, 1938); Linnie Marsh Wolfe, *Son of the Wilderness: The Life of John Muir* (New York: Alfred Knopf, 1945); Stephen Fox, *John Muir and His Legacy: The American Conservation Movement* (Boston: Little Brown and Company, 1981); Michael P. Cohen, *The Pathless Way: John Muir and the American Wilderness* (Madison: University of Wisconsin Press, 1984); Frederick Turner, *Rediscovering America: John Muir in His Time and Ours* (New York: Viking, 1985); William F. Kimes and Maymie B. Kimes, *John Muir: A Reading Bibliography* (Fresno: Panorama West Books, 1986).

The editor acknowledges Gregory Summers for his work in preparing the Chronology.

MY FIRST SUMMER IN THE SIERRA

I.I–2   MY FIRST . . . SIERRA]   For this book Muir significantly revised the diary that he kept during his first visit to the Yosemite and its environs in 1869, linking entries with carefully constructed transitional passages and adding episodes from other summers.

17.9   "wee, . . . beasties"]   Cf. Robert Burns, "To a Mouse," line 1.

33.14   "bank to brae."]   Robert Burns, "Winter": "While, tumbling brown, the Burn comes down, / And roars frae bank to brae"; a "burn" is a rivulet and a "brae," the slope of a hill.

51.20–21   Once I . . . Bonaventure graveyard]   During his walk to the Gulf of Mexico in 1867.

57.22–23   "He giveth his beloved sleep."]   Psalm 127:2.

66.29–30   Samson's riddle . . . sweetness."]   Cf. Judges 14:5–8, 14–18; the solution to the riddle is: "What is sweeter than honey? And what is stronger than a lion?"

90.38–39   "I sift . . . mountains below."]   "The Cloud," line 7.

100.7   Grip]   A parrot in Charles Dickens' *Barnaby Rudge* (1841).

101.5–6   Tenaya . . . company of soldiers]   Tenaya was chief of the Ahwahneechee Indians who were removed from Yosemite in 1851; he was killed in 1853.

108.9   Professor J. D. Butler]   James Davie Butler was professor of classics. He helped to introduce Muir to the works of Emerson.

110.6–7   Mrs. Hutchings]   Elvira Hutchings, who became a close friend of Muir's.

110.31   General Alvord]   Benjamin Alvord (1813–84), a career soldier, was brevetted brigadier general of the Union Army in 1862 and served as paymaster general for the U.S. Army, 1872–80. He taught mathematics and physics at West Point early in his career, served in numerous conflicts, including the Seminole War, 1835–37, and was the author of many articles, notably on math and geography.

112.10–12   "As the sun . . . walks to-morrow."]   Johann Christoph Friedrich von Schiller, *The Death of Wallenstein*, Act 5, scene 3.

128.20–21   "still singing . . . for joy."]   Cf. Job 38:7.

132.10–11   "It's coming yet . . . a' that."]   From Burns' untitled song that begins: "The Honest Man the best of Men."

SELECTED ESSAYS

165.1   *Yosemite Glaciers*]   Aside from a very brief botanical listing in the Boston *Recorder* in 1866, this was Muir's first publication.

176.23–26   Hutching's . . . Black's]   James M. Hutching's and A. G. Black's hotels.

177.6   Hill's painting]   Thomas Hill (1829–1908) emigrated from England in 1840 and settled in California around 1871; he was famous for his landscapes of the Yosemite Valley region.

180.1   *A Geologist's Winter Walk*]   This was an excerpt from a letter to Jeanne Carr. She submitted it to *The Overland Monthly* without Muir's knowledge.

183.17   'benmost bore']   Robert Burns, *The Jolly Beggars. A Cantata*, 2nd recitative; the words mean "inmost crevice (or cranny)."

186.1   *Flood-Storm in the Sierra*]   Muir later revised this essay for *The Mountains of California*, Chapter XI.

196.22–23   "it is . . . for a' that"]   From Robert Burns' "The Honest Man."

197.1   *Living Glaciers of California*]   Muir revised this essay for *The Mountains of California*, Chapter II.

198.1–7   The first Sierra glacier . . . my discovery]   The bulk of Muir's writings about his geological "discoveries" appeared, like this essay, in popular journals. But at a time when science was just beginning to professionalize itself into the academic disciplines that characterized it in the 20th century, Muir was taken quite seriously as an amateur geologist, principally for his work in applying Louis Agassiz's theories of glaciation to the mountain landscapes of the American West. His more explicitly "scientific" work appeared in the *Proceedings of the Boston Society of Natural History* with the help of Dr. Samuel Kneeland, who shared Muir's interest in Yosemite geology. Muir also published his work in the *Proceedings of the American Association for the Advancement of Science.*

200.13–18   lateral moraines . . . channel.]   Moraines are the piles of gravel that accumulate along the front and sides of glaciers as their ice moves forward. Every glacier is always moving forward as the weight of snow and ice renders its base plastic, even when the front of the glacier remains fixed at a stable location (the front will remain fixed as long as the rate at which snow and ice accumulate in the winter matches the rate at which they melt in the summer). Moraines form as the forward moving ice transports rock to the stable front of the glacier, where the load is deposited to form heaps of gravel on the margins of the ice. Terminal moraines lie at the outward leading edge of the glacier, marking its farthest forward extent; lateral moraines lie along its edges.

201.13   *névé*]   Or firn, the granular, partially compacted snow located at the upper end of a glacier.

201.14   *Bergschrund*]   A crevasse, a fissure extending deep into the ice of a glacier.

203.35   Professor Joseph Leconte]   Le Conte (1823–1901) was a leading geologist at the University of California at Berkeley.

205.15   Schlagintweit brothers]   German naturalists, explorers, and writers Hermann von Schlagintweit (1826–82) and Adolf Schlagintweit (1829–57); they explored the Alps in 1846–53.

205.22   Clarence King]   King (1842–1901) was considered the leading geologist of his generation; he served as the first director of the U.S. Geological Survey, 1879–81.

208.1   *God's First Temples*]   This is the first article in which Muir protests the destruction of natural resources and wild country in the mountain West.

208.19–209.9   The practical importance . . . them.]   Muir's argument about the role of forests in regulating streamflow was already familiar to many

19th-century readers from the work of George Perkins Marsh (1801–82), whose *Man and Nature* (1864) ascribed the fall of ancient Greece and Rome to the environmental degradation resulting from their indiscriminate cutting of Mediterranean forests. *Man and Nature* was crucial in building a national consensus about the need to protect American forests, leading eventually to the establishment of the Adirondack State Park in New York and to the 1891 Forest Reserves Act which laid the foundation for the national forests. Muir's efforts to defend wilderness areas in the West were a part of this national movement.

226.34   Sisson]   Proprietor of the hotel at which Muir was staying.

228.1–2   *Features . . . National Park*]   Muir began to emerge during the 1890s as the leading proponent of permanent federal protection of Yosemite as a national park. In 1864 the United States had given the Yosemite Valley to the state of California. It was the nation's first wild land park, and leading landscape architect Frederick Law Olmsted (1822–1903) had played a key role in designing that park. Muir was among those who by the 1890s were arguing for setting aside a much larger tract of land than just Yosemite Valley itself and in 1892 he became a founder of the Sierra Club as part of the lobbying effort to protect the Yosemite and other parts of the Sierra high country.

242.1   *The American Forests*]   This is Muir's most sustained essay on the lands that eventually became the core of the national forests. It is an outgrowth of his service as a consultant to the National Forestry Commission, chaired by Harvard botanist Charles Sprague Sargent (1841–1927) and with members such as as Yale scientist William H. Brewer (1828–1910), Alexander Agassiz (1835–1910), and Gifford Pinchot (1865–1946). The essay, which was commissioned in 1897 by *Atlantic Monthly* editor Walter Hines Page, is essentially a précis of the Forestry Report's major arguments, rendered livelier and more accessible by Muir's prose. In arguing for government ownership and regulation of forested lands throughout the nation, Muir aligned himself with the work that Gifford Pinchot (who would become Theodore Roosevelt's Chief Forester and founder of the United States Forest Service) was beginning to pursue in promoting permanent federal management of forests on public lands. The echoes of Marsh's *Man and Nature* (see note 208.17–209.9) also are evident here. Pinchot and Muir would soon diverge in their visions of how such forests should be managed and used, with the struggle over Hetch Hetchy providing the occasion for a final break that in fact reflected longstanding philosophical tensions between the two men; the two actually came into conflict over grazing policy in the western forests not long after this piece was written.

248.20   timber culture act]   Passed in 1873, the act was another legacy of George Perkins Marsh's *Man and Nature*, the theory being that by encouraging settlers to plant trees in grassland and desert environments, "rain would follow the plow" and barren land would be made fertile for agriculture.

250.38–39   *A change . . . 1901.]   "The American Forests" was first published in August 1897.

262.1–2   *The Wild Parks and Forest Reservations of the West*]   This essay was originally published in *The Atlantic Monthly* as the first in a series of nine articles on wild parks of the American West that Walter Hines Page commissioned from Muir following the success of "The American Forests"; all ten essays were collected, with some revisions, in *Our National Parks*.

269.40–270.1   buffalo . . . described by Parkman]   In Francis Parkman's *The Oregon Trail* (1849).

282.39   p. 277]   The page number has been changed to conform to the present volume.

289.28–33   Dr. Johnson's . . . something."]   In James Boswell, *Journal of a Tour of the Hebrides* (1785), entry of October 19, 1773.

303.16   Emerson came.]   This is Muir's first published account of his 1871 meeting with Emerson, who was vacationing in the West as part of a cross-country railroad trip with family and friends. Emerson had become exhausted by his teaching and writing schedule and the trip has been credited with prolonging his life.

303.26   'gang tapsal-teerie.']   Go topsy-turvey, from Burns' "Green grow the Rashes."

303.27   'Good-by . . . home,']   "Good-Bye," line 1, in *Poems* (1847).

304.6–7   "Come listen . . . saith,"]   Cf. "Woodnotes II" in *Poems* (1847).

305.6   Galen Clark]   Clark was appointed California's state guardian of the Yosemite Grant in 1866. He was heavily involved in promoting the area for tourist use.

307.1   *Hetch Hetchy Valley*]   This essay is Muir's most important single piece on the Hetch Hetchy controversy. For it, Muir edited and expanded the closing section of his 1890 article "Features of the Proposed Yosemite National Park" (pp. 235–241 in this volume).

315.19–20   "Forgive . . . do."]   Cf. Luke 23:34.

Index

The Library of America Paperback Classics Series

American Speeches: Political Oratory from Patrick Henry to Barack Obama (various authors)
Edited and with an introduction by Ted Widmer
ISBN: 978-1-59853-094-0

The Education of Henry Adams by Henry Adams
With an introduction by Leon Wieseltier
ISBN: 978-1-59853-060-5

The Red Badge of Courage by Stephen Crane
With an introduction by Robert Stone
ISBN: 978-1-59853-061-2

The Souls of Black Folk by W.E.B. Du Bois
With an introduction by John Edgar Wideman
ISBN: 978-1-59853-054-4

Essays: First and Second Series by Ralph Waldo Emerson
With an introduction by Douglas Crase
ISBN: 978-1-59853-084-1

The Autobiography by Benjamin Franklin
With an introduction by Daniel Aaron
ISBN: 978-1-59853-095-7

The Scarlet Letter by Nathaniel Hawthorne
With an introduction by Harold Bloom
ISBN: 978-1-59853-112-1

The Varieties of Religious Experience by William James
With an introduction by Jaroslav Pelikan
ISBN: 978-1-59853-062-9

Selected Writings by Thomas Jefferson
With an introduction by Tom Wicker
ISBN: 978-1-59853-096-4

The Autobiography of an Ex-Colored Man by James Weldon Johnson
With an introduction by Charles R. Johnson
ISBN: 978-1-59853-113-8

Selected Speeches and Writings by Abraham Lincoln
With an introduction by Gore Vidal
ISBN: 978-1-59853-053-7

For more information, please visit www.loa.org/paperbackclassics/

☆ The Library of America

The contents of this Paperback Classic are drawn from *John Muir: Nature Writings* (William Cronon, editor), volume number 92 in the Library of America series, which also includes *The Story of My Boyhood, The Mountains of California, Stickeen,* and selected essays.

Created with seed funding from the National Endowment for the Humanities and the Ford Foundation, The Library of America is a nonprofit cultural institution that preserves our nation's literary heritage by publishing, and keeping permanently in print, authoritative editions of America's best and most significant writing. Hailed as "the most important book-publishing project in the nation's history" (*Newsweek*), this award-winning series maintains America's most treasured writers in "the finest-looking, longest-lasting edition ever made" (*The New Republic*).

Since 1982, over 220 hardcover volumes have been published in the Library of America series, each containing up to 1600 pages and including a number of works. In many cases, the complete works of a writer are collected in as few as three compact volumes. New volumes are added each year to make all the essential writings of America's foremost novelists, historians, poets, essayists, philosophers, playwrights, journalists, and statesmen part of The Library of America.

Each volume features: authoritative, unabridged texts • a chronology of the author's life, helpful notes, and a brief textual essay • a handsomely designed, easy-to-read page • high-quality, acid-free paper, bound in a cloth cover and sewn to lie flat when opened • a ribbon marker and printed end papers.

For more information, a complete list of titles, tables of contents, and to request a catalogue, please visit www.loa.org.